Object Databases

An ODMG Approach

Related titles

Published titles

Ed Ashley and Beth Epperson *Sybase SQL Server on the World Wide Web* 1-85032-815-3

Mitchell Gurspan *Upgrading and Migrating to Sybase SQL Server 11* 1-85032-861-7

Thomas C. Hammergren *Data Warehousing: Building the Corporate Knowledge Base* 1-85032-856-0

John E. Kirkwood *Sybase SQL Server 11: An Administrator's Guide* 1-85032-287-2

Sidharan Kotta *Understanding Sybase SQL Server 11: A Hands-on Approach* 1-85032-852-8

Karen Paulsell *Sybase SQL Server Performance and Tuning Guide* 1-85032-883-8

Forthcoming titles

Angelo Bobak *Very Large Databases with Intranet and Internet Applications* 1-85032-888-9

Thomas C. Hammergren *Official Sybase: Data Warehousing on the Internet* 1-85032-857-9

John E. Kirkwood *Official Sybase Internals: Designing and Troubleshooting for High Performance* 1-85032-334-8

Ian Richmond and Derek Ball *Sybase Adaptive Server Anywhere: A Developer's Guide* 1-85032-860-9

Object Databases

An ODMG Approach

Richard Cooper

INTERNATIONAL THOMSON COMPUTER PRESS

I ⓣ P ® An International Thomson Publishing Company

Boston • London • Bonn • Johannesburg • Madrid • Melbourne • Mexico City • New York • Paris •
Singapore • Tokyo • Toronto • Albany, NY • Belmont, CA • Cincinnati, OH • Detroit, MI

Object Databases: An ODMG Approach
Copyright © 1997 International Thomson Computer Press

I ⓣ P A division of International Thomson Publishing Inc.
The ITP logo is a trademark under licence.

For more information, contact:

International Thomson Computer Press
20 Park Plaza
13th Floor
Boston, MA 02116
USA

International Thomson Computer Press
Berkshire House
168–173 High Holborn
London WC1V 7AA
UK

Imprints of International Thomson Publishing

International Thomson Publishing GmbH
Königswinterer Straße 418
53227 Bonn
Germany

International Thomson Publishing Asia
60 Albert Street #15-01
Albert Complex
Singapore 189969

Thomas Nelson Australia
102 Dodds Street
South Melbourne, 3205
Victoria
Australia

International Thomson Publishing Japan
Hirakawacho Kyowa Building, 3F
2-2-1 Hirakawacho
Chiyoda-ku, 102 Tokyo
Japan

Nelson Canada
1120 Birchmount Road
Scarborough, Ontario
Canada M1K 5G4

International Thomson Editores
Campos Eliseos 385, Piso 7
Col. Polenco
11560 Mexico D.F. Mexico

International Thomson Publishing South Africa
PO Box 2459
Halfway House
1685 South Africa

International Thomson Publishing France
Tour Maine-Parnasse
33 avenue du Maine
75755 Paris Cedex 15
France

ISBN 1-85032-294-5

Typeset by Hodgson Williams Associates, Tunbridge Wells and Cambridge, England

Pubisher/Vice President: Jim DeWolf, ITCP/Boston
Marketing Manager: Christine Nagle, ITCP/Boston
Projects Director: Vivienne Toye, ITCP/Boston
Manufacturing Manager: Sandra Sabathy, ITCP/Boston

Contents

Foreword

Object databases have been in the research world as for more than twelve years, and on the market for more than six years. They have evolved from the initial prototypes and early products to industrial-strength mature products. They have moved from technology evaluation, to pilot projects, and to application development and deployment. They have changed from small single-user applications to very large databases with large numbers of users. They have evolved from a set of different systems to a common architecture and interface.

This common architecture and interface was defined and specified by ODMG (Object Data Management Group). This organization, which consists of object database vendors, users and researchers, has defined a portability standard for object databases that allows ODMG-compliant applications to be ported from one compliant object database system to another, thus securing the application development investment. At this time, six vendors are offering products with a variable degree of compliance. O_2 Technology is committed to providing the strongest level of compliance, compliance which is widely recognized in the industry.

Object databases have been used in areas such as defense, telecommunications, financial industries, manufacturing, CAD/CAM, multimedia, geographical information systems and software engineering.

The benefit of this book is to provide an extensive coverage of this essential field. Richard Cooper manages to cover both the theoretical aspects and the practical aspects of object databases. Most of the presentation is based on actual examples of the ODMG interface, using the O_2 example. This makes it a useful and highly practical learning tool.

The combination of a comprehensive text and an accompanying CD-ROM, which includes a tutorial and a demonstration, provides the reader with a complete vision and understanding of this field. This makes it a unique tool for users, researchers and professionals who need to understand object database technology and its benefits.

François Bancilhon
O_2 Technology

Preface

In writing a book on object-oriented database systems (OODBMS), I have attempted to provide an up-to-date account of the current status of these new systems for managing data. OODBMS have arisen from a need that data management be based on more easily understood descriptions. The need arises because database systems are increasingly being used to manage more complex kinds of data and therefore ease of description becomes a more pressing requirement. OODBMS are believed to offer easier forms of descriptions because object orientation models the data in use mechanisms which mirror the ways in which we manage information in the real world more directly. Furthermore, the object-oriented paradigm provides better facilities for integrating computation (application code or data behaviour) with the data.

The book, and its accompanying CD-ROM are designed to bring together the main concepts of object-oriented systems and database systems in a single coherent discussion. Since object orientation was initially introduced into software systems to manage in-memory data, it is not surprising that extending the paradigm to encompass long-lived data has required changes to some of the underlying ideas. There is a continuing discussion about how these two contrasting views of data are brought together in practice.

In writing the book, I have attempted to demonstrate several major ideas:

- Database systems have been successfully used to underpin certain kinds of enterprise which rely on well-supported access to potentially huge amounts of data. Such enterprises have so far been restricted to those whose data can relatively easily be reduced to simple forms. The success of these enterprises has led to the desire to use database technology to manage other enterprises which have complex information that is not so easily reduced to simple structures.

- Object orientation provides a suitable paradigm in which to describe databases and their applications, including those which need to use complex information structures. In database research terms, object orientation can be thought of as building on work on semantic data models, since it provides a semantically rich model as its main mode of data description.

- Object-riented database systems, although apparently revolutionary, are better thought of as an evolutionary extension of existing database management systems, re-using implementation techniques and providing similar user interfaces, but providing a much more extensive and supportive superstructure to contain these, and adding an increased range of data storage and user interaction facilities.

- It is a vital and fundamental requirement of database management systems that increasingly they manage values which takes the form of code as well as data in the traditional sense. Application programs, object behavior and active values should all be managed by the same system as that which holds the data. Without this it becomes unnecessarily difficult to maintain complex applications which use large amounts of long-lived data. One of the main benefits of object orientation is that it supports the maintenance of both code and data.

- Given the importance of managing code, the programming interface becomes increasingly vital. One section of the book is given over to the programming interface: the requirements of an appropriate programming language; and the ways in which the two main object oriented languages – C++ and Smalltalk – can be used for programming database applications.

- The interoperability of database systems (and indeed other software) is also a vital issue. It is increasingly the case that critical information used by an enterprise is being managed using different kinds of software that, as yet, does not interact well. Document production software, spreadsheets and database systems all need to be able to share their data freely. OODBMS are well suited to play an integrating role in managing data that arises in older forms of DBMS and in non-database software.

- One of the principal reasons that traditional DBMS have been so successful is that they are built on well defined standards. It is one of the drawbacks of object orientation that it has so many varieties and, therefore, the integration of data arising in different object-oriented systems can be difficult to integrate. Much of the book will be taken up in discussing standards for OODBMS – a vital issue if they are to be effectively usable.

- A new paradigm suggests both novel implementation techniques and novel ways for using the data. The final section of the book discusses these issues.

The book is divided into five parts:

Part 1 introduces the main ideas of database systems and of object orientation. A chapter is devoted to each subject and a third chapter discusses what it means to bring them together.

Part 2 discusses the Object Data Management Group standard for OODBMS. It starts with a chapter on standardization in database systems and continues with two chapters on the data model proposed by the ODMG, one describing the model in abstract and the other using the model to describe a small application. Finally, there are two chapters on one of the ODMG-compliant commercial OODBMS – the O_2 system. One describes the system in general and the other discusses how it is used to manage the sample application.

Part 3 discusses querying an object-oriented database. A query language is an important feature of any DBMS, and OODBMS need to provide a standard language. The part comprises two chapters – the first discussing querying in the object-oriented context, the other describing OQL, the language proposed by the ODMG, together with the way that it is used in O_2.

Part 4 discusses programming language interfaces to OODBMS. Perhaps the main difference between a traditional DBMS and an OODBMS is that the programming language is much more important in the latter. There are three chapters in Part 4. The first discusses the principal issues in providing programming interfaces to database systems. The other two discuss how C++ and Smalltalk can be used for this purpose – again using the ODMG proposals and the O_2 implementation to make the discussion concrete.

Part 5 discusses some of the OODBMS issues in more depth. It has a chapter on implementation, one on the user interface and one which surveys the other major commercial OODBMS. The final chapter summarizes the whole book.

The CD-ROM contains a hypertext version of the book, but extends this in two ways. Firstly, there is an interactively-accessed glossary of the main terms met in the book. Secondly, there are two interactive tutorials – one showing how the ODMG data model is used to design a database application and the other showing how the O2 system is used to implement it.

Part One

Objects and databases

An object-oriented database system is one which brings together the organizational structures of object orientation with techniques for the persistent storage of large amounts of data. This introductory part of the book is intended to bring together discussion of the main concepts underlying database systems and object systems.

Database systems form the start point and Chapter 1 discusses both current practice and research in database systems, beginning with those systems which reliably underpin commercial activity. The discussion then turns to other kinds of data-intensive application and finds that present database systems do not provide effective management of the kinds of data of which such applications make use. Different ideas for making database systems more effective and more powerful are then discussed, before object databases are introduced.

Chapter 2 then provides an overview of the main concepts of the object-oriented approach, showing how it provides a suitable data model for complex applications.

Chapter 3 brings the two areas together by demonstrating the kinds of ways in which object systems can be used as the basis for database management.

1 Developments in database technology

Database systems are a success!

The development and application of software to hold massive amounts of information has been one of the main factors in the considerable transformation which our society has undergone during the last 20 to 30 years. The explosion of the global economy has depended upon fast access to commercial information. The growth in the use of transport systems has necessitated the management of large amounts of booking information. Government services have required the storage of massive amounts of information to underpin an increasingly complex administration. All of these information management tasks have grown to such a size that they can only be successfully accomplished with the use of computers. However, the tasks require not only fast computer hardware, but also finely tuned software systems to provide access to massive amounts of data in reasonable time. Such systems are called database management systems (or DBMS).

A DBMS is designed to hold data from many different kinds of application areas with equal ease. It achieves this by reducing all of the information stored to a common set of data structures, which are not application specific. The DBMS – the software to store, retrieve and manipulate the data in this form – can then be created as a single programming task. This brings a considerable saving of implementation effort when compared with writing data management programs one application at a time.

However, the data structures which are used by most currently operating commercial DBMS are extremely simple. This raises a difficulty when setting up a database and when creating and maintaining applications which operate using the database. Real-world information comes in a wide range of varied and complex structures. The database can only hold simple structures. The principal task in using a DBMS consists of transforming the complex information into the simple database structures. Eliciting a simple representation of complex information is a difficult task, since, with the limited expressive power implicit in data structures, important distinctions are lost and much detail must be omitted.

In fact, this task is so difficult that a large organization which makes heavy use of database systems will hold much of the information that it uses outside of the DBMS, since it does not fit well with the simple database structures. Furthermore, there are a whole range of application areas whose practitioners are impressed by the successes of DBMS and find that they too need to store large amounts of data arising from their information handling. Computer-aided design, computer-aided software engineering and spatial information management are only three such areas. In these domains, all of the information is complex – really too complex for currently operating DBMS to manage with total success.

There is therefore a need for new kinds of DBMS, which build on the success of current systems, but which are better able to manage complex information. This chapter will examine this need and survey the responses to it, culminating in the introduction of object-oriented database management systems.

■ 1.1 Record-based DBMS

In this section, the principal facilities which are provided by a DBMS will be described and the nature of current DBMS will be discussed. Then the new application areas whose practitioners wish to use database systems will be described together with the new requirements that these new uses bring.

■ 1.1.1 What is a database system?

The starting point for a discussion of the new kind of database system called an object-oriented database management system (OODBMS) is to look again at what a database system is and what it does. In this section, the main attributes and facilities expected of a DBMS will be described, as well how they are structured. This will not be a detailed description, since there are many excellent text books which the reader can consult.

A DBMS is a coordinated package of software which permits large amounts of structured data to be managed. A DBMS will usually provide the following set of facilities:

- *Application generality.* The DBMS will be able to handle data from many different application areas equally easily. There is no need to have one DBMS for banking applications, one for booking systems and so on.
- *Efficient data access.* The data will be stored in such a way that it can be accessed as quickly as possible. The principal storage structures used to hold the data will be designed so that individual data items can be found quickly. Furthermore, the store will be augmented by supporting structures such as indices so that the most common uses for the data are achieved quickly.
- *Security.* There will be privacy mechanisms securing the data against unauthorized access and misuse. Individual users may be given access restricted to parts of a database. Some users may be able to change data, while others can only consult the data.
- *Data consistency.* Any changes made to the data will be organized in such a way that the database always remains consistent, i.e. no changes will be allowed to violate the organization imposed on the data by the database designer.
- *Resilience.* Hardware or software failures while the database is running are never allowed to make the database inconsistent – at most a few of the most recent changes will be lost if the system crashes.
- *Concurrency control.* Many users can access the database at the same time without interfering with each other's work.
- *Multiple views.* There will be a facility for providing apparently different or more focused representations to different kinds of user. Thus a database may be accessed using a detailed view by staff working intensively with a set of data, while a manager may see a less detailed view.
- *User interfaces.* Appropriate user interfaces will be provided to allow databases to be designed and used by a wide variety of users. Among these will be:

  - *Parametric interfaces.* These are specific interfaces which may be added to the system and which allow particular repetitive tasks to be carried by non-computing personnel, simply by inputting a few small values. Automated teller machines (ATM) provide the most prevalent example of this kind of interface.

- Ad hoc *querying*. The DBMS will provide a general purpose query language which gives users a fairly simple textual method for specifying the database structure, updates to data and retrievals of data from the database.

- *Graphical interfaces.* In order to simplify the interaction, there are a variety of emerging interface styles including node-and-arc graphs to represent the data structure, window systems which support a manipulable form-based representation of the data, and direct manipulation techniques for creating changes to the data and its structure.

- *Programming interfaces.* For more complex work, there will be a facility for permitting applications written mostly in a high level programming language to access the data in the database.

- *Administrative interfaces.* In its most extensive form, a DBMS is intended to support many different kinds of activity simultaneously. In this case, there will need to be a privileged user role – called a database administrator – whose job it is to control the definition of databases and the privileges of users. Such tasks call for specific interfaces.

- *Integrity.* There may be the facility for imposing integrity constraints which limit the values which the database can take – thus maintaining the meaning of the information stored.

- *Distribution.* It may be possible for the DBMS to handle data which is distributed across more than one computer joined in a local network or even across a number of sites joined in a wider network.

To provide these facilities, the DBMS requires that the data be structured in a particular way, which is usually described using a three-level architecture, shown in Figure 1.1, which emerged as an abstract standard proposed by the SPARC committee of the American National Standards Institute (ANSI). In this architecture, the same data can be thought of as being structured in three different, but equivalent ways:

- In the *external layer*, different views of the data can be provided to particular user groups, potentially using application specific interfaces. At the external level, the user may perceive the data as bank accounts, airline tickets, and so on.

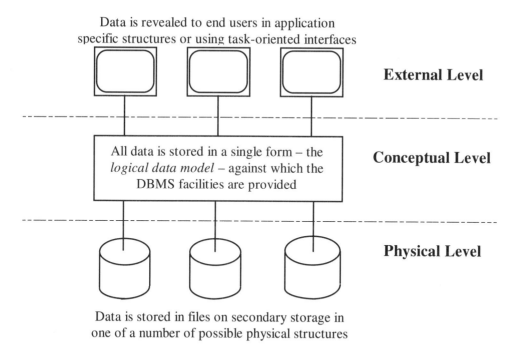

Data is revealed to end users in application
specific structures or using task-oriented interfaces

External Level

All data is stored in a single form – the
logical data model – against which the
DBMS facilities are provided

Conceptual Level

Physical Level

Data is stored in files on secondary storage in
one of a number of possible physical structures

Figure 1.1   The ANSI-SPARC three-layer model.

- In the *conceptual layer*, all of the data are described using a single logical data model, i.e. they are all represented as being structured in one form no matter what the application area is. In the relational model, for instance, all of the data is structured in the form of tables of records.
- In the *physical layer*, the data are described as they actually are stored on the disk. The physical layer determines the order in which the data are stored and which files they are stored in and so is important for efficiency reasons. Thus a set of data which appears to be a single table at the conceptual layer may in fact be split up into a number of files held on the disk. The same logical representation can be stored in any of a number of logically equivalent physical forms.

The primary idea which makes this a useful model of database storage is *data independence*. This means that the data can be manipulated at each of the three different levels (whether directly by users or indirectly by programmers) without any need to understand the representation at the other levels. This has several beneficial effects. First, the storage management software can change how the data is stored in files without changing its logical representation. Thus the same data can be re-organized for efficiency purposes without changing how it is used at the upper two levels. Second, the logical representation can be changed without affecting how users at the external levels view the data. Finally, the user can access the external representation and have no idea of how the data is actually structured from the DBMS point of view.

The central component of this structure is the *logical data model*, which describes the structure of data at the conceptual layer. A data model is a set of constructs for describing data (see Section 1.2 for more detail). The implementation of the facilities listed above is achieved with reference to the logical data model. To create a database, its structure must be specified using the modeling constructs available. Such a specification is called a *schema* and the particular logical data model used restricts the ways in which a schema can be organized. After the schema has been set up, any change to the database must leave it in the form specified. Thus the notion of consistency now means "as specified in the schema".

The other important concept used by a DBMS is the *transaction*. A transaction consists of one or more changes to the database which take the database from one consistent state to another. To take a simple example, the transfer of a sum of money from one bank account to another would be a transaction. This transaction is made up of two updates – debiting a sum of money from one account and crediting the same sum to another account. It is vital that both of the changes are made or, in the case of failure, neither of them is. Otherwise the total sum of money in the system would change. If all of the component updates in the transaction are successful, the transaction *commits* its changes to permanent store. If anything goes wrong during the transaction, it is *aborted* and all of the changes are undone.

To enable the DBMS to function correctly, transactions must have the following four properties (jointly known as the ACID properties):

- *Atomicity.* If a transaction is made up of a number of component updates, then every update must take effect or none of them should. The sum of money must not be debited without being credited or vice versa.
- *Consistency.* The total effect of all of the components of the transaction must take the database from one consistent state to another. The total sum of money represented in the database must remain unchanged.
- *Isolation.* Each transaction must not affect the smooth and correct running of any other transaction. Thus no two transactions are allowed to try to change the same account at the same time, for fear of corrupting each other.

- *Durability.* After the transaction has successfully completed, nothing will permit the changes made to be lost – not even a system crash.

By organizing changes into transactions, a DBMS can successfully provide three of the main facilities listed above:

- *Resilience* is achieved by ensuring that all of the transactions which complete have their changes made permanent in some way before the crash, while the effects of any half-completed transactions are completely undone.
- *Concurrency control* is achieved by isolating each transaction through the use of *locks*. Each piece of data that the transaction is changing is made inaccessible to any other transaction and so no two transactions can conflict. On the other hand, transactions can jointly access data they are only going to read but not change. In this case, no transaction is permitted to try to change a piece of data that another transaction has locked for reading.
- *Integrity* is maintained since the effect of each transaction can be checked to verify that none of the constraints have been violated at the end of the transaction. Violations may result in the transaction being aborted or in automatic or user-directed compensating actions.

In summary then, a DBMS works by holding all of its data in a single form – using the logical data model – and then rigidly controlling access to data in that form. The next section discusses the most common logical models that are used.

1.1.2 Record-based DBMS

The kinds of database currently used for storing large amounts of information make use of the *record* as the principal data structure. A record, also frequently called a *tuple* or a *structure*, is a small collection of values which are stored together. The structure of a record consists of a number of *fields*, each of which has a name and can hold one value of a particular kind – called the *domain* of the field. In most database systems domains must be *atomic*. This means that the values held in the field are non-decomposable – they are usually either numbers of some kind or small textual strings. In particular, the value of a field cannot be a set and cannot be a record. To take an example, a small record held about a person in the database might include fields for the person's name, age and occupation. A suitable structure for this would be to have a string field called *name*, an integer field called *age* and another string field called *occupation*. If the record also had a field for the address of the person, this could only hold a string and could not itself be decomposable.

In order to manage the totality of information in a database, record-based DBMS partition the data into collections of records of the same kind. Thus there may be a set of records representing persons, all of which have these same three fields. There are two principal kinds of DBMS based on records:

- Network DBMS organize the collections of similar records as linked lists each holding a descriptive header record. Thus the set of person records will appear as a header record which points to the first person record. This in turn points to the second record and so on until the final person record points back to the header.
- Relational DBMS organize each collection of similar records as a table, with one column for each field and one row for each record, and furthermore require that one or more fields of the table have unique values for each record, i.e. a table is a set of records. In the case of the *Person* table, there are two possibilities. The first alternative would be to decide that the names are unique – no two people have the same name. However, this will be insupportable for an application of any size, so it is more likely that an extra field will be added which uniquely identifies a the person. In either case the identifying field is called the *primary key* of the record.

Figure 1.2 shows how the two kinds of DBMS organize a set of records. The primary key for the table is underlined.

Either of these organizations is fine provided that the sets of records all represent simple information about a real world entity – these can be called *entity records*. However, databases must also represent the relationships between these entities – for instance that a person works for a particular company.

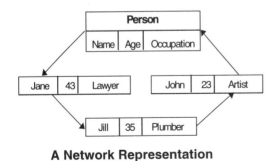

A Network Representation   **A Relational Representation**

Figure 1.2 Two organizations for a set of records.

Assuming that there is a parallel set of entity records for companies, the way that the two kinds of DBMS represent the relationship is shown in Figure 1.3.

- Network DBMS add an extra field to each *Person* record which is a pointer to a *Company* record – the relationship pointers are shown using thicker lines.
- Relational DBMS also add an extra field to the *Person* record, but this time it is a simple value which identifies the *Company* – this value contains the primary key of the *Company* record – the copy of the value in the *Person* record is called a *foreign key*. Thus the fact that Jane works for the company SGR is represented by the 17 in the *worksFor* column.

Already both representations are becoming somewhat difficult to understand either through having extraneous numbers in the relational case or by producing a complex web of pointers in a network representation. As will be seen in a succeeding section, the situation becomes significantly more complex and difficult to understand for more complicated kinds of relationship.

Designing a database in either of these systems consists of defining the organization into which the records will be put. In the network case this means specifying the record structures which will be supported and the links between them. In the relational case this means creating a set of tables which will hold the records. The most common approach to this design is to use some kind of diagrammatic tool. In the network case, the technique is called a Bachman

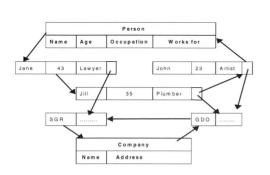

Person

Number	Name	Age	Occupation	Works for
5432	Jane	43	Lawyer	17
3467	Jill	35	Plumber	25
7531	John	23	Artist	25

Company

Number	Name	Address
17	SGR	....
25	GDC	....

A Network Representation   **A Relational Representation**

Figure 1.3 Two organizations for a simple relationship.

diagram. In the relational case, the entity relationship approach (described in Section 1.2.3) is used as a first step. Relational database design also uses a normalization technique in which the data is successively split into smaller and smaller tables which are well connected, maintain the semantics of the data and limit redundancy.

Manipulating a database is carried out rather differently in the two cases. In a network DBMS, some extra commands are embedded in a programming language which allow the programmer to navigate about the network, adding, removing, changing and displaying records. Thus a network DBMS is easier to use for those tasks in which it is required to access data which is related to the data already found. Relational databases are most commonly manipulated with the query language SQL. This permits queries to be written which retrieve or manipulate all or part of tables, which are connected using the foreign key mechanism. Alternatively for more complex tasks, SQL can be embedded in a full programming language.

Using either of these mechanisms, huge databases of commercial data have been set up and managed extremely effectively. This has been possible because large amounts of commercial data can easily be stored in records with atomic fields. However, the very success in these areas has motivated a whole range of new potential customers for DBMS, whose data cannot so easily be transformed into these simple structures.

■ 1.1.3 New applications areas for database systems

Traditionally, database systems have been used for a fairly restricted range of activities – mostly for holding commercial information arising in the context of banking, booking systems, payroll and so on. In fact, even these activities often place requirements which are beyond the capabilities of traditional DBMS. For instance, a stock-keeping system for an engineering company may very well wish to hold the notion that some stock items are components of others. The price of a composite stock item (one made out of others) may then need to be calculated partly from the sum of its components, which may in turn have components of its own. This kind of recursive calculation is beyond the range of many relational DBMS. Similarly a photograph of each account holder would be, for security purposes, a useful addition to a banking database. Yet most DBMS currently being used cannot manage pictorial data.

This section looks at some of the new kinds of data-intensive application – these will be called *advanced applications* – that involve data management activities which, at first sight, would seem to benefit from the use of a DBMS. In fact, they also have features which make the use of record-based DBMS extremely problematic. This is because they require facilities which are not among those described above or are different variations of those facilities. The next section will then summarize the new requirements which the advanced applications will make on the DBMS.

Computer aided design (CAD), computer aided engineering (CAE) and computer integrated manufacturing (CIM) all involve the creation and maintenance of the complex structures which describe technical objects. A group involved in design work may need to store securely a large number of such designs (each design potentially being a large and complex value) so that they can be worked on by a group of designers. This seems to point to the use of a DBMS to manage the data, but in this case the structures will be much more complex than those for the traditional applications and will probably also have a diagrammatic element as an essential component. Cooperative working must also be supported.

Computer aided software engineering (CASE) improves the process of producing and maintaining software by providing operations for storing and retrieving software components in a systematic way. These components are organized in complex graph structures which are very different from those handled by traditional DBMS. Moreover, an ideal CASE tool would allow documentation, designs, specifications and test data to be linked automatically. More complex structures for project management may be added on top and this would require a description of a complex organizational structure. Again cooperation between users will be important.

These two application areas are usually referred to as design applications, because they share common characteristics of managing complex design information as data.

Office information systems (OIS) manage the kinds of information traditionally housed in a paper-based office – documents, messages, lists, etc. The documents handled will not merely be long text strings, but may have a great deal of structure imposed on them – perhaps described using a mark-up language such as SGML or HTML. Once more there is the need to store large amounts of information and this will have a much richer structure than simple records of numbers and short text strings. There is also the need to store the processes with which these data are managed, since the tight integration of office data with the operations which use them will greatly simplify the overall organization.

Geographic information systems (GIS) are used to hold the basic information underlying various kinds of spatially and temporally related information. GIS increasingly play an important role in transport systems, the organization of power and telecommunications utilities, land management and underwater exploration. The information they rely on, deriving from survey and satellite pictures, is likely to be vast and employs not only the complex structures already mentioned, but adds to these spatial and temporal relationships and complex pictorial modes of visualization.

Hypermedia systems hold interlinked textual, numerical, pictorial and aural data and provide functions for traversing these structures. A museum information system, such as that provided in the Louvre, allows the user to find information about a given picture, artist, school, etc. and, since it holds the images of the pictures, will contain a considerable quantity of data, even after compression techniques have been used on the larger kinds of data. It is one of the most penetrating criticisms of prevalent DBMS that the largest "database" in the world – the World Wide Web – has developed with little or no use of database technology.

■ 1.1.4 Requirements arising from complex applications

The record-based DBMS emerged to suit business applications, for which they have been so successful. The importance of each of the facilities described above was recognized and so they were integrated into the development of a state-of-the-art DBMS. Most of these features are equally important to the advanced applications. However, some of these requirements need radical transformation, while there are, in addition, some completely new requirements.

The basic requirements which carry over include all of the ones listed in Section 1.1.1, of which the following appear in a somewhat modified form:

- The use of transactions remains crucial. However, transactions in traditional applications are typically short, being the few milliseconds it takes to move cash from one account to another, book a seat, or check out a library book. In contrast, transactions in advanced applications may very well be long – for instance, update to a design or a piece of software may well take several hours or even days to complete, since it is probably carried out by a user working on-line with an editor.
- Traditionally, isolation is a vital aspect of transactions since they are expected to compete for resources. Thus only one transaction at a time can

change a bank account – this is an effective strategy so long as the transactions are short. With long transactions, traditional concurrency control becomes infeasible since it is not practical to wait until a long transaction is finished for another to start. Compensating this, however, the transactions involved in design applications may very well be collaborative or cooperative rather than competitive, in which case a different strategy which involves new kinds of shared access may be needed.

- Many DBMS pay lip-service to the use of integrity constraints. However, advanced applications make much more use of integrity constraints since the data being described are related using far more constraining information. Advanced applications require a DBMS which allows complex constraints to be asserted and which automatically checks that all updates preserve the integrity of the database.

- The range of user interfaces must be greater. The reason for this is to mitigate the adverse effects of users having to interact with complex data using complex software. In particular, graphical interfaces will be more necessary and computationally complete interfaces need to be more seamlessly integrated with the system, in order to compensate users for the greater complexity of the applications.

At the same time, there are some requirements which advanced applications bring which are not found in traditional applications:

- Traditional applications have the implicit assumption that all data can be described using simple structures – in advanced applications, there is a strong requirement that complex data structures be available.

- In particular, the complexity of the data can only be managed tractably if the system provides data structures which more accurately mirror real-world information structures. For instance, representing one real world entity with a single denotable value in the database (*object identity*) and allowing direct *references* between objects, rather than using the indirect foreign key mechanism.

- Traditional applications further assume that there will be large numbers of database objects, each of which is fairly small and each of which belongs to a fairly small number of structures. Thus a large relational database will typically hold millions of records in up to 20 relations, each record being perhaps 200 bytes long. Advanced applications on the other hand will often require the management of large numbers of data structures holding small numbers of large objects. For instance, compare the values found in a database of nautical equipment parts held by a ship's chandler with a database supporting a company which designs ships and boats. The former will have many items, each of which carries very little information – a catalog number, a price, a supplier and so on. The latter will hold relatively few items, the designs of a few hundred craft and their components, but each item is likely to have a great deal of component information.

- Advanced applications place a much greater emphasis on holding pictorial and aural data. The use of multimedia underlies all of the advanced applications listed above.
- Furthermore, the complexity and dynamic nature of the data may be so great that it is best represented by application code inside the database. The semantics of a data type in traditional DBMS is expressable only in terms of the structural description achievable using the logical data model and as constraints imposed on this structure. In describing the semantics of design data, for instance, more emphasis is placed on how the data can be changed, how they can be displayed and so on, rather than solely in what forms they should be stored. Furthermore, office information may consist of information which is inherently procedural and is best represented as code.
- Whereas traditional applications rely on the idea that there is only one correct value for each piece of data at any one time, design databases require the notion of concurrent *versions* of some pieces of data. For instance, there may be several different versions of the sorting algorithm in a piece of software or of the design of a yacht.

To sum up, the new applications place a much greater emphasis on the complexity of the data, the involvement of multimedia types, non-competitive modes of access and a closer involvement with the code which operates on the data.

■ 1.1.5 Shortcomings of record-based DBMS

In terms of the advanced applications that have just been discussed, the record-based models have three significant deficiencies all of which greatly impede their applicability. First, they lack modeling expressiveness, which makes database design difficult for complex information structures. Second, they do not make it easy for users to express complex computations on the data. Finally, they do not integrate the computational aspect of an application with the data at all well. These problems, which are certainly encountered even for commercial applications, become much more pronounced for advanced applications since complex information structures and the computational aspect both are more important. In this section, these three problems are elaborated upon.

Data modeling deficiencies

The record-based DBMS provide a few simple structures and yet are being required to store information from the real world which is inherently complex. It is not surprising that they are difficult to use. There are two ways of looking at the shortcomings. The first way is to consider what is to be modeled and observe the difficulties in creating an appropriate model. The second way is to look at each construct in the record-based models and see what it is used for. The former demonstrates inelegancies and confusing indirection of expression. The latter reveals the overuse of constructs for multiple purposes so that looking at a schema does not easily reveal the meaning of each component.

Looking first at what is to be modeled:

- It is necessary to store information about real-world entities in a coherent way, but they turn out not to be well-modeled by records of numbers and strings. One record seldom holds all of the information about an entity. An entity may be represented by a single record, may have its component values scattered around a number of records, or may be just part of a larger record.
- Storing the properties of entities can be difficult to achieve unless they are numerical or textual. A property which has multiple values cannot fit easily, nor can a property which can take more than one type of value. For instance, the owner of a car may be a company or a person. It is difficult to model this.
- Storing the relationships between entities is achieved in a variety of ways. In Figure 1.3, the *worksFor* relationship is modeled by pointers in the network model or by foreign keys in the relational case. This works reasonably well as long as on at least one side of the relationship the entities are related to exactly one entity on the other side (a one-to-one or one-to-many relationship). In the *worksFor* example, each person works for exactly one company.

If the database were to reflect the more realistic situation in which people can work more for than one company, then this method breaks down. This means that each person potentially works for many companies and each company employs many people – this is called a many-to-many relationship (see Section 1.2.3 for more on this). In both network and relational databases, an extra set of records must be added to pair up the related entities. There are two bad effects of this. First, the extra set of records greatly complicates the schema. Second, this means that relationships in general are modeled by two completely different methods.

- Naming and entity identification is not well represented. In order to interrelate records in a relational database, it is necessary that each record have some component value which can be used as a primary key. This can be either naturally occurring information, such as a name, or an otherwise meaningless identifier (which may be human or system-created), but which is made visible in the schema.

If a naturally occurring key is chosen:

- uniqueness cannot be absolutely guaranteed, since the actual values of newly added data might violate this;
- existence cannot be guaranteed either, since new data may be encountered for which the value is missing;
- systems cannot easily be merged in case the unique identifiers lose their uniqueness – one example is trying to combine two sets of staff numbers after a company merger;
- the identifier field should not be updated, since all foreign key references will have to be sought and changed as well.

If an otherwise meaningless identifier is chosen:

- either a new identifier must be generated by the human process for which the database is supplied, which is additional work required only to overcome a weakness of the system which is supposed be saving effort;
- or there is a system-produced key which has no semantic value and yet resides in the same conceptual space as apparently similar information which does have a meaning.

The problem boils down to the "semantic overloading" of the constructs found in record-based DBMS. There are essentially two ways in which the relational model allows us to record the fact that two data values are related in some way:

(a) they are both fields in the same record; or
(b) they are in two records which are connected by having a common value in one of their columns.

Both of these mechanisms are used to model all kinds of relationships between the two entities.

The former is used for:

- gathering together the simple properties of an entity – these will usually appear as a column in the main relation representing the entity type;
- gathering together the components of a composite value – if one value is made up of other components (an address for instance), the components will appear as fields of the same relation;
- representing one-to-one relationships – here two entities can be put together in the same record;
- representing many-to-many relationships – here a special relation is used and related items are paired by having their primary keys be fields of the same record in the relation.

The latter is used for:

- representing multi-valued properties – a separate relation is provided which pairs the primary key of an entity with one of the values;
- representing one-to-one or one-to-many relationships – here the two entities will be in two tuples linked by the foreign key;
- subtyping – the records of the super- and sub-typed information are joined by a common value – note however that which is the subtype and which the supertype can be lost.

So the same mechanisms are used for different purposes and, moreover, there is no way of knowing when looking at a given relational schema which of these purposes is intended by each use of the mechanisms. In fact too much of the semantics of a record-based schema resides entirely in the names chosen for the components of the schema. Even worse, some of the meanings above can be represented either by being in the same relation or by being joined by key fields.

Expressing complex computation

Eventually users of any long-lived database will develop a need to carry out complex computations over the data. However, performing general computations with a record-based database involves some kind of embedding of a database-oriented language in a normal programming language. This leads to a complicated programming environment in which two largely different conceptions of data fit together uneasily. This is called the *impedance mismatch problem*, conveying the notion that moving data between the two systems encounters a deterring force.

A more helpful approach is to unify the two notions of data so that data in the database and data in the programming language look the same. Unifying the data model of the database and the type system of the programming language would permit complex database programming to proceed in a much simpler, efficient and reliable manner.

The key notion here is *persistence*, which can mean different things in different contexts, but essentially refers to a system in which programming language data can be stored without transformation. Given a programming language X, the term *persistent X* means an implementation of the language in which any of its data can be stored without transformation, although many so-called persistent languages restrict which of their values can be stored. In such a system, the impedance mismatch goes away, since the database specific model is eliminated. The database is organized according to the constructs provided in the language. In this case, many of the problems of accessing data through complex computations goes away.

Chapter 3 discusses different aspects of persistence in more detail.

Integrating computation and data

Even given a language whose programs store their data, there remains the question of what happens to those programs. In most currently used DBMS, all programs, even those written in a query language, cannot be stored along with the data in the database. Instead they must be placed in a file system or some other external repository. Traditional DBMS have no way of storing code.

Clearly, a more reliable method would be to integrate the code, which may be application code, queries, transactions and so on. To hold the code in the DBMS along with the data enables the system to ensure more readily the integrity of code and data. The main motivation for the development of DBMS in the first place was that, by placing all data under the control of a single software system, greater control over data integrity could be achieved in the first place. It is a natural consequence that a DBMS would be even more effective if it also managed the code that accessed that data.

Given the need to bring code into the DBMS, there are a number of ways in which this could be achieved:

- The structure of the database could be extended to include ways of integrating code together with the particular kinds of data that it uses.
- An application storage structure could be added to the DBMS, so that application code has a place inside the DBMS, but one separate from the data.
- Code could be considered as just another kind of data which the data model of the DBMS can recognize. In this case code and data can be freely intermixed thus creating whatever structures are deemed useful.

OODBMS follow the first of these possibilities, by creating objects as instances of classes which encapsulate both properties and operations. Any up-to-date DBMS should also follow the second possibility, whatever kind of logical data model it uses. A DBMS without good software engineering support has extremely limited appeal. In the view of the author, the final possibility is the one that DBMS will eventually follow. Values which are themselves code will ultimately be seen to be important in their own right and to require the same storage possibilities as other data. The distinction between "code" and "data" will increasingly be seen as an unfortunate and anachronistic irrelevance.

Summary

Record-based models, although extraordinarily successful in managing simple kinds of data, are not quite as applicable to complex data. They can of course be used for complex data. It is possible to turn software, designs, structured texts, maps and so on into atomic records. The problems lie in the intellectual complexity that is required to manage the translation between the intuitive information structure and the set of records in the database and to integrate the code that maintains that data.

One proposal for assisting with the first of these problems is to use a more intuitive, semantic data model as an intermediary device between the users' understanding of the real world and the database. It is this kind of data modeling that the next section describes.

■ 1.2 Data modeling

Data modeling is the process of creating a description of a database which is intended to hold a collection of related information. Originally, data modeling concentrated on the creation of a description of the *structure* of the database, but increasingly it is used to describe restrictions which are to apply to the data – *constraints* – and also some aspects of how the data is to be manipulated – often called the *behavior* of the database.

The database description is framed in terms of the constructs of a data model. One of the principal problems discussed above is that data modeling is difficult using the relational data model if the information being described is in any way complex. One response to this problem is to make use of more intuitive data models to cope with the complexity since they are held to capture more of the meaning of the information being modeled than do the record-based models. This section describes the nature of semantic data models and how they are used as a preliminary step in designing record-based databases. It contains some amplification on the nature of data modeling, a categorization of the constructs which might be found in a data model, a description of the most popular model – the entity relationship model – and a survey of some other important models which add extra facilities to those found in the entity relationship model.

■ 1.2.1 What is data modeling?

Data modeling is the activity of describing information so that it can be stored and manipulated as data in a computer system. The description is called a *schema* and is created in terms of a *data model*. The data model consists of a small number of *constructs* or structures using which some aspects of the nature of data can be described. A schema is a set of instances of these constructs. Thus the network data model contains constructs for describing linked lists of records and pointers between them, but not tables, while the relational data model contains constructs for describing tables of records, but not linked lists.

It is useful here to say a little more about the relationships between a database, a schema and a data model. A database is a set of related data which is an instance of a schema. The database is one of many different databases which could be created out of the schema. Thus a schema which describes a library system could be instantiated as one database for Glasgow Public Libraries, another for the British Museum, and so on. A schema is a set of *metadata*, or descriptions of data, and this is an instance of a data model. The same data model could be used to create the library schema or a nautical schema. Confusingly, a schema is also called a model of its data. In this sense, a data model is a model of data or a *meta-model*.

There are data models which are concerned with various aspects of the database system. In particular there are data models which are appropriate for describing a database at each of the three layers shown in Figure 1.1. For instance, there will be a *physical data model* for describing the structure of data as stored on the disk – this will have constructs for describing files and how the data is partitioned into files. There is a *logical data model* for describing the conceptual structure of the data. At the external level, there are data models which allow views to be described and also data models which provide a more meaningful representation. One of the key concerns that should be noted is that the same database can be described in more than one way for different purposes.

The current section, however, will concentrate on a particular kind of data model, called a *semantic data model*. Such a data model is designed to have constructs which are more closely related to the kinds of structuring that humans are thought to use when conceptualizing about the real world. The motivating factor behind the use of semantic data models is that the data modeling process will be easier to accomplish using more familiar constructs.

Initially semantic models were intended to be used as off-line tools as the first step in the design of a record-based database. The semantic model is used in conjunction with the logical model as follows. The database is designed using the semantic model, since this is easier to work with in the first instance. The resulting design is mapped into the logical model, by a (semi-)automatic process. The logical model is then entered into the DBMS and is used for the lifetime of the database. Increasingly, however, semantic data modeling tools have been integrated as key components of the DBMS. The database specification is entered into the computer using the semantic model and the logical model is produced as an implicit part of creating the database from the semantic design. In some systems, the logical model is hidden completely and all interaction with users occurs through the semantic model.

What aspects of the real world are to be modeled? Consider, for instance, a nautical application. The information to be managed consists of things, such as vessels and ports; properties of things, such as a vessel's tonnage or a port's name; relationships between things, such as that between a vessel and its home port; and perhaps also properties of these relationships, such as when the vessel was registered there. There are also restrictive statements that can be made about the things, such as "only small boats are registered in Helensburgh"; changes that can be made to the data, like "change the port of registration for a given vessel"; and questions that can be asked, such as "how many vessels are registered in Helensburgh?".

An adequate data model should be able to express as much of this as possible without requiring the user to make involved contortions to fit in with an implementation-oriented structure. Note that natural language, with its nouns, adjectives, verbs, adverbs, statements, commands and questions, is highly tuned for the job. Unfortunately, the structure of human language is still too little understood for humans to be able to instruct computers accurately using it.

■ 1.2.2 A categorization of fundamental modeling constructs

A data model has been defined here to be a set of descriptive constructs with which a body of data can be described. This section will list some of the kinds of construct which a particular semantic data model might provide. There are three aspects of this description:

(a) the *structure* of the data to be managed,

(b) *constraints* that limit the number of states that the database can take and how the data can change, and

(c) the *computations* which will be performed on the data – the behavioral part.

The relational model has very simple structural constructs – relations as sets of records. It also can be used as a basis on which to specify constraints (using the SQL *assert* command, for instance), while using interfaces such as SQL, there are ways of specifying updates and queries. In general, data models tend to concentrate on the first of these three parts, since the ideas involved in data structuring are the most fundamental, in that once the data has been set up, the other two aspects can be added later. Data structure is also rather simpler and better understood than is constraint handling and the description of computation. However, the coherent integration of all three parts is clearly desirable from a software maintenance point of view.

Within this categorization, a number of concepts will now be distinguished.

Structural constructs

The structural constructs of a data model provide different kinds of organizational structures into which data can be fitted. They can describe what kinds of data can be stored and how they are related. In general, values in a database are grouped into types for ease of description, so that many different instances can be described by a single type description. A *type* is the description of a set of values together with the kinds of operation which can be used to manipulate these values.

In general there are two kinds of type found in a data model:

- *Entity types* describe the things in the real world which are to be stored in the database. These may be further categorized into:

  - *base* entity types (also called *literal* or *printable* or *lexical* types). These are entities, such as numbers or strings, which are the fundamental building blocks of the database and will be associated with a discrete sequence of memory and be capable of being displayed or printed.

  - *abstract atomic* (or *non-lexical*) entities. These are entities which are designed to model one complex real world entity as an identifiable and indivisible database value. Although they themselves have no printable

representation, they are related to printable entities, which might, for instance, be properties of the entity.
- *composite* (or *bulk*) entities. These are entities which are made up of component values. Examples of bulk entities include records or sets.

- *Link types* connect two or more entity types of the database. A link type may be thought of as a function and may have attributes defined on it. Some kinds of link which can be usefully distinguished include:

  - *attribution* – the link between one entity and another that is a property of it;
  - *part-of* – the link between a bulk entity and an entity that is a member of it;
  - *inheritance* (or *subtyping*) – the link between two entity types that one is a more specialized version of another; and
  - *instantiation* – the relationship between a data value and its type.

For a nautical database, vessels and ports would be represented by abstract entity types; the names of the vessels and ports, the tonnage of the vessels, etc. would be base entity types which are related to the vessels and ports by attribution; the set of ports visited would be a bulk entity type attribute of each vessel; there may be entity types for passenger vessels and cargo vessels each of which are subtypes of the vessel entity type; and so on.

Constraint constructs

The next aspect of a database which should be described is the constraints which limit the number of acceptable states of the database and also how the data may change. In traditional database systems, constraints are added after the data modeling process – as separate assertions or as fragments of application programs built on top of the database. Providing the constraints as a coherent part of the schema is superior since the constraints will then be more explicit and easier to maintain.

There are many different kinds of constraint found in database systems, but constraint management is, in general, poorly understood and poorly provided by current DBMS. Even semantic models provide insufficient facilities in this respect. Yet, as has already been mentioned, for advanced applications, the complexity of the meaning of the data is best captured by constraints.

A constraint is essentially a predicate held in the DBMS. There are many possibilities concerning what it refers to, how it is specified and how it takes effect. Here are a few of the issues:

- Constraints can be either *static* (i.e. they place limits on data) or *dynamic* (they limit, instead, changes to the data). That the age of a person must be less than 150 is a static constraint, that the age can only be increased is a dynamic constraint.

- Constraints can be *inherent* (built into the DBMS), *implicit* (expressible in the data model) or *explicit* (expressible outside of the data model). In the relational model, the fact that all fields must hold atomic data is inherent, the ability to identify key fields is implicit, and the ability to assert constraints on records is explicit.

- Constraints can limit data or metadata. Thus to assert that the age of a person is less than 150 limits the data, while to limit the values in a table to be numbers or strings is a constraint on metadata.

- One important class of constraints are the *integrity constraints*. These are general constraints which state what it means for a database to be well formed. In the relational model, a *key constraint* asserts that the values in key fields are indeed unique. The important kind of constraint, called a *referential constraint*, asserts that a foreign key value will exist. Whether or not such constraints are enforced by the database is an important issue.

- Constraints may be implemented in a variety of ways – in the DBMS software, using a query language, in application code, or using the constraint constructs of a data model. The more explicit a constraint is the more control the programmer will have over its effect.

- The effect of constraint violations can be: to abort the transaction which causes it, to initiate some repair activity, or to alert the user.

- Constraints can be used to interact with the behavior of the database in a number of ways:

  - They can be used as *pre-conditions* which are checked before an operation is allowed to take place, or as *post-conditions* which are checked after an operation has completed and which, if violated, cause the effects to be undone.

  - They can *trigger* an operation. If a violation is found because of an update, the operation will be invoked as a result.

  - They can be used as part of an *exception* handling mechanism. In this case the constraint signals an unusual condition and a separate operation, called an exception handler, takes over in place of the currently operating code.

Behavioral constructs

Finally, the ways in which the data is to be manipulated must be described. Traditionally, this has been completely separated from the data modeling process. Simple manipulations are described in the query language, while more complex computations are described in a programming language which has been tacked on to the database system. There is a strong argument, again in terms of maintainability, for a closer integration between the data structure and the code which manipulates it. This becomes more pressing for the kinds of complex application which were described in Section 1.1.3.

Some of the behavioral aspects of a database which can usefully be brought into an integrated structure include:

- *Derived data*. This includes the description of properties which are calculated rather than stored and of data sets whose membership is calculated from other sets.
- *Storage techniques*. The integration of storage structures and their access mechanisms inside the DBMS would make physical data re-organization easier to automate.
- *User interaction techniques*. It would, equivalently, be easier to configure the user interface given DBMS components which could be customized.
- *Queries and transactions*. The ability to store these alongside the data would make their re-use easier to support.
- *Parametric interfaces*. These could also be maintained as an extensible set of database values.

In general, then, the ability to maintain some kinds of code fragment inside the DBMS creates a system which is easier and more reliable to manage.

This section has described in general terms some of the kinds of construct which a data model might have. Any particular data model will have different flavors of these with different degrees of detail and emphasis. The next section describes the most common semantic data model – the entity relationship model – and is followed by a more general survey.

▓ 1.2.3 The ER model and its usage

The entity relationship data model (ER) is by far the most popular design tool for the creation of relational databases. Introduced in 1976 by Chen to overcome the problems discussed in Section 1.1.5, ER is a diagrammatic modeling system, which allows an end-user to design a database without having to understand much about the DBMS. ER is, in fact, a family of different models, since the original proposal has been extended in a variety of ways. In this section, the original ER model will be described, while some of the extensions will appear in the next section.

The ER model has three principal constructs:

- entity types – meaning specifically abstract entity types in the terminology given above;

- attributes – base entity types; and
- relationships – composite types each of which connects two or more entity types.

These are linked in three ways. Each entity type is connected to a set of attributes which are properties of the entity. Similarly, a relationship may have one or more attributes. Finally, relationships are connected to the entity types which take part in the relationship.

The ER model supports three kinds of constraint:

- an attribute of an entity type can be identified as being a key – i.e. each instance of the entity has a unique value;
- an attribute can be identified to be single-valued or multi-valued; and
- the number of times that an entity instance can take part in a relationship can be restricted.

Figure 1.4 shows an example of an ER schema.

The diagram shows the design of a database to hold the information about a shipping company's fleet. It has three main information structures – the entity types represented by rectangles. Each of these has a number of attributes represented by ovals and they are connected by relationships represented by diamonds. The relationship *registered at* also has an attribute – the date on which the registration took place. For each entity type, the key attribute is underlined. The *Dependents* attribute of the *Crew* entity type has a double oval indicating

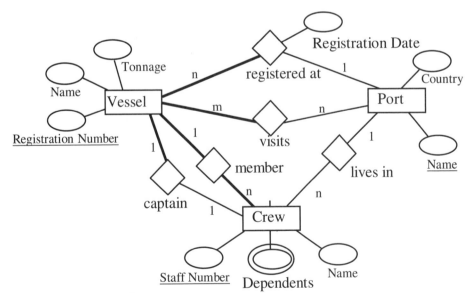

Figure 1.4   An ER schema.

that the attribute may have more than one value – all of the other attributes must be single-valued.

Five relationships are represented and the connecting lines are decorated in two ways:

- Some lines are emboldened. This means that each entity of the type connected must take part in the relationship at least once. Thus every vessel must have a captain, although not every crew member is a captain.
- The lines connecting entity types to relationships all have either "1", "m" or "n" by them. These partition the relationships into:
  - one-one relationships: those labeled with a "1" on both sides of the relationship – each entity from each type is associated with at most one entity of the other side – thus a vessel has only one captain and a captain has only one vessel,
  - one-many relationships: those labeled with a "1" on one side and with an "n" on the other – a single entity in one type is associated with many entities of the other – thus each crew member works on one vessel, but each vessel has many crew members; and
  - many-many relationships: those labeled with an "m" on one side and an "n" on the other – entities from each side may be associated with many entities from the other – thus each vessel visits many ports and each port is visited by many ships.

An ER diagram is a moderately detailed description of a collection of information that should be stored. This description can then be used systematically to produce a relational schema suitable for the task of maintaining this information. This is achieved by the following steps:

1. Every entity type will become a table in the relational schema, with the key from the ER diagram used as the primary key of the table. Thus there will be tables for *Vessel*, *Port* and *Crew*.
2. Every single-valued attribute of an entity type will become a column in the table. For instance, *Port* will have the two columns *Name* and *Country*.
3. Every multi-valued attribute of an entity type will become a table in its own right with one column for the primary key and another for the attribute. Thus the *Crew* table will not have a column for *Dependents*, instead there will be a table with columns for *Dependent* and *Staff Number*.
4. Every one-many relationship will be represented by placing a column in the entity type table for the many side which is the primary key of the one side. Thus there will be a column in the *Vessel* table holding the name of the port it is registered at.

5. Every one-one relationship will also be represented by a foreign key in one of the tables. If only one of the entity types must take part in the relationship then the foreign key should go in that side. Thus, the *Vessel* table will have a column holding the staff number of the captain. If neither or both sides must take part, then the decision is more finely balanced – the technique requires some guidance as to which representation would create more redundancy.

6. Every many-many relationship is represented as a table in its own right with columns for the primary keys of the participating entity types. Thus there will be a table for the ports that ships have visited, with one column for the ship's registration number and another for the port name.

7. Finally, every attribute of a relationship will appear in a column next to the column representing the relationship. Thus the *Vessel* table will have a column for the port it is registered at and another for the date of registration.

The full relational schema is therefore:

```
relation Vessel( registration: string; name: string; tonnage: string;
       captain:  integer; registeredAt: string; registrationDate: date )
relation Crew( staffNumber: integer; name: string;
       membershipRegistration:    string; livesIn: string )
relation Port( name: string; country: string )
relation Dependent( staffNumber: integer; dependentName: string )
relation Visit( registration: string; portname: string )
```

In summary, the ER approach permits a relatively intuitive design process to lead to a well structured relational database. However, for information structures of any complexity, the constructs provided are insufficient. The ER model soon becomes unwieldy as different kinds of relationship appear, whose constraints the ER model cannot express. Moreover, the ER model takes no account at all of the behavioral aspect of an application.

■ 1.2.4 More complex data models

The simplicity of the basic ER model is at once its great strength, being relatively easy to master, and its weakness, since it quickly runs out of expressive power. It is not surprising therefore that a variety of other semantic data models have been proposed which intend to be alternatives to ER or to extend it in some way. The differences considered in this section fall into four categories: a change to the underlying paradigm of expression, the provision of different constructs, the ability to express more detail (usually in the form of constraints), and the inclusion of a behavioral element.

Changing the paradigm

The functional data model (FDM) is typical of data models with a different paradigm. FDM brings out the semantic interrelationships in the form of functions. Everything in FDM is a function. There are functions for entity types (for instance in our example there will be a function *Vessel* which takes no arguments and returns the set of vessels in the database). Attributes and relationships are also expressed as functions, so there would be functions *Tonnage*, which takes a vessel as an argument and returns its tonnage, and *RegisteredAt* which takes a vessel and returns the port at which it is registered. Note that FDM does not clearly distinguish base-valued attributes from relationships with other abstract entities. This distinction which is so clear in ER has not always been found to be useful at the design level and so tends to disappear from later models, including the object-oriented models. It will be seen later that the distinction is important at the implementation level for reasons of efficiency.

Adding constructs

The extra constructs provided by some models include the ability to describe bulk types explicitly – thus there are types for sets or lists in some data models – and to express part-of and inheritance relationships. The IFO data model, for instance, provides an aggregate type to model part-of relationships – an aggregate is similar to a record. In IFO, it would be appropriate to model an address as an aggregate having components which hold the house number, street, city and postal code. The most important additional construct, found in many models, is inheritance.

Inheritance is an important expressive device for semantic modeling, all the more so since it is one which people are accustomed to use in the real world. The basic idea of inheritance is best introduced by an example. If the nautical database must be extended to distinguish passenger ships and cargo ships, the one expectation of the resulting database is that all the instances of the set of cargo ships are also instances of the set of ships. Moreover all of the properties of ships are also properties of cargo ships. In data modeling terms this is stated as "*Cargo Vessel* inherits from *Vessel*.". The newly created entity types can have further attributes of their own. Thus passenger ships have an attribute which is the maximum number of passengers that they are allowed to carry, whereas cargo ships do not have this attribute. The extended entity relationship data model (EER) adds inheritance to the basic ER constructs. An EER schema is shown in Figure 1.5 (using the notation of Elmasri and Navathe) which distinguishes the two kinds of vessel and also two different kinds of port.

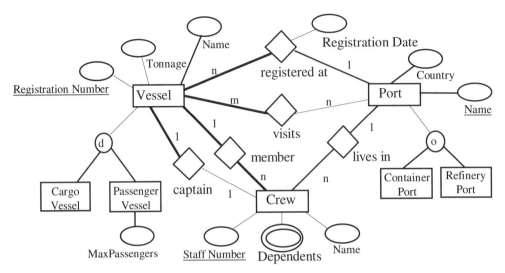

Figure 1.5 An EER schema.

Adding more implicit constraints

Extra constraints provide more detail and a clearer description of the nature of the information being managed. For instance, some models permit further assertions to be made about the nature of an attribute. One common example is the constraint that a particular attribute must have a value for every instance – there can be no missing values. Every vessel must have a registration number, for instance. Another kind of constraint is on inheritance relationships. The EER diagram in Figure 1.5 shows two kinds of inheritance relationship. The "d" in the inheritance relationship between ships symbolizes the assertion that the set of cargo ships and passenger ships are disjoint – a vessel is either one or the other. On the other hand the "o" in the inheritance between ports signifies that ports can be both refinery ports and container ports – the subtypes overlap.

Including a behavioral element

Finally, there has been a growing tendency to attempt to include some computational aspects into data models. This can mean including a number of different kinds of computations.

The first aspect which can usefully be included is *derived data*. There are at least two kinds of derived data:

- A *derived attribute* is one which is calculated from other stored data, rather than being stored redundantly. For instance, given a date of birth, it would be redundant and inflexible to store the age of a person as well. Some data models can express the fact that an attribute is derived. Less frequently, the derivation formula can be expressed.

- A *derived type* is one whose membership is calculated, usually by filtering the membership of some other type. For instance, the type *Child* might be defined to be all members of the type *Person* whose age is less than 17. The semantic data model (SDM) of Hammer and McLeod has elaborate mechanisms for this.

More ambitiously, some data models attempt to provide constructs for describing values which are essentially fragments of computation. TAXIS is typical of this approach. TAXIS is a textual database design language. The following fragment of TAXIS shows how an abstract entity type is defined in TAXIS:

```
PERSON_CLASS PERSON with
  keys: person_id: (name, address)
  characteristics  name: PERSON_NAME
                              address: ADDRESS_VALUE
                              phone#: PHONE_VALUE
  attribute_properties:   age: AGE_VALUE
                                  sex: SEX_VALUE
end
```

In this description, the attributes of *PERSON* are defined in terms of whether they are keys and whether they must have a value (in which case they are characteristics). Using the same kind of language, TAXIS also permits the definition of transactions:

```
TRANSACTION_CLASS RESERVE_SEAT with
parameter_list reserve_seat: (p, f);
locals  p:PERSON;
        f:FLIGHT;
        x:INTEGER;
prereqs
        seats_left: f.seats_left > 0
actions
        make_reservation:
                insert_object_in RESERVATION with
                    person  <- p, flight <- f;
        decrement_seats: f.seats_left <- f.seats_left - 1
        assign_aux_vars: x <-f.seats_left
returns
        rtrn: x
end
```

which specifies a transaction in terms of its input and output parameters, the pre-conditions which must hold before it can be executed and the component actions which comprise the changes the transactions will make to the database.

However, having once started to include some aspects of computation into the database description, the designer quickly feels the need for more facilities and ultimately the seamless integration of data structure description and behavioral description. This is one of the main motivating factors behind the development of object-oriented databases.

■ 1.3 Advanced DBMS

Although object-oriented systems are the most discussed alternative to the basic record-based DBMS, there are a number of separate developments, each of which attempts to deal with one or more of the problems stated above. The research in each of the areas to be discussed is an important contribution to the development of database systems. Many of them have had a strong influence on OODBMS and all will contribute to emerging database standards in the long run.

■ 1.3.1 Historical DBMS

Historical DBMS provide facilities for retaining all past states of a database. Thus every time a value is updated or deleted, the old value is not removed. Instead all values are time-stamped with a creation and destruction date and so it becomes possible to find out what values were current at any time. POSTGRES is one system which provides this facility.

Historical DBMS are an initial attempt at providing multiple versions of data. However, they are limited in this respect as they do not permit multiple **coexisting** versions. At any one time, only a single version of a datum is valid and this will not be sufficient for design databases.

■ 1.3.2 Complex object DBMS

Complex object DBMS, also known as non-first normal form relational DBMS, are relational DBMS in which values in the tables may themselves be records. For instance, if companies are only a subsidiary element of the database of people, then the *worksFor* field could contain the whole of the company record. Such DBMS provide significantly improved modeling power, since the artificially contrived foreign key mechanism need not be used and referential integrity constraints are directly represented. RM/T is one example of such a system.

Extended relational DBMS, such as POSTGRES, take this approach a little further by permitting fields of tables to be calculated by functions (programmed in a programming language). In this way derived data can easily be integrated.

POSTGRES allows user-defined abstract data types to be added to the system, but once more the operations of the type must be programmed outside of the database.

Complex object DBMS provide a significant step towards object orientation and solve many of the problems discussed in Section 1.1.5. Moreover they can be made to fit on top of relational systems, with simple mapping operations between the two forms. However, they do not fully integrate the behavioral aspect of the data into the DBMS.

1.3.3 Deductive DBMS

Deductive DBMS (DDBMS) concentrate on the importance of derived data and integrity constraints and provide mechanisms for describing data in terms of these constraints. They are mostly developed as persistent forms of the language Prolog, which is a language which permits the description of the data as simple facts and rules to generate other facts. Since the simple facts look very like records, it has proved possible to combine Prolog with a relational DBMS to provide persistence. In fact, mathematically speaking, a description in terms of facts and rules is an extended form of the relational model. Datalog is the best known example of a deductive database language and systems such as CORAL are useful mechanisms for researching constraint management, but are somewhat lacking in data modeling tools.

DDBMS and OODBMS have developed in different directions since they attempt to tackle different sub-problems posed by advanced applications. DDBMS tackle the need for better constraint handling powers, while OODBMS concentrate on behavioral modeling. Clearly, the ultimate database systems will integrate these two approaches.

1.3.4 Persistent programming languages

Persistent programming languages (PPLs) attempt to eliminate the "impedance mismatch" between data structuring tools and programming languages. However, instead of starting from data structuring and enhancing it with programming components as do OODBMS, PPLs start from the programming language and extend this with database capabilities. In a PPL, the type system provides the data model and, given that the PPL has a modern type system with parameterized types, polymorphic types and multimedia types, rich structuring mechanisms are available for describing the data. In their most advanced form, such as Napier88, PPLs include procedures as a first class data type and so it is straightforward to manage program fragments in the same way as other data values.

There are two important ideas which act as the basis for PPLs. First, in a PPL values of any type can be stored with equal ease, including multimedia and procedural values. Second, the data do not require their structure to be changed when they are stored. The complexity of building data-intensive applications which have a considerable computational aspect is usually intensified since two different data structures are required – one for data storage and one for in-memory programming. The classical example of this is the use of a query language embedded in a programming language. Each has different data structuring devices and so the programmer must manage both representations and the translation between the two. PPLs, having a single representation for in-memory and on-disk data, remove the need for this.

The research into PPLs has been of considerable influence on the development of OODBMS and the degree to which the different OODBMS comply with the principles of persistence will form part of the discussion in this book.

■ 1.3.5 Active DBMS

The term active DBMS means a DBMS which contains some behavioral component, most frequently in the form of triggered activities. The activity is usually some kind of update to the database or output to database users. Most DBMS, even if they can store activities rely on a user action to cause them to be executed. Thus a debit transaction is triggered by a customer requesting money from an ATM. In an active DBMS, the activity may be started off by another change to the database or by an automatically detectable event such as the passage of a period of time. The description of a change will have two parts: an event and a condition which is checked when such an event occurs. In the banking example, the debit transaction may be the event and the condition may be that this debit brings the balance below the credit limit. When a debit event causes the condition *balance < credit limit* to be true, then an activity such as send a letter to the customer or alert the bank manager will occur.

Active DBMS are another attempt to bring computation and integrity checking into the DBMS. Such a system can be used to maintain the integrity of a system by causing integrity violations to trigger repair actions. Once more, such mechanisms will be ultimately included in all DBMS and some record-based and object-oriented DBMS already include effective triggering mechanisms.

1.3.6 Domain specific database systems

One last response to the problems outlined in Section 1.1.5 is to create application-area specific DBMS. Two domains have been subject to considerable research: spatial databases and temporal databases.

Geographic information systems (GIS) and other spatial data management systems play an increasing role in a variety of activities – telecommunications, utility planning and leisure activities for instance. If the spatial aspect of data dominates the activities, it may very well be sensible to provide a system in which the particular integrity constraints that hold for spatial data are embedded deeply (and therefore more efficiently) into the software that maintains the data. GIS include different physical storage techniques, spatial user interfaces, query languages and spatial data structures to assist in the development of spatial applications.

Temporal databases attempt to bring a more complete account of the nature of time into databases. For instance, they provide mechanisms for distinguishing the time that a piece of data is valid for in the real world (*valid time*), from when it becomes stored in the database (*transactional time*). They also provide query languages in which the user can use concepts such as "before" or "during" in writing queries.

Both of these kinds of DBMS are attempting to provide new structures inside the DBMS data model and new facilities to use these structures. Much of the research carried out in these areas has made use of the object-oriented paradigm and so spatial and temporal components of OODBMS can be expected to emerge in the near future.

1.4 Object-oriented database management systems

This section introduces OODBMS in the context of the foregoing discussion of database systems, their problems and some of the techniques being proposed to deal with them. The section starts by outlining the main ideas behind object orientation and then looks at how this fits with previous database techniques and why it might be a suitable paradigm for database systems.

1.4.1 What is object orientation?

Object orientation is a paradigm for the implementation of computer systems which has emerged separately in the context of programming languages, artificial intelligence and data modeling. The programming language history begins with the language Simula in the mid-1960s and emerges in full force with the languages Smalltalk and C++ in the early 1980s. Similar structural ideas arose in the field of artificial intelligence (AI) in the form of frame-based systems and actor systems. AI programs are among the most complex to design and so researchers in this field felt a pressing need to develop paradigms which simplified their tasks by using familiar conceptual structures.

The framework which has come to be known as the object-oriented paradigm, is built around a small number of powerful constructs for data description. These are:

- *Object identity*. Every real world entity being stored will be represented by one indivisible structure, called an *object*, which is the base point for all of the information about that entity. This structure is uniquely and consistently identified by an internal identifier.
- *Classification*. Every object will be an instance of a class of objects all of which will have the same *properties*.
- *Encapsulation*. Each class will also have associated with it a set of operations which manipulate objects in the class. Thus the full description of the class will include not only a set of properties (which resemble the attributes in an ER diagram), but also a set of operations, each including an interface specifying the parameters involved and a code fragment specifying the implementation.
- *Information hiding*. Some parts of the class description are made inaccessible to any part of the application outside of the class description itself. One common scheme is to allow only the operations to be available to other parts of the system and to keep the properties hidden.
- *Inheritance*. The classes take part in an inheritance hierarchy, so that a new class can be defined as inheriting all of the properties and operations from a previously existing class, together with adding some additional ones.
- *Overriding* and *late binding*. In defining a new class as inheriting from an old one, it may be possible to redefine some of the definition – usually the operations. In this case, when an operation is invoked for a given object, the particular version of the operation which is executed depends upon which class the object belongs to.

Chapter 2 will elaborate on these ideas in detail.

Programming an object-oriented system consists almost exclusively of defining new classes to add to the inheritance hierarchy or of adding new properties to already existing classes. A start-up system comes with classes for the base entity types and a variety of system classes, such as bulk entity types, storage structures, user interface components and so on. The next section will describe how these ideas compare with other semantic data modeling methodologies.

1.4.2 An example of a class

To illustrate the ideas given above briefly, here is the description of the class of passenger ships, which extends the design of the entity type shown in Figure 1.5.

```
class PassengerVessel
isa Vessel
properties
   public maxPassengers: integer
   private passengers: set(Person)
   private purser: Person
operations
   public takeOnBoard( newPassenger: Person )
   public display
end class
```

The first line introduces and names the class. The second line places it in the inheritance hierarchy as being a subclass of *Vessel*. Lines 4 to 6 list the properties of the class. Note that the first of these is a base entity, the second a composite entity and the last an abstract entity. The free mixture of base values and objects is characteristic of the object-oriented approach. The eighth and ninth lines each give the interface of an operation – one which adds a new passenger to the set of passengers and one to display the properties of the class. There may well be a *display* operation for the *Vessel* class as well, in which case, this one will override it. Access to the *passengers* and *purser* properties has been restricted, by marking them "private". This means that only the code bodies of the operations in the *PassengerVessel* class can access them. The *maxPassengers* property and the two operations can be referenced from any code using the class.

1.4.3 Comparing object models with other data models

The primary feature that object orientation carries over from the semantic data models already discussed is that the database will be described mainly in terms of abstract entity types. An object in an OODBMS is very similar to an entity in an ER schema. However, instead of mapping the abstract object down into tables in which the data associated with the object becomes scattered over a number of records, an OODBMS will preserve the unity of the object. The description of the object in terms of a number of properties will remain the definition of its structure throughout its lifetime. It will never get decomposed – at least in the programmer's eyes. (At the physical level, the system may reorganize the data in any way appropriate to the improvement of efficiency.)

Inheritance has been introduced into data modeling to improve the conciseness of the description. Inheritance has the same effect in an OODBMS schema as it does in an EER schema. The example in the previous subsection would have been much longer if all of the properties and operations which belong to the *Vessel* class had to be recreated here.

The main advantage that the object-oriented model provides over the semantic models is the coherent inclusion of behavior in the form of the operations which are part of the class definition. As has been seen, some semantic models attempt to provide behavioral components, but at best this only consists of parts of the computational aspects of a database application. OODBMS provide a mechanism for integrating all of the computation into the database description.

■ 1.4.4 Object orientation as the basis for data management

An OODBMS is characterized by having an object-oriented logical data model and by using an object-oriented programming language as its principal interface (hopefully backed up by an appropriate software engineering environment). The description of the database in terms of classes and their properties in an inheritance hierarchy is a much more direct representation of real world information than is a record-based description. The integration of a behavioral element means that applications can be developed in a manner which has much increased coherence and can also be more tightly coupled with the data description.

However, there are a few caveats in the use of OODBMS, which explains why they have not quickly replaced record-based database systems. Some of the problems are:

- Large enterprises have a great deal of investment in current database systems, in the forms of computer systems and expertise, but more crucially in the form of *legacy data*, stored using these systems. Migration to a new form of database cannot be allowed to entail significant amounts of data entry. The process of seamlessly migrating data from an older form of database system to a newer one is an active area of research at present.
- The term "object-oriented data model" does not denote a single, universally accepted definition of data structures. There are several different models

which all have the features listed above, but which vary in the precise meaning of each of the terms. Standardization of object-oriented models is one of the principal topics of this book.

- Over 20 years of intensive research have gone into making record-based systems highly efficient. OODBMS are still a relatively immature technology. Although the development of OODBMS can and does make significant use of the implementation techniques of previous systems, they inevitably require the development of new techniques as well.

- At the same time, the object-oriented model is much more complex than are the record-based models, so it is clear that the techniques to implement them efficiently will be more sophisticated and difficult to achieve.

- The user environments provided with early OODBMS were poor in quality compared with more mature products. More attention is now being paid to the user side of things.

■ 1.5 Summary

This chapter has looked at database systems, how they are used and why current systems are inadequate for applications which manage information which is inherently complex. The chapter has demonstrated the need for a new kind of database system in response to a range of new requirements. The principal ideas behind object-oriented database systems were then discussed.

Here is a list of the most important points made during the discussion:

- Database systems have been successfully used to support commercial applications.

- The successful record-based DBMS have depended for their success on the reduction of all data to a small set of simple structures.

- A new range of applications need to use the database approach and yet are not well supported by the kinds of DBMS which are currently prevalent.

- The essentially novel aspects of the advanced applications are: much more complex information structures (including the widespread use of constraints); a reliance on multimedia data; a requirement for multiple versions of data, a need for cooperative use of the database; and a more urgent need to integrate code and data better.

- The record-based DBMS are difficult to use for these applications because of their simple model of data; because they do not allow computationally complete programming languages direct access to the data; and because they cannot integrate code with the data inside the DBMS controlled store.

- The standard approach to solving the first of these problems is to use a semantic data model, with which the user is better able to produce a design for the database. The semantic schema is then mapped into a record-based representation. There have also been proposals for the integration of constraints and a computational aspect into the data model.
- A range of different extensions to or replacements of the record-based models have been proposed. These include: the use of more complex data models, support for spatial and temporal data, the ability to handle more powerful kinds of constraint and the seamless integration of persistence with complex data types.
- An object-oriented data model is one which extends a semantic model by integrating the code which manipulates data into the overall structure.
- An OODBMS is one which can be seen either as using an object-oriented data model as the logical model for the DBMS or as making an object-oriented programming language persistent.

2 An introduction to object orientation

Unfortunately, unlike relational database systems, the term object-oriented database system is only loosely defined. The relational model is exactly and rigorously defined and so to speak of a relational DBMS is to be very specific at least in terms of its logical model and the consequent facilities which must be provided. Unfortunately the object-oriented data model is not an exactly specified single model. Rather the model underlying each object-oriented system is subtly distinct from any other. There are, however, features which are common to all object-oriented systems – object identity, the encapsulation of operations with the data structure, and the structuring of the whole application and its data as a class hierarchy. Furthermore, an object-oriented system should also include the other features discussed in Section 1.4.1 – information hiding and late binding. The specific semantics of each of these concepts does, unfortunately, differ from system to system.

This chapter will discuss each of these features in greater detail. Unfortunately, the lack of uniformity also extends to nomenclature, and so some discussion of the names of the various components will also be included. The chapter will be illustrated with occasional code fragments. These will be written in no specific language, but attempt to put the main constructs into a Pascal-like setting. The material concentrates on design issues which are not specific to database systems but general to all object-oriented systems. Database specific issues are left to the following chapter, but where the requirements of database systems impose a particular view on some of the open questions, these will be mentioned.

Before launching into the discussion of concepts, it is important to distinguish the following:

- An *object system* or *object-based system* is one which supports the modeling of data as abstract entities, with object identity. This includes object-oriented systems, but also includes complex object systems, semantic data models and persistent programming languages.
- An *object-oriented system* is an object system in which all data is created as instances of classes which encapsulate properties and operations and which take part in an inheritance hierarchy.
- An *object-oriented database management system* (OODBMS) is a DBMS with an object-oriented logical data model.
- An *object-oriented database* is a database made up of objects and managed by an OODBMS.

■ 2.1 Object identity

■ 2.1.1 Object identifiers

The first and most important feature of object-oriented systems is that they permit the programmer to preserve a one-to-one mapping between the entities in the real world and representations in the computer system. For anything which is being modeled, the programmer can introduce a computer representation, called an *object*, which logically brings together all of the information that is to be stored about that entity. One of the principal claims for the superiority of object-oriented systems over record-based systems is that this information is kept together rather than scattered over a number of records joined with foreign keys.

Each object in the system is made distinct from any other object, by providing it with an *identifier* which is:

- system generated;
- unique to that object;
- invariant for the object's lifetime; and
- never visible to the programmer or end user.

This is the property known as *object identity.*

The unique identifier is variously called an object identifier (oid), a persistent identifier (pid) or a low-level identifier (lli). The function of the oid is to ensure that the object can be found wherever it happens to be and the oid is used wherever a reference to the object is needed. Thus if a *Book* object has a *Person* object as its *author* property, then the slot in the data structure for the author of the *Book* object whose title is "Emma" will be the oid for the *Person* object, whose name is "Jane Austen".

The system must therefore link the oid to the precise location of the object. This may be in memory or on the disk and there will be a mechanism which locates an object given its identifier. Sometimes the oid will be a virtual address, which can represent disk or memory locations. In many systems, the oid is more abstract and the lookup mechanism takes the form of a table – called the *object table* – which maps oids to either a memory location or a disk location. In the former case, the object is simply found by consulting the memory location. If the object is on the disk, then the object must be brought into memory. This results in a copy being made into memory with a corresponding change to the object table entry in order to indicate that the object is now in memory. The operation of changing the address map is often called pointer swizzling.

The information which an object brings together includes a set of properties. Properties are like the fields of a record in that they are component data of the object. Thus an object representing a person might have properties which represent an address and a name. Unlike a record, however, the properties are not forced to be atomic values – they can be more than just numbers or strings. A property of an object can be an atomic value, a composite value or another object. In this way richly structured information with interconnected part-of and attribution relationships can be represented directly. The properties are brought together by being held in a unified structure. If the properties are literals, they will be held in this area. If they are objects, the oid will be held instead.

2.1.2 Objects and literal values

In order to clarify the nature of objects, it is necessary here to clearly distinguish them from normal computer values. The term *literal value* (or just literal) will be used to cover the standard kind of stored representation, used in languages like C or Pascal. Literals may have a complex structure with several components, but they do not have object identity. To find them, the system needs to know their address and, although this may be relocatable, any reference to the literal will be via this address. Objects, on the other hand, have an object identifier and are usually found indirectly, for instance by using the object table.

To illustrate the point further, consider two definitions of an object representation of a person, in both of which the person has two properties – a name, which is a string, and an address. In the first representation, the address is held as a record literal. In the second the address is an object. Figure 2.1 shows a diagrammatic representation of these two representations.

In the diagram, an object is represented as a rounded rectangle in which all of the properties are shown, while a literal is represented by a right-angled rectangle. On the left-hand side, the person object, whose oid is 12345, contains the string "John" for the name and a subsidiary literal – a record containing the two components of the address. On the right-hand side, the person object contains the name as before, but instead of the address details it contains an object identifier. This identifier, 23456, is the oid of an address object and to find the two components of the address, it is necessary to look up the oid in the object table and to follow the pointer found there.

One important consequence of this difference is that objects can be *shared*. It is possible to have multiple coexisting references to an object in the data. Given either of the representations of John in Figure 2.1, it would be possible to have John be the manager of the company, MultiSuperSave, the father of Jean and the owner of a VW car. This is achieved by placing the oid, 12345, as the properties of the objects representing MultiSuperSave, Jean and the car. Now if John were to change his name, this would simultaneously be a change to the name of the manager of MultiSuperSave, the father of Jean and the owner of the car.

Comparing again the two representations of the address and the effect of setting Jean's address to be the same as John's address. If the address is represented

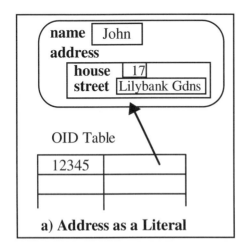

a) Address as a Literal

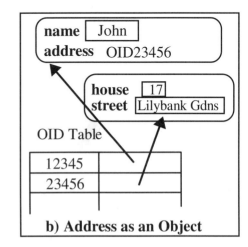

b) Address as an Object

Figure 2.1   The difference between a literal and an object.

as a literal, then the object representing Jean must take a copy of the address. Subsequent changes to John's address (say a change to the street name) will not automatically affect Jean's address. If the address is an object, then the object for Jean will take a copy of the oid and just be another reference to the same object. Now changes to John's address affect Jean as well.

One of the principal considerations when designing a system built around object orientation is to decide whether or not to make everything an object. Certainly from a design point of view, an object-oriented system should present everything as though it were an object. The literal types will be provided as system classes and the programmer will notice no difference between the way a *Person* is referred to and the way an integer is referred to. At the implementation level, on the other hand, it is likely that the distinction will be maintained for efficiency purposes. This is even more important in the context of object-oriented database systems than it is for object-oriented programming languages, since their main activity is to access large numbers of literals. The addition of indirection to this process is likely to prove unacceptable. This discussion will be returned to in a later chapter.

Here is a list of differences between literals and objects. The later entries in this table will be discussed in succeeding sections.

Literals	Objects
are simple structures	are packaged structures
are addressed (relocatably) by a physical address	are addressed through an object identifier
cannot be shared	can be shared
will be embedded in any containing structure (as in example)	will be stored separately – the oid will be stored in the containing structure
are instances of types	are instances of classes
properties are all public	properties have different levels of visibility
no operations can be defined against types of objects	new operations can be user-defined for classes

■ 2.1.3 Copying and equality semantics

One of the critical differences between objects and literals is the meaning of the operations to copy a value and to test two values for equality. Consider the following which both copy values:

```
O1 := O2
```
and
```
L1 := L2
```

The first of these creates a copy of an object in which O1 is set to the oid of O2. From this point both O1 and O2 refer to the same object. In the second case, the value of a literal, L2, is copied to the literal L1. If L2 refers to a literal record, for instance, then L1 now refers to a new record, but one whose fields contain copies of the values of the fields of L2.

An assignment of this form can, in fact, have three different semantics as illustrated in Figure 2.2.

The diagram illustrates three different copies which have been made of the *Person* object, P1. The three kinds of copy are:

- *Pointer copying*. The assignment "P2 := P1" has created another reference to the same object.

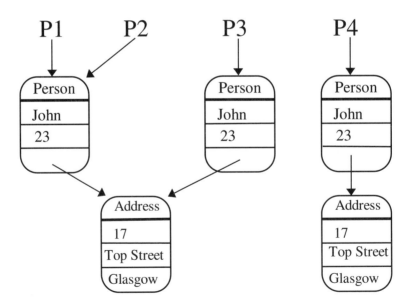

Figure 2.2   Three meanings of a copy operation.

- *Shallow copying*. This form of copying (illustrated by the effect of P3 := P1), creates a new object, but one in which each of the properties of the new object are copies of properties of P1. If one of these properties is an object, then only its reference will be copied as shown.
- *Deep copying*. The final form of copying (shown as P4 := P1), also creates a new object and copies the values of the fields of P1. However, if the fields are objects, then new copies are created for these also.

Object copying is pointer copying, while literal copying is usually deep copying. All three modes of copying have their uses and so some systems provide system operations to achieve each of them. A deep copy of a complex value can create a lot of new data, so it should be used judiciously.

*　*　*

Equality testing can have the equivalent three semantics:

- *Pointer equality*. This tests whether or not two references refer to the same object. Thus P1 does equal P2, but not P3 or P4.
- *Shallow equality*. This form of equality tests whether the properties of the two objects are the same. If a property is an object, then the property must refer to the same object. In the example, P1 equals P2 and also P3, but not P4, since the third field points to a different object.
- *Deep equality*. The last form of equality testing tests all of the literal values which are embedded in the structure. Using deep equality testing, all four Ps are equal.

Again all three forms of equality testing are useful in different circumstances. Equality on objects uses pointer equality, while literals usually use deep equality testing. The deep form can give surprising results if there are cycles in the object structure.

▦ 2.2 Classification

▦ 2.2.1 Describing objects

Classification is the process of grouping together objects which have common features. Conceptually, at least, it would be possible to describe a different data structure for each literal and object in the database, but this could not be tractably managed. Consequently, most computer systems have some mechanism for describing a group of values all of which have the same properties. Programming languages have type systems and database systems have data models.

The name used for the classificatory group of values is usually either *class* or *type*. The differences between the meanings of these two words can be quite subtle and, in any case, will vary from system to system. This will be discussed in the next subsection, but at first the word "class" will be used.

Classes in object-oriented systems are introduced as in the following example:

```
class Person
properties
   name: string
   age: integer
   address: Address
end Person
```

which states that all *Person* objects will have the three properties *name*, *age* and *address*. Objects of the class will then be created by executing an operation (usually called *new*) which uses the class description as a template to generate a new data structure. Note that this description is very like the description of a relation with the obvious difference that the *address* property will hold a reference to an object rather than an atomic piece of data.

There are three other features of classes which may be provided.

- In some object-oriented systems, the properties are divided into two types:

  - *Member properties* are properties of each object in the class (like *name* and *age* in the example); while
  - *Class properties* are properties of the class as a whole – such as the number of objects in the class or the average age of the people in the class.

- It is usual to divide the class definition into two parts:

  - an *interface* part which describes the aspects of the class to which other parts of the application can refer; and
  - an *implementation* part, which provides detail on how the classes will actually be constructed.

  As this distinction is particularly important with regard to operations, this will be discussed more fully later in the chapter.

- It is an open question whether or not a class itself is an object – in some systems, there are some distinguished classes called **metaclasses** whose members are themselves classes – this can be a useful way of grouping descriptions which hold for a number of classes – see Section 2.7 for more on this.

▨ 2.2.2 Types and classes

As previously mentioned, the terms type and class are often confused and have different meanings in different systems. This section provides a brief description of the usually accepted distinctions between the two.

A *type* is the abstract description of a set of values. The description is written in terms of the constructs of the *type system* and so, for each type, a standard, non-extensible set of system supplied operations are available for manipulating the instances of the type. The type system will include a set of base types and a set of constructors for bulk values such as records or collections. The type conveys no implications for the ways in which the values of the type might be stored. Encapsulation (Section 2.3) and information hiding (Section 2.4) are not part of a type, nor is the explicit specification of inheritance relationships (Section 2.5).

A *class* on the other hand, extends the notion of type with the availability of facilities for packaging its instances into objects. As will be seen, class descriptions can be augmented with the definition of user-defined operations on the class and its instances. Properties and operations of classes can be made invisible outside of the class. Classes take part in an inheritance hierarchy.

One further issue concerns the *extension* or *extent* of the type or class. This is the set of instances which exist at any particular time. The question is whether or not the system will automatically maintain the extension of a class or type. The usual answer to this question is "no" for types. For classes, the provision is different from system to system. In some systems, the set of currently existing objects of a class will automatically be maintained. Others force the programmer to maintain those extensions which are useful. For database systems, it is probably too expensive to maintain the extensions of all classes. This issue will appear again when persistence is considered in the next chapter.

One other way in which the difference is often represented is that a class is a particular kind of type, with the added features already mentioned. If this is the view taken, then the class hierarchy becomes a special part of the type system and a class can be described as being based on a type which describes its properties.

▨ 2.2.3 Accessing objects and components

Once a class has been described, objects of that class can be created. This is achieved by calling a system-provided operation, usually called **new**. Thus the instruction

```
john := new Person
```

will generate a new object with a structure which has space to hold all of the properties which have been defined on class *Person* and make the identifier *john* refer to it. The properties will start with either default or indeterminate values depending upon the system.

Given an identifier which refers to an object, it then becomes possible to access the properties of the object as in:

```
myAge := john . age
john . name := "John"
```

in which the dot operator is used to indicate the action of extracting a property from its object.

As a further example, given the class *Address*, defined as follows:

```
class Address
properties
   house: integer;
   street: string
end Address
```

the address property of *john* can be set by the following

```
CSaddress := new Address
CSaddress . house := 17
CSaddress . street := "Lilybank Gdns"
john . address := CSaddress
```

in which the last line has the effect of placing the object identifier of *CSaddress* into the *address* slot of the object *john*.

An important benefit bestowed by object-oriented systems is that objects can be shared. Supposing there is another resident of 17 Lilybank Gardens, the person *jane*. This is implemented by:

```
jane . address := CSaddress
```

Unlike a literal-based programming system, since *CSaddress* is an object, there will only be one copy of its properties in the system – the oid will be replicated wherever multiple references to the object are required. The effect of this is that having changed the house number of Jane's address, thus:

```
jane . address . house := 19
```

then John's address will also change and so, given a print operation over the printable values, the following

```
print john . address . house
```

will result in the number 19 being printed.

■ 2.3 Encapsulation

This section describes how a behavioral element is integrated into a class description. Firstly the term operation is defined and examples of the kind of operation that might be used are given. The other subsections describe how operations are specified, how they are used and the context in which they are programmed.

■ 2.3.1 Operations

The next vital feature of object-oriented systems is that they permit the integrated description of the behavior of the application together with the structure of the data managed by the application. This is achieved by including a computational component into the description of a class. This component is made up of the set of *operations* (often called *methods*) which can manipulate instances of the class. The integration of the description of data structure and operation is called *encapsulation*. Taken together the properties and methods constitute a single set of class components, which are often given the name *characteristics*.

In fact, the only place for describing computation in a truly object-oriented system is within the operations of classes. Programming an object-oriented system therefore requires an inversion of procedural programming concepts – instead of creating a data structure to hold the values of the computation, the computation is created to fit in with the data structure.

The operations defined on the class carry out the following sorts of task:

- *Object construction*. The programmer can redefine the behavior of the *new* operation – for instance, setting the initial values of some of the properties or recursively creating component objects.
- *Object destruction*. These operations carry out clearing up tasks after an object is removed from the system.
- *Property assignment*. Such operations change the value of a property to a new value provided as a parameter.
- *Property retrieval*. Equivalent operations for returning the value of a property to a calling program.
- *Display operations*. An operation of this kind is used to provide the user with displayed information about the object.
- *Calculations*. Some operations return values calculated from the object's properties. Clearly, any of the operations above might also include a calculation component.

The *Person* class may well include the following operations:

- a constructor which takes the initial values for *name, age* and *address* as parameters;
- a destructor which removes the address of deleted person if no-one else lives there;
- operations to change the name, age and address of the person;
- operations to return the name, age and address of the person;
- an operation which displays the three properties as a form on the screen;
- an operation which returns the length of the name for formatting purposes.

■ 2.3.2 Describing operations

Operations are coded as part of the description of the class. Thus the class specification above can be extended to include an operation which sets the *age* property:

```
class Person
properties
   name: string
   age: integer
   address: Address
operations
   setAge( newAge: integer )   ! interface of the operation
      self . age := newAge     ! body of the operation
end Person
```

in which an operation is defined which changes the *age* of a *Person*.

An operation has two parts – an *interface* and a *body*. The interface provides enough information to allow a call to the operation to be written. Thus the interface contains the name of the operation and a description of the parameters. The body contains the code implementing the operation.

In the example above, the interface and body are specified together, but it is usual to find the two separated. In this case, the class description contains only the interfaces of the operations, while the bodies are provided separately. In particular, C++ code is usually written in this way, which provides a close correspondence with the header files and code files of the C language. Providing a clear separation between the two effectively isolates the design process from its implementation. This provides software engineering benefits and it also softens the distinction between properties and operations.

The class description can now be seen to have two parts:

- A *class interface* contains the list of properties and their types together with the operation interfaces.

- A *class implementation* contains the bodies of the operations and, in some systems, may also include further detail on the implementation structure to hold the data, such as the byte length of an integer or the underlying structure used to represent a collection.

Usually, an integrated language is used to code both the class interface and the implementation, but some systems have been created in which a class interface is written in a more abstract language, while its implementation is written in a lower level language such as C.

To sum up, a more complete interface of the class *Person* which includes the list of operations given in the previous section, might be:

```
class Person
properties
   name: string
   age: integer
   address: Address
operations
   new( initName: string; initAge: integer; initAdress: Address)
   delete()
   setName( newName: string )
   setAge( newAge: integer )
   setAddress( newAddress: Address )
   getName( ): string
   getAge( ): integer
   getAddress( ): Address
   display()
   nameLength():integer
end Person
```

The separation of the interface from the body permits one further valuable aspect of object-oriented systems – the ability to provide multiple or evolving implementations of the same operation. The important feature is that as long as the interface remains unchanged, then any other piece of the application using the operation can continue unmodified.

■ 2.3.3 Invoking operations

Having created an operation, such as the ones listed above, the code required to call the operation is constructed as an invocation of the operation against a particular object by supplying actual values for the parameters. This process is often called *message passing*, a term which refers to the sending of the parameter values (the message) to the object. The execution of the operations then constitutes the object's response to the message.

In the example, the following would set Jane's age:

```
jane->setAge( 17 )
```

in which the arrow operator indicates message passing and the actual parameter values are given in brackets.

Thus the command specifies an object to be operated on, an operation and any parameter values. The syntax emphasizes the similarity between invoking operations and retrieving properties. Indeed, in many object-oriented languages, including those proposed by the Object Data Management Group (ODMG), the same operators can be used for both.

◼ 2.3.4 The programming context of the operation body

The operation body is coded using the syntax of a programming language. Part Four will consider the nature of object-oriented languages in more detail, but this section describes the features that are available to the programmer of an operation body.

The programming language will provide the normal kinds of programming constructs for looping, conditional execution and so on. The code will be written in terms of program identifiers, which are drawn from the following:

- the operation parameters;
- local variables;
- the properties and operations of the current class;
- some of the properties and operators of other classes (for which ones see the next section); and
- a distinguished variable usually called **self** or **this**.

self is an identifier which refers to the current object. Thus in the example given above, the line:

```
self . age := newAge
```

means change the age of the object against which the operation was invoked. In the previous section this was the object *jane* and so the effect of

```
jane->setAge( 17 )
```

is to make **self** refer in this instance to *jane* and so to set the age of Jane to 17.

In an OODBMS, there must also be some identifiers which allow access to the database. These will be globally available persistent roots and may, for instance, be the names of extents of the classes. This is discussed in greater detail in Section 3.3.

2.4 Information hiding

2.4.1 Public and private identifiers

An object-oriented application is written entirely as a set of class descriptions, with their constituent properties, operation interfaces and interface bodies. The application program is developed by adding new classes to the existing set. A critical question concerns which parts of the application so far written can be accessed when writing the new code bodies.

One possibility is to allow the programmer of a new class to have access to the whole of the application structure that has been defined so far – i.e. all of the identifiers and interrelationships in all of the classes so far defined. However, this is unlikely to be a sensible way to proceed and is, indeed, unlikely to be possible. To take an example, the following adds a new class for describing a set of cars being insured:

```
class Car
properties
    registration: string;
    make: string;
    owner: Person
operations
    display()
    ...        etc.
end Car
```

In this example, the *display* operation has been designed to display the make and registration of the car as well as the owner's name and address. How is the programmer allowed to code this?

This boils down to a question of which identifiers of the program are in scope. The first thing that can be taken for granted is that all of the identifiers which have been introduced in the current class description will be available. Thus the property and operation names of class *Car* can be used. Therefore, given a generic print operation over the printable types (such as integer and string), the following is acceptable:

```
print self . registration
```

This should then be followed with

```
print self . owner . name
```

i.e. print the name of the owner of the car and then:

```
print self . owner . address . house
```

to print the house number of the address of the owner of the car. However, there is an overriding reason why the property names of other classes should not be made accessible.

Consider an application development environment in which a team of programmers are jointly working on a product. In order to allow the team to work together effectively, one of the crucial issues which must be taken into account is the way in which the programming task can be partitioned. An important goal is that the effects of minor implementation decisions by one team member must not require further compensating effort by another team member.

Assume now that the *Person* and *Car* classes are being developed by separate programmers. One effective way of working in this situation is to have the team design a set of *public* interfaces to the classes in the application. All of the identifiers in the public interface of a class will be accessible to the programmers of other classes, while any other identifiers will remain *private* – inaccessible to other classes.

All object-oriented systems provide ways of partitioning the property and operation names into public and private sets. The restriction of other code bodies from accessing the private names is called *information hiding*. This principle is even more important when a distributed development system is considered. If some of the classes are installed in the system when delivered and others are bought in from other vendors, local developers will have no access to implementation detail. In general then some of the structuring information from previously existing classes can be expected to be hidden.

■ 2.4.2 Information hiding and encapsulation

In some systems, notably Smalltalk, the ideas of encapsulation and information hiding are brought together. In such systems, the properties are always private and only the operation interfaces can ever be public. Therefore, the actual data structure used may be changed without affecting any exterior programs which use the class.

In this case, the set and get operations of the class become crucial. In the example of displaying the car, the following would be used:

```
print self . registration
        print self . owner -> getName()
        print self . owner -> getAddress() -> getHouse()
 . . .
```

Indeed, so vital do these operations become that some systems automatically generate them.

More generally, the system might allow the description of the class to be subdivided into parts which are and are not accessible outside the class description:

```
class Person
private
 properties age: integer
 operations nameLength( ): string
public
 properties name: string
 operations setAge( newAge: integer )
          self . age := newAge
end Person
```

in which *age* and *nameLength* are not accessible outside of the class, but *name* and *setAge* are.

▓ 2.4.3 Other controls for information hiding

Not all systems rigidly enforce the partition that all **properties** are private while only **operations** can be public. As the last example showed, it is often permitted for the programmer to determine exactly which operators or **properties** should be private and which public. However, other systems provide an intermediate position between the two extremes.

C++ has the idea of *friends* to the class. A friend may be another class, an **operation** of another class or even an individual object. Such friends must be declared and they have access to all of the private information of the class. The provision of friends is a compromise introduced when the discipline of information hiding was felt to be too harsh. The general controls for information hiding are broken with the consequence that software decisions can no longer be localized with any certainty.

Some systems make use of the inheritance hierarchy to limit information access. In such systems, all subclasses (see below) of a class are automatically friends. This is more disciplined than the use of friends, but begs the question of how local users are supposed to find out about the private information of externally provided classes of which they wish to create subclasses.

Finally, some systems permit read-only access to parts of the information. In this case, there is not just a dichotomy between private and public, but an intermediate read-only state which may be asserted about any aspect of the class. Thus read access might be provided to the fields of the *Address* class so that components of an address can be displayed, but not modified.

In short, information hiding is a highly desirable feature of a software engineering system, particularly when development is to be shared between groups of programmers who have no mutual contact. Internally, however, the firewalls that are set up between classes which are developed together can be something of an irritation and so the compromises described have come into existence. The author's preference is always for the most direct programming representation and so placing some of the properties directly into the interface seems to be superior to hiding all properties. The indirection introduced by the compulsory use of set and get properties is a small, but irritating, inelegance.

■ 2.5 Inheritance

■ 2.5.1 Inheritance in object-oriented systems

A further important distinguishing feature of object-oriented systems is that they make very heavy use of *inheritance* (which was first discussed in Section 1.2.2). A new class is usually described in terms of one or more previously defined classes from which the new class inherits properties and operations. For instance, the following defines a new class *Student*:

```
class Student isa Person
properties
        matric: integer
operations
        register( C: course)
end     Student
```

The class *Student* is said to be a *subclass* of *Person*, which in turn is called the *superclass* of *Student*. Several features of the relationship between these two classes will be supported automatically:

- all objects created to be members of *Student* will also be members of *Person* – the "isa" relationship demonstrates the artificial intelligence ancestry since AI systems have traditionally supported specifications such as "Student isa Person";
- all properties and operations of *Person* are also defined on *Student* although they may be replaced by alternative versions (see Section 2.6);
- wherever a *Person* object is expected, a *Student* object is acceptable;
- whenever a *Student* object is created, then it is not only added to the set of existing *Student* objects but also to the set of existing *Person* objects.

There are two very important reasons why inheritance brings significant benefits when incorporated in a software development system. Firstly, there is a great saving in the quantity of code which needs to be written. The fact that the properties and operations of the class *Person* are automatically available for the class *Student* saves the programmer from rewriting the same code for the two classes. Secondly, the construct is familiar even to novice programmers, since it is one that people use continually to structure real-world information in a way which makes it manageable. Therefore, the assertion "Student isa Person" communicates a significant semantic content in a concise form. The system must then automatically maintain constraints between the data in order to support these semantics.

Inheritance is used in object-oriented systems for a variety of purposes

- to express the semantics of a subset in the application, i.e. that there is a set containing some of the instances of a particular class which needs to be separately distinguishable (as above);
- to refine a definition without recompiling already existing code – thus to add a *title* property to *Person* it is possible to create a class *Person2* with this extra property and nothing else is disturbed;
- to create more restricted values – user interface designers do this a great deal – for instance a class *Pane* may be refined to different kinds of *Menu* and *Window*;
- to create different implementations of the same kind of object – thus there might be one subclass for *Person* implemented on a Sun, another implemented on a Macintosh.

■ 2.5.2 Single and multiple inheritance

In the student example, the new class was declared to be the subclass of just one superclass. In many object-oriented systems, there is an enforced restriction that each class can only have one superclass. Such a system is called a *single inheritance* system. In this case, the set of classes usually forms a *tree-shaped hierarchy*, with a single most general class at the top. Some systems do not have a most general class, instead they provide a number of coexisting trees – this is usually called a *forest*.

Of course, in the real world, any class of objects can be expected to have multiple superclasses. For instance, extending the teaching model, there might be a class *Teacher* and then there arises the need to have a class of those people in the database who are both teachers and students. In this case, the class

StudentTeacher must inherit from both *Student* and *Teacher*. A system which permits this is called a *multiple inheritance* system.

If multiple inheritance is provided, the inheritance graph is more densely connected than for single inheritance as it forms a lattice. However, in either case, it is usual to call the graph the *inheritance hierarchy*, even though this is not strictly accurate for the multiple inheritance case.

There is some debate about whether or not multiple inheritance is a desirable property, although it seems clear to the author that it is, at least for data modeling purposes. Why then do not all systems provide it?

The reason is that inheritance from more than one class can cause name clashes. In the example, it might be required to add a property to the *Teacher* class holding the room number that the teacher works in and simultaneously, to add to the *Student* class the room number of the home room of the course which the student is attending. It is reasonable (remembering that each class is possibly being developed by a separate programmer) to expect that both of these will be called *room*. Now the creation of *StudentTeacher* results in a class that inherits both of the *room* properties. If *ST* is an object of the *StudentTeacher* class what is meant by *ST . room*?

If the system provides multiple inheritance then there are a number of possible solutions to this problem:

- forbid the creation of a class inheriting from more than one class with a common property name – in order to create *StudentTeacher* one or other of the *room* properties must have previously been renamed;
- inherit the property from the first named superclass in the definition – thus the room number of the teacher will appear but not the home room of the student;
- inherit both and automatically rename both to clarify which is which – calling them *roomStudent* and *roomTeacher*, for instance.

It is clear that none of these alternatives is entirely satisfactory – restricting the programmer, requiring retroactive modifications, changing automatically the programmer's specification or requiring that the programmer obtains more knowledge about other parts of the application than should be necessary. However, a system without multiple inheritance may impose overly severe limitations on the programmer and the author believes the last of the approaches to be the least of the various evils.

■ 2.5.3 Generalization and specialization

When constructing the design of an inheritance hierarchy, there are two ways to proceed – top-down or bottom-up. Working in the two directions corresponds to using two rather different conceptual devices – specialization and generalization.

Specialization is the addition of an extra class as a subclass of an already existing class. It is the method of working best supported by object-oriented systems and was the concept illustrated by the "Student isa Person" example. In this case the *Student* class was created to create specialized instances of the *Person* class.

Generalization is the opposite way of working – taking a set of classes and creating a superclass which generalizes them. For instance, the design of a transport application might start by constructing a set of classes for cars, boats, planes, etc. and out of them extract common features and create a common class of vehicles. Although this is an important way of working in creating the design of a database, it will rarely be supported as the implementation path in an object-oriented system. In the case of the example, it will instead be necessary to create a vehicle class first and then each of the subclasses in turn.

One way in which generalization is supported by object-oriented system is by the use of abstract classes. These are described more fully in Section 2.6.3, but the principal idea is that the generalized class will have no members which are not in one of the subclasses and contain operations which have no implementations. Instead the subclasses each implement the operations separately and the late binding takes care of matching an object with the operation body appropriate to it.

■ 2.5.4 Inclusion polymorphism

One consequence of inheritance is that object-oriented systems exhibit *inclusion polymorphism*. A programming system is *polymorphic* if a single operation can be executed against values of more than one type. Languages such as Pascal are *monomorphic* in that each user-defined procedure that is written runs only against parameters of the exact type specified.

Several kinds of polymorphism can be distinguished. Given an operation O which operates over a number of types T_1, T_2 and so on:

- *Ad hoc* polymorphism is the kind in which for each of the T_i there will be a different piece of code implementing the operation. The *write* command in Pascal is an example of this. It accepts values which are reals, integers or strings and clearly the code to display the internal representation of each of these on the screen will be different, yet the programmer is not aware of this.

- Parametric polymorphism is the kind where some part of the type is abstracted over by being parameterized. All of the T_i are actually instances of one type constructor. It is common to provide bulk types as parameterized types. For instance, a list type can be defined over values of any component type. Such a type may be written as "List[T]" and the T_i will be, for instance, List[integer], List[string], List[Person] and so on. It is then possible to write a polymorphic operation as long as it does not need to access values of the list element type. For instance, an operation to return the length of the list can be written since this is just a matter of counting the elements no matter what values they have. Some object-oriented systems provide this kind of polymorphism in places.
- Inclusion polymorphism is the kind of polymorphism in which one operation can act over values of not only one specified type but also over any of its subtypes. Thus the operation O is implemented with regard to T_1, say, and the other T_i are subtypes of T_1.

It is the last of these that inheritance provides. Consider the name length operation that was defined over the *Person* class. Clearly, given an object of the *Person* class, identified by *john*, then the following calculates the length of John's name:

```
lengthOfJohn = john->nameLength( )
```

However, if there is also *jane* of class *Student*, then:

```
lengthOfJane := jane->nameLength( )
```

is also allowed since the class *Student* inherits from the class *Person*. Thus the *nameLength* operation can be executed against *Person* objects or *Student* objects or objects from any class that inherits from *Person*.

■ 2.5.5 Inheritance and subtyping

There is another use of the term "subtyping" which, although similar to inheritance, arises in a slightly different way. A number of systems, including languages such as ML, automatically infer the subtype relationship from the context.

To take an example, supposing a program module has been created which takes, as an argument, a record which has two string fields called *name* and *address*. In languages like ML, an acceptable actual value would be a record which has those two fields plus additional fields, for instance an integer field called *age*. The reason why this different structure is acceptable is that its type (i.e. a record with the three fields mentioned) is a subtype of a record with just the two fields *name* and *address*. This subtype relationship has been inferred by the system by a rule which states that any record type with a certain set of fields is a supertype of a record type with those fields and some others. There are several rules which can be used to infer similar relationships.

Note that there is a clear difference between subtyping in these systems and inheritance in object-oriented systems. Inheritance is asserted by the programmer, while subtyping is constructed by the system. The kind of subtyping just described is inferred by the system from types fully constructed by the programmer. There remains the possibility, in the object-oriented context, of the system automatically building inheritance links by inferring subtype relationships, which had been set up by the programmer unconsciously. This might lead to a more efficient system, but could cause unforeseen complications.

▨ 2.6 Delayed binding and overriding

▨ 2.6.1. Overriding

The previous two sections showed how the operations defined in one class can be used in any of its subclasses. This section refines that idea by adding that whereas this is the default case, it is also possible to redefine the operation in the subclass.

Suppose that *Person* is given an operation to display the values of an object:

```
class Person
properties
   name: string
   age: integer
operations
   display()
   begin
     print "The name is ", self . name
     print "The age is ", self . age
   end
end Person
```

It is then possible to redefine the *display* operation in the class *Student* as follows:

```
class Student isa Person
properties
   matric: integer
operations
   display()
   begin
       print "The name is ", self . name
       print "The age is ", self . age
       print "The matriculation number is ", self . matric
   end
end Student
```

Replacing an operation by a different version in a subclass is called *overriding*. The value in this is that appropriate forms of the same operation can be provided at different levels of the inheritance hierarchy, while these can all be invoked by the same piece of code by a process called *late binding*.

2.6.2 Late binding

Given a set of *Person* objects in a set variable called *People*, then the following fragment calls the display operation on each of the members of the set:

```
for X in People
       X -> display()
```

The second line in the fragment behaves differently depending upon which class the object *X* is in. If it is in *Student* class, the matriculation number will be displayed as well. This means that the binding between the object and the code that runs against it is delayed until run-time – this is the notion of *late* or *delayed binding*. Note also that *display* exhibits *ad hoc* polymorphism as there are separate pieces of code for each class that a displayed object can be in. Note in particular that it is not possible to look at the piece of code "X -> display()" and know for sure which version of *X* will be executed.

2.6.3 Abstract classes and operations

One final feature which may be provided in an object-oriented system, is that it is sometimes possible to define an operation abstractly in a class, but to assert that its implementation will only be provided for each subclass. Such an operation is called a *deferred* or *virtual* operation, and a class all of whose operations are deferred is called an *abstract class*. For instance, here is part of the definition of a class for vehicles:

```
class Vehicle
operations
   register()
      deferred
end Vehicle
```

This means that there is to be a *register* operation for all vehicles, but the keyword, **deferred**, indicates that this cannot be written generically for all vehicles, since each kind of vehicle has a different registration process.

Later, class definitions must be supplied for the different kinds of vehicle including:

```
class Car isa Vehicle
operations
   register()
      code to register with the Driving Authorities
end Car
```

and

```
class Boat isa Vehicle
operations
   register()
      code to register with the Shipping Authorities
end Car
```

Again delayed binding will be used whenever a vehicle is registered, executing one of the code bodies defined in the subclasses. There is a potential pitfall here. If the program can create objects of class *Vehicle*, which are not also instances of one of the subclasses then the *register* operation had better not be invoked against that object, since the **deferred** keyword indicates an absence of code to cope with the invocation. More usually, the system will prevent the creation of instances of abstract classes.

■ 2.7 Software re-use

■ 2.7.1 Classes and software libraries

One of the primary reasons for the development of the object-oriented paradigm has been to encourage the re-use of software. Software is expensive to produce. It is therefore important to make as much use of each completed component as possible. For software to be re-usable, it must meet two criteria. First, it must have been rigorously tested and thoroughly documented, but second it must have been put into a form in which it is easily accessible. This is where object orientation comes in.

The class hierarchy has been found to be a highly suitable structure in which to place software so that it can easily be accessed. By implementing algorithms as the operations of classes, it has proved possible to create libraries of, among other things, user interface tools, graphics functions, access mechanisms and bulk type libraries as classes. Two examples are:

- A set of classes for user interface widgets. At the top of such a hierarchy is the pane. This is a rectangular portion of the screen and so has dimensions and little else. Below this come alert boxes, windows and buttons. Windows can be scrollable or not. Menus are a kind of window, which again can be scrollable or not. Each class adds extra properties and extra operations.
- A bulk type library. The top of the hierarchy is now a class of generic bulk objects, called *Container*. This has the number of objects in the container as the sole property. It also has deferred operations to insert and scan the objects in the container. Underneath this come a variety of bulk classes, sets as ones for sets or lists, each having slightly different properties and operations, as well as different implementations of the operations.

Bulk libraries such as these will be supplied with the object-oriented system, but one important benefit of using an object-oriented system is that it will usually be possible to obtain other class libraries from a wide range of sources. Therefore, if the expected usage will have a significant spatial aspect, then it should be possible to find packages of classes for spatial objects.

▓ 2.7.2 The system library

Each different OODBMS will come with its own class library. When the OODBMS is installed, the user will find a set of classes available for use. Chapter 16 will discuss particular OODBMS, but here are some of the class libraries that may be found:

- A bulk type library will almost certainly be included, at least containing sets, bags and lists.
- A library of access functions, such as B-trees, grid files and so on make the database aspect of the system easy for the system programmers to configure.
- User interface tools are also necessary for the kinds of application which OODBMS are designed to support.
- In some systems, a printable type library will be supplied. Although for database use, it would be insupportable to store literal values as objects, for programmer ease, there may be a set of classes – Integer, String and so

on – which make the programming of objects and literals appear to be the same – thus simplifying the software.

Examples of these will be found in later chapters.

■ 2.8 Metadata and metaclasses

The term *metaclass* can mean two different things. Either it is a class whose members are themselves classes or it is a class whose members describe classes. The former, for which the term metaclass will be reserved for the rest of this discussion, are available in those systems which consider classes to be objects. The latter is a way of making metadata available to programmers in systems where classes are not themselves objects. These will be called *metadata classes*.

In either case, there may, for instance, be a metaclass for all of the classes in the system (including itself). In general object-oriented systems will vary in how they provide metaclasses. In particular, they may vary in how many metaclasses are available to the programmer:

- none – most C++ systems do not support the concept;
- one – there is just the single metaclass, *MetaClass*, which contains all of the classes;
- many – the programmer can generate other metaclasses which group together classes with different properties.

Metaclasses provide a very powerful method of system evolution, which mixes well with inheritance, but can be difficult to understand. Metadata classes allow the metadata to be made available within the same programming context as the data and these, being somewhat simpler, will be dealt with first.

■ 2.8.1 Metadata classes

In a database system, it is usually considered important that the metadata be available for use in order, for instance, to generate system administration data and in order to allow generic user interfaces to be built without prior knowledge of the actual databases which will be used. Metadata classes are very important for these purposes. In this section, some of the main concepts will be discussed – a working system using these ideas will be discussed in Chapter 7.

The starting point for using metadata is an operation, defined on the most general class *Object*, which returns an object which describes the class of the object. So if given the object *john* of class *Person*, then the instruction

```
PersonMetaData := john->getClass()
```

will make *PersonMetaData* hold an object which describes the *Person* class. The class that *PersonMetaData* is a member of will hold operations to return such details as the names and classes of the properties and the names and parameters of the operations.

In this case, the following:

```
PersonProperties := PersonMetaData->getProperties()
for P in PersonProperties do
   print P -> getName( )
```

would print the names of the properties of the class that *john* is an instance of.

One final facility is provided by the O_2 system, which makes this even more useful. That is the ability to send a command to the system in the form of a string. Such a string can create new classes or modify existing classes. Since the string can be built up by programming and since the program can access the metadata as shown, this is a powerful mechanism for developing generic software in advance of the creation of databases.

■ 2.8.2 Metaclasses

A metaclass is a class whose members are classes and these can be used to imbue different sets of classes with different functionality. Such a system has three levels of value:

an **instance** is an object	(123456, "John Smith", "CS")
this is an instance of	
a **class** which defines methods and properties available on all instances of a class	employee(staffNo: integer, name: string, dept: string)
this is an instance of	
a **metaclass** which defines methods and properties of sets of classes	keyed_class(Key: ...)

By using the two relationships, inheritance and instance_of, a great deal of code structuring and re-use is made possible.

The power of the system is built around a consistent application of the **new** method for the creation both of objects and of classes. This is built around two intuitions:

(a) if sending **new** to a class generates a new object as an instance of the class then sending **new** to a metaclass ought to generate a new class;

(b) if the class contains a description of the structure and facilities of the objects which are its members (i.e. the class determines what properties and methods are available), then a metaclass can contain a description of the structure and facilities of the classes which are its members.

Taking such a view, performing the **create class** operation is in effect doing the same as calling the new operator on a Metaclass and providing it with the descriptions of the properties and operations:

```
new MetaClass( class name, property descriptions, operation descriptions )
```

So for instance **create class** Person might be seen as:

```
new MetaClass( "Person",
               list( ( "name", "string" ), ("age", "integer"),
                             ( "address", "Address" ) ),
               list ( "setAge", ) ) )
```

So in this case, *Meta_class* has three properties: the name of the class; a list of property descriptions and a list of operator descriptions.

Now, just as it is possible to specialize an ordinary class to add more features, so it is also possible to specialize *Meta_class* to add more features. For instance, to create a set of keyed classes:

```
create class Keyed_Meta_class isa Meta_class
   add a new property which describes a key
```

so that now if the creation of a class is an instance of *Keyed_Meta_class*, then the **new** method will expect a key to be described for the class.

■ 2.9 Object-oriented design methodologies

The object-oriented approach has become widespread over the last 10 or 15 years. However, the creation of an object-oriented model of an enterprise has some aspects which are not particularly intuitive. Just like any other modeling system with a powerful set of constructs, the most appropriate use of the constructs requires a backing methodology.

There have, consequently, been a number of methodologies for object-oriented design (OOD) which have been proposed and have received considerable acceptance. This is notably the case for the methodologies of Booch, Coad and Yourdon, and Rumbaugh. The methodologies have as their main purposes, the identification of the essential aspects of the application domain being modeled followed by a systematic transformation of those aspects into elements in the object model being used.

One of the main problems of using object orientation is the decomposition of the application into operations and the placement of those operations with the appropriate classes. In order to achieve this a certain number of elements are distinguished, which include:

- the *entity types* required;
- the *responsibilities* of those entity types;
- the *collaborations* which must occur between the entity types; and
- *subsystems* of frequently collaborating types.

The entity types will provide the main classes which will be needed. The collaborations and responsibilities provide the start points from which to identify relationships, the operations required and the parameters of those operations. The subsystems partition the application into sections which (a) can provide the strongest boundaries for information hiding; and (b) can be assigned to different groups of programmers to implement.

Another important design technique is the use of *patterns*. These are frequently recurring components of the design. There are patterns for generalization and specialization, handling bulk values, managing a class which has only one instance, managing generic algorithms and so on. By use of a pattern, a complex design problem can often be reduced to a systematic process.

The subject of OOD is already a large one and is growing rapidly as new techniques become understood. There is, unfortunately, insufficient space here to go into the issues more deeply, but it is recommended that an OOD methodology be used as the starting point for the design of an application to run using an OODBMS.

■ 2.10 Summary

This has been a very quick tour of the basic concepts involved in an object-oriented system. Fuller treatments can be found in many textbooks. The chapter has aimed at providing sufficient detail to ground the demonstrations of object-oriented programming of a database system which will follow.

The main points covered in the chapter were:

- Objects are distinguished from other values since they are accessed by an object identifier and can be shared.
- Objects are members of classes, which describe the common characteristics of all of the members of the class.

- A class description encapsulates both the structure and behavior of the objects, in that the characteristics include both properties, which hold the component data of the object, and operations, which are code fragments that can be executed against members of the class.
- Information hiding can be used to restrict access to a subset of the characteristics of a class.
- Inheritance relationships are explicitly set up by the programmer in order to assert that one class is a specialized version of one or more classes that have already been defined. Inheritance is used to reduce coding since the characteristics of the new class will automatically include the characteristics of all of the classes that it is specialized from.
- The new class can, however, override (i.e. redefine) any of the inherited characteristics.
- The inheritance hierarchy can be used to provide libraries, which either form part of the delivered system or which can be bought in from third-party vendors.
- Some systems provide support for metaclasses – classes whose members are themselves classes – although this may, in practice, either mean objects which describe classes or objects which actually are the classes.
- There are a number of useful object-oriented design methodologies which are appropriate for early schema design.

3 Persistence and objects

This chapter deals with the important issues which must be tackled when turning an object-oriented system into a database system. Most object-oriented systems are built around programming languages which manage the persistence of data in much the same way as more traditional languages. An object-oriented program is built as a class hierarchy and its data is a network of objects. An object-oriented database similarly uses the class hierarchy as its schema and a network of objects as its data. What does it take to allow the extension of the use of the classes and objects so that they also become the basis of data storage?

The term *persistence* is used to describe the ways in which systems allow data to be stored between program runs. In the case of OODBMS, the persistence mechanism must support the movement of classes and objects between memory and secondary storage. The main problems in providing a persistent system are: how are the data to be stored distinguished from data which can be discarded?; how can objects be accessed efficiently?; how is the application code managed?; and how do objects get deleted? In this chapter, these questions are examined. First of all, however, some terms need to be introduced.

3.1 What is persistence?

The term *persistence* has two meanings. With respect to a piece of data it means the length of time for which that datum exists. With respect to an information system, it means the ability of the system to store its data – or to prolong the data's persistence beyond a single execution of a program.

The persistence of a data item can vary considerably. Some data are created in one line of a program and used in the next, after which they may be removed and the space they occupy re-used – for instance, by the scoping mechanism of a block structured programming language. Other data must outlive not only the program run, but also the lifetime of the program that created them and even the lifetime of the computer system on which they were created. Increasingly, information systems bear legal requirements which insist that data be kept for a lengthy minimum period of time.

In general, programming languages provide mechanisms which are best suited to the management of data which does not outlast the program run – short-term or *transient* data – and have relatively inappropriate mechanisms for dealing with long-term or *persistent* data. Database systems on the other hand are designed to manage persistent data, rather than transient data. The consequent differences in the ways that database systems and programming languages treat data have given rise to the term *impedance mismatch*. Most applications need both to be able to compute with their data and to be able to store their data. This means that they must attempt to bring together programming language and database capabilities. Impedance mismatch arises in that the mechanisms for dealing effectively with transient and persistent data are different enough that implementing software that must meet the two requirements causes difficulties.

When a system is a *persistent system* it can have a range of expected features. At the very least a persistent system is one which, in some way or other, can make its data outlast the execution of the program which created it. However, it has come to mean somewhat more than that. The term *orthogonal persistence* has been used to describe persistent systems with two added features:

(a) The data which are stored on the disk retain the same structure, at least logically, that they have in memory.
(b) Any data value can be made persistent or transient no matter what type it is.

When considering the different OODBMS, an important issue will be the degree to which they accord to these two principles. The first one means that the object-oriented class hierarchy will be used both as the in-memory representation of data and as the stored representation. The second principle means that objects from any class can be stored. The next section deals with some of the ways in which persistence is provided by computer systems.

▓ 3.2 Kinds of persistence

This section deals with mechanisms by which the programmer achieves the transfer of data between memory and the disk. The principal goal is, of course, that when the program quits some or all of the data that it has been manipulating finds its way onto the disk in a structure from which it can be retrieved. Future runs of this or other programs will be able to locate the data and bring it back into memory so that it has the same structure and hence the same meaning as it did in the original program.

There are three main ways in which programming systems achieve this:

(a) At the end of the program run, the area of memory being used by the program is copied out in total onto the disk, from where it can be retrieved – also in total. As this can be thought of as saving the current session, or run of the program, this is called *session persistence*.

(b) During its run, the program can write out the data into one or more files. This is called *file persistence*.

(c) At the end of the program, the set of values, which have in some way or another been indicated to be persistent, are written out to disk along with their structure. This is *orthogonal persistence*.

The next three subsections examine these three methods of persistence and are followed by sections which discuss how the programmer can indicate which data is to be kept and which is to be thrown away.

The discussion is based around a particular way of using the data, which proceeds as follows:

1. The database is opened for use. This may be by launching an application or initiating a standard DBMS interface using the database.
2. The data is manipulated.
3. From time to time, the data is saved using a commit or save operation.
4. Eventually the current session is quit, which will usually include a final commit.

■ 3.2.1 Session persistence

Perhaps the most primitive form of persistence that a system can offer is to allow the user to save the current workspace of the program for re-use. Such a form of persistence is usually associated with single-user interactive systems, such as many Smalltalk implementations. Figure 3.1 shows how this works.

In the figure, the area of memory which is the workspace of the application is copied to the disk. In Smalltalk, this will include the system software, the program that the user is developing and the data that this program is using. There are obvious benefits of this form of persistence. It is very easy to implement; the user has to do very little to save work; the saving retains the structure of the data; and the program and data remain securely bound together.

However, for most purposes in which data storage is a key aspect, this will not be adequate in two fundamental respects. First, the user has no control over what is stored and what is not. Everything in the workspace is kept whether or not it is valuable data. More importantly, the data is not shareable. There can be only one copy of the whole working environment and short of developing elaborate mechanisms for moving data between the workspaces of different users, there is no way that many users can jointly access the same copy of a piece of data.

In summary, this form of persistence, although valuable for some kinds of single-user system, has little or no value as a basis for the development of database systems.

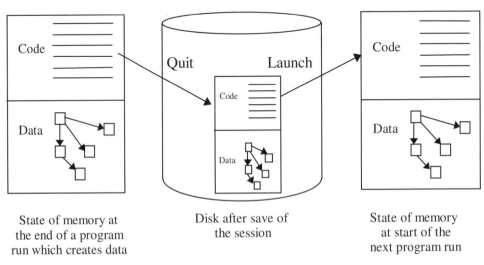

| State of memory at the end of a program run which creates data | Disk after save of the session | State of memory at start of the next program run |

Figure 3.1   Session persistence.

▮ 3.2.2 File persistence

Most programming languages concentrate on providing mechanisms for the manipulation of in-memory data. They are not well tuned for making data persistent. Instead they offer facilities to store the data in files. At the end of the program or whenever a "save" operation of the application is invoked, the data is transformed into a structure suitable to be stored in files and written out to the disk. Equivalent operations, for instance "open", are then used to transform the file(s) back into the internal data format for the program to resume working on. Figure 3.2 illustrates file persistence. Note that the data is in a different form on disk and is now separated from the code. Before the program can "start", the data must be explicitly read in.

One problem with this is that each program must have its core functionality augmented with additional components to save data to files and to retrieve data from files. Surveys have estimated that this consumes 30% of the programming effort to produce and maintain the application. Another problem is that the data in the file is then potentially open to access and corruption by other software.

However, the main problem with file persistence is the existence of two different formats for the data. There will be an in-memory format and a file format. The programmer therefore has to deal with three conceptualizations of the information – the understanding of the real world being modeled and the two computer representations. Keeping these three consistent is intellectually more challenging than maintaining a single computer representation, since now

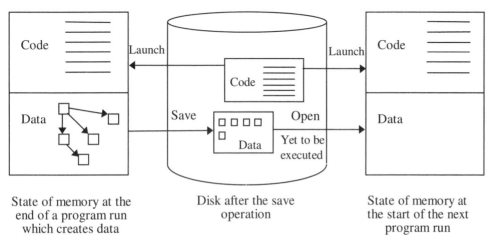

State of memory at the end of a program run which creates data

Disk after the save operation

State of memory at the start of the next program run

Figure 3.2　File persistence.

there are six possible transformations between models of the information (as shown in Figure 3.3), instead of the two that there would be between the real world and a single computer representation.

In summary, the development of a database system around the type system of a programming language could imply the use of file persistence since that is the traditional way of making programming languages persistent. However, this would be to throw away one of the main aspects of the inherent simplicity of databases – the single model of data. It is preferable to retain the single model structure when making an object-oriented language persistent. This means using some variety of orthogonal persistence.

In passing, it should be noted that the three-representation model also underlies the reason why the use of embedded query languages is so tricky. The programmer of such languages has typically to master the set-oriented SQL (disk) representation and the value-oriented programming language (memory) representation. The main difficulty of using such languages is the maintenance of consistent representations in the two languages.

■ 3.2.3 Orthogonal persistence

As stated above, the provision of orthogonal persistence is embodied in two principles. First, the commit operation stores the data in the same form on the disk as they had in memory and so can be manipulated by the same code, wherever it resides. Second, any of the in memory data can be stored without transformation. Figure 3.4 illustrates this and shows how a mixture of code

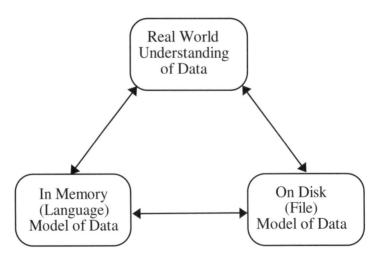

Figure 3.3   Too many representations!

(circles) and data (squares) can coexist in memory and on the disk. Launching an application brings in a leading piece of code, which then retrieves the other code modules and the data as the process accesses them. The figure shows that only some of the code modules and data have been retrieved from the disk, two of the data and one of the code modules shown have not been brought back into memory, instead pointers to disk locations are placed wherever they are referred to, so that they can be fetched when required. A great deal of saving in disk traffic is made possible because of this. Notice also that the persistence of code and data is achieved in the same way.

This is a much more suitable model for database work and carries over from traditional systems the notion of a single logical model of data. This time the logical model is the type system of the programming language. The data structure is created in this type system. Application code is written against the data structure. Data storage uses the same data structure.

In object-oriented languages the type system is the class structure. Therefore, the logical data model of an OODBMS is also the class structure and the database is a class hierarchy. Application code is written against the class hierarchy and is stored as operations in the database alongside the data. In this way, a single representation of code and data permeates the whole database environment and greatly simplifies it.

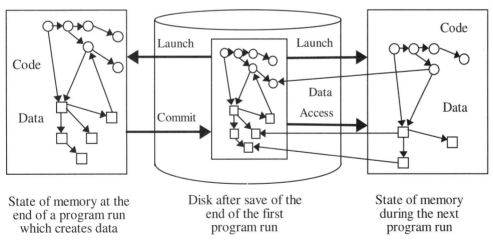

Figure 3.4 Orthogonal persistence.

■ 3.3 Distinguishing transient and persistent data

■ 3.3.1 Programmer efficiency vs. data access efficiency

The next point which must be dealt with is how the system determines which of the data are to be preserved and which not. In this matter, OODBMS vary significantly amongst themselves and there are two offsetting concerns which need to be taken into account: the efficiency of the storage of data and the amount of effort which the programmer has to make to ensure that the data is stored.

In some systems, concern for storage efficiency is felt to be the more important. If this is the case, the programmer can indicate not just which data is to be stored, but how and where the data is to be kept. The programmer can, for instance, cluster data that will be used together. The thinking behind this is that the programmer must know best how to make the storage efficient.

The alternative line of thinking is that programmer time is too valuable to spend on internal details of data storage. Apart from permitting the programmer to indicate where indices are to be used or which access structures are required, such systems put the load of deciding questions of data storage detail on the system software, which is expected to tune storage structures according to an analysis of the ways in which the data are used.

■ 3.3.2 Explicit and inferred persistence

This section describes mechanisms which have one main task – permitting the programmer to indicate which data should be stored and which should be discarded when the application closes or when a commit operation is called. At that time, all of the data in memory should clearly be identifiable as "to be stored" or "not to be stored". There are several different methods for achieving this, which vary in two ways: the degree to which the programmer has to explicitly state which objects are persistent, and how the programmer states that objects persist. These two aspects are discussed in this and the following subsection.

For an object to persist one of two things must have occurred. Either the programmer has explicitly stated that it is persistent, using one of the methods which will be listed in the next subsection, or the system will infer that the object must also persist as a result of its relationship to explicitly persistent objects. The relationship usually used is called *reachability*.

Persistence by reachability means that, if an object is persistent, then any other object or literal value which it refers to must also be persistent. Thus properties and components of persistent objects must also persist. The mechanism starts from a set of *persistent roots* – explicitly determined persistent objects – and ensures that any object which can be followed by any path of references from a persistent root is also persistent. All of the other objects – ones which cannot be reached from the roots – are transient. One kind of persistent root that is commonly used is the extent of a class. For instance, the extent of the class *Person* may be a persistent root (either explicitly or because all extents of classes are roots). All of the members of the class will automatically be stored together with their properties and any objects referred to.

Figure 3.5 shows how reachability works. Diagram (a) shows some data that has already been made persistent and a transient data structure which has a header *H* and four components. The persistent data shown starts from a root which holds a collection of items (shown as a vertical line), one of which is shown to have three components, including one labeled *C*. Diagram (b) shows the effect of bringing *C* into memory and making a reference from it to *H*. Diagram (c) shows what happens at the end of the program run. *C* is transferred back to the disk and is followed by *H*, since there is a reference from *C* to *H*. Moreover, all of the other components of *H* also are moved to the disk, as shown in diagram (d).

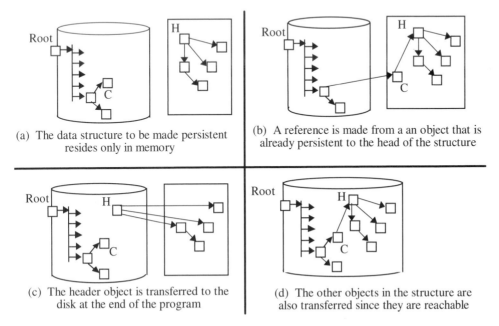

(a) The data structure to be made persistent resides only in memory

(b) A reference is made from a an object that is already persistent to the head of the structure

(c) The header object is transferred to the disk at the end of the program

(d) The other objects in the structure are also transferred since they are reachable

Figure 3.5 Persistence by reachability.

Systems vary in the degree to which they use reachability. Some do not use it at all, forcing the programmer to save every persistent object explicitly. Others use reachability completely, so that the only way to make an object persistent is by making it reachable from a root by referring to it from another object already known to be persistent. Some systems take an intermediate path. For instance, they may automatically force the persistence of the components of a persistent collection, but not cause the properties of a persistent object also to persist.

The principal benefits of reachability are that referential integrity constraints are consistently enforced and that a great deal of programmer effort is saved. (The effort saved is similar to that required in file persistence – writing code to store each piece of data.) It is particularly problematic in persistent object systems if a referenced object is not saved. For instance, if a person is stored together with a reference to the company for which he or she works, but the company object is not stored, then any attempt to access the name of the person's employer will result in some kind of run-time problem.

The problem with reachability is that it might cause too much unwanted information to be stored. If there exist some globally useful objects, it can very easily be the case that if they are stored they bring with them as much unwanted data as does session persistence.

■ 3.3.3 Methods for indicating persistence

Even if the system makes full use of reachability, there has to be a starting point for the reachability process – one or more denotable data items which are either always provided by the system or which the programmer has explicitly stated to be persistent. There is a great deal of variability in the way in which the object-oriented data structure is used for this. The explicitly persistent objects are identified in one of the following ways, each of which is demonstrated by indicating how a person object called *john* would be stored:

- *Persistent classes*. When a class is created, it is declared either to be a persistent class or not. Any object created to be a member of that class is automatically stored. Members of other classes are not stored automatically, although individual members of the class might be stored as well by reachability. In this case, *Person* must be declared persistent.
- *Persistent shadow classes*. For each class, there is an automatically created persistent version. Only members of the persistent versions of classes automatically persist. The E language, designed as part of the Exodus project, uses the term *dbclass* to indicate the persistent versions, and only objects declared to be instances of dbclasses automatically persist. Thus as

well as the class *Person* there will also be a dbclass with the same name. To make *john* persistent, it will be created as a member of the dbclass *Person* rather than the class *Person*.

- *A persistent root class.* Some systems use the class hierarchy to determine which classes are persistent. These systems provide one root class which carries with it all of the mechanisms which support persistence. Any class declared to be a subclass of this class is also persistent, since it will inherit the persistence mechanisms. If this is done, then any instances of the class will persist. If the persistent root class is called *StoredObject*, it will be necessary to create *Person* as a subclass of *StoredObject*.

- *Persistence declared at object creation.* Instead of declaring persistence on a class by class basis, some systems allow any object to persist, but force the programmer to declare whether or not each object is to persist as it is created. This is achieved by making the persistence of the object a parameter to the *new* operation. In the example, the object *john* must be created as a persistent object.

- *Persistence by explicit storage.* An alternative to this, which is similar to file persistence in traditional languages is to allow the programmer to instruct the system to store particular objects. The language will be augmented with a *store* command which will include an indication of how to store the object. Using this mechanism, it would then be possible to store *john* in the database at any time.

- *System provided persistent roots.* Another popular scheme is for the system to provide certain objects to be roots of persistence. These are continuously maintained disk locations which hold bulk values. Any objects which are made components of these root objects will persist automatically. In this case, the extent of the class *Person* could be created as a collection which is inserted into a persistent root object.

- *Named root objects.* Finally, there may be a facility for naming specific objects which become roots of persistence. This can be provided in two ways. Either the named root is specific to a database, in which case this is similar to persistence declared at object creation. Alternatively, the named root can be part of the schema, in which case there will be a value for each different database. In a company database, there may be such a named root object holding the manager as a *Person* object. In this case, if John is the manager, then this root can be set to *john*.

Given the division of data into persistent and non-persistent sets, the system will transmit the persistent data to disk. In general, this will be a continuous activity, controlled by the transaction system. During the run of the program, changed pages of data will be written back to disk in order to make room for other pages of data to be brought in. At the end of the program any changed persistent data will be written out.

■ 3.4 Storing code and data

One other point to be made about data storage is how application data and code are related when they are stored. This section will look at how this is managed for traditional programming languages, traditional database systems, persistent programming languages and object-oriented databases. Figure 3.6 shows these different organizations.

In the figure code is shown as ovals, while data is shown as rectangles. A file system (a) is an unprotected but flexible environment in which code and data can be freely mixed. A traditional DBMS (b), on the other hand, controls part of the file system which it uses to store and protect data. Application code remains outside the control of the DBMS. An orthogonally persistent language (c) allows code to be protected as well and for data and code to be freely mixed. OODBMS (d) provide a class structure in which the mixture of code and data is controlled.

The importance of this section is that the advanced kinds of application which now require database treatment must include a significantly greater computa-

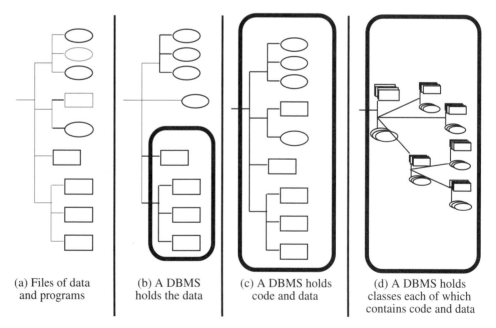

(a) Files of data and programs

(b) A DBMS holds the data

(c) A DBMS holds code and data

(d) A DBMS holds classes each of which contains code and data

Figure 3.6 Storing code and data.

tional component to cover the richness and complexity of the information they hold. Systems which exclude the program code from the supportive kinds of structuring which database systems have brought to data management, can be expected to increasingly fall into disuse because they make the creation and maintenance of the applications a task which is far too onerous, costly and error-prone.

Programming languages with file persistence store data in one set of files and programs in another. The difficulty in keeping the data files coherently organized was one of the motivating factors behind the development of database systems. Both data and program files are organized using the directory structure of the file system. This is an open and flexible structure, but one which provides no integrity facilities for ensuring that nothing gets lost or corrupted. Accessing the data files coherently is entirely the responsibility of the application program. Accessing the program files coherently is the responsibility of the software development environment tools, such as the UNIX tools *make* or SCSS. Indeed these may be seen as application programs with code as data.

Traditional database systems are much better organized with regard to data. They provide a rigidly enforced structure to the data and perform all of the organization of the data for the application programmer. However, when it comes to the application code, they are not so supportive. The application code lives entirely outside the database, back in the file system. No structure is provided in which data and code can be kept together. Therefore, although there is a transactional mechanism for keeping data consistent, no such facilities are available for keeping application code modules consistent either with themselves or with the data.

Orthogonally persistent programming languages tackle this problem by removing the distinction between code and data. Program code is just another kind of data and should be manipulable in precisely the same way as any other data. Thus code can be stored in the database, retrieved, passed as data to other programs (such as software development tools) and so on. The traditional distinction between the ways in which data and code are handled means that indirect and obscure techniques sometimes have to be used when developing advanced forms of software with strong data storage needs. However, persistent languages do not enforce any particular structure on the organization of the code and the data and so, in a similar way to file systems, throw this organization back on the application developer.

Object-oriented databases can be seen as halfway between the traditional systems and persistent languages. For sure, code and data are not treated the same in OODBMS. However, both are stored together in a coherent structure – the class hierarchy. One of the most important benefits of using OODBMS is that they provide a structure in which both code and data are consistently structured and cannot be separated. Moreover, all of the software engineering advantages for cooperative software development will be available to the users of an OODBMS.

■ 3.5 Removing data

■ 3.5.1 Explicit and automatic removal of data

One of the important facilities that a database system must provide is the ability to get rid of data that are no longer useful. To do this there must be some way of identifying data which are to be removed. The process of identifying redundant data parallels the identification of persistent data. Redundant data can either be explicitly deleted by the programmer or they can be removed automatically by the system after they become no longer usable – which means that they are no longer reachable from the roots of persistence. Therefore, data management systems either provide explicit delete (or destructor) operations or they remove data by the use of garbage collection or they use a combination of these.

Traditional database systems provide explicit deletion. There will, for instance, be operations which remove records from tables, remove tables from the database (drop operations) or remove whole databases. The system may then re-use any of the storage area of the deleted items for newly created data. It is one of the features of relational systems most helpful to implementors, that there is a very precise and fixed structure for the data, so that it is relatively easy to locate areas of store which have been freed by deletion. However, there is a negative impact of explicit deletion in that it is possible for the user to remove a record to which there is a useful reference (using a foreign key) from other records – thus violating the integrity of the database.

With object-oriented databases, the situation is considerably more complicated. It is this complication which lies at the heart of the worries of traditional database researchers, who in essence, believe that the complexity of an object database is too difficult to manage efficiently. An object-oriented database is a complex web of interrelated objects. The effect of deleting one object from this web may violate the integrity of the database in the same way that deleting one record from a relational database can. Even if the deletion is sound, it may prove difficult for the system to re-use the freed space easily, since objects are of different sizes and may be scattered around the storage area. Thus the management of both memory and the disk in object-oriented systems is much more difficult to achieve.

The next two sections will compare the automatic and explicit methods of deletion. In doing so, the same issues of efficiency will come up.

■ 3.5.2 Explicit deletion of data

Some systems permit the explicit deletion of objects and of classes. The motivation for telling the system which data to delete is the same as that for explicit storage of data – the programmer can achieve this in the most efficient form possible. For instance, deletions can be batched so that whole pages get removed at a time with a considerable saving in time. Thus if all of the graduating students in a university database are removed and if the objects representing the students have been clustered, then the set of pages containing them can be removed, instead of removing the student records one at a time.

Furthermore, the integrity violations can be fixed up by good programming. C++ is the most common language around which to build a DBMS. C++ classes have a specific operation called a *destructor*. This is an operation which is called when an object is explicitly deleted and it can be used to clean up the data. C++ database classes are usually implemented with destructors which will restore any integrity constraints which are violated by the deletion. In the case of the students, there may be objects representing the courses that the students are enrolled in. Using a destructor on the class of course objects, when a school class is deleted, all the students in that course can be removed as well. Therefore instead of making one call to delete each student, there could be just the fewer calls needed to delete the courses.

■ 3.5.3 Garbage collection

The other alternative which systems provide is to use some form of automatic *garbage collection*. Garbage collection tends to be used by the OODBMS which make use of persistence by reachability. In these systems it becomes possible for updates to a database to cause a stored object to become unreachable. For instance, if one of the departments in a company is closed down and all of the personnel are relocated, then the department attribute of the employee objects will be changed to their new departments. After all of the objects representing the personnel of the department are updated, no references will be left from employee objects. Finally, the reference to the old department object will be removed from the object holding the set of departments and now no references will be left to the object and it will become unusable data. Figure 3.7 shows an object graph with garbage and non-garbage.

Garbage collection has two phases to it – the identification of garbage and the freeing up of the area used by the unwanted objects. In the simplest kind of garbage collector, these two phases are kept separate. Other more complex forms interleave the two phases so as not to interrupt the application. The two phases are sometimes called *mark-and-sweep*.

The identification phase begins with the persistent root objects – these are never garbage. It proceeds by marking everything referred to by these roots as wanted, and then recursively marking further objects referred to by already marked objects. Eventually no more objects will be marked. Anything left unmarked is garbage. The second phase consists either of constructing a free list of unused locations, or of compacting the store to create larger areas of space.

One other technique which can be used is called *reference counting*. To use this method, every object must keep a count of all the references which are made to it. Every time a new reference is made, the count is incremented and every time a reference is removed it is decremented. Objects with a reference count of zero are unreachable and so are garbage and can be removed. A garbage collector can therefore easily be implemented which runs round the store, finding objects

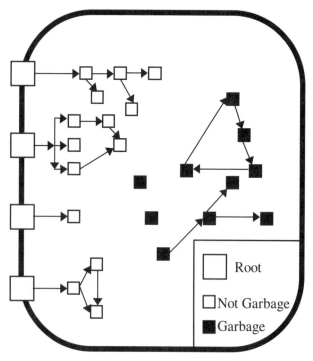

Figure 3.7   Garbage and non-garbage.

with zero reference counts and reclaiming the space they use. There are however two problems with reference counting as a means of managing garbage collection. First, it takes space to hold the counts and time to maintain them. The second reason is much more serious. In Figure 3.7, there is a cycle of objects, which although unreachable from the roots, will all have a non-zero reference count indefinitely. These can never be detected as garbage and so the space they occupy can never be freed up. This means that reference counting can only at best be used as a temporary device, which must be augmented with a more effective form of garbage collection.

There is another difficulty with respect to garbage collection. It is needed for two reasons – because there is no more memory left and to make room in the store. In the former case, space used by data with which the process is finished can be freed up. This must happen during the run of the application. To prevent the store filling up, unreachable data must be periodically flushed from the disk. This will usually happen as a separate process from the application being run – perhaps concurrently or, in some cases, requiring the suspension of any running programs. The most useful kinds of garbage collector run concurrently, but may not find all of the garbage.

■ 3.6 Database requirements

With all of this in mind, what does it mean to turn an object-oriented system into a database system? The response to this question considers first the requirements which are provided by traditional database systems and then the new requirements posed by the advanced applications.

■ 3.6.1 Traditional requirements

In Section 1.1.1, the features expected of a database system were described. This section revisits these features in the context of an object-oriented environment.

The first feature was the ability to be general enough to describe and manage data from *multiple applications*. Clearly object-oriented languages are at least as general purpose as are relational languages. In fact, they can be used both to model the data, using the type system, and to implement the applications. The class hierarchy of an OODBMS can be used to house classes from a wide variety of applications.

Efficiency of data access is another matter. One of the critical questions for the long-term success of any form of database system is whether or not it can provide fast access to large amounts of data. Some of the problems concerned in achieving this are:

- *Efficiency of object lookup.* The number of objects which is potentially large for an OO language, becomes potentially huge in an OO database. The object lookup mechanism must be fast to find the object wherever it is. This can be achieved by using one of the efficient indexing structures already developed for relational systems.
- *Efficiency of inter-object navigation.* Queries which contain long paths of references could easily become very slow – requiring many lookups. It is vital that appropriate indices and other mechanisms are available in the background to speed up query processing.
- *Efficient use of the disk.* The most important aspect of any database system is the amount of disk traffic generated. It is vital that this is kept to a minimum which can be achieved by putting together data which will be accessed together (clustering) and by splitting data which, although logically part of the same object, is rarely accessed together (partitioning).

Security of access is also important for a database system to be usable in a commercial setting. Relational systems make a great deal of use of views to control access, typically providing mechanisms to give the users access control over these virtual tables. Object-oriented systems have a richer structure and therefore have more potential techniques for providing accessing control. It is at least potentially possible to provide control on an object-by-object basis, on a class-by-class basis or by making access control operate over sections of the class hierarchy. View mechanisms have also been proposed for object systems. However, the range of possibilities here means that there does not yet exist a common method of providing security.

Maintaining data *consistency* and *resilience* against hardware or software failure can be expected to make use of many of the same techniques as traditional systems – principally the maintenance of some shadowing of the database, such as a log system, and building updates into atomic transactions.

Concurrent access by multiple users is another vital feature of database systems. Users of early versions of OODBMS have not always fared well in this regard. It is very much easier for the vendors to provide single-access systems. However, OODBMS are increasingly built on top of a client/server architecture which makes multi-user access available in current systems.

Appropriate user interfaces should be easier to provide in object-oriented systems since they have a programming language built in. The close integration between the user interface and the data is one of the key benefits of OODBMS. Moreover, database systems should, by using object orientation, be able to re-use a great deal of the human–computer interaction research in which object-orientation is the dominant paradigm.

Querying capability is one of the contentious issues between OODBMS developers and relational developers. The debate centers around the two kinds of querying which users of databases typically need:

- *ad hoc querying* requests a summary of all or part of the database – such as "Tell me about all of the people over 30";
- *navigational querying*, on the other hand, works by starting from a particular piece of data and moving to related data – "OK, I have a reference to Jane, now tell me about the company that Jane works for".

Both of these forms of querying are useful in different circumstances, but each requires rather different support mechanisms.

Returning to the debate, the most usual form of the claim of relational superiority over object systems is that relational systems were initially successful because they are better at *ad hoc* querying than are network systems. This advantage is due to the fact that it is much easier to construct *ad hoc* queries over a set of tables and to execute these queries efficiently than it is over a network of data references. Since OODBMS also manage a network of references, the same claim is made for the superiority of relational systems. Indeed, this is extended with the claim that information hiding must get in the way of query optimization. However, several responses can be made in support of OODBMS:

- The efficiency of relational queries depends to a large extent on the use of the relational algebra to support equivalences between different forms of the same query. This only points to the need for equivalent algebras for object systems and indeed these are forthcoming.
- Versions of SQL for object systems have been developed which integrate the object-oriented paradigm seamlessly. See Part Three for details.
- Information hiding would indeed prevent the expression and optimization of queries. However, most OODBMS provide a flexible approach so that only parts of the structure not required in queries are hidden. Moreover what is hidden from the user may still be available to the system to guide optimization. Furthermore, as long as querying is restricted to retrieval then the query processor may be allowed access denied when using other kinds of interface.

- The kinds of application at which OODBMS are targeted require navigational querying at least as much as *ad hoc* querying. In this regard OODBMS perform better than relational systems since they provide both kinds of query facility.

OODBMS provide much better means for enforcing *integrity* constraints. In exactly the same way that a foreign key is expected to exist in a relational database, any reference to an object should imply the existence of an equivalent entry in the object table and that the object's data actually exists in the address that the object table entry refers to. Many OODBMS will not permit a referenced object to be deleted thus enforcing referential integrity.

Distribution is an area in which object systems struggle to compete with relational systems. A distributed relational system, even one where the underlying DBMS is different at each site, is relatively straightforward to provide by linking the sites using SQL. Any query which cannot be satisfied locally is fired off to a remote site – the result being a table. Tables can be partitioned and foreign keys can refer to tables on other sites.

In a truly distributed object system, there is the potential for many references to be between sites and the retrieval of information to include much network traffic. Furthermore, the notion of integrity described above will be difficult to maintain in the case where sites have the potential to disappear and reappear from time to time. To create a truly resilient distributed object system is one of the most important of the current research issues in information systems.

■ 3.6.2 Advanced requirements

This section considers how OODBMS are evolving to respond to the advanced requirements described in Section 1.1.4.

Long cooperative transactions are a requirement of design databases. Much of the research into providing different kinds of locking mechanisms is taking place in the context of OODBMS.

Clearly, object-oriented systems provide *complex data structures* and their design is motivated by the need to mirror real-world information structures. The class hierarchy, being easily extensible, can either hold large numbers of classes with small numbers of instances of each or vice versa.

Object-oriented systems provide more flexibility for storing *multimedia* data in a coherent form than do relational systems, since these are limited to the storage of atomic data. Relational approaches to the treatment of multimedia typically provide an atomic type which references a file holding the data. Thus they reintroduce a discontinuity between parts of the data, which seems to backtrack on the basic principles of databases.

OODBMS automatically provide the *storage of code* as well as data. Code fragments persist and are also easily accessible and clustered with their data. Section 3.5 dealt with this matter.

Multiple *versions* of data are potentially supportable in relational and object systems, but OODBMS have gone further in their implementation since the applications they are trying to support have more need of them. Moreover configuring versions of objects would appear to be easier in object systems with their rich command of reference structures.

Thus, object systems hold their own in many, but not yet all, of the areas in which relational systems have prospered. Moreover, they begin to tackle some of the key requirements of advanced applications.

■ 3.7 Summary

This chapter has considered some of the issues in turning an object-oriented language into an object-oriented database system. An object database consists of an interlinked collection of persistent objects. Most of the discussion concerned how new objects were to be added to the collection and how they were to be removed. In general, there are two approaches.

One approach is to give the programmer control of which data are stored and which data are removed. This is held to improve the run-time efficiency particularly as fine control over object placement can be included in the facilities provided. The other approach is to use reachability, so that any objects which can be referenced from a set of persistent roots will be kept and anything else will not. Such systems save the programmer from a lot of tedious programming, but need very well-designed underlying mechanisms to be fast enough to make the system usable for significant quantities of data.

The bias of the author is for those systems which can hide low-level detail from the programmer. It should not require the mastery of intricate programming skills to set up a database and its application. DBMS have traditionally been intended for a wide range of users and given both the continual improvements in hardware and our growing understanding of appropriate data modeling techniques, it should be possible to provide high-level access to a DBMS without forfeiting good performance.

The main points of this chapter include:

- Persistence is the property of a computer system which permits data to outlive the process which created them.

- This can be achieved by storing an image of the memory, by using files or by use of orthogonal persistence.
- Orthogonal persistence means that any kind of data can be stored without transforming its structure.
- Persistent data can be distinguished from transient data either explicitly by the programmer or automatically by the system.
- Programmers can indicate persistence by a number of mechanisms including indicating that some classes are persistent, by making particular objects persistent at creation time, by executing a store command or by making objects components of already persistent objects.
- Persistence by reachability requires that one or more persistent roots be available. Persistent roots can either be automatically provided by the system or be created by the programmer explicitly naming them.
- Code can be stored alongside the data in a database.
- Data are either removed from the store explicitly by the programmer or automatically when they become unreachable by using garbage collection.
- Persistent object systems are capable of supporting all of the requirements made by both traditional and advanced applications.

There does remain a problem if the OODBMS aims to support more than one programming language – for instance, C++ and Smalltalk. These two languages have somewhat different semantics attached to aspects of the object-oriented model – indeed they have significantly different models in some respects. If multilingual working is to be an issue, then the OODBMS will have to live with more than one logical model. However, it will be usual for the OODBMS to insist on one of the models being dominant.

This can be achieved by making one of the language models the dominant one. Thus we might have C++ with Smalltalk tacked on at the side. The alternative is to have one model – *the* object model for this DBMS – and to map each language to the model. In doing this, an object model can be designed that is more influenced by traditional data models and database requirements.

The other issue which develops from this is that of inter-OODBMS working. As mentioned above, it is relatively easy to create a distributed database which uses more than one relational DBMS. Presumably, this is another requirement that should be made of OODBMS – the interworking of OODBMS from different vendors. This will only really be feasible if there is an object model which is independent of any particular object-oriented database. The development of such a model is the subject matter of Part Two of this book.

Part Two

The ODMG standard

The second part of the book turns to a major effort at standardizing the structure of object-oriented databases – the standard being produced by the Object Data Management Group (ODMG). In this part, the main features of the standard will be described along with one of its implementations – that provided by the O_2 OODBMS.

The next chapter provides some context for the ODMG effort – what others are doing and who the ODMG are. This will be followed by two chapters on the ODMG data model – one describing the model and one illustrating how it can be used to design an application. In order to demonstrate the practical use of the data model, the O_2 database system is then introduced, followed by a chapter describing how the application would be built in O_2.

4 Standardizing and the ODMG

The goal of the ODMG is to create a standard for object-oriented database management systems. This chapter puts the activities of the ODMG in context, firstly by discussing the reasons why standards for OODBMS are important. Then follows a brief overview of other related standardization efforts. Finally, the nature of the ODMG will be described.

4.1 The need for standards

One of the principal shortcomings of the object-oriented approach is its lack of standards. When someone speaks of a fully relational database system, then, without mentioning any particular system, they will be referring to a DBMS whose logical model and principal features are well defined. The databases will all be sets of tables of atomic values. The system will supply an SQL interface for data definition and manipulation. There will be support for views, indexes and transactions. There may be some differences in the flavor of SQL provided, there may be different additional user interfaces in different systems and there may be different storage structures, optimization techniques and other details at the physical level, but in certain fundamental respects all relational DBMS will be the same.

This has not been true of OODBMS.

Yet the standardization of the main aspects of different relational systems has been beneficial in a number of respects – usability in terms of transferable skills, data sharing between systems and a supportive context for third-party software.

When a new user becomes acquainted with the workings of one relational system, crossing over to another relational system can be accomplished relatively easily. The basic model of data and many of the methods of working will be much the same. Therefore extensive retraining of data-processing staff is not required if the company switches its relational DBMS. This stability makes relational systems very attractive to potential customers.

It is not unusual for different enterprises to want to share their data resources. If they all have relational databases, then, no matter which system they are using, it will be a relatively straightforward task to link up the databases, creating the effect of a single overall database which contains all of the tables from all of the sources. Distributed access using SQL can then permit data to flow between the sites relatively seamlessly. Furthermore, if a particular company wishes to switch DBMS, then they will be able to do this without needing massive data re-entry.

The DBMS is not the whole story as far as clients are concerned. The customer also needs to use application programs built on top of the database. This can be achieved either by hiring staff to build the applications or by buying in third-party software. Third-party software may provide the whole of the completed application or it may consist of libraries or tools which make application development much easier. Using third-party software will usually prove to be the more effective strategy for any company that does not wish to make a major investment in IT staff. The availability of so much third-party software is another benefit of using relational systems.

The vendors of third-party software have a vested interest in making their products as generally saleable as possible and so they create their products so that they can work in the context of a variety of different relational platforms. The third-party vendors therefore design their software against the lowest common denominator of the database systems that potential customers might be using. It is greatly to the advantage of relational systems that this lowest common denominator is reasonably rich in features. This means that third-party software can be written at a relatively high level – in a standard mix of C and SQL. Indeed this is one of the major disincentives for the addition of new features by relational vendors, since many of the application developers which can be run on them will avoid the new features as they are not (yet) part of the common denominator.

As has been stated already, object-oriented database systems are greatly at a disadvantage in this respect. Chapters 2 and 3 contained a necessarily imprecise set of descriptions of the principal structures and facilities that an OODBMS is supposed to provide. Within this generality there is a great range of variability in that different systems: make use of different ways of making the concepts more precise, structure their data differently, and provide methods of access which are different. Consequently, skill transfer, data sharing and the creation of third-party applications all become much more difficult to achieve.

There are at least three reasons why relational systems have more extensive standards than do object-oriented systems. First, relational DBMS are more mature, having a history whose duration is more than twice that of OODBMS. Second, as a result there has been a significant effort by a number of organizations to create a usable set of standards. Finally, the relational model is much simpler than an object model and has a strong mathematical background. On the other hand, the object-oriented community have had to explore a range of possibilities in defining the basic concepts of the model, whereas the relational model had a precise start point. The exploration has resulted in a wealth of ideas, which it is now time to make concrete.

Clearly, the lack of standards cannot be allowed to continue if OODBMS are ever to become a viable technology and to claim a significant share of the marketplace. The main OODBMS vendors described in Chapter 16 were quick to realize this and, under the leadership of Rick Catell of Sun Microsystems, have begun to propose a solution – a standard for OODBMS. Accordingly, the ODMG was set up by a number of these companies and this part of the book describes their efforts.

Before the ODMG is examined, it is useful to look at their activities in terms of the general development of object system standards.

■ 4.2 Approaches to standardization

Standardization of the various aspects of object database systems is taking place in a number of ways, both by collaborative groups and by individual organizations. This section describes some of the various interacting efforts. First, the bodies which are involved will be described and then standardization in four areas will be discussed: system architecture (CORBA and ODBC), object models (the OMG model), query languages (SQL and its derivatives) and document structure (mark-up languages and compound document architectures).

■ 4.2.1 Other standardization bodies

Standardization in information technology has had a patchy history at best. This is not surprizing since it is a very young discipline in which theory, techniques, methodologies and tools are evolving extremely quickly – often too quickly for standards to keep pace with them. At the same time, market forces and competitive business practices have led to the premature delivery of products which become *de facto* standards of inferior quality. Standards can evolve in two ways – deliberately through the concerted effort of a group of interested parties or as a by-product of overwhelming user acceptance of a particular product. Network database systems are an example of the former, while the emergence of SQL as the standard database query language is an example of the latter. The practical use of object orientation in information systems is currently witnessing both of these kinds of approaches.

Standardization "by committee" can be seen in the efforts of the Object Management Group (OMG) and the various SQL committees as well as the ODMG, while some companies, notably Microsoft, are attempting to develop *de facto* standards which will then be spread through the popularity of their products.

The main standardizing authorities for computer systems are the International Standards Organization (ISO) and the American National Standards Institute (ANSI). These have both set up committees (ISO JTC1/SC21/WG3 and ANSI/X3H2) for standardizing in the database area, which jointly provide standards for SQL – see Section 4.2.4.

They have also set up the OODBMS Task Group. Originating in 1989, this group produced a report in 1991 which contained a glossary of object orientation terms, a reference model characterizing OODBMS and a set of recommendations for standardization. They fell short of specifying actual interfaces, however. They further recognized that object orientation is arizing in areas other than database systems as well and that integration may thus be difficult. They recommend a set of composable standards rather than one monolithic standard. This has led on to a further ANSI venture in the form of the X3H7 Object Information Committee which was formed in January 1992. It is considering how to accommodate application-specific differences in object data models and how to manage the reality of a multiplicity of object models. This committee promises the construction of a features matrix which will compare the different features of object models in the form of a rectangular grid with object models as the rows and different features as the columns. At the time of writing the matrix contains 20 models and 29 features.

The OMG is a collection of more than 300 companies including manufacturers like DEC, Bull, IBM, etc.; database vendors – like O₂ and Informix; and end-users – like BT, American Airlines, etc. It was formed in 1989 and has produced a common architecture (Object Model Architecture – OMA) linking services with applications through a shared OO interface – CORBA. Section 4.2.2 will briefly describe the architecture proposed.

The OpenDoc initiative to standardize inter-document architecture is being managed by a non-profit organization called Component Integration Labs (CI Labs) which was founded by Apple, IBM, and Novell Inc. CI Labs is acting as the focal point for the collaborative design of the proposed structure, which will involve more than 300 companies, including the OMG as a major contributor. Section 4.2.5 includes a description of OpenDoc.

The Microsoft Corporation can be considered another standardization body, although they take the contrasting go-it-alone approach. Instead of collaborating with potential competitors and producing a standard by committee, they install design decisions into their products and, since they are the dominant software manufacturer, anticipate that these will become a *de facto* standard. It will be interesting to see if the limited personnel that even Microsoft have at their disposal can effectively compete with the combined expertise of their competitors.

▪ 4.2.2 Standardizing the architecture

The main goal of the OMG was to provide an industry-wide architecture to which all object-oriented systems can conform. The architecture proposed was created through a process in which all the main computer firms presented an architecture and the "best" one was chosen. This became the OMA which is shown in Figure 4.1.

The OMG architecture is centered round the Object Request Broker (ORB) which is a distributed "software bus" that enables objects to make and receive requests and responses. An application written in the OMG architecture uses the ORB to locate external data and components, which may be distributed. Consequently, the application developer has transparent access to information that might otherwise have required explicit programming, using features such as remote procedure calls.

All of the system software, application software and data are then built using an object-oriented approach. The object classes are divided into three categories:

- *object services* – these are the basic functions for the maintenance of objects;
- *common facilities* – these are a collection of classes and objects that provide general-purpose capabilities useful in many applications;

- *application objects* – these are application specific classes, which does not mean that they are not shareable, since it is a common finding that facilities developed for one application may be useful in other applications.

The object services include:

archiving	implementation repository	persistence	security
backup and recovery	interface repository	properties	startup services
change management	licensing	queries	threads
concurrency model	lifecycle	relationships	time
data interchange	naming	replication	transactions
event notification	operational control	sagas	

OMG then proceeded to produce a more detailed definition of the ORB – Common Object Request Broker Architecture (CORBA). Some of the elements of CORBA are:

- an interface definition language (IDL), which permits the description of the class interfaces independent of any particular DBMS or language;
- a type model for defining the values which can be passed around the network;
- an interface repository in which all interfaces are stored;
- methods for getting the interfaces and specifications of objects;
- methods for transforming oids to strings and back again;
- a sophisticated name-scoping mechanism.

There is not space here to deal with these in detail, but the type model and IDL influence the type model of ODMG and its interface language, ODL. These will be discussed in the next chapter.

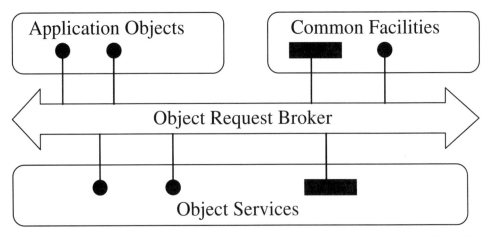

Figure 4.1 The OMG object model architecture.

Another important architectural standard is Open Database Connectivity (ODBC), which has emerged from Microsoft, but is spreading industry wide. ODBC is an application programmer interface which unifies the ways in which a variety of different DBMS can be used, thus permitting applications (such as spreadsheet programs) to be written which can operate against databases stored in different DBMS transparently. Figure 4.2 shows how this is achieved. The application accesses data using calls to ODBC functions, which transmit SQL statements. These are executed by the driver manager which sends the SQL across the network to the appropriate DBMS, using an ODBC driver specific to that DBMS. The database is then used by the application as required.

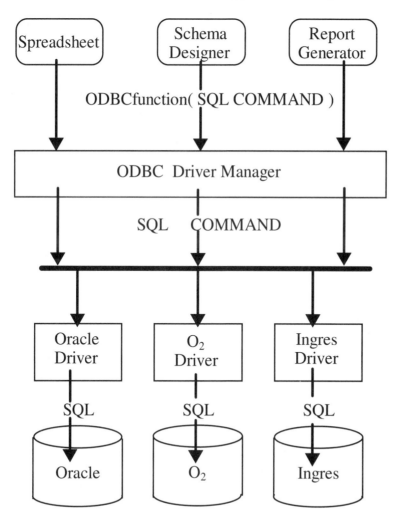

Figure 4.2 Open database connectivity.

ODBC uses a purely relational view of data and was designed so that users of Sybase, Informix, Oracle and so on could all make use of the same application programs without having to modify them. The importance of ODBC in the context of object-oriented systems is that users will want to continue to use the interfaces and applications that they are currently using, even if they switch to the new technology. By supporting ODBC, OODBMS vendors can allow this to happen with no effort on the users' part. The OODBMS comes with an ODBC driver, which flattens the object-oriented data to a relational structure.

■ 4.2.3 Standardizing the object model

There are two approaches to providing a standard object model:

- create a core object model at the design level and expect actual systems to provide more extended versions for implementation;
- create a complete object model which enables both designs and implementations to be ported between compliant systems.

OMG have proceeded down the first path and ODMG down the second – their model is the subject of the next chapter.

The OMG core object model had the following features:

- object identity;
- object types are described in terms of their interface, i.e. the set of legal operations available on them;
- non-object types – the set is not specified but are expected to include all of the usual printable and constructed types;
- operations have a name, a set of named and typed input parameters and a set of named and typed output parameters;
- subtyping between types means that all of the operations on the supertype are also operations on the subtype – and that the number and types of input and output parameters are the same, an unusually severe requirement, since contravariance is usually held to suffice;
- a type may have multiple supertypes;
- multiple inheritance provided by declaring types to be in a subtyping relationship;
- the possibility of multiple implementations for a type.

The ODMG object model is intended to be more detailed, but to include the OMG model as a subset.

■ 4.2.4 Standardizing the query language

The existence of a standard querying language is one of the main strengths of relational DBMS. The language SQL emerged through a sequence of precursors – SQUARE, SEQUEL (1974), etc. SQL86 was the first attempt to standardize the language and the current standard is SQL89 which added referential integrity checking.

SQL2 is the standard with which the next releases of relational database systems intend to comply – it adds dynamic SQL; outer join; cascaded update and delete; temporary tables; the set operations union, intersection and difference, domain definitions in schemata; built-in data types (including Datetime, National and Varchar), transaction consistency levels, deferred constraint checking, scrolled cursors and SQL diagnostics.

Much more ambitious is the move to SQL3 and the attempts to bring objects into SQL. SQL3 is a massive increase in the scope of SQL. Not only does it include objects through an abstract data type mechanism, but it is computationally complete. It supports multiple inheritance, public, private and protected members and operations, parameterized abstract data types (ADTs) and relationships. It has a completely flexible approach to object identity allowing oids, user detectable keys or internal oids which may be neither unique nor immutable! It aims to provide a standard set of ADTs including vectors, matrices, geographic and spatial types, text, document, graphics, pictures, video, audio, hypermedia and ASN.1 data types.

There are many similar attempts to add objects to SQL, including: Object SQL, which was developed as part of the IRIS system by Hewlett-Packard; and OQL, which is part of the ODMG standard and is the subject of Part Three of this book.

Object SQL is a computationally complete language which is based on a functional model. Objects are instances of types situated in a multiple inheritance hierarchy. The top of this hierarchy includes types for: types, surrogates (objects with an oid), aggregates (values with components), literals and transients. Transients are objects which never need to be stored – system examples of this include transactions, savepoints, sessions and cursors. The properties of a type are all modeled as functions – including stored and derived attributes and relationships and other computations. The definition and implementation(s) of a type are kept separate.

*   *   *

It is clear that the **select ... from ... where ...** structure of queries in SQL is here to stay. SQL has become such a cornerstone of user interaction with DBMS that to abandon it would be to throw away a large part of the expertise which has been built up on how to use databases. All serious attempts to add a query language to an OODBMS recognize this and, although there have been different flavors of "object SQL", they are all similar in many respects and can be reduced to a single standard given time. OQL is the standard which is being developed by OODBMS vendors to unify the ways in which they are used.

■ 4.2.5 Standardizing document structures

A further motivation for creating object standards arises from outside the database world. This is the need to provide a standard for sharing documents – a document being a set of data created by an application such as a word processor, spreadsheet, etc. In order to allow documents created by different applications to be freely mixed, and embedded within each other, it is necessary that there is a common descriptive structure for all such documents. As it is increasingly common to create document descriptions in an object framework, this amounts to creating an object standard for documents. There are two dominant strands in the attempts to provide such standards – standardized mark-up languages, which permit the structure of a single document to be specified, and compound document architectures, which permit the documents arising from different applications to be combined in a clean manner.

The need to identify the logical structure of documents has led to a class of languages called *mark-up languages.* These identify fragments of a document as having some logical meaning and indicate this with tags which delimit the fragment. The reasons for marking a fragment vary from indicating the syntactic properties, such as labeling which parts are headings, titles, quotes and so on, to indicating semantic properties, such as specifying that this section is a census record and in it is a person's name, date of birth and so on.

In order to cope with this variety, Standard Generalized Mark-up Language (SGML) has been created as ISO standard 8879. In fact SGML is not really a language but a meta-language built around a data model for documents, in which different types of tags and attributes of tags can be specified. Using SGML it is possible to define an application specific language, called a Document Type Definition (DTD) by identifying a particular set of tag types together with how they interrelate. The relationships between a marked-up document, a DTD and SGML mirrors that between a database, a schema and the ER model.

For use with the World Wide Web, a dialect of SGML called HTML has been produced, since a web-specific DTD was found to be insufficient for an application which embodied great generality. The spread of HTML usage has been as dramatic as that of the web itself. The importance of mark-up languages is that they provide a model for documents which can be reproduced easily in the object-oriented context and this will be of increasing importance as OODBMS vendors integrate web access mechanisms into their products. Section 7.5.9 includes the description of an OODBMS tool for using the web.

*   *   *

A *compound document architecture*, on the other hand, creates a uniform structure within which documents which arise out of different applications can coexist. Examples of such documents include spreadsheets, diaries, drawings, audio and video clips. The ability to create documents out of such components has a gradually evolving history, from cutting and pasting by hand, through specific closed multi-purpose packages, such as Lotus 1-2-3, and open system support tools such as clipboard mechanisms. With the emergence of object systems, a conceptual framework has become available which is simple enough to turn the problem on its head. Instead of forcing applications to know the specifics of each other's data structure, a generic data structure is provided to which any contributing application must conform. This is a much more powerful and extensible architecture in that it is continuously open to the emergence of new applications, whose data will immediately be able to coexist with already existing applications.

Object Linking and Embedding (OLE) is a document architecture which forms the standard interface for sharing objects in Microsoft's Windows 95. In OLE documents, such as spreadsheets or word processing texts, are objects with properties that can be manipulated. The documents are accessed and edited by operations which summon the usual kinds of document preparations tools. Documents produced by applications conforming to OLE can share their data in one of two ways. If one document, *A*, produced by the word processor, *MegaWord*, has a link to another, *B*, produced by the spreadsheet program, *MicroSheet*, then *B* remains a *MicroSheet* document and an attempt to manipulate *A* may involve access to *MicroSheet* if the component part is to be changed. If, on the other hand, *B* was embedded in *A*, then the embedded copy can only be manipulated by *MegaWord*.

OpenDoc, managed by CI Labs, is a cross platform (at the moment this means Windows, the MacOS, OS/2 and Unix) standard for documents, to enable applications to inter-communicate their data more easily. The OMG has been a major contributor to the technical design and so OpenDoc has access to many of the features of the CORBA architecture, such as networking and security. OpenDoc provides a generic user interface which relies on drag-and-drop to create compound documents out of components. It is a superset of OLE with many more features, being the product of a large collaboration effort. One example is that OpenDoc components are not forced to be rectangular – embed a round drawing in a text and the text will flow around it.

The requirements of office information systems mainly concern the management of stored documents. The developments discussed here concern the formation of standard structures both within and between documents. These have all been based on object concepts and clearly fit better with object systems. Consequently, it is to be expected that OODBMS will provide the persistent storage of application data.

4.3 The ODMG

4.3.1 Who is involved in the ODMG?

In contrast to the OMG, the ODMG is a much more tightly knit enterprise. It was initiated by Rick Cattell of Sun Microsystems, who invited the most important OODBMS vendors to club together to create a standard with which they could all work. The companies committed leading technical staff to an intensive phase of discussion which led to the first standard, ODMG-93. Further work is moving towards a second more detailed standard.

The structure of the ODMG is built around a small core of voting members, originally five in number but currently comprising GemStone Systems, IBEX Computing, O_2 Technology, Object Design, Objectivity, POET Software, UniSQL Inc. and Versant Object Technology. Three criteria apply to voting members:

- They must be the manufacturer of an OODBMS system.
- They must commit 20% of the time of a leading technical expert to the development of the standard.
- They must implement the ODMG-93 standard in their product.

This core is enhanced with two sets of "reviewers" – a group of distinguished academic theorists and a wider range of companies, mostly hardware companies, telecommunications companies, database manufacturers and other customers. To be a reviewing member, a company needs only to commit 10% of the time of a technical expert.

▨ 4.3.2 What are the ODMG doing?

The ODMG have been designing an architecture for OODBMS together with the key components of that architecture. The work of the ODMG proceeds in the context of the OMG efforts. ODMG proposals are expected to comply with OMG standards, but to be somewhat more detailed, since OMG have a wider remit than the database aspect of object systems. This has influenced the ODMG model to include some features (for instance enumerated types) which otherwise might have been omitted. Furthermore, the ODMG proposals are intended to support the porting of code between compliant systems, whereas the OMG proposals are only intending to support the porting of designs.

The proposals of the ODMG define:

- an architecture for OODBMS;
- a data model which will act as the logical model for all OODBMS and thus achieve a similar level of inter-operability to that found in relational systems;
- a data definition language, ODL, which will form a concrete specification of the operations permitted over schemata defined in the data model;
- a query language, OQL, which provides an interface for posing *ad hoc* queries (but not for doing data definition or data manipulation); and
- a number of bindings to existing object-oriented programming languages, such as C++, Smalltalk and Java.

▨ 4.4 Summary

This chapter has concentrated on the issue of standards in the object database field – why they are needed and what is being done to bring them about. This leads naturally into the work of the ODMG, which is attempting to achieve a similar level of agreement between different kinds of OODBMS to that already found among relational systems.

The important points made in the chapter include:

- A standard is necessary to allow different platforms implementing a particular kind of DBMS to coexist.
- This standard should include definitions of the architecture, data model, querying and other ways of using the system.
- Relational systems have increasingly good standards, partly because they are simpler and partly because they are more mature.
- OODBMS have not had standards and, in particular, "the" object model is, in fact, a group of related models which differ significantly among themselves.

- Standards bodies such as ISO and ANSI have initiated work in standardizing object models.
- Manufacturers have set up the OMG to define object standards at the design level.
- There are also emerging standards for document structures which are object based.
- The ODMG is a group of OODBMS vendors who are putting together a standard at the application coding level.

The next chapter will discuss the object model proposed by the ODMG. Later chapters will deal with the languages which they have proposed for object definition and querying, together with how the database is to be integrated with the object-oriented languages C++ and Smalltalk.

5 The ODMG data model

This chapter and the next describe the object model proposed by the ODMG which is intended to provide the basis for all subsequent OODBMS development. Chapter 5 defines the data model while Chapter 6 illustrates its use. It should be noted that the ODMG standard is work in progress. The first version of the standard appeared in 1993 and is known as version 1.1 or ODMG-93. Version 2 is still under development at the time of writing, but the most recent release (version 1.2 in December 1995) is a small update to the ODL specification from 1993. The description given here is primarily drawn from version 1.1, but occasionally updates will be mentioned.

5.1 The context of the ODMG model

The ODMG proposal includes a number of components, of which the data model is the one that binds everything together. This section describes the framework within which the data model is used.

■ 5.1.1 The ODMG architecture

The architecture, proposed by the ODMG and shown in Figure 5.1, defines the way in which data is stored and the different kinds of user access to the store which will be available. There will be a single store which is accessible by a data definition language, a query language and a number of manipulation languages. The architecture emerged early and naturally in the ODMG discussions, since it more or less approximated to the architecture which all of the collaborating vendors were already using.

The data model is central to the proposal since it is the organizing structure within which all of the information managed by the OODBMS will be stored. The data definition language, the query language and the manipulation languages are all designed to make the data model central to their facilities. The architecture then permits a variety of implementation structures to hold the data modeled, but importantly all software libraries and all support tools are provided in the object-oriented framework and so are coherently stored alongside the data.

The principal components of the architecture are:

- *The object data model*. All of the data held by the OODBMS is structured in terms of the constructs of the data model. The data model specifies the precise semantics of the concepts described in Chapter 2. This chapter will describe the data model.

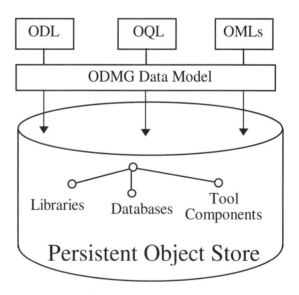

Figure 5.1 The ODMG architecture.

- *The object definition language (ODL).* Schemata are described in terms of the ODL, in which the constructs of the data model are made concrete in the form of a definition language. ODL allows a schema to be described as a set of object type interfaces, i.e. the properties and interrelationships of the types together with the names and parameters of the operations of those types. The ODL is not a full programming language – the implementations of the types must be performed in an OML. It should be noted that the ODL is also a virtual language, which will not necessarily be implemented in the ODMG compliant products. Instead, the OODBMS products will contain equivalent definition languages, containing all of the facilities in ODL, but tailored to specifics of the particular system. ODL is, however, important in that it makes concrete the features of the data model and so it is used in the examples in this chapter and the next. Section 5.1.4 describes the ODL.
- *The object query language (OQL).* This is an SQL-like query language which can be used as a stand-alone querying language or be embedded in one of the OMLs. OQL contains only querying commands, unlike SQL which also has commands for data definition and updating the data. Chapter 10 is devoted to OQL.
- *Object manipulation languages (OMLs).* The coding of operation implementations and application frameworks requires the availability of the features of an object-oriented programming language (OOPL). An OML is the integration of a programming language with the ODMG data model and this is achieved by a *language binding*. OOPLs by themselves are not naturally persistent. In order to enable them to interact with stored data, they need to be extended, either by additional language constructs or by library elements. The language binding provides this.

  The system may provide more than one OML in order to exploit the differing programming skills of users. The ODMG initiative recognizes the importance of C++ and Smalltalk and so proposals for bindings to those languages are an important part of the standard. Part Four of this book describes these bindings. The importance of the newly arrived language, Java, is also recognized and version 2.0 is intended to contain a binding to that language.
- *The persistent object store.* The storage used by an ODMG-compliant OODBMS uses the data model as its logical organization. The physical organization will vary from product to product, but all will provide appropriately efficient data structures to store the type hierarchy and the

objects which are instances of the types. The type hierarchy holds not only the data but also the various libraries and components of the tools which support application development. Thus an ODMG-compliant store constitutes an integrated system in which all data and code are kept in a coherent organization.

- *Tools and libraries.* Tools, such as browsers, application development environments and user interface management systems are written in an OML and stored as part of the class hierarchy. Libraries of access functions, user interface toolkits, arithmetic functions and other useful application components are also stored in the type hierarchy and are accessible in a uniform manner to the application developer's own code. The ODMG makes no attempt to determine which tools and libraries a vendor should supply.

■ 5.1.2 An object model for database systems

The ODMG model is an object data model, which includes the ability to describe both objects and literal values. The fact that the model is intended to support database work influences its design, since efficiency of data access becomes of primary importance. Most object models have been developed for programming languages which are expected to manage all data in memory. In this context, implementing all data as objects is acceptable. When large amounts of data on disk must also be managed some compromise with the "purity" of the object model is essential.

There are four ways in which the object model is geared towards database systems:

- There are built-in object types for databases, schemata and sub-schemata.
- The model includes a number of built-in structured types, which permit traditional database modeling to be used.
- The model includes both objects and literals.
- The model distinguishes relationships between objects from attributes of objects in an analogous manner to the ER model.

Of these the last two points are more important and need some explanation.

Objects and literals

As explained in Section 2.1, an object is distinguished from a traditional computer value by having object identity. This implies the space and time overheads of dereferencing objects, which, if made to apply to basic data values, would fatally slow down a database application. The ODMG model therefore permits the description of all data in terms of objects and the traditional kind of value – called a *literal* value in the model. Thus the age of a person can be specified to be an integer literal, not an object so that the age property would then be stored as part of the person object data structure rather than be stored separately as an object. In particular, as discussed in Chapter 2, a primary difference is that objects can be shared while literals cannot. A schema in the ODMG model still consists primarily of a set of object types, but the components of these may be literal value types.

The other concept which is used to distinguish objects and literals in the ODMG model is that of *mutability*. This needs careful consideration, which is best achieved by returning to the example of the address property (Figure 2.1). The ODMG model would distinguish the two cases as follows:

- If an address is modeled as an object then its components (house number, street name, etc.) can be updated, while it remains the same object – this is therefore a *mutable object*.
- If an address is a literal structure and one of its components is changed, then the whole address is considered to become a different value. If it is to remain the same value, the components may not be changed, i.e. it is an *immutable literal*.

That is, an object's identity is the oid, which is completely separate from its component values, while the identity of a literal is entirely determined by its component values. It is not too obvious that this distinction is very useful to a user, because in both cases it is possible to change the value of an address property, whether it is modeled by an object or a literal, but it is used as a main labeling concept in the ODMG type hierarchy.

Relationships

One of the primary criticisms of object orientation made by the data modeling community is the treatment of relationships. In most object models, these are implicitly modeled as properties whose values are objects. Thus if a person works for a company, there may be a property for each person, perhaps called *worksFor*, whose value is a company object. The problem then arises if there is also a property of each company (*employees*, say) which holds the set of employees. As far as the system is concerned, these two properties are unconnected and maintaining consistency between them becomes an irritating and error-prone programming problem.

The ODMG model, on the other hand, follows the ER model in distinguishing two kinds of property – attributes and relationships – although the distinction between them is somewhat different. *Attributes* are properties whose inverses are not required. Often these will be literal values, although objects can be attributes too, as long as the reverse reference is not required. *Relationships* are properties with inverses. In this case they must be object values since literals do not have properties. Thus a person's age will usually be modeled as an attribute, while the person's company, would be modeled as a relationship. When a relationship is declared, its inverse must be given. In the example just given, the definition of *worksFor* as a relationship must indicate that *employees* is its inverse, while the definition of *employees* must mention *worksFor*. The database system is then expected to maintain the consistency of relationship values – a clear saving of programmer effort and an increase in reliability. If the *employees* property is not required then *worksFor* can remain an attribute.

■ 5.1.3 Introduction to the data model

The ODMG data model describes a database as a collection of *denotable values* of which there are two kinds – *objects* and *literals*. As usual, objects have identity and a separate existence, whereas literals are components of objects. The data model has constructs for the specification of object types and literal types. Object types inhabit an object type hierarchy, whereas literal types are similar to the kinds of type specifiable in a language such as Pascal or C.

One consequence of the inclusion of objects and literals concerns the type structure. Section 2.2.2 was a discussion of classificatory constructs and, in particular, the terms "type" and "class". In the ODMG model, the classificatory construct is called a "type" and types describe both objects and literals. The term "class" is not used in this model. What has previously been called a "class" is, in the ODMG model, a particular kind of type – an object type. As will be seen, individual systems will retain the word "class" to mean object type.

The model includes a range of *literal types* – some basic scalar types for numbers, characters and booleans (called atomic literal types and described in Section 5.2.1) and some constructed types for literal records (called structures) and collections (Sections 5.2.2 and 5.2.3). The constructed types can be built out of any literal or object type, but are considered to be immutable as discussed above. Dates and times are built as literal structures.

An *object type* consists of an interface and one or more implementations. The *interface* describes the external appearance of the type – what properties it has, which operations are available and what are the parameters of those operations. An *implementation* consists of the data structures which implement the properties and the code bodies which implement the operations. The interface is the public part of the type, while the implementation may introduce further private properties and operations if required. This chapter and the next are mainly concerned with type interfaces. All of the object types, whether user-defined or system-provided, form a lattice headed by the type *Object*.

An object type interface has the following components: a *name*; a set of *supertypes*; the name of a system-maintained *extent*; one or more *keys* for associative access; a set of *attributes* – each instance of which is a component object or literal value; a set of *relationships* – each instance of which is a link to another object; and a set of *operations*. Attributes and relationships are jointly called *properties*, while properties and operations when considered together are called *characteristics*.

Just as there are atomic and constructed literal types so there are atomic and constructed object types. Types themselves are atomic objects, as are exceptions (described in Section 5.4.2) and iterators (variables that take each of the values in a collection in turn). The constructed object types include the structure types and a number of collection types, which are described in Section 5.2.2.

Figure 5.2 is a type hierarchical representation of the data model indicating all of the main components. In fact, the figure is the structure which holds the meta-information in an ODMG database, since types are themselves objects. Thus, when a user defines a new type, it not only becomes a new type in the hierarchy (held as subtype of *Object*), but the type description, in some systems, also becomes an instance of the atomic object type *Type*, where it is accessible for querying.

The figure shows the different kinds of object there can be and also shows that the main components of a type (characteristics) are also values in the data model, but not ones that are denotable. Thus it is not possible to redefine an attribute or an operation. It is however possible, for instance, to query a type to discover its attributes and then to find the name of the attribute.

■ 5.1.4 The object definition language, ODL

The Object Definition Language, ODL, is the data definition language for the ODMG data model. This section introduces ODL, which will be used extensively in the examples given in this and the next chapter. The syntax will be introduced gradually by example. Section 5.5 will then bring the language together with an informal syntax and a full example. A formal syntax for the language is given in the ODMG-93 book.

ODL is used only to describe the interface of the types in the application and not to code the implementation. It is not a programming language, but merely a

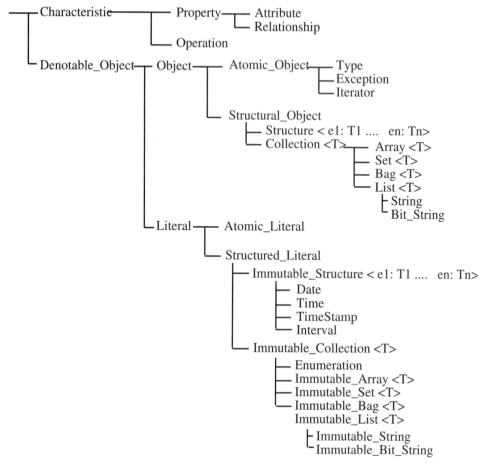

Figure 5.2 The ODMG object model.

schema description language. In fact, ODL modules resemble the header files of C++, containing the type descriptions, including the properties and the operation interfaces. ODL is an extension of the OMG definition language – the differences mirroring the differences between the two data models.

Unlike OQL, the query language, ODL is not intended to be implemented in an ODMG-compliant OODBMS as it stands. Rather it is a vehicle for expressing the schema operations which must be provided by the interfaces which are available in the OODBMS. The exact form in which this will be provided varies from system to system, but it could take the form of a stand-alone data definition language or be part of the facilities of a manipulation language.

ODL programs are collections of definitions of types, constants, exceptions, type interfaces and modules. Type definitions allow the creation of types which are locally available. Type interfaces define object types and put them permanently into the type hierarchy, while modules form a nesting mechanism for gathering together definitions.

To start building a small example, in which some employment details are to be stored, a module will be specified for holding the whole structure:

```
module Employment
{
}
```

creates the module. The specifications of the various types will be placed in between the curly braces.

5.2 The built-in types

The built-in types provide the basic building blocks for the construction of databases and applications. There are a number of literal types which are built-in, including both types for scalar values and constructors for compound values. There are also constructors for compound objects. This section will discuss three kinds of built-in type: the atomic literal types which describe the basic scalar values available; collection types, which hold multiple objects or literals; and record types.

5.2.1 Atomic literal types

In common with other data models, the ODMG model provides a set of built-in atomic literal types – which have also been called base types, scalar types and printable types in other contexts. These types appear as subtypes of the type *Atomic_Literal* in the type hierarchy and they form part of the definition of ODL, in which they are keywords. The atomic types provided in the ODL specification constitute a general guideline, but it is not clear that all vendors will provide exactly the same set.

The types in the ODL specification are listed in Figure 5.3. Mostly these are straightforward, but the type **any** requires a little explanation. This is a dynamic type, which can be used as the domain of a component whose actual type is either unknown or irrelevant. This is the least likely aspect of ODL to be implemented in a particular system.

Numbers

Integers

Long – a signed integer with a large range of values
Short – a signed integer with a small range of values
Unsigned Long – an integer with a large range of positive values
Unsigned Short – an integer with a small range of positive values

Reals

Float – a single precision real type
Double – a double precision real type

Booleans

Boolean – true or false

Character

Char – the type of a single character

Octet

Octet – the type of a single byte

Any

Any – the type of a location which can hold any value.

Figure 5.3   The atomic literals in ODMG / ODL.

■ 5.2.2 Collections

Multi-valued properties call for the use of *collections*. There are collections which are themselves objects and collections which are literals – as will be seen by referring to Figure 5.2. The main difference between the two is that collection literals are immutable – it is not possible to insert new values into the collection, or to remove values from the collection. Collection literals are useful, for instance, to hold the result of a query.

In order to support different kinds of data structure, there are five kinds of collection:

- *Sets* are unordered collections which do not allow duplicates. They support operations to perform set union, intersection and difference; to copy the set; to test for subset and superset relationships; and to (object sets only) insert and remove elements.
- *Bags* are unordered collections in which duplicates are allowed.
- *Lists* are ordered collections in which duplicates are allowed. These support a variety of retrieval operations and (object lists only) insertion and removal operations.

- *Arrays* are indexed lists of fixed size. They support indexed retrieval and insertion operations. Deletion operations on object arrays merely replace the value with nil.
- *Enumerations* are literals which contain an explicitly listed group of values. In our example, the title of a person is one of "Mr.", "Ms", "Mrs", "Miss" or "Dr.", i.e. an enumeration type of five strings. Enumerations are not supported by all ODMG "compliant" systems.

The five kinds of collection are implemented as types which are parameterized on the element type and which are subtypes of either *Collection* or *Immutable_Collection*, both of which are abstract types – i.e. they do not have any direct members. All collections must be members of one of the types supporting one of the five collection kinds listed above.

A string is considered to be a list of characters and as such is a constructed value. In fact, its position is somewhat more ambiguous since most often it will be used as if it were an atomic value.

To describe a collection type in ODL, it is necessary to specify which kind of collection it is and the type of the elements. Here are some examples:

```
List<Float> Immutable_Bag<Person> Array< List< Set< Vehicle > > >
```

In order to support operations on all of the members of a collection, the type *Iterator* is provided. Iterators are objects which keep track of which member of a collection is currently being used. They support operations which generate the first, last and next member, test if there are more members, reset the iteration and so on. In implementing a code fragment which iterated over a collection, for instance:

```
for all X in C do Command
```

the following sequence of operations would be followed:

```
I := C -> create_iterator()    ! Generate an iterator for the collection
X := I -> first()              ! Make X the first member of the collection
repeat Command
    while I -> more?()          ! Is this the end of the collection?
      do X := I -> next()       ! Make X the next member of the collection
```

▓ 5.2.3 Records

Records have been fundamental to database construction and the ODMG recognizes this by including built-in classes for records – the class *Structure* for record objects and the class *Immutable_Structure* for record literals. The latter are particularly used for returning the result of a query – perhaps a projection of some of the attributes of a type.

A structure has a name and a number of elements and each of these is a name, type pair. The latter can be any object or literal type, giving rise to the possibility of nested records. For example, it seems appropriate to model an address attribute as a structure. This will have elements including an integer house number and strings for street name, city, country and postcode. The ODL definition of such a type is:

```
Struct Address { Unsigned Short House; String street,
              String city, String postcode}
```

Such a definition can be used in a schema in one of two ways:

- Either the type specification can be supplied in line as part of the property definition, as in:

```
attribute Struct Address
    { Unsigned Short House; String street, String city,
     String postcode} address
```

in which the domain specification includes all of the definition,

- or a type specification can be given a name if it is to be used globally, as is the case for the example schema. The definition of a new type name looks like:

```
typedef Struct Address
    { Unsigned Short House; String street, String city,
     String postcode} address
```

following which *Address* can be used in:

```
attribute Address address;
```

As an address type will be useful for the example being developed, the second alternative will be used and the *typedef* statement will be placed in the module definition, from which it can be used by any type interfaces that are developed. Note that using *typedef* in this way does not add a new type to the hierarchy – only an object type interface does that.

There are a number of built-in subtypes of *Immutable_Structure* which are of general use for modeling dates and times. These provide in-built types for decomposable temporal data, thus avoiding the necessity of recoding these in each application.

■ 5.3 User-defined object types – modeling state

The first task when creating a schema is to describe the structure of the data. In an object-oriented data model this mainly means describing the interfaces to a set of object types in terms of a type hierarchy. This section will examine more closely the structure of an object type and how objects and literals can be jointly used to create a database description.

■ 5.3.1 Object type interfaces

An object type interface describes the structure of a set of data, how that data can be manipulated and how it is related to other types of data. To define a type interface, it is necessary to specify: its name, the name(s) of its superclass(es), some type properties, the attributes of the class, the relationships of the class, and the operation interfaces. Abstractly, a type interface definition looks like:

```
interface typeName : supertypes
{
type property specifications;
exported item specifications;
};
```

The exported items include attributes, relationships and operations. They can also include exceptions, types and constants which are to be exported as part of the type interface. The next section describes how operations and exceptions are specified, this section concentrating on the other aspects of the type interface.

In the example being developed, the interface definitions will be placed inside the module. As usual the first thing to be specified is a name of the type. In ODL, a type interface begins with a line such as:

```
interface Person
```

or

```
interface Company
```

The first line also places the new type in the type hierarchy, by indicating its supertype(s). The previous two examples had no such indication so, by default, both the *Person* type and the *Company* type will be placed directly as a subtype of *Object*. The construction of an extra class, *Adult*, to appear as a subtype of *Person*, would start:

```
interface Adult : Person
```

The next part of a type interface defines what are called *type properties*. These are additional aspects of a type which concern its use in a database. At present, there are three properties defined: an extent, one or more keys, and an indicator of the persistence of the instances.

An *extent* is a collection of all of the instances of the type which will be maintained automatically by the system. The extent is an optional component and there may be types whose extents do not need to be maintained. This does not mean that instances cannot be stored, merely that this is not automatically carried out, neither are all of the instances kept together in a logically distinct collection. The principal reason for defining the extent is to provide a persistent root to act as a start point for accessing the database – equivalent to the names of tables in a relational system. This is one aspect in which the object model is more flexible than relational systems, since the latter force the extents of all tables to be maintained, even though many will never be used as the basis of querying.

A *key* is, as usual, a data value created out of properties of the type. A *simple key* uses just one property, while a *compound key* uses more than one. Either attributes or relationships can be used as parts of keys.

The *persistence indicator* of a type specifies the expected lifetime of instances of the type. At present this can either be "persistent" or "transient". The most important consequence of this type property is that, if a type is declared to be persistent, then its instances will be created and managed by the storage manager of the OODBMS, while the instances of a transient type will be managed by the run-time system of a programming language. In this way, transient objects will disappear as the memory is de-allocated, while persistent objects will remain under the control of the storage manager even after the current process stops.

The extent and key properties appear in round parentheses following the first line and are followed by the persistence indicator. The three classes that were started above can be extended to:

```
interface Person
(    extent People
     key socialSecurityNumber ) persistent

interface Company
(    extent Companies
     keys companyID, companyName ) persistent

interface Adult : Person
(    key ( worksFor, staffNumber ) ) persistent
```

in which system maintained extents are specified for people and companies. There is no explicit extent for *Adult*, since the instances will not need to be queried separately. All adults will, of course, be stored in the extent *People*. The type *Person* has one key, while *Company* has two alternative keys – an identifier and the company name. *Adult* also has two keys – the social security number inherited from *Person* and a compound key made out of the company that the person works for and the staff number within that company.

5.3.2 Attributes and relationships

The next aspect of a type to be described is the set of properties which instances of the type will have. The ODMG data model distinguishes two kinds of properties – attributes and relationships. An *attribute* is a property which is part of the object, whereas a *relationship* is a binary link between two objects, in which traversal in both directions is required.

Neither kind of property is "first-class". That is, neither a relationship nor an attribute value can stand on its own. For instance, a property value cannot be the value of a programming variable, or be stored separately from the object. The hierarchy shown in Figure 5.2 shows this by separating characteristics off from the denotable values in the ODMG model.

Returning to the three classes, the following specify the attributes which could be made available in each class:

```
interface Person
   attribute String socialSecurityNumber;
   attribute String name;
   attribute Unsigned short age;
   attribute Address address;

interface Company
   attribute Unsigned short companyID;
   attribute String companyName;
   attribute Adult manager;
   attribute Address address;

interface Adult : Person
   attribute Unsigned short staffNumber;
```

in which the attributes are a mixture of strings, integers ("Unsigned short"), structured literals (*Address* – which was specified in Section 5.2.3) and objects (the *manager* property requires no inverse in the *Adult* type). The structure of an attribute specification consists of a domain specification followed by the attribute name. The domain specification can be a type name or a full type specification.

Relationships in the ODMG data model are always binary, but, as in the ER model, there are three kinds of these:

- One-to-one relationships pair two single-valued object classes. The relationship instances pair two object instances.
- One-to-many relationships pair a single-valued object class with a collection class. The relationship instances pair an object with a collection.

- Many-to-many relationships pair two collection classes. The instances of the relationship pair up two collections.

In the example, it is required to model the marriages of people, the parent-child relationships and the employment relationship with companies. The following show the relationship parts of the three classes to achieve this.

```
interface Person
    relationship Set<Adult> parents inverse Adult::children;
    relationship Company worksFor inverse Company::employees;

interface Company
    relationship Set<Person> employees inverse Person::worksFor;

interface Adult : Person
    relationship Adult spouse inverse Adult :: spouse;
    relationship List<Person> children inverse Person::parents;
```

The three kinds of relationship are all shown here. The *spouse* relationship is reflexive and pairs up individual adults. The *worksFor* and *employees* relationships pair up one company object with a set of person objects. The *parents* and *children* relationship pairs up a list of children with a set of adults.

▨ 5.3.3 Other kinds of exported item

As well as properties, described above, and the behavioral items (operations and exceptions, to be described in Section 5.4), there are two other kinds of exportable item – types and constants.

To export a constant, a line such as:

```
const Unsigned Short maximumAge = 150
```

can be added to the type interface.

To create a subsidiary type, the **typedef** operator is used. The construction of a record type, *Address*, has already been seen. It is equally possible to create another name for an atomic type or to create a collection type. Here are examples of these:

```
typedef Unsigned Short Smallint
```

and

```
typedef List<Company> EmploymentRecord
```

Continuing the example, the latter will be installed in the type *Adult*. It is placed there, since it will not be used outside of this type. After adding it, it becomes possible to add an attribute to *Adult*:

```
attribute EmploymentRecord pastEmployers
```

■ 5.3.4 Names

Sometimes in a database application, it is useful to identify individual objects and give them names, which are independent of any particular database, and thus are part of the schema rather than the database. In the ODMG model any object can be given one or more names, although the same name cannot be used for more than one object.

For instance, if the *Person* type is intended to be used for genealogical purposes, in which each database is to house the descendants of a particular couple, this could usefully include as named objects: *FirstWoman* and *FirstMan*. This looks like:

```
name Person FirstMan;

name Person FirstWoman;
```

The most important use of named objects is that they are persistent root objects and can be used as the start points to database access. In the ODMG model, all persistent roots are either named objects or extents of object types.

■ 5.4 User-defined object types – modeling behavior

The ODMG model provides two levels of computational construct. An application program is considered to be made up of a number of queries and a number of transactions which make atomic changes to the database in order to keep it consistent. At a lower level, the data is manipulated by operations and these form the building blocks out of which transactions and queries are constructed. The operations available on an object are described in the type interface along with the properties of the class. One other computational category provided by the ODMG data model is the exception. An exception describes a situation which the normal code sequence is unable to deal with, and it is paired with an exception handler, which is a piece of code which can respond to that situation.

This section discusses operations, transactions and exceptions, leaving queries to Part Three of the book.

■ 5.4.1 Operations

An operation is a code fragment which manipulates the properties of an object, as discussed in Section 2.3. There are two parts to an operation: its interface and its implementation (of which there may be more than one). The *interface* of the object is a description of the arguments it takes and the results it returns. The *implementation* is a piece of code which manipulates the data as required. The interface is described as part of the type interface, while the implementation is provided separately using any of the object manipulation languages supported by the OODBMS.

Extending the example above, consider the following four operations:

- an operation, *birthday*, defined on *Person*, which adds 1 to the age;
- an operation, *employ*, which is defined on *Adult*, and sets the *worksFor* property;
- an operation, *addChild*, which adds another person to the children of an adult; and
- an operation, *isChild*, which tests if one person is the child of another.

To specify these in the type interfaces, then the parameters must be added:

- For the operation, *birthday*, there are no parameters. The operation merely adds 1 to the *age* attribute and does not require any input or output for the purpose.
- For the operations, *employ* and *addChild*, it is necessary to indicate that these take a *Person* object as argument. In both operations, the parameters need to be named – *newEmployee* and *newChild*, respectively will suffice.
- The operation *isChild* has both an argument and a result. The former is a *Person* object, called *testChild*, say. The latter is a boolean.

In ODL, these are added to the type interfaces of the classes as follows:

```
interface Person
    void birthday();

interface Company
    void employ( in Adult newEmployee );

interface Adult : Person
    void addChild( in Person newChild );
    boolean isChild( in Person testChild );
```

In these specifications, each operation appears in a line which includes: the type of value returned by the operation (or "void" if nothing is returned), the name of the operation, and parameter specifications in round brackets. Each parameter specification describes whether or not the parameter value will be modified, the type of the parameter, and its name.

The ODMG model has nothing to say about whether or not an operation updates the data in the class. Operations such as the first of the three above are called *side-effecting*. This term has as its basis a functional model of computation. In such a model, all data manipulation performed inside a function must be explicitly passed back to the caller, rather than be stored. If all programming is carried out in this way, important correctness properties of the code can be proved. In a database context, the term means that querying the data is considered to be the main function of an operation and the change of data is considered to be a side effect of running the operation. The *isChild* operation is not-side-effecting, since it merely returns a calculated value, without changing anything. The fact that there is no indication of whether or not an operation is side-effecting is somewhat unfortunate since if these are clearly distinguished, then queries which do not cause side effects can be optimized rather more thoroughly than can side-effecting queries.

▪ 5.4.2 Exceptions

The normal flow of control of an object-oriented program consists of sequences of operation invocations. The initiating program calls an operation on an object, which in turn may call other operations. When an operation is completed, control passes back to the calling operation and continues at the next instruction following the operation call, ultimately returning to the initial program.

Whereas this has been found to be a very productive way to structure software, sometimes this structure makes programming particular tasks difficult. One difficult kind of task involves making an operation react differently to special situations. It is possible to deal with this by putting tests at various points of the code, thus complicating the program and making it more error-prone and difficult to debug. This is particularly tedious if a test occurring deep into a call sequence requires the unwinding (and aborting) of many of the surrounding operations. For example, the syntactic analysis of file input is best implemented as a set of operations which ultimately depend upon an operation to read the next character from the file. If there is no next character, immediately jumping out of the analytical operations would be extremely desirable as it would save a lot of coding of tests.

A different scheme is to treat one sequence of events as the normal one, while any others (such as reaching the end of the file) are regarded as exceptional. Each operation is programmed to deal only with the normal case. If any other situation is found to occur, an *exception* is signalled to the system and some data indicating the reason for the exception is passed back. This is called raising an exception. The system will then find a piece of software which will deal with the exceptional situation.

An exception is therefore made up of three components:

- an *event* which causes the exceptional situation to occur;
- *exception data* which is a (possibly empty) structure holding information

about the reason for the problem; and

- an *exception handler* – a piece of code which, using the exception, deals with the unusual situation in some way.

To illustrate how the mechanism works, consider the following fragment of pseudo-code.

```
Implementation of Operation A of type T
    define exception E to be event N which passes back a string as the
        exception data and is handled by handler H which just prints the
        string it has been given
    ...

    print 1
    call operation B on object X of type U
    print 2
    ...

    end of operation A
```

```
Implementation of Operation B of type U

    ...
    print 3
    call operation C on object Y of type V
    print 4
    ...

    end of Operation B
```

```
Implementation of Operation C of type V

    ....
    print 5
    if event N has occurred raise exception E, passing back "N"
    print 6
    ...

    end of Operation C
```

The fragment shows that operation *A* calls *B* which in turn calls *C*. The normal sequence of events would cause the following list of characters to be printed: "1, 3, 5, 6, 4, 2". The odd numbers appearing as the operations are called, and the even numbers appearing as the operation calls unwind. If, however, event *N* is found to occur, then something different happens.

Operation *A* starts normally and prints 1, before calling *B*. *B* prints 3 and calls *C*. *C* prints 5, but then detects that *N* has occurred and raises the exception *E*. Now instead of continuing with the print of 6 and so on, *C* is aborted and, as *C* does not have a handler for *E*, control returns to *B*. *B* in turn finds it has no handler for the exception and so it also aborts and returns to operation *A*. *A* does have a handler and this it now executes, causing the "N" which has been passed back to be printed. After the handler is executed, in some models, control passes to the next instruction in *A* after the call to *B*. So the program would print

"1, 3, 5, N, 2". In other models, *A* is aborted as well.

In the ODMG model, there is a most general exception, which is used if no handler is found in any of the operations which are in progress. This prints out a message to say that the exception has happened and then aborts the current process. This most general exception is an instance of the most general exception type. Defining a new exception consists of defining a new exception type as a subtype of *Exception*. Exceptions can be specified either in modules or in type interfaces.

In the example, the operation *birthday* could encounter a problem if it attempts to increase the age beyond the specified maximum. Setting the *age* property outside of the legal range 0 to 150 is an example of an exceptional event. The most sensible place to put the exception handler is with the *Person* type, since it is only the operations of *person* that will be allowed to change *age*. The declaration of this type is extended with:

```
exception ageLimit[ Unsigned short wrongAge ];
```

which indicates that the incorrect age will be returned. (This exception can then be used by any operation which changes the *age* property.)

The specification must also indicate that the exception can be raised in *birthday*, so the specification of that operation is changed to:

```
void birthday() raises (ageLimit);
```

■ 5.4.3 Transactions

The ODMG model supports the traditional ACID transactions, familiar to database users. Transactions lock the data they access with the normal kinds of shared and exclusive locks, so that many readers or one writer are allowed on each piece of data. Pessimistic concurrency control is the standard for the ODMG model, although other protocols may be supported at a later date.

Transactions are started with a **begin transaction** command, which is similar in some ways to the *new* command which creates objects. Transactions must be explicitly initiated – they do not just spring into being when the application starts up or when the current transaction quits.

The following operations are allowed on a transaction:

- **begin** initiates a transaction (and specifies the concurrency control protocol where this is allowed).
- **commit** completes a transaction, releasing all of the locks held by that transaction and making the changes accessible to any transactions in which this one is nested. If the transaction is a top-level transaction, all other

transactions can now access the changes.

- **abort** quits the transaction, releases locks and undoes any changes.
- **checkpoint** makes any changes permanent, but does not release any locks or quit the transaction.
- **abort-to-top-level** quits and undoes not just the changes of the current transaction but of all transactions in which this one is contained.

5.5 ODL reference

In this section, the details of ODL are brought together, first as an informal syntax and second by drawing together the various examples into a complete module specification.

5.5.1 An informal syntax for ODL

The overall structure of a program in ODL is a list of definitions, separated by semicolons, in which each definition is one of six possibilities:

(a) a module, which is used to group definitions as follows:

```
module <moduleName>
{
<list of definitions>
}
```

(b) a type declaration, which defines a new type name with a type expression, using a definition of the form:

```
typedef <typeExpression> <typeName>
```

(c) a constant, which is defined using:

```
const <type name> <constant name> = <expression>
```

(d) an exception is declared as follows:

```
exception <exception name>[ <list of elements> ]
```

where an element is a pair of a type and a name.

(e) a name for a persistent root is declared as follows:

```
name <typeExpression> <rootName>
```

(f) a type interface.

The definition of a type interface is as follows:

```
interface <typeName> [: <SupertypeName(s)>]
( <type properties> )[ : <persistence indicator> ]
{ <list of export items> }
```

There are only two type properties which can appear inside the round brackets in the current specification of ODL – the extent of the type and the key of the type. The extent is specified in a line of the form:

```
extent <extentName>
```

while the key(s) appear as either:

```
key <theKey>
```

or

```
keys <key_1>, ..., <key_n>
```

if there are more than one key. A simple key is a single property name, while a compound key is shown as a bracketed list of property names.

The persistence indicator must be one of "persistent" or "transient".

The list of export items is separated by semicolons. There are six kinds of export item:

(a) a type declaration – defined as for a module, but local to this type;
(b) a constant – defined as for a module, but local to this type;
(c) an exception – defined as for a module, but local to this type;
(d) an attribute, which is declared with a line of the form:

```
attribute <domain type spec> <attribute name>
```

in which the domain type name may be a type name from the hierarchy, a type name defined in any surrounding module or interface, or a type specification;

(e) a relationship, which is declared as follows:

```
relationship <object type spec> <relationship name>
   [ inverse <inverse type name> :: <inverse relationship name> ]
```

in which the object type spec is either the name of an object type or a object type expression.

(f) an operation, which is specified as follows:

```
<result type name> <operation name> ( [<parameter list>] )
   [ raises <list of exception names> ]
```

where a parameter has three components – a name, a type and a specification of whether it is updated or not. (A parameter can be marked input only (**in**), input and output (**inout**) or output only (**out**).)

■ 5.5.2 A three-type schema in ODL

Here are the examples given above gathered together to provide an example of the syntax.

```
module Employment
{
typedef Struct Address
{ Unsigned Short House; String street, String city,
  String postcode} address
interface Person
( extent People
  key socialSecurityNumber ) persistent
  exception ageLimit[ Unsigned short wrongAge ];
  const Unsigned Short maximumAge = 150;
  attribute String socialSecurityNumber;
  attribute String name;
  attribute Unsigned short age;
  attribute Address address;
  relationship Set<Adult> parents inverse Adult::children;
  relationship Company worksFor inverse Company::employees;
  void birthday() raises (ageLimit);
}
interface Company
( extent Companies
  keys companyID, companyName ) persistent
  attribute Unsigned short companyID;
  attribute String companyName;
  attribute Adult manager;
  attribute Address address;
  relationship Set<Person> employees inverse Person::worksFor;
  void employ( in Adult newEmployee );
}
interface Adult : Person
( key ( worksFor, staffNumber ) ) persistent
  typedef List<Company> EmploymentRecord
  attribute Unsigned short staffNumber;
  attribute EmploymentRecord pastEmployers
  relationship Adult spouse inverse Adult :: spouse;
  relationship List<Person> children inverse Person::parents;
  void addChild( in Person newChild);
  boolean isChild( in Person testChild );
} }
```

■ 5.6 Summary

The main points made in this chapter are:

- The ODMG data model places a precise meaning on the concepts discussed in Chapter 2.
- It is the core component of an architecture in which various kinds of languages are available.

- ODL is the data definition language which makes the concepts in the data model more concrete, but is not necessarily expected to be implemented.
- OQL is a language only used for querying the database. It is a key component of an ODMG-compliant OODBMS and is used both as a stand-alone interactive component and embedded in any OML.
- An OML is an object-oriented programming language extended both by adding persistence and by adding access to the ODMG data model. This is achieved by a language binding.
- The ODMG data model provides both immutable literal types and mutable object types.
- It includes a range of atomic literal types, collection types and a structure type for records.
- Definitions in ODL permit local types, constants, exceptions and object type interfaces to be grouped together in a nested module structure.
- An object type interface contains local types, constants and exceptions, but mainly includes properties and operations. Properties may be attributes which are uni-directional references, or relationships which have automatically maintained inverses.
- Operations have a result type and one or more parameters. Parameter values may themselves be updated.
- Type interfaces have properties: an extent which holds all the instances of the type; one or more keys, and a persistence indicator.
- The model supports two kinds of persistent root – the extents of object types and explicitly named objects.

The next chapter will give a more extensive example of the use of the data model and of ODL.

6 Developing an application in the ODMG model

This chapter illustrates the use of the ODMG proposal with the design of a database to support an electronic mail facility. The first section describes the intended application. The second and third sections describe the structural and behavioral design of the application and the chapter finishes with a complete ODL description.

6.1 The informal specification of an example

Here is the kind of specification that might arise as the start point of the design of an OODBMS application:

> The application is intended to support the use of electronic mail between a local group of computer users. The application must support the operations of sending and receiving mail messages between the users as well as allowing users to store and reply to the mail. The application must also provide a privileged user, called the superuser, with the ability to add and remove users and to perform some management tasks.

Figure 6.1 shows the kind of system that is being described. Each of the four users is shown with an incoming mailbox and a collection of storage mailboxes. Jim is sending a message, shown as *M1*, to June – the message ending up in June's incoming mailbox.

The application must provide all users with the following functions:

- logging on – the user becomes the current user of the application;
- logging off – there is now no current user;
- send a message – to any other user or collection of users;
- summarize mailbox – to see what messages are there;
- read a message – select a message, display it and deal with it first by either replying to it or not and second by holding it in the incoming mailbox, storing it in one of a number of storage mailboxes or destroying it;
- delete a message – when it is no longer useful;
- create a mailbox – as a new member of the collection of storage mailboxes;
- remove a mailbox – and its messages;
- flush a mailbox – destroying all messages.

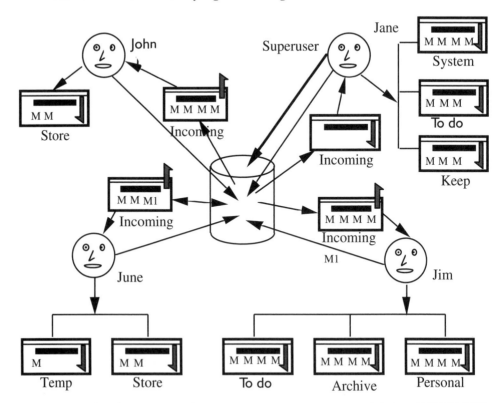

Figure 6.1 An electronic mail system.

The application recognizes a single superuser, who, when logged in, can also:

- create a user – add a new user to the system;
- remove a user – and his or her mailboxes and stored messages;
- summarize usage – listing all of the users and the messages held by each user.

These 12 facilities will provide the core functionality of the application which manages the mail database.

To support this, the application will store a collection of users, each having a name, login and password together with an incoming mailbox of messages and a collection of mailboxes for storing messages. Each mailbox has a name and records the number of messages in the mailbox and which messages are in the mailbox. Each message consists of the sender, the recipients, a subject line, the main body of the message, and the date on which it was sent.

■ 6.2 Structural design

There are three aspects of the structural part of a schema: the types used, the properties of those types (including identification of keys), and the persistent roots. This section will describe how these can be extracted from the informal specification of the mail application.

■ 6.2.1 Choosing the types

The design process starts by identifying the main object types required. Object design methodologies usually concentrate, for this purpose, on the noun phrases to be found in the requirements specification. In this case, there must be types for users, mailboxes and messages.

The application also needs to distinguish the superuser from other users and one effective way of doing this is to make it an instance of a special type – one which is a subtype of the user type.

There are other types which will be required in the application – certain scalar values and collections for the representation of the storage mailboxes, the messages in a mailbox and the users who are recipients of a message. All of these together with a type for the date of a message are available in the ODMG type hierarchy and can be expected to be in any ODMG compliant OODBMS. The body of a message may be a held as a string, albeit a long one. Alternatively, an OODBMS may provide a type for structured texts, in which case this might be preferred.

Figure 6.2   The electronic mail inheritance hierarchy.

The beginnings of the ODL specification is therefore:

interface User
interface Superuser **:** User
interface Mailbox
interface Message

and the inheritance hierarchy is shown in Figure 6.2.

■ 6.2.2 Identifying the properties

The second step is to identify the properties of these types. Some consideration reveals the following properties are needed:

- each **user** has a **name**, a **login**, a **password**, an **incoming** mailbox, and a collection of **storage** mailboxes;
- each **mailbox** has a **name**, the **number** of messages held, and **holds** a list of messages;
- each **message** has a **subject**, a **sending date** and a message **body**, is **held in** a mailbox, is **sent by** one user and is **received by** many users.

Figure 6.3 summarizes this in the form of an ER diagram augmented with a thick arrowed line representing a subtype relationship. The properties with scalar values are shown as attributes and the properties which refer to other types are shown as relationships.

Representing this in ODL is achieved by adding properties to the types. Recall that there are two kinds of these, also called attributes and relationships, but with a different distinction between the two than that found in the ER model. Attributes are those which do not have inverses while relationships do.

All of the ER attributes, since they are literal values, will be attributes with the exception of the number of messages in a mailbox. This will not be stored but derived. It will therefore be dealt with when operations are discussed. It remains to consider how each of the relationships in Figure 6.3 will be represented:

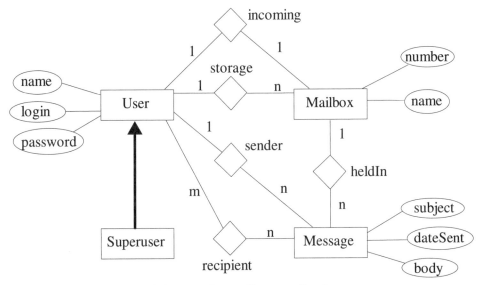

Figure 6.3 The structural design of a mailbox application.

- *sender* links a message to the person who sent it. Clearly, it will be necessary to find the sender from the message. Is it going to be useful to find all of the messages which a user has sent? If so it will be necessary to put inverse relationships in *User* and in *Message*. It seems, however, that maintaining all of the messages sent by any user is not going to be necessary and therefore *sender* will be presented as an attribute of *Message*.
- *recipient* is treated similarly. Storing a list of all the messages which have ever been sent to a user is unlikely to be valuable and so *recipients* will be represented as a multi-valued attribute of *Message*.
- *heldIn* needs a different treatment. If it is going to be necessary to delete a message, then the message must be able to find the mailbox object that holds it, so that it can be removed from the collection of messages in the mailbox. *heldIn* will therefore be represented as a relationship.
- *incoming* is an attribute of *User*. Mailboxes will be accessed from users, not the other way round.
- *storage*, similarly, is a multi-valued attribute of *User*. In fact, if there needed to be an owner property of mailboxes, then this would be quite difficult to model as a relationship, since it would be the inverse of not one but two properties of *User*. This could perhaps be achieved by making the incoming mailbox one of an all-embracing collection of mailboxes, distinguished by its name. However, this does not seem particularly useful in the current context.

There is another important consideration in creating the inverse links which are involved in relationships. This is how such links will affect the reachability (and hence the persistence) of the data. For instance, if the sender and recipients of a message are represented as relationships, then there will be links from users to messages. These links will be maintained even after a message has been "deleted", i.e. removed from all mailboxes. Thus either such links must be explicitly broken (an additional programming task) or the message will be retained until all of the users it was sent to and from are removed from the system. It is therefore clearly important that relationships should only be used where both links are really useful. Some systems will assist with this by removing both sides of a link when either of them is removed, but extra work is still required.

The result of this analysis is that the following properties must be provided:

- User
  attributes – name, password, login, incoming, storage;
  relationships – none;
- Superuser – no extra properties;
- Mailbox
  attributes – name;
  relationships – holds (the inverse is *heldIn*);
- Message
  attributes – sender, recipients, subject, dateSent, body;
  relationships – heldIn (the inverse is *holds*).

Three of the properties will use collections, but which collection types should be used? The three properties involved are:

- *storage* – this indicates a collection of mailboxes. These are in no particular order, nor will they be duplicated, and so using a **set** is appropriate.
- *holds* – the collection of messages in a mailbox. This is usually regarded as being ordered and thus a **list** is appropriate here.
- *recipients* – the collection of users receiving a message is unordered and should not contain duplicates and so, once more, a **set** is the right choice.

The type specifications therefore now include for their property part:

```
interface User
{ attribute String name;
  attribute String login;
  attribute String password;
  attribute Mailbox incoming;
  attribute Set<Mailbox> storage;
}

interface Superuser : User
{ }

interface Mailbox
{ attribute String name;
  relationship List<Message> holds inverse Message heldIn;
  Unsigned Short number();
}

interface Message
{ attribute String subject;
  attribute Date dateSent;
  attribute Text body;
  attribute User sender;
  attribute Set<User> recipients;
  relationship Mailbox heldIn inverse Mailbox holds;
}
```

■ 6.2.3 Selecting the persistent root objects

The description of the database structure must also identify which values will be explicitly stored and named in the database. These will be the root objects from which all other persistent data can be accessed. In trying to find which roots might be useful, the place to start is to examine all of the values which are globally identifiable.

In this case, there are five candidates:

- the collection of all users;
- the collection of all mailboxes;
- the collection of all messages;
- a distinguished user who is the superuser; and
- the current user – the one who is logged on in the current process.

In choosing which of these to use, the guiding question is:

When the process starts up, what must be available so that all of the data can be accessed by following references?

A secondary question is:

Are there any other ways into the data that will also be useful (to cut down programming or access times, for instance)?

In this case, it is important to retrieve all of the messages, mailboxes and users, and to be able to find the superuser. If all of the mailboxes are accessible, then all of the messages will be accessible as well, since each message will be reachable as one of the contents of a mailbox, unless the message has been deleted in which case it is no longer needed. Perhaps, it might be thought useful to maintain a reference to the collection of all of the messages so that they can be queried over, but this is not a facility that is expected of a mail system and indeed violates the basic privacy desired by users unless passwords are attached to messages as well. Therefore, it is not necessary to keep the collection of messages as a persistent root.

A similar argument follows for the collection of mailboxes. They are all reachable from a *User* object and if the collection of users is persistent the mailboxes will be as well. Neither is there any reason to query the collection of all mailboxes. Therefore, the collection of all mailboxes will not be used as a root.

The collection of users must, on the other hand, be persistent. The extent of the type *User* is typical of the kind of root object expected of databases of all kinds.

The superuser is also a useful root. The superuser object is already persistent since it is in the collection of all users, but here it is indistinguishable from the other user objects. One way of identifying the superuser would be by using a boolean attribute, combined with a query which filters the collection of users based on this attribute. This seems like overkill though. It is better to place a root object for ease of access.

The current user must be treated differently. Much of the same argument for distinguishing this user follows in the same way as for the superuser. However, a key difference between the two cases, is what is to be expected to be available at the start of the process. It is clearly an expectation that the database retains an indication of who is the superuser between program runs. That person might be changed, but the current value must be available in order for the whole application to run. Conversely, there can be no expectation that the current user will be retained. An implicit consequence of halting the process is to log out the current user. If the current user is made persistent then the application must nullify the value when it quits to achieve this. Moreover, if there is one current user object, centrally held in the database, this implies no multi-user access to the database, since this object will be locked by the first process to start up. What would be useful is for the application structure to enable the current user object, although transient, to be declared to be global to all of the constituent transactions and queries. In Chapters 7 and 8, a method for achieving this will be described.

There are therefore two persistent roots which will have to be named in the schema:

- the collection of users, which will be specified as the extent (and therefore this will be a set) of the type *User*, and called *theUsers*;
- the superuser, which will be an explicitly named root – *superUser*.

Although only the extent for *User* has been made an explicit root, this does not mean that the other types are not persistent. Recall that the use of the keyword **persistent** determines whether the object of the type will be managed by the storage manager or by the language run-time system. In this case, all of the objects should be handled by the storage manager so that they can be saved in the database.

The type properties of the four types therefore begin:

```
interface User
( extent theUsers ) persistent

interface Superuser : User
( ) persistent

interface Mailbox
( ) persistent

interface Message
( ) persistent
```

The object representing the superuser must be explicitly named as a persistent root, *superUser* say:

```
name Superuser superUser;
```

▪ 6.2.4 Choosing keys

Identifying which properties are to be used as keys is based largely upon querying requirements. A key can be used to gain associative access to a collection. The collections which might be queried include the three collection properties discussed in Section 6.2.2, as well as the extents of the types, discussed in Section 6.2.3. The extents of *Mailbox* and *Message* have already been discarded, so they will have no impact, which leaves:

- *theUsers* – This set will be queried to find a user by login and possibly also by name. Both of these should therefore be keys of the type *User*.
- *storage* – This set will also be queried using the mailbox name. However, the sets involved will be small so it is questionable whether or not a key would be particularly useful. However, there is no pressing argument against this, so *name* will be made a key of the *Mailbox* type.

- *holds* – This will be queried, but by position and, as this is already supported by the list type, there is no need for a key.
- *recipients* – This is unlikely to be queried and has no impact on the need for keys.

Therefore, two keys will be added to *User* and one to *Mailbox*, which means that the type definitions now begin:

```
interface User
( extent theUsers
    keys name, login ) persistent

interface Superuser : User
( ) persistent

interface Mailbox
( key name ) persistent

interface Message
( ) persistent
```

6.3 Behavioral design

In this section, the structure of the application will be discussed, and the operations and exceptions which are useful will be identified. In creating the application, a command-driven interface will be used, rather than a graphical and menu-driven mechanism. Either interface relies ultimately on a similar collection of data access operations.

6.3.1 Application structure and transactions

Although different systems might implement application structure in different ways, an application is always, in effect, a collection of transactions and queries. The ways in which these can be combined will vary from system to system, but most will provide some kind of high-level structure to ease the creation of applications. In Chapters 7 and 8, the O_2 application structure will be shown as an example of the kind of framework likely to be available.

In the current example, the list of 12 facilities developed in Section 6.1 constitute the collection of transactions and queries required. This collection will be embedded in the application framework, but the implementation of the facilities will rely on the availability of appropriate type operations to implement the basic computational components. Which operations are actually required will be discussed next.

■ 6.3.2 Operations

Identifying the operations which should be provided for each type is a more complex task. There are at least two ways to proceed:

- Start with the types and determine the operations which might be usefully provided for members of the type. This is often called identifying the responsibilities of the type instances.
- Start with the application and, in top-down fashion, arrive at the operations which must be made available.

In this section, the second approach will be taken, although a mixture of the two approaches is often appropriate.

The problem is one of positioning each part of the computation by making it an operation of a particular type. In doing this, the guiding principle is to maximize the information hiding capability of the type. Wherever possible, the operation should be placed in the type which has the properties that it makes use of. For instance, the facility to display the headers of a mailbox could be coded entirely as an operation on type *User*, but then it would need to fetch the messages and their components. It is much better in this instance to break the code down into an operation on *Message*, which displays the details of a particular message; another in type, *Mailbox*, which iterates over the collection of messages held; and one on *User* controlling the whole facility.

The starting point, then, is the collection of facilities which the application is intended to support. From these, it gradually becomes clear which operations are needed. The transactions and queries are all expected to operate in a context which includes the persistent roots and any globally available values. As discussed above these include the set of users, *theUsers*; the superuser, *superUser*; and the current user, a global variable called *currentUser*.

Each of the transactions or queries in the application will now be examined to determine which operations they need.

Logging in

This transaction changes the value of *currentUser*. To achieve this it requests that a login and password be entered. It then queries the set of users to find the appropriate user object. This is best carried out by a direct query on the collection, *theUsers*, which can be achieved in most systems by an embedded OQL query of the form:

```
currentUser := OQLquery( "select U from theUsers where login = param1
                                      and password = param2" )
```

If this facility is not available, then a query must be written as an iteration in the programming language:

```
for each U in theUsers do if U. -> testUser() then return U
```

and this would require an operation on *User* to test if this is the one wanted:

object type	name	op type	parameters
User	testUser	Boolean	testLogin and testPassword both input only

Logging out

This transaction sets the current user to nil and requires no type operations to assist with this.

Sending a message

This transaction must create a message, gathering all of the information to instantiate its attributes and then put the message in the incoming mailbox of the recipients. This is perhaps best implemented primarily as an operation on the *User* type, which creates a new message and then calls an operation on the *Message* type to set up the property values. The sequence of control is therefore:

1. An operation, *sendMail*, of type, *User*, is called.
2. This calls a constructor operation of type *Message* sending the *User* object itself as a parameter, so that this can be used as the value of the *sender* attribute.
3. The constructor requests its property values interactively from the user who is logged in. Mostly, these are scalar and are created directly from the input, but the specification of the recipients requires a selection from the set of users, which is similar to that required for logging in.
4. The completed message is sent to the recipient *User* objects, by calling a receiving operation of that type.
5. The receiving operation, in turn, sends the message to the incoming mailbox object, by calling an insertion operation.

In this sequence, the information hiding principles are firmly adhered to – the mailbox object is responsible for accepting and storing a message, user objects are responsible for initiating the creation process and for receiving objects, and message objects are responsible for instantiating their properties. In all cases, the properties which must be accessed are local to the type of the operation.

The following operations have therefore been identified:

object type	name	op type	parameters
User	sendMail	void	none
Message	create	void	sendingUser (input)
User	receive	void	theMessage (input)
Mailbox	insert	void	theMessage (input)

Summarizing a mailbox

This transaction summarizes one of the mailboxes of the current user. It requests a mailbox name and displays the number, the subject and sender of all messages in the mailbox. Again this is basically an operation (called *summarize*) on type *User*. It must take in a name and find the mailbox with that name This is a query on the collection of storage mailboxes and, for the reasons discussed under logging in, above, this might require an operation to test a mailbox by name, similar to *testUser*. Finally *summarize* calls an operation on the mailbox to execute the summary. This operation in turns calls a summarizing operation on each message.

This requires:

object type	name	op type	parameters
User	summarize	void	none
Mailbox	testMbox	Boolean	testName, an input string
Mailbox	showHeaders	void	none
Message	summarize	void	number, an input integer

Reading a message

The current user must select a mailbox. The headers will be displayed and the user selects a message by inputting the number shown against it in the summary. The body of the message will then be shown. Finally the user is given the options of replying to the sender and of storing the message.

This is again best implemented as a call to a void operation on the *User* type. This starts by calling *summarize*. It then requests a number from the user, and then needs to be able to retrieve the message from the mailbox by passing the number of the message to a mailbox operation. It must then display it using a display operation on the *Message* type.

If the user chooses to reply, then a new message must be created and its attributes must be instantiated in a different way from the *create* operation used to send an original message. The recipients will be the sender (and optionally the recipients) of the original message and the subject will be "Re:" concatenated with the original subject. This means there will have to be a different operation on the *Message* type. This will then use the *receive* and *insert* operations already discussed for sending original mail.

The storage options may result in the message being added to a storage mailbox (*insert* can be used for that) and removed from the incoming mailbox. Therefore a delete operation is required to remove a message from a mailbox.

The following are therefore needed:

object type	name	op type	parameters
User	readMail	void	none
Mailbox	getMessage	Message	number, an input integer
Message	display	void	none
Message	reply	void	replier, sender both input Users and oldSubject, an input string
Mailbox	delete	void	the message to be deleted is input

Deleting a message

The user who is logged in will choose one of the storage mailboxes and then one of the messages, in the same way as for reading a message, but the operation will delete the message, by calling the *delete* operation of the mailbox. This will be controlled by an operation of type *User*. This operation will re-use the *summarize*, *getMessage* and *delete* operations which are already defined.

object type	name	op type	parameters
User	deleteMsg	void	none

Creating a mailbox

This is primarily a *User* type operation, which requests a name for the mailbox and creates it in the set of storage mailboxes. It calls a create operation on the mailbox to set the name and clear the list of messages. Insertion of the new mailbox into the storage set will be carried out using an operation which will be available on the system-provided collection type which will be used to implement the set. It requires, therefore:

object type	name	op type	parameters
User	createMbox	void	none
Mailbox	create	void	mailbox name as an input string

Removing a mailbox

This is another *User* type operation, which requests a mailbox and then removes it from the set of storage mailboxes. The deletion operation of the system-provided collection type will be available for the removal. Note that the messages in the mailbox will automatically be removed as well, as long as the system implements persistence by reachability.

object type	name	op type	parameters
User	removeMbox	void	none

Flushing a mailbox

This transaction also calls an operation on the user type. This operation requests a mailbox name and then calls a flush operation on that mailbox:

object type	name	op type	parameters
User	flushMbox	void	none
Mailbox	flush	void	none

Creating a user

This is an operation declared on the *Superuser* type. It creates a new user object and then calls an operation to request the details of the user and to set up the user attributes. This in turn must create a new incoming mailbox and a default storage mailbox, which has no name. As well as the mailbox operation, *create*, it therefore requires:

object type	name	op type	parameters
Superuser	makeUser	void	none
User	create	void	none

Removing a user

Another *Superuser* operation, this requests a user name, finds the user (using a query or the *testUser* operation) and deletes it from the set of users, using a system-provided collection operation. This only requires:

object type	name	op type	parameters
Superuser	deleteUser	void	none

Summarizing usage

This iterates across the set of users and displays the user name and for each mailbox, the mailbox name and the number of messages held. It is controlled by a *Superuser* operation and this calls an operation on *User* to display the name and another on *Mailbox* to display the name and the number of messages. The last operations required are therefore:

object type	name	op type	parameters
Superuser	summarize	void	none
User	displayName	void	none
Mailbox	display	void	none

This completes the identification of operations. As a result, the operation parts of the various types will appear as follows:

```
interface User
{ Boolean testUser( in String testLogin, in String testPassword );
  void sendMail( );
  void receive( in Message theMessage )
  void summarize( );
  void readMail( );
  void deleteMsg( );
  void createMbox( );
  void removeMbox( );
  void flushMbox( );
  void create();
  void displayName( );
};

interface Superuser : User
{ void makeUser();
  void deleteUser();
  void summarize();
};
```

```
interface Mailbox
{ Unsigned Short number();
  void insert( in Message newMessage );
  Boolean testMbox( in String testName )
  void showHeaders();
  Message getMessage( in Unsigned Short number );
  void delete(in Message theMessage );
  void flush();
  void create( in String theName );
  void display();
};

interface Message
{ void create( in User sendingUser );
  void summarize( in Unsigned Short number );
  void display();
  void reply( in User sender; in User replier; in String oldSubject );
};
```

6.3.3 Exceptions

An exception is used to provide an escape mechanism for unusual events. In this application, it will be assumed that the software is well formed and, therefore the data will never be in an inconsistent state. In this case, it is end user input that might cause exceptional behavior – in particular requesting data which is not in the database.

For the current purposes three exceptions, from among several possibilities, which might occur will be identified:

- *badMessageNumber* – in this case, the user requests a message with a number which is larger than the number of messages in the mailbox;
- *badMailboxName* – similarly, the user inputs the name of a non-existent mailbox;
- *userNotFound* – this happens when a user login (or login and password) is given which fails to match any of the stored users.

badMessageNumber occurs as part of the *readMail* and *deleteMsg* operations, when a user types in a message number which is incorrect. The exception is raised in both of these operations and a handler will be provided at the top level which is required to print "There is no message numbered N". As the number input is required for this, the exception is given the number as an element. Since the handler is placed at the top level this will abort the read mail operation. If this is not the required behavior, the exception handler can be implemented in both of the operations, which can then be attempted again.

badMailboxName occurs in all of those operations which attempt to manipulate an existing mailbox – *readMail*, *deleteMsg*, *removeMbox* and *flushMbox*. Each of these can raise the exception and, when they do, they pass back the incorrect string as an element of the exception. The top-level exception handler then prints "Mailbox named XXX cannot be found" and the operation is aborted.

userNotFound occurs widely. In particular it occurs when:

- *logging in* – In this case, either the login or password could be wrong. The exception is raised in the transaction and an exception handler at the top level prints out a message stating that a user with that login is not known. The exception needs the user login to be supplied as an element to facilitate this.
- *sending mail* – This occurs if the login of a supposed recipient is not found. It is raised in the *create* operation of the message. It should also be handled there or otherwise the whole message construction process would be aborted.
- *deleting users* – In this case, the login of the user to be deleted is not found. Now aborting the process is probably the right thing to do so that the top-level exception handler can be re-used.

Thus, the application needs three exceptions with an element which is used for the reporting process. The application also needs three handlers, one for the incorrect message number error and two for the failure to find the user.

The schema will therefore start with the definition of these exceptions:

```
exception userNotFound( String supposedLogin );
exception badMailboxName( String supposedName );
exception badMessageNumber( Unsigned Short supposedNumber );
```

and the appropriate operation definitions will be extended, for instance:

```
interface User
{ ...
        void readMail( ) raises BadMessageNumber;
... }
```

■ 6.4 Specification in ODL

This completes the schema design. It now consists of a number of types with their properties, operations and exceptions.

Here is the full schema gathered together as an ODL specification.

```
module Email
{
exception userNotFound( String supposedLogin );
exception badMailboxName( String supposedName );
exception badMessageNumber( Unsigned Short supposedNumber );
name Superuser superUser;
interface User
{ extent theUsers
  key login): persistent
{ attribute String name;
  attribute String login;
  attribute String password;
  attribute Mailbox incoming;
  attribute Set<Mailbox> storage;
  Boolean testUser( in String testLogin, in String testPassword );
  void sendMail( );
  void receive( in Message theMessage )
  void summarize( );
  void readMail( ) raises badMessageNumber, badMailboxName;
  void deleteMsg( ) raises badMailboxName;
  void createMbox( );
  void removeMbox( ) raises badMailboxName;
  void flushMbox( ) raises badMailboxName;
  void create();
  void displayName( );
};
interface Superuser : User
{ void makeUser();
  void deleteUser() raises userNotFound;
  void summarize();
};
interface Mailbox
{ attribute String name;
  relationship List<Message> holds inverse Message heldin;
  Unsigned Short number();
  void insert( in Message newMessage );
  Boolean testMbox( in String testName )
  void showHeaders();
  Message getMessage( in Unsigned Short number );
  void delete(in Message theMessage );
  void flush();
  void create( in String theName );
  void display();
};
interface Message
{ attribute String subject;
  attribute Date dateSent;
  attribute Text body;
  attribute User sender;
  attribute Set<User> recipients;
  relationship Mailbox heldin inverse Mailbox holds;
  void create( in User sendingUser ) raises userNotFound;
  void summarize( in Unsigned Short number );
  void display();
  void reply( in User sender; in User replier; in String oldSubject );
};
};
```

■ 6.5 Summary

In this chapter, the complete development of an ODL schema was demonstrated. The stages involved included: the design of a type hierarchy; the identification of appropriate properties, keys and persistent roots; a selection of the transactions and queries which together will constitute the application; an analysis of the computation into appropriately placed operations; and the specification of exceptions to handle unusual behavior.

The main points covered in this chapter include:

- Starting from an informal specification of the application, the first task is to develop a schema as a collection of types.
- The types required are identifiable from the noun phrases found in the specification.
- The types should be organized into an inheritance hierarchy in order to cut down on the coding required.
- The properties required for each type should be identified. If they can be derived from other data, they should be represented as operations.
- Of the other properties, some are attributes and some are relationships. All of the literal values will be attributes.
- Of the object properties, only those which have useful inverses should be identified as relationships. The rest are attributes.
- Where persistence is implemented using reachability, the creation of unnecessary inverse relationships can make object deletion more problematic.
- The schema must also include the definition of one or more persistent roots. These are either type extents or named objects.
- In selecting the roots, it is vital that all data be reachable from at least one of them. Additional roots which reduce access paths should also be provided.
- The operations provided for each type can be identified either by determining the important facilities which the type should provide or by starting from the application and identifying which operations are needed to support it.
- In positioning the code with particular types, it is important to maximize the information hiding aspect.
- Exceptions should be identified to handle unusual behavior without complicating the code.

The design thus created is still an abstract specification. Even the ODMG members have no intention of providing an ODL interface. Rather, they will provide equivalent schema design interfaces. The next chapter introduces the O_2 system which is one of the leading ODMG-compliant products. In examining O_2, the application designed in this chapter will be turned into a concrete OODBMS application.

7 | O$_2$: an object-oriented database system

This chapter concentrates on one of the commercial systems which realizes the concepts that have been discussed so far. The first part of the book introduced the main ideas involved in object-oriented database systems in abstract, while the previous three chapters have demonstrated an emerging standard abstract model to structure those ideas. This chapter describes a concrete realization of this structure – the O$_2$ object-oriented database system.

O$_2$ is being marketed as an ODMG compliant product. This means that the model discussed in the previous three chapters is supported. However, O$_2$, in common with the other commercial OODBMS, provides much more than this. In particular, O$_2$ extends the ODMG model in a variety of ways which include a database structure centered around the schema as the fundamental construct and versioning. Furthermore, O$_2$ contains a model for applications built on top of schemata, which means that applications and data can be more coherently organized in a tightly integrated manner. O$_2$ also extends the persistence model, by supporting persistence by reachability. Finally, O$_2$ includes a number of support tools for user interface management, metadata management, web access, graph editing and so on. All of these facilities are built on top of the object-oriented primitives and so are tightly integrated with the databases they support.

O$_2$ is particularly interesting as a commercial product in that its development has been consciously carried out in the public eye. The development of most products in our competitive economic system occurs in secret. The predominant ethos is that to show one's hand too soon conveys a clear benefit to competitors in that they can "steal" the best ideas. An alternative approach is that to produce a public account of product development lays the product open to criticism which, although painful, can create improvements in design and implementation which is likely to result in a better product when finally delivered. This is the manner in which O$_2$ is being developed.

The O$_2$ initiative started as a research project funded by both public and private money. The product has evolved through a number of different versions and the details of the model on which it is based have changed, but at all times, the O$_2$ company has contributed research reports to the academic community and has been one of the most consistent and productive groups contributing to database research over the last 10 years.

The first section of this chapter will discuss the history of this development. In succeeding sections, the structure of the O$_2$ system and its various components will be discussed – the architecture, the database engine, the application structure and, finally, the tools and libraries. The next chapter will then show how O$_2$ is used to develop a database application.

■ 7.1 The history of O$_2$

■ 7.1.1 Company history

The start point for the creation of the O$_2$ system was the setting up of the Altaïr research consortium in Versailles in September 1986 headed by François Bançilhon who had already had a distinguished career in database system research, both in France and in the USA. The consortium was funded by IN2 (a Siemens subsidiary), INRIA (the French national institute for IT research) and LRI (one of the computer science laboratories at the University of Paris-Sud). The project also played a full role in a number of European Commission Esprit funded projects, as the company continues to do. Altaïr ran for five years, from 1986 to 1991 and represented a total initial R&D investment of $20 million and a product development effort of some 130 man-years. This included not just paid company employees, but also a number of database experts from Europe and North America who spent short periods of time in Versailles and contributed many of the ideas which emerged in the prototypes and in the final commercial product.

The results of the Altaïr work were sufficiently encouraging that it was decided to market an O$_2$ system and, to achieve this end, O$_2$ Technology was created in 1991, also in Versailles. O$_2$ then became one of the five initial members of the ODMG design team and the model presented in Chapter 5 shows the influence of the O$_2$ data model. In 1994, O$_2$ extended their operation to North America by opening an office in Palo Alto, California.

■ 7.1.2 Product history

Technically, the O$_2$ system has evolved considerably. The ODMG compatible version of O$_2$ is version number 4.6 of the system and this indicates the number of very different systems which have been produced. However, some common threads can be seen in the various designs from the very early days, all of which are either central to or compatible with the ODMG standard:

- a commitment to object orientation;
- the centrality of a data model which supports database work and object-oriented programming;
- constructs in the data model for both literal values and objects;
- the use of orthogonal persistence by reachability from named roots;
- a client/server architecture;
- the potential availability of more than one programming language;
- interactive textual command language and graphical programming interfaces;
- a query language interface;
- the importance of multimedia data;
- the provision of support tools.

The evolution of the O$_2$ system can be seen in the following phases:

1. The design and development of the first prototype in 1987, described in various research papers in the late 1980s.
2. A working prototype in 1989, which included a programming environment, a textual interface, a set of user interface generation tools, a query processor and support for multiple languages. Initially these were supposed to be a range of traditional programming languages – CO$_2$, BO$_2$ (Basic), LO$_2$ (Lisp), etc. – enhanced with persistence and the O$_2$ data model, but only CO$_2$ was practically usable. The underlying architecture included a schema manager, an object manager and a disk manager. This version is described in the book, "The Story of O$_2$".

3. A commercial product which evolved around the data model and the use of O_2C, a development of CO_2, which is also a persistent, object-oriented form of C. During a number of releases, this has gradually developed into a full database system supporting multiple clients, transactions and so on. A database and application structure, described in Section 7.4, was developed, together with an architecture, described in Sections 7.2 and 7.3 and a set of support tools, described in Section 7.5. In order to support the existing programming standard, a C++ interface was added, but application development using C++ was, at that time, clearly more limited than by using O_2C.

4. With release 4.6, O_2 Technology met their commitment to support the ODMG standard. The differences between the ODMG data model and the previous O_2 model are largely superficial, but there is some change in the terminology with which the data model is discussed. Therefore a brief description of the previous O_2 data model will now be given, particularly since it has clearly influenced the ODMG standard. The major change is to use the ODMG binding to C++ and to also support Smalltalk. Version management also appears for the first time in release 4.6. Despite the new promotion of the ODMG model, the release is intended to be backwards compatible with release 4.5.

■ 7.1.3 The O_2 data model

The O_2 data model, built into the releases up to and including release 4.5, clearly distinguished literal values and objects and provided a similar type system to the ODMG model. However, the original O_2 model was superficially different from the model given in Chapter 5. In discussing the O_2 system and its components, the original O_2 nomenclature will be used (classes not object types, methods not operations), but it should be borne in mind that these are different from the ODMG standard in name only. The most important differences include: the provision of types and classes, the labeling of public and private data, the nature of O_2C, and the availability of functions and programs. Each of these will be discussed in turn.

Types and classes

In the nomenclature of the O_2 system, the term *class* is used instead of object type, with the term *type* being reserved for literal types. The type system (i.e. the set of literal types) is similar to the *Literal* sub-hierarchy in Figure 6.1 and allows literal values to be built up by use of the type constructors, set, bag, list and record, ultimately out of base types such as integer and string as well as out of classes. In this model a class is an encapsulated type which describes a potential set of objects. It is therefore specified as a literal type together with a set of methods. The extent of a class is not automatically maintained.

To return to the example from Chapter 5, a *Person* class would be described as a type for the structure of the data and then augmented with the set of methods:

```
type Address
tuple ( house: integer; street, city, postcode: string )

class Person
type tuple (
   socialSecurityNumber, name, age, title: string;
   address: Address
   spouse: Person;
   children: List[Person];
   employer: Company
   )
method
   birthday;
   marry( newSpouse: Person );
   procreate( newChild: Person );
   isChild( testChild: Person ): boolean;
end
```

This example shows the usual structure of a class but one in which the structure of its members is explicitly indicated as being a record (as shown by the "type tuple" introduction). However, there is no reason why the type underlying a class should not be a set or a list, which gives the same effect as constructed objects in the ODMG model. Note also that the more usual object-oriented term "method" is used to mean operation.

The O$_2$ model in its original form made no attempt to distinguish attributes and relationships, but the ability to indicate inverses has been added in the most recent version.

Public and private data

The labeling of public and private parts of the class structure is explicit in the O$_2$ model. In the ODMG model, the same effect is achieved by putting public properties and operations in the interface and private characteristics in the implementation. In O$_2$, any property (i.e. field in the type structure) or operation can be preceded by either **private** (not accessible outside of the operations of this class or one of its superclasses); **public** (fully visible everywhere); and **read** (readable everywhere, but writeable only by the direct or inherited operations of the class). Notice that the meaning of **private** here corresponds to that of **protected** in C++.

O₂C

The principal programming language for previous versions of O₂ was the O₂C language. This is a superset of C, which is used to code: the class operations, functions, programs and transactions, and interactively entered programs. Each of these has a body containing local declarations and lines of C. Local declarations are of the form:

```
o2 typeName variableName = expression;
```

in which *typeName* may be a class or type name and the initializing expression can be omitted. However, one of the forms that the expression can take is the keyword **new** and this is the way in which new objects are dynamically created in O₂C.

O₂C is incrementally compiled. New methods can be input, compiled and run all in a single session without having to leave the system into order to link the new code into the application. This gives the comfort of an interpreted language with the security of a compiled language.

As O₂C has the O₂ model so tightly bound into it, it remains an appropriate language with which to program O₂ applications, however, the emphasis of the present book will be on C++, since this is the more standard language.

Constructors

When *new* is called in O₂C, a class operation called *init* is called. The first thing that this operation does is to create the object. That is indeed all that the default version does, installing default values for all of the properties. However, the programmer can redefine *init* to achieve other tasks. Two common tasks which are performed by *init* are to insert the new object into the database and to initialize some of the properties with values other than the defaults. This initialization can be achieved by putting some user interaction into the code body of *init* or by parameterizing the operation, in which case a call to *new* supplies the actual parameters.

Thus if *init* for the *Person* class is programmed with parameters which hold initial values for the name and age properties, then the following:

```
o2 Person jane = new Person( "Jane", 21 );
```

creates a new *Person* object. The left-hand side creates a variable of the *Person* class. The right-hand side is an initializing expression, one which invokes the appropriate *init*, i.e. the one for *Person*. In other circumstances, it is sometimes useful to use the *init* from a superclass.

Functions and programs

In a fully object-oriented programming system, all of the code must be programmed as the operations of the types. There is no other kind of code object. Just as O_2, in common with other OODBMS designs, compromised the purity of the data model by allowing values to be distinguished, so also the computational model is compromised by allowing other kinds of code value into the model. These include:

- Functions – these are free standing code fragments (exactly as provided in C++) which can be installed in a schema and then called from any other code fragment in the schema.
- Programs and transactions. An application is a set of these, programs being queries, while transactions change the database. The system provides a mechanism for binding these together to form an application. It also provides automatically generated menus to choose which one to execute.
- Interactive programs. The programmer can initiate an activity by creating a "run" program. The code in a run program, is not stored but instead is immediately executed. It may call any public operations or access any public properties. This is an ideal way to develop applications incrementally. For instance, its operations can be debugged as run programs, before being installed.

All of these can be coded in any of the programming languages provided.

7.2 The architecture of O_2

The O_2 system as delivered, as shown in Figure 7.1, comprises a database engine and a set of libraries and tools, provided as schemata, which are already installed when the system is delivered. The database engine enhances a basic record-based data manager with the ability to store objects in terms of the O_2 model of applications and data. This is described in Section 7.3.

The functionality of the database engine is provided as an application programming interface (API) library. Using this, programmers can customize the data storage software in order to make appropriately efficient use of the data particular to a given application.

Using this engine, a set of schemata can be stored, each of which contains a logically connected set of classes in the form of a hierarchy. A schema may be used either to store the classes which make up an application, or a library of classes to support some particular general-purpose activity. All application development takes place in the context of a particular schema, although the

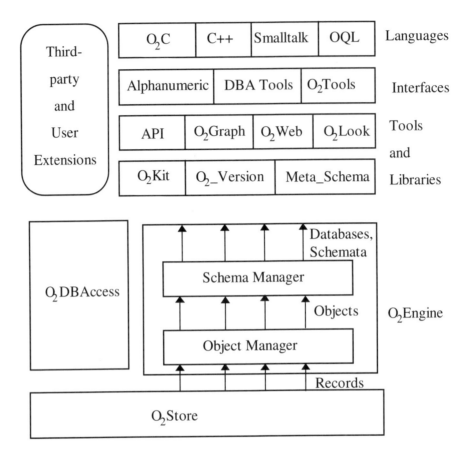

Figure 7.1 The architecture of O₂.

contents of one schema can be imported to others. Section 7.4 describes the O₂ model of database and application structure.

The system comes with pre-populated libraries, described in Section 7.5, which contain:

- user interface objects and date and time classes – *O₂Kit*;
- a graphical editor – *O₂Graph*;
- version management software – *O₂Version*; and
- metadata access facilities *Meta_schema*.

There is also a tool for automatic generation of form interfaces to objects, called *O₂Look*. This will create appropriate browsers and editors for a class – for instance, laying out slots for each attribute in the class. The structure of the forms can be customized. *O₂Look* is described in Section 7.5.4.

O₂Web is an O₂ application for managing World Wide Web data. It provides a gateway to the web and classes so that HTML documents are stored as objects instead of files. This is described in Section 7.5.9.

Use of the system can be performed by one of a pair of user interfaces:

- the alphanumeric interface, an interactive textual interface;
- or O₂Tools, a form-based interface, built on top of *O₂Look*.

Using each of these, the user has access to interactive commands to create, edit, query and delete the data, databases, schemata and applications which are in the store. Using the alphanumeric interface this is carried out with commands such as "create schema EMAIL". Using *O₂Tools*, equivalent tasks are achieved in a windowing environment, controlled by selecting light buttons and menu options. *O₂Tools* is described in Section 7.5.5.

There are also special modules, *O₂dba* and *O₂dsa*, which permit a database administrator to fine tune O₂ databases and schemata. These are described in Section 7.5.1.

O₂DBAccess is a schema of classes which enable O₂ users to gain access to data in a relational database. This is described in Section 7.5.3.

O₂ is designed to be used with equal ease by a variety of mainly object-oriented languages. At present this is restricted to O₂C, C, C++ and Smalltalk. O₂C is designed to support the O₂ data model described above, while the others are installed by language bindings to be described in Part Four of the book. There is also an implementation of the OQL query language which will be described in Chapter 10.

■ 7.3 The O₂ database engine

This section will describe the database engine in more detail. The engine is constructed in three layers. The lowest layer, *O₂Store*, deals solely with the storage of data. The middle layer provides an object-oriented framework on top of this. The top layer installs the O₂ model of databases and applications. Each layer will now be described.

■ 7.3.1 O₂Store

The database component of O₂ is provided by the data manager, *O₂Store*. This has the following features:

- the storage of data structured as a set of **records**;
- indexes;

- ACID transactions;
- a page based client/server architecture;
- independence of the data model, i.e. this level can equally well support a wide variety of data models at the next level.

All data is stored centrally using the following structures:

- sequential files of variable length records to hold the numerical and textual data;
- an 8-byte record identifier (RID) which locates a record by volume, page and slot (a slot is an address within a page);
- B-trees to hold indexes;
- a special structure to hold long data items for the storage of multimedia data (up to 4 gigabytes);
- a special structure, called a scan, for managing the access to data sets.

These are grouped into volumes. A volume is either a raw disk partition or a UNIX file, which holds files, B-trees and long data items, organized in a single-level directory.

The client/server architecture is based on the transmission of pages across the network. This means that when a collection of data is required, the client is responsible for identifying the page or pages needed and requesting them from the server. This keeps the server process simple and fast, the complexity being in the client process. This makes good sense since the client process has only to support one user process, whereas the server is required to support many clients running concurrently. Figure 7.2 illustrates this. When client C requires object O, it requests the page P that O is on and the server S sends this page across the network.

Data update makes use of a transaction mechanism which supports the basic ACID principles. The transaction manager has the following features:

- concurrency control using two-phase locking on files and pages – locks on pages have the usual shared and exclusive forms, while files also support intention locks;
- recovery using a write-ahead log which is mostly used to redo committed transactions;
- update is usually to pages held in a local cache in order to minimize disk and network traffic.

In summary, the data manager provides reliable storage of records. Creating the appearance of an object structure is the responsibility of the next layer – the object manager.

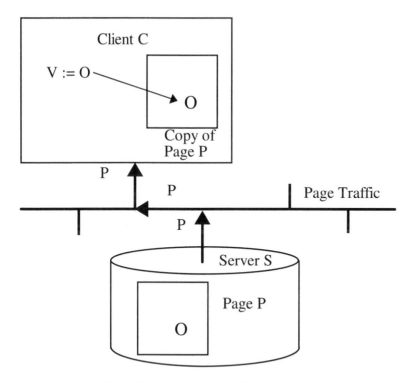

Figure 7.2 A page-based client/server architecture.

▓ 7.3.2 The object manager

In order to support an object database, the object manager has to carry out the following tasks: mapping the objects into records, providing an addressing scheme to permit inter-object references to be maintained, assigning the data to appropriate disk pages, and creating indexes as required.

The mapping of objects into records is similar to, but more complex than, the mapping of an ER model into relations. The process includes:

- for each object, the creation of a record to hold the small atomic properties;
- for large string attributes, the creation of additional records;
- for non-atomic properties, the creation of additional records, with appropriate pointers stored in the parent record;
- for small collections (i.e. those that can be held in one page), the creation of a sequence of component records; and
- for larger collections, the creation of B-trees for sets, positional B-trees for lists and sequential files for bags.

Figure 7.3 shows how this works in practice. Figure 7.3(a) shows a set of users, together with a message that Jim has sent Jane and which is still in her incoming mailbox. (Objects are shown as rounded rectangles, collections as shadowed rectangles.) Figure 7.3(b) shows the physical storage of this logical arrangement.

The collection of users, being potentially large, is held as a B-tree, identified by CID213. The user, "Jane" is represented as the record, RID765, the five fields of the record corresponding to the five properties. The scalar properties are stored directly, while the incoming mailbox is another record. The identifier of this record, RID534, is stored in a field of Jane's record. The storage mailboxes are a collection, CID246. As this collection will almost certainly be small, it is just stored as a sequence of records. The collection of messages held in the incoming mailbox (CID429), on the other hand, could be large, so it is stored as a B-tree (in fact a positional B-tree as the collection is a list). The message shown, RID923, has fields referring back to the sender, RID632, the record holding Jim's properties, and the mailbox, RID534. The recipients of the message form another small collection, CID531, so these are stored in a sequence, currently consisting solely of a reference to Jane as the only recipient. The subject and date are scalar fields, but the body is held separately as a long data item.

Thus, a web of objects can be stored as a set of normalized records, with the foreign key mechanism being used to manage object identity. The O₂ storage manager can therefore make use of the record storage techniques which have proved so effective in other DBMS. Notice, however, the considerable difference in cognitive complexity between the upper and lower representations of the same set of data. There is no obvious reason why a programmer should be forced to manage the lower structure to have access to efficient storage mechanisms.

Objects are located by use of the record identifiers managed by the data manager if the data is held on disk and by a special transient addressing identifier called a *handle* while in memory. O₂ does not use an object table. Instead when an object is created, since this happens initially in memory, a handle is created and this is used as the reference for the object until it is stored. When it is stored, a record identifier is created and this replaces the handle. When the object is retrieved, a hash table is used to create a fresh handle for it in memory.

The persistence of data on the disk is entirely determined by reachability. In the ODMG model, persistence is indicated at object creation time, since many systems represent persistent and transient objects differently and cannot change this representation during the lifetime of the object. Although this simplifies the system, it is also makes it less flexible to program, since the programmer must know at the outset which data is to persist and which not. In O₂, persistent

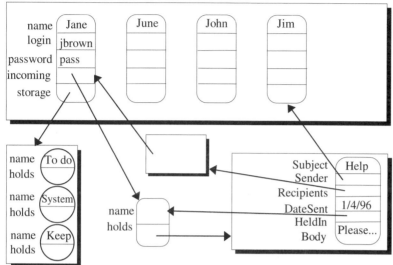

(a) Some Objects in the Mail Database

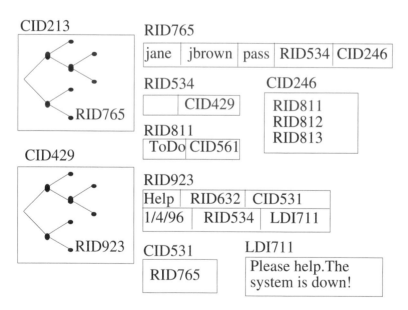

(b) A Record Store for those Objects

Figure 7.3 A record store for objects.

objects can become transient and vice versa – all according to their reachability from the persistent roots. Note that this provides a superset of the possibilities available with the ODMG proposal. Using O$_2$, it is possible to adopt a protocol in which persistence is never altered during the lifetime of an object.

Persistent objects are assigned to pages using a clustering algorithm, which puts component objects as near as possible to their parent objects. O$_2$ provides this as a default algorithm, but it also permits the DBA to supply a different clustering strategy for specific purposes.

Garbage collection of memory occurs incrementally – when an operation is completed, any transient values created are removed. Garbage collecting on the disk is a more difficult problem. Previous versions of O$_2$ supported an automatic reference counting garbage collector, but this was found to be too inefficient. The current system provides the garbage collector as a utility which must be explicitly invoked when space needs to be reclaimed.

■ 7.3.3 The schema manager

The schema manager is responsible for the creation, retrieval, update and deletion of all of the schema items in the O$_2$ store, i.e. classes, types, operations, functions, applications and names. The schema manager is designed to support the incremental development of schemata, databases and applications. It has three useful features to support this – the ability to extend any definition at any time, the ability to make a definition depend upon identifiers which have yet to be defined, and automatic data update as a schema evolves.

The editing functions permit any part of a schema to be extended or removed at any time. This means that not only can new classes or types be added, but new characteristics can be added to previously existing types. For instance, a new property or operation can be added to a type.

Second, it is not necessary for all of the component identifier names in a new definition already to have been defined. For instance, in creating a new operation in type X which has a parameter whose type is Y, it is not necessary that Y already exists before the new operation can be added. In displaying a schema, those parts of the schema which have still to be defined are clearly marked. It is at run-time when all definitions must be complete – attempts to run code against a database of an incomplete schema will prevent the program from being run.

Schema evolution is something of a Holy Grail among database researchers. The goal is that, after populating a database, it would be useful to be able to modify the schema and yet have the data in the database be continuously maintained and to have the data automatically migrate to the new structure. O$_2$

provides this in a "lazy" way. That is, when the schema is changed, the data remains in the old form until it is used. The first use of any data will cause the transformation. This may well save a considerable period of unavailability for a very large database, which may not be acceptable if it is permanently required. (This is often referred to as 24 × 7 availability, meaning 24 hours a day, 7 days a week.) In the change, data contained in deleted properties and classes will be removed, while additional properties are set to a default value.

■ 7.4 Data and application structure in O₂

The ODMG standard, although fixing the data model, still leaves flexible the structure of the database management and the structure of any applications using a database. In O₂, the schema is the principal database structure and a database (called a *base* in the O₂) is a set of data conforming to the schema. An application in O₂ is associated with a schema and is a set of programs and transactions. This section describes the interrelationships between these components in detail.

■ 7.4.1 Database structure

The fundamental entity in an O₂ store is the *schema*. Everything is defined in terms of a schema. Figure 7.4 illustrates the interrelationships between the components of an O₂ store, placing a schema at the top. The figure is an extended ER diagram in which the relationships are labeled with letters to indicate their meaning. The "definition" node represents an entity which may be a class or a type – thus a property can either be an object of a class or a literal value of a type, for instance.

A schema defines the structure of a database and consists of the following:

- a set of object types, called classes, each consisting of a set of characteristics;
- a set of literal types, called types;
- a set of names, which are persistent root values; and
- a set of functions, which are code fragments which can be called from any operation or application.

The set of schemata logically partition the store in that the type of every object in the store will be defined as part of a schema. Schemata are used not only to define the structure of databases, but also to form object type libraries. In particular, the system comes with a standard library of useful types, called *O₂Kit*

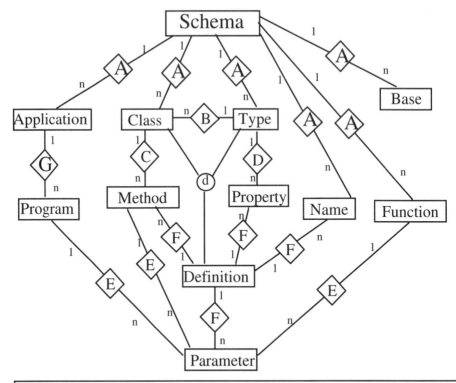

Key to Relationships

A A schema is composed of applications classes, types, names and functions
B A class is based on a type
C A class has methods
D A type has properties

E Methods, functions and programs have parameters
F Methods, properties, parameters and names have type or class definitions
G an application is composed of programs

Figure 7.4 The main components of an O₂ store.

– see Section 7.5.2 for more details of this. Users can build their own libraries as schemata and these can be shared by use of the **import** command.

A schema is also associated with:

- a set of databases, each instantiating the schema by providing actual values for the structures defined in the schema; and
- a set of applications, each of which provides controlled user access to any of the databases, in the form of a set of programs and transactions.

The development of database and application structure is incremental and takes place in the context of a *current schema*. Editing takes place either through the interactive textual interface or through the graphical interface, *O$_2$Tools*. The commands which these provide include the following:

- commands to create and remove schemata;
- a command to select one schema to be the current one;
- commands to create and remove databases, applications, types, classes and functions;
- commands to add and remove attributes from types and classes;
- commands to add and remove methods from classes;
- commands to add and remove programs from applications;
- commands to install code bodies for methods, functions and programs.

The schema manager provides a set of operations to achieve these tasks which are built into the two principal programming interfaces. In the alphanumeric interface these take the form of a command language which supports commands such as "create class X ..." to create a new class, or "method body Y ..." to define the implementation of an operation. In *O$_2$Tools*, the commands are invoked by the use of light buttons and menus.

Testing takes place in the context of a *current database* and code can be initiated by running a stand-alone program, by invoking an operation or by running an application. No code can be run without a current database being specified.

■ 7.4.2 Application structure

An application consists of a set of programs and transactions, a program being a code module which accesses the database, while a transaction is a program with an implicit *begin transaction ... commit* placed at its start and end. Transactions are used for updates and programs for queries. There is, however, the possibility of placing explicit *begin transaction, commit* and *abort* commands in a program or transaction.

To illustrate the structure, here is part of a mail application which embodies some of the facilities discussed in the previous chapter. The application framework includes:

```
create application harness
   o2 User currentUser
   program public makeUser( name: string, login: string ),
           public showUser( login: string ),
           public sendMessage
end
```

Notes:

1. Any global variables shared by the programs, such as *currentUser*, can be declared between the create application and the program lines.
2. Programs and transactions can have parameters.
3. At this point all programs are declared to be programs – transactions are distinguished at the implementation stage.

The programs will be implemented in one of the programming languages provided and installed in much the same way that methods are installed. When the application is complete, it can be used by issuing a command to run it. Running the application results in the presentation of a menu of all of the programs which have been specified. In *O₂Tools* this means bringing up a menu window, with the commands as options. In the alphanumeric interface, a menu is printed and each of the programs can be used as commands. The application is then exited by the quit command. Chapter 8 gives examples of this.

Each application contains some default system programs, which can be replaced by user defined versions:

- *init* is a program executed when the application starts. It may, for instance, initialize any global variables. *init* can be given parameters in which case the actual parameter values must be given in the run application command. For instance, the application could be given a boolean parameter, which, if set, causes the automatic saving of all messages sent by users. In the alphanumeric interface, *init* displays the programs available.
- *restart* is a program called when the application is restarted after a crash. It will typically test what caused the crash and react differently to each cause.
- *dashboard* is the program which controls the use of the application. It is called when each program quits, at which point a new program selection is required.
- *exit* is the program called when the application is quit. The tasks it accomplishes include tidying up the database and the screen.

■ 7.4.3 Metaclasses

O₂ has a system-provided schema called *Meta_schema*, which can be used to gain access to metadata from within an application. This contains a set of object types containing operations for retrieving meta-information about the current schema. From the current schema, there are methods to find the classes, types, names and functions. From a class, there are operations to retrieve the names and types of attributes and methods, and so on.

Using *Meta_schema*, it is possible to build different sorts of general-purpose tool, among which are:

- management and database administration tools which provide summary information about the database and facilities for database creation;
- generic end-user facilities for the automatic building of interfaces.

Thus if the facilities described in Section 7.5 are insufficient or unsuitable for a particular installation, the database administrator can use *Meta_schema* to install new tools.

Section 7.5.7 describes the facilities of *Meta_schema* more fully and provides examples of their use.

▮ 7.4.4 Versions

Version management is one of the emerging requirements which database systems will increasingly have to support. There is, as yet, no uniformly accepted model of versions and so version management is not a part of the ODMG standard. However, commercial OODBMS are increasingly supporting some form of versioning and O_2 is no exception.

In O_2, there is a class of versionable objects, *O2_Version*, each of which holds a derivation graph of configurations – a configuration being a set of objects. To make such a configuration versionable, a versionable object is created by calling *new* on *O2_Version* and the objects which make up the configuration are installed into the configuration. There are then operations to derive new versions, edit the data in a version, merge versions and remove versions. There is also a labeling facility for versions and an operation to select which version is the one currently being used by an application.

In all of this, O_2 is only providing a management structure for versions. Thus to create version 5 as a derivation of version 2 only asserts a link in the version derivation graph. It does not imply any automatic relationship between the data in the two versions. This is the responsibility of the programmer. There is however, a facility to return the differences in the data values between two versions. In short, the facility enables the programmer to maintain multiple versions of the same set of objects, without the need to construct the version graph structure as well.

Section 7.5.8 describes the facilities of *O2_Version* in more detail, together with an example.

■ 7.5 Components of the O₂ system

Extensibility is a vital aspect of any information system. An appropriate data model for representing the data together with languages for manipulating the data will provide the basic features, but many of the mechanisms which are useful for managing databases can best be provided on top of the DBMS. Ideally, this will be achieved using tight integration with the database system, rather than by providing components which live outside of the DBMS and, as such, are outside of its control.

Object orientation provides a suitably open structure in this regard. Since classes contain operations, the functionality of support tools can be provided using the class structure. All OODBMS make heavy use of the class hierarchy in this way – all but the most basic facilities appear as system classes. Most of the facilities of the O₂ system are provided in this way. There are a number of schemata which are supplied with the system and which exist for the purpose of providing support tools and libraries. These include:

- O₂Kit – the system library;
- O₂DBAccess – a set of classes to support access to remote relational databases;
- O₂Look – a set of classes which support the graphical presentation of data;
- O₂Graph – a set of classes which support the editing of node-and-arc graphs;
- Meta_schema – classes for managing metadata;
- O₂Version – classes to support multiple versions of data;
- O₂Web – classes to support World Wide Web access.

This section is devoted to the description of these classes in order to demonstrate the ways in which these kind of facility can be provided seamlessly in the database.

■ 7.5.1 DBA tools

This module permits a database administrator to perform the management tasks typical of running a database system. There are three sets of commands: a set of operating system commands to set up the O₂ environment; *O2dba*, a program which manages databases and their access; and *O2dsa*, a program consisting of a set of commands which manage schemata.

The operating system commands allow the DBA to:

- start an O₂ server and an O₂ client;
- dump and load databases or schemata to and from files;

- copy a database;
- monitor usage;
- set and structure user volumes and system logs; and
- create a *tar* backup of the system.

O2dba is a program which can be summoned from the system and permits the management of applications, databases, clusters, groups, indexes, owners, rights and volumes. *O2dsa*, on the other hand, has commands to manage the components of schemata, their owners and access rights.

7.5.2 O₂Kit

O₂Kit is the schema which contains the system classes and is under continuous development. These can be imported for use in the current schema by issuing a command such as:

```
import schema o2Kit class Date
```

The classes include the following:

- *Date* is a class for dates, with methods defined to break the date up into its component day, month and year; to perform various calculations on dates; to produce dates in different formats and to convert the date to a string.
- *Box* is a class of user dialogs which can be integrated with *O₂Look*. Among the methods available are ones to: display a message until an OK button is pressed, display a yes/no question with buttons for "yes" and "no", provide a text entry box, and select an item from a list.
- *Component* is the class of widgets usually used within a dialog box. It has subclasses for light buttons, radio buttons, selection from lists, labels and pictures.
- *Dialog.box* is the class of dialog boxes built out of members of *box* and *component*.
- *Text* is the class of text items, which are lists of strings. The class has methods to read and write pieces of text to and from files, to display the text and to edit the text.
- *Drawable* is the class of screen displays. It has two subclasses: *bitmap* is the class of X-windows bitmaps; while *image* is the class of colored pixmaps. Any of these may be loaded from a file and may be displayed.

■ 7.5.3 O₂DBAccess

Access to legacy data is one of the most vital concerns for users of OODBMS. Any organization intending to make substantial use of an OODBMS is very likely already to have a considerable quantity of data managed by other kinds of database system. All of the major OODBMS products provide methods of accessing relational data. In fact, as one of the strengths of relational systems that, via the use of SQL, it is relatively easy to organize remote access in the forms of queries. The primary mechanism consists of making a connection, submitting a query and fetching the results, turning them into objects as they arrive at the OODBMS.

$O_2DBAccess$ is a set of classes arranged in a standard O_2 schema, called *o2dbaccess*, which permits O_2 users to access data in relational databases and, in particular, to fetch them into the O_2 environment as objects. The schema consists of five classes:

- $O_2DBAccess$ is a virtual class whose members are the objects involved in connecting to a relational database. It provides an operation which can return an error message if a problem arises.
- *Connection* is a subclass of $O_2DBAccess$ which manages the connection of the O_2 system to the relational databases. It has operations to connect to the system, to disconnect, to log on a particular user and to log off.
- *Session* is also a subclass of $O_2DBAccess$. This manages the interaction within a particular session and provides operations to commit updates, rollback to the last commit, submit an SQL query, and to open and close a context.
- *Context* is the third and final subclass of $O_2DBAccess$. A context is an environment for a query. The class contains operations which specify a query, bind parameter values, define which variables are to be returned and execute the query.
- *Parameter* is a virtual class which must be a superclass of any classes which are parameters of a query.

These classes make use of a *configuration file* which contains details of the systems to which connections can be made. The details include the number of contexts which can be supported, whether type checking will be enforced, the network protocol, host name and other particulars of the protocol chosen.

The steps in accessing the data are:

1. Obtain a connection.
2. Log on as a user, thus creating a session.
3. Create objects which hold the data which are to be submitted in the query.

All of these must be members of subclasses of *Parameter*, even if they are scalar – see the *stringParameter* example below.

4. Create objects to hold the results of any queries, also as members of subclasses of *Parameter*.
5. Create an SQL query as a string.
6. Choose which properties of the return object are to hold the results of the query (projections) and specify these also as strings.
7. Either submit the queries directly by the *Session* operation, *sqlquery*, or open a context, building the context out of the query, parameters and projections, before submitting the query. The latter method is to be preferred if several similar queries are to be submitted.

To illustrate the process, here is some code to retrieve the names and login identifiers of users with the title, "Dr." from a table, called *users*, in a relational database, *Accounts*, which has, at least, the fields, *UserName*, *UserLogin* and *UserTitle*. In the example, the data is displayed, but the results could be used as the start point for a new database supporting the Email system, by copying them into *theUsers*.

```
class ImportedUsers inherit Parameter
   type list( User )
end;
class stringParameter inherit Parameter
   type string
end;
o2 ImportedUsers result = new ImportedUsers;
o2 stringParameter title = new stringParameter;
host -> connect( "AccountServer", "jbrown", "Janespassword" );
session = host -> logon( "Accounts", "password" ) . session;
context = session -> open . context;
context -> associate(                    // set the query
   "SELECT UserLogin, UserName,
      FROM users WHERE UserTitle = ?" ); // "?" means parameter
*title = "Dr.";
context -> define_bind( title, 1 );      // set the parameter value
context -> define_projection( result,    // indicate where the results are to
      list ( "login", "name" ) );        //   appear in objects - in this case
                                         //   using property names of User
context -> exec;                         // execute the query remotely
context -> fetch(O2DB_ALL);              // fetch all of the resulting records
result -> display;
```

In this way, relational queries can be specified locally, executed remotely and the results be fetched according to need. The *fetch* operation, for instance, can be used to fetch only a limited number of records.

The resulting data can be used as if it were object oriented. Imported data can be merged with O₂ data and can be managed using any of the interfaces which are available in O_2. Therefore, this kind of feature eases the development path from organizations adding an OODBMS to their information technology toolkit.

■ 7.5.4 O₂Look

O₂Look is the generic graphical form user interface manager with which O_2 applications can be built. *O₂Look* runs under X windows and the Motif graphics manager. The core function provided by *O₂Look* is the ability to generate automatically a window, called a *presentation*, containing the properties of an object. The structure of the presentation is a nested form whose fields match the properties of the type of the object. For instance, Figure 7.5 shows a form which would be generated for the *Person* class. Using the presentation, the data associated with the object can be displayed, input or edited. As such, it bears a distinct resemblance to query-by-forms.

The figure shows the data associated with a *Person* object. Each property name appears alongside a box holding its value. Where the value is itself complex, this box is broken down into sub-components – as shown for the *address* property. Above the set of properties is a box, labeled *methods*, which can be selected to bring up a menu of the methods defined on the class – choosing a menu option causes that operation to be executed. Above that are the *Pencil* and *Eraser* icons. The *Pencil* button causes the object to be saved, while the *Eraser* icon causes the presentation to be removed from the display.

In an object-oriented database, the problems of managing generic interfaces are somewhat greater than they are for a relational database, since an object can be arbitrarily deep and complex (even infinitely deep, if cyclically related to itself). How much of the object should be displayed? *O₂Look* allows the depth of display to be controlled, using a *mask*. A mask controls how much of the object is displayed and how the parts of the presentation appear.

The basic method that the system uses to build a presentation is:

- For each base type of data (integer, string, etc.), a standard presentation is defined.
- For each type constructor, there is a method of constructing an equivalent presentation out of component presentations. For instance, a record will be represented by a subsidiary box with its fields displayed inside.
- For object types, there is a standard way of creating presentations, i.e. a standard way of laying out the properties.
- In creating any of the standard kinds of presentation, the depth of data

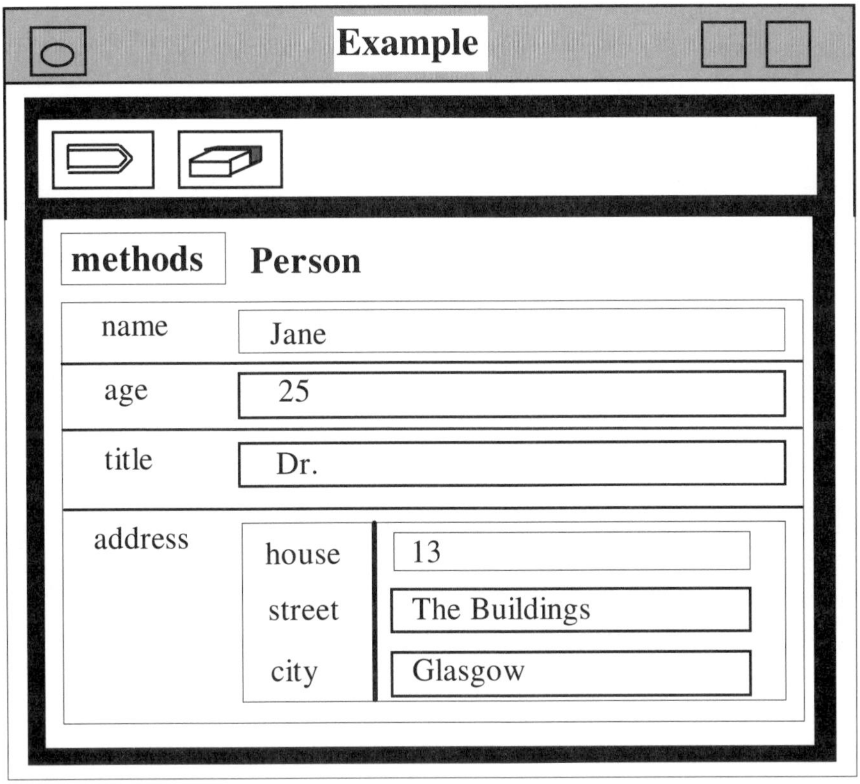

Figure 7.5 An O₂Look presentation.

which is used is controlled by the mask.

- The look of any particular component of the data is also controlled by the mask, which can determine presentation "resources" such as coloring, typeface and protection.

O₂Look is provided as a set of system functions and a set of operations defined on type *Object*. Since the operations are defined on *Object*, they are available to all objects by inheritance. These operations allow the programmer to:

- display the object using a default mask;
- put up an editor of the same form, again using a default mask;
- create a presentation for subsequent display;
- display the presentation created;
- update the object with the values currently being displayed in a presentation

window;
- refresh all of the displayed presentations of the object;
- erase all the presentations of the object;
- clear the presentation; and
- disable or re-enable a method in a presentation.

The other control the programmer has over the behavior of an O_2Look interface is by overriding a number of standard operations. These are:

- the operation called when the *Pencil* icon is selected – by default this saves the values displayed, but the programmer may cause it to perform other actions if desired;
- the operation called when the *Eraser* icon is selected – this removes the presentation, but again it may be programmed to do other things;
- the operation which determines the title of a presentation, which would, by default, be the title of the object type it was presenting, but the programmer can cause it to be something other than this;
- the operation which displays an iconic representation of the object, for which the default would be a null icon;
- the final operation brings up a menu of the operations of the object type when the "methods" button is pressed – by default, this is a menu of all the operations plus system operations to display and edit the object, but the programmer can change this behavior too.

By changing these, the behavior of a presentation can be customized for particular purposes for which the standard presentation structure is considered inadequate.

O_2Look is an example of the kind of software tool which can be provided seamlessly in an object-oriented environment. System object types are declared for presentations, masks and resources, such as color and font. Operations to implement the functionality are added to the *Object* type and this makes them available everywhere, without a complex software structure. Thus O_2Look is provided system wide, so that end-user applications can be constructed using it, as are system facilities, such as O_2Tools. This can be used to create a uniform mode of data access across a variety of different interfaces.

■ 7.5.5 O₂Tools

O_2Tools is a window-based programming environment built on top of O_2Look. It includes the following features:

- form-based browsers and editors for schemata, classes, applications, functions, persistent types and named root objects;

- editors and debuggers for program source;
- an editor to run alphanumeric sessions;
- a cross-reference manager to maintain application coherence.

O_2*Tools* is invoked by issuing the command

```
toolsgraphic
```

in the alphanumeric interface.

This brings up the *dashboard*, which is shown in Figure 7.6. The dashboard window is made up of an information pane, a set of browser buttons and a set of miscellaneous buttons. The information is at the top left and this displays the current schema, database and volume in use. The browser buttons bring up windows to browse and edit the schemata, applications, names, classes, types and functions.

The other buttons have the following effects:

- O2Tools brings up a window for configuring the environment.
- O2Shell brings up a window in which alphanumeric commands can be entered.
- O2Debug will bring up a graphical debugger.
- Help brings up help on the command language and the graphical environment.
- Lock freezes the O_2*Tools* window.
- Commit makes any changes permanent.
- Abort loses any changes since the last commit.
- Alpha returns to the alphanumeric interface.
- Quit exits from O_2 and returns to the containing environment.

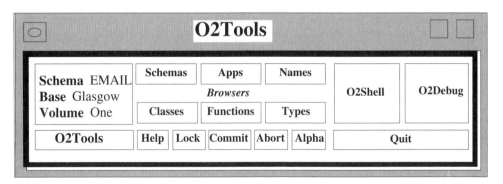

Figure 7.6 The O_2Tools dashboard.

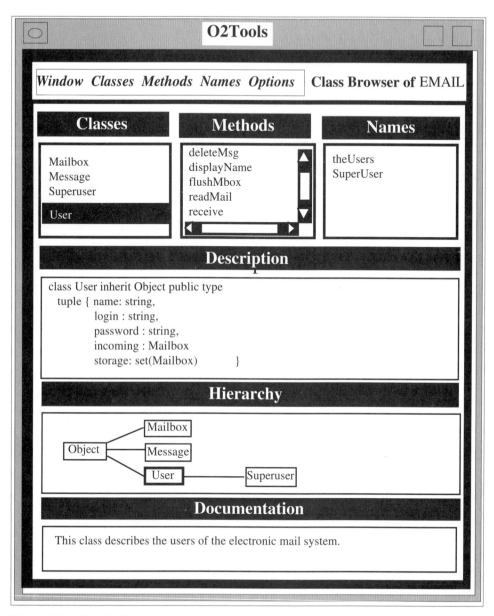

Figure 7.7 The O₂Tools class browser.

There is no space here to provide much detail about the *O₂Tools* facilities, but a single illustration will suffice to indicate the general mode of use. The class browser is shown in Figure 7.7.

From top to bottom, the window contains:

- a menu bar – the options allow the user to create, edit and delete classes and to compile and commit any changes;
- three panes containing menus – at the outset, the list of classes is visible and when a class is selected the operations in the class appear, while the third list contains any persistent named roots;
- the description pane contains a textual specification of whichever meta-object is selected using the scrollable menus – this may be a class description or an operation interface;
- the class hierarchy pane shows the class hierarchy of the current schema – if a class is selected this is highlighted (as *User* is in the figure) and this pane is an alternative way of selecting a class;
- a documentation pane contains whatever descriptive text has been stored with the currently selected meta-object.

From the browser, editors can be reached which allow the class description or the operation code bodies to be edited. The other browsers similarly allow components of system meta-objects to be viewed and edited. For instance, the Application Browser allows the set of programs and transactions to be edited.

■ 7.5.6 O₂Graph

O₂Graph is a set of classes, built on top of *O₂Look*, which provide facilities for editing node and arc graphs. A typical example of a fragment of such a graph is shown in Figure 7.8. *O₂Graph* has features which allow such a graph to be displayed and edited.

O₂Graph is built around four main classes:

- *Node* is a virtual class in which there are properties for the x and y positions of the nodes in real space and operations to set and retrieve those positions.
- *Link* is also a virtual class, with properties describing the two nodes being joined, as well as a set of x, y positions of any intermediary points, if the link is not a straight line. Operations in the class allow the connected nodes to be changed or retrieved.
- *Graph* is a virtual class of graphs, each having as properties: the origin and size in real space, the size of the screen area it is to be mapped to, a back-

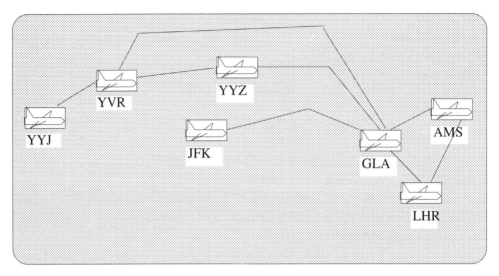

Figure 7.8 A node and arc graph.

ground image, and the sets of nodes and links involved. Operations in the class allow the origin and size properties to be changed and the two sets of components to be modified.

• *GraphDialoguer* is a class which contains methods for controlling user interaction with the graph, determining what should happen if a node is selected, for instance.

To create a particular graph, the three virtual classes must be subclassed. The subclass of *Node* that is created must have an extra property, *content*, added which holds the object represented by the node. The subclass of *Link* has a *label* property added; while *Graph* is subclassed so that it refers to sets of the subclassed node and link classes.

The graph, when displayed, will show up as the *O₂Look* presentations for the nodes and be linked using a particular kind of mask, which determines the width of lines, arrowing, color and so on. A graph can be laid out either automatically, using a layout strategy, or by using the x- and y-positions in the *Node* objects. Layout strategies that are provided include showing the nodes as a tree, in a rectangular grid, using a spring and repulsion algorithm, or as a directed acyclic graph.

A graph dialoguer is required only if interactive editing of the graph is needed. The functionality of a dialoguer is based around a list of triggered methods – each trigger containing an event type (such as dragging a node or selecting a link), an object which will be affected by the event; and the method of that object which will be invoked by the event.

To generate an editor for the graph shown in Figure 7.8, the following steps would be taken:

1. Create subclasses:

```
class AirportNode inherit Node
    type tuple( content: Airport )

class Airway inherit Link
    type tuple( from, to: AirportNode; label string )

class AirportGraph inherit Graph
    type tuple( dialoguer: GraphDialoguer,
                nodes: set(AirportNode),
                links: set(Airway) )
```

2. Create an object of type *AirportGraph* and populate its *nodes* and *links* properties with appropriate nodes containing airport objects with links between them.

3. Create a presentation for *Airports* – in the figure, the presentation shows an aeroplane labeled by the airport's call letters.

4. Create methods for the *AirportGraph* class which implement the required behavior which should follow each kind of interaction with the graph.

5. Create and invoke a presentation for the graph.

O₂Graph is typical of the kind of generic interactive tool which OODBMS can easily support. Object orientation has proved a very supportive paradigm in which interactive software can be written. Inheritance is very powerful in this area, since the successive refinement of interactive behavior both reduces the amount of coding required and provides a manageable structure in which to maintain the code. Storing interaction objects in the database further reduces the complexity of the environment with which the programmer is faced.

■ 7.5.7 Meta_schema

The schema *Meta_schema* is the library of metadata access facilities. These are provided as the operations of a number of object types whose members are schemata and various kinds of types. The object type hierarchy held in *Meta_schema* is:

Meta – the object type whose members are O₂ schemata;

Meta_definition – a class which is the generalization of *Meta_class* and *Meta_type*;

Meta_class – the class of all O₂ object types;

Meta_type – the class of all O₂ literal types, which has two subclasses;

Meta_collection – the class of all collection types (sets, bags and lists);

Meta_tuple – the class of all tuple types.

To access the metaclasses in O_2 it is necessary to import these types, together with a persistent root to the meta-information, called *Schema*. This is achieved with the following O_2 commands:

```
import schema Meta_schema
  class Meta, Meta_definition, Meta_class, Meta_type, Meta_collection,
              Meta_tuple
  name Schema;
```

It is then necessary to initialize the variable *Schema* with:

```
Schema = new Meta;
```

in which the *init* method picks up the correct metadata structure corresponding to the schema which is currently in use. Now all of the metadata from the current schema are accessible through the variable *Schema*.

For instance:

```
Schema->classes
```

returns a list of the classes.

Here are the methods provided for each of these classes.

The Class Meta

The class *Meta* contains objects which describe the schemata which exist in the current O_2 system. For instance, a description of the *EMAIL* schema is an instance of this class. At any time, the current schema description is available using the variable *Schema* (as long as this has been imported as described above).

The class has operations to achieve the following:

- return a list of pairs of class names and class descriptions;
- return a list of pairs of type names and type descriptions;
- return the set of persistent names and their type or class;
- given the name of a class, type or persistent name, return its definition;
- given a value return a description of the type of which it is an instance;
- take in an O_2 command, execute it against the schema and return the number of errors.

For instance, the command:

```
schema -> command( "display classes" )
```

will print out a list of all of the classes in the schema.

Class Meta_definition

The class *Meta_definition* is the generalization of the classes *Meta_class* and *Meta_type*. It is used everywhere in the schema where something which may be a class or a type is required. For instance, any property can be described as being either one of the members of a class (*incoming* is of class *Mailbox*, for instance) or a value of a type (*login* is of type **string**). Therefore, to refer generally to the domain of the property, there is a need for a type which generalizes the notion of type and class – the class *Meta_definition* does this. (NB – this is a typical case of using inheritance to support generalization where references to the general class are required.)

Meta_definition has the following methods defined on it:

- test if the definition is of a class or a type;
- test whether the type or class is completely defined or not;
- return the name of the type or class; and
- a virtual method to test how this type or class compares with another.

Class Meta_class

This is the class of descriptions of classes in O₂. Operations to carry out the following are defined:

- test the relationship between the class and another class provided as a parameter (the result indicates if the two classes are in an inheritance relationship or not);
- return a list of the names, visibilities and types of the attributes of the class;
- return a list of descriptions of the operations – each containing the name, result type and a list of input parameters for the method;
- return the type definition underlying the class;
- return a list of descriptions of the subclasses of the class;
- return a list of descriptions of the superclasses of the class.

Class Meta_type

This is the class of all type descriptions in the schema. It supports the following methods:

- return a description for the kind of this type – one of "boolean", "char", "integer", "real", "string", "bits", "tuple", "list", "set", "bag", "undefined";
- compare two types to see if they are the same, are in a subtype relationship or are unconnected.

Class Meta_collection

This is the class of type descriptions of types which are bags, sets or lists. It is only used to find out the type or class of the elements by use of an operation which returns the definition of that type or class.

Class Meta_tuple

This contains the type descriptions of types which are tuples. It can be picked apart using a method which returns the list of names and types/classes of the fields of the tuple.

Here are two examples which show how these facilities might be used.

Example 1 – a program to add a new class

Consider the construction of a program which creates a new class as a subclass of an old one adding one extra attribute. The interface to such a program is:

```
program subclass( newClassName: string,      /* The name of the new class */
                  oldClass: Meta_class,        /* The old class description */
                  newAttName: string,          /*The name of the new attribute */
                  newAttType: Meta_definition ) /* The type of the new attribute */
```

The flow of such a program would be:

1. Call the definition operation on the current schema to check if the class already exists and report an error if it does.
2. Extract the class name of the old class and the type name of the new attribute, and then build up a string containing a command to create the class.
3. Send the command to the schema using the *command* operation.
4. Check that the command has succeeded and issue a success or fail message.

Example 2 – adding methods to traverse the metastructure

The next example shows how to write methods which look recursively into the metadata structure. The example searches for a string which is provided as a parameter and prints out where this occurs as a component name in a schema.

A program to carry this out is implemented as a series of statements each of which examines one of the kinds of schema component – the classes, the types, the names and so on. To do this it calls a lookup operation which is added to each of the *Meta_schema* classes. The program therefore looks like:

For every class C in the set of classes in the schema, call the lookup operation of class *Meta_class*.
For every type T in the set of types in the schema, call the lookup operation of class *Meta_type*.
etc.

The lookup operations must be added to each of the classes in *Meta_schema*. The one for *Meta_class*, for instance, will:

1. Check if this class has already been checked and exit if it has.
2. Check if the input string is the class name.
3. For each property of the class, check if it ha the input string as its name.
4. For each property, call the lookup operaticn on its type or class.
5. For each operation, check if it has the name sought after.
6. For each operation, check if any of its parameters have the required name.
7. For each parameter, call the lookup operation on its type.
8. Indicate that the class has now been checked.

The recursion terminates since ultimately all schema objects are built out of atomic types or will cycle back to metadata which has already been checked.

■ 7.5.8 Version management in O₂

Versionable objects are members of the class *O2version* which is to be found in the system schema *O2_Version*. A versionable object is a labeled directed graph in which the nodes are versions and the arcs are derivation paths. Orthogonal to this structure is the data which is being versioned. Each node in the graph contains particular values for the same set of objects. For instance, in the mail system, it might be useful to have versions of messages and each node would then contain a version of a message. It might further be useful to include a small textual description of the reason for the version, in which case a string would be added to each node. Figure 7.9 illustrates this situation. The initial version shows a message and a description. Versions 2 and 3 are derived from this; version 4 is derived from version 3 and version 5 merges versions 2 and 4. Version 4 is highlighted to indicate that it is the one currently in use.

The graph has the following features:

- each node has a parallel version of the data associated with the same set of objects – this set is called a *configuration*;
- each arc is a logical link indicating that one version has been derived from another;
- the graph has a root version – the first one created;
- all other nodes are created either as the derivation from another node, or as a derivation from two nodes (merging);
- each node has a label associated with it, which the programmer can set;

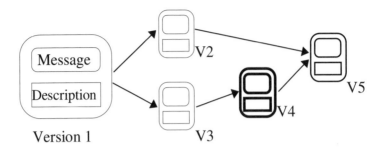

Figure 7.9 A version graph.

- one of the nodes is the one which would be used if an application were to access one of the objects in the configuration – which version this is being under programmer control;
- each version can be write locked (but not read locked).

Once a versionable object has been created, by calling *new* on class *O2_Version*, then a number of operations are available on it, which mostly make changes to the graph structure. Among the operations available are ones to:

- add a new value or object to the configuration being versioned;
- create a new version as a derivation of the current version;
- remove a version;
- return the versions derived from this one or the versions which this one is derived from;
- merge two versions;
- return a list of differences between the data values in two versions;
- copy the values from one version to another or nullify the component values;
- destroy the version graph and return the currently selected version – in effect, turning a versionable object into a non-versionable one;
- retrieve object values from a version;
- label a version and retrieve a version by label;
- set and retrieve the default version and the access mode;
- return the root version of the graph.

Finally, there is an operation attached to class *Object* which given an object which has been made versionable, returns the currently selected version.

Example – versionable mail messages

Returning to the example, shown in Figure 7.9, this is how a versionable message would be created:

1. Create a message, *M* say, by calling *new* on class *Message*.
2. Create a version graph, *BaseMessage*, by calling *new* on *o2_Version*.
3. Append *M* to *BaseMessage*.
4. Append a string value, *Description*, to *BaseMessage* – the configuration is now *M* and *Description*.
5. Set the fields of *M* (the receivers, subject, body and so on) and set *Description* to "First most general version".

So, there is now a single version of the message. To add a second version:

6. Create a new version, *JaneMessage*, by calling the derive operation on *BaseMessage*. *JaneMessage* has the same values as *BaseMessage*.
7. Select *JaneMessage* to be the current version and change the fields of the object so that Jane is the only recipient and the text of the message has additional comments on it. Also change *Description* to "Bosses' eyes only".

Now there are two versions and more could be added.

■ 7.5.9 O₂Web

The World Wide Web has often been called the largest database in the world – a database that consists of documents, which are identified by URLs (universal resource locators). It has, however, grown up without having much recourse to database technology. Most web site servers use the file system to organize documents (the URLs are file pathnames) and the mark-up language, HTML, to organize the contents of documents. *O₂Web* provides the tools to build web servers which organize their data in an object-oriented database.

To do this, the server must have two capabilities:

- a method of using database queries as URLs; and
- a way of returning the results of database queries in HTML.

To achieve the first of these, the database system provides a form of URL which logically looks like:

```
http://system path/database/query
```

in which the system path locates a program which can deal with the database query. The query is an OQL query and this will retrieve data from the database and return it in HTML.

Creating the HTML is a similar process to creating an *O₂Look* presentation. For each kind of data there is an equivalent HTML structure – scalar values are printed as themselves; tuples become HTML lists of field name, value pairs; collections become HTML lists; objects are dealt with according to their underlying type; and component objects become separate HTML fragments, referred to as an HTML anchor.

The simplest way to use *O₂Web* is to start with a persistent root as the query. For instance, access to the Email database might start with the simple query "theUsers". This returns HTML describing the set of users. The web browser will display this as a form and further browsing can be initiated by selecting the fields of the form.

Whereas *O₂Web* can be used directly in this way, it can also be customized so that it reacts differently. This is achieved by creating and using an object of a class called *O2WebInteractor*, which allows the different parts of the HTML text (a prolog, page header, body, page footer and epilog) to be produced in nonstandard ways. It also allows the effect of connection and disconnection to the server to be modified.

A web server connected to an OODBMS provides an opportunity for mixing database data with data not usually found in a database. It also provides the opportunity to make database style access available to more data and to allow other search mechanisms to be added to the repertoire of the DBMS.

■ 7.6 Summary

This chapter has described the features available in the O₂ system in order to demonstrate the kind of facilities likely to be found in an OODBMS. Here are some of the main points to be emphasized:

- O₂, like any of the other compliant OODBMS, supports the ODMG standard, but enhances it in various ways.
- The primary data structure used is the class which holds a set of objects together with the operations with which they may be manipulated.
- In order to ensure a sufficiently fast response, there are also subsidiary data structures which hold atomic values and some kinds of constructed value in non-object form.
- Database access structures are built in below the object-oriented framework, again leading to increased efficiency.
- Persistence by reachability is supported, so that any data item can be stored merely by making it a component of an already stored data item.

- In order to produce appropriate software engineering flexibility, additional computational structures (applications and functions) are supported.
- The class hierarchy is embedded in a standard database superstructure in which schemata are the fundamental construct and databases are instantiations of those schemata.
- The system as delivered comes with several sets of classes which provide useful features, including:

  - extensions to the basic data model including a date class, versions and metadata access;
  - tools including access to legacy data, graph management, web access and user interface management.

- A variety of user interfaces including one that is purely textual and one which is window-based, of which the latter is built on top of the user interface facilities.
- A variety of programming interfaces including a query language.

Most importantly, all of the above are provided in a single coherent and interlocking set of structures all held within the database, rather than as a disparate collection of components held variously in the database and the file system. This is perhaps the single most important contribution of object databases.

The next chapter will show how the O_2 system can be used to build the mail application.

8 An O₂ application

This chapter returns to the electronic mail example introduced in Chapter 6 and demonstrates how to build an application which will manage a mail database using the O_2 object-oriented database management system. The chapter will discuss application development at the interface level. That is, the database and application structures will be specified, but the implementation of the code fragments will be held over to Chapters 12 and 13.

In Chapter 6, an ODL description was produced for the application structure. O_2 does not support the ODL language and therefore it is necessary to transform the ODL schema into a description that O_2 recognizes. Section 8.1 discusses how to start up the O_2 system, Section 8.2 discusses the ODL to O_2 transformation. The two main sections then discuss the creation of a schema and database to hold the data (Section 8.3), and the creation of an application to provide the mail functions in a coherent and usable form (Section 8.4).

In the book form of this chapter, the O_2 alphanumeric interface will be demonstrated. The CD-ROM contains an equivalent treatment using the O_2Tools interface.

■ 8.1 Getting started with O₂

This section will briefly describe how to get started with O₂. Details of such matters are only of importance to those planning to use the system and so the chapter contains just sufficient information for the reader to understand the ways in which O₂ is used, with detail being left to user manuals. Section 8.1.1 discusses the steps required to set up the environment to give a flavor of how this is achieved. Section 8.1.2 describes the alphanumeric interface.

■ 8.1.1 Setting up the environment

O₂ comes with a variety of operating system level functions to achieve tasks such as: monitoring usage, bulk dumping and bulk loading a database, checking the consistency of a database, copying one system to another, shutting down a server process, and starting client and server processes. Most of these will not be described here. Instead the section concentrates on the relationship between database systems, schemata, databases, and client and server processes.

The O₂ environment can be distributed about a network of machines and contains the following:

- one or more physical volumes, which are areas of disk storage;
- a set of schemata, each of which is held in a particular volume and thus is associated with a particular system;
- a set of databases, each of which is an instance of schema, but may span more than one volume of the same system;
- one or more database systems, which can span more than one volume and can hold many schemata and many databases;
- one or more server processes, each of which is attached to one system and must be the only server for that system;
- one or more client processes, each attached to one of the server processes.

Figure 8.1 shows an O₂ environment in which a network of six machines with color names supports two O₂ systems and is being used by three users. System B has eight volumes, one of which holds the electronic mail schema and part of a first database for mail data. This database also uses a second volume. A second mail database is spread over three volumes and there is a also a parts schema and database.

In order to set this up, three things must have been done:

- a configuration file matching systems to machine names must have been created by the database administrator;

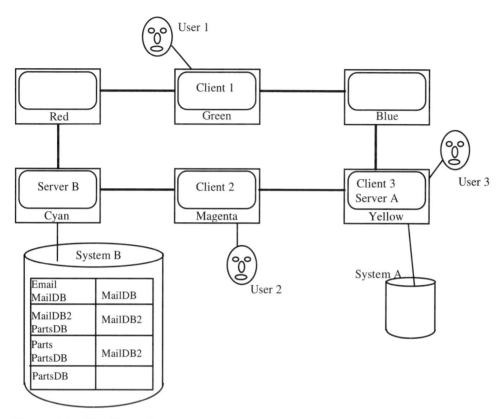

Figure 8.1 The O₂ environment.

- the server processes must have been started also by the database administrator;
- the client processes must have been started by the users.

Starting a server process is achieved by the *o2server* command which is run as follows in a UNIX environment:

```
o2server -system B
```

The command also has an option to determine the concurrency control protocol.

Starting the client process on any of the nodes of the network can then be achieved by use of the *o2* command as in:

```
o2 -system B
```

and there are other options to summon O₂*Tools*, set the library directory and to set the network node on which to send graphical displays.

■ 8.1.2 Using the textual command interface

There are several parts to the material which the user is working with – the databases, the schemata, the application code and the data. In manipulating a database, the user is determining which volumes it uses, clustering information, applications, indexes, etc. The schema manipulation determines the classes, properties, method interfaces, names, libraries, privileges and owners of the different parts of the schema. The coding part determines the code bodies of methods, functions and application programs.

The textual interaction to achieve all of this is split between a number of components: the *o2dba* tool is used for manipulating databases and the *o2dsa* tool is used for manipulating schemata. Coding is achieved using the component which manages the particular language required. If the language used is O₂C, the interface completely integrates all three parts – thus the O₂C interface subsumes *o2dba* and *o2dsa*. If the program is to be written in C++ or Smalltalk, then (as described in Chapters 12 and 13) schema and database management is not available in the language component. In those cases, *o2dba* and *o2dsa* must be used to perform tasks like creating a database and creating a schema. In this chapter, commands drawn from *o2dba* and *o2dsa* will be used.

Using the textual interface, there are two ways to specify component items (such as the methods of a class, or the programs of an application) – either immediately by specifying them as part of the command which creates the containing item (the class or the application), or by using a create command for the component (the method or the program). For instance, it is possible to create method *M* in class *C*, in either of the following two ways:

```
create class C
   ...
   method
      M ...
   ...
end
```

or

```
create method M in class C
```

The latter method permits the environment to be incrementally extended at any time. In this chapter, both methods will be shown.

All commands are executed in the context of an environment which contains currently open instances of the main categories of O₂ constructs – schema, base, application, class and so on. "create" commands make the new item current, while "set" commands change which item is current. Many of the create commands have an "in" clause, for instance:

```
        create program P in application A
or      create class C in schema S
```

In these cases, the "in" clause can be omitted if there is a currently open instance of the construct and this is to be used. Thus, if application *A* and schema *S* are the current instances, then the commands above can be reduced to:

```
        create program P
and     create class C
```

The keyword "create" can always be omitted, resulting in the above becoming:

```
        program P
and     class C
```

8.2 How the ODL specification is used

Section 6.4 contained an ODL representation of the schema of the mail application. This description centered around the definition of four object types – those for users, the superuser, mailboxes and messages. It is now necessary to transform this into appropriate O_2 structures to hold the data and the application code.

In O_2, the first structure that must be created is a schema – which corresponds roughly to the module in the ODL representation. When the schema has been set up, the following can also be added:

- the components of the schema – in particular classes for the object types;
- one or more databases – each corresponding to a different mail system;
- some named persistent roots;
- an application structure to hold the facilities, such as sending and receiving messages, described in Section 6.1.

The mapping of the ODMG description to an O_2 description is fairly direct. The object types become O_2 classes, the literal types become O_2 types, operations become methods and so on. Instead of simply listing the properties of a class, O_2 supports the specification of properties in a slightly unusual manner, which makes explicit that the set of properties form a record. In the O_2 description, the class is described as having members whose state is an instance of an attached record (or tuple) type. Each field of a record structure is described using the syntax <name>: <type> rather than <type> <space> <name>. Thus an ODMG description which looks like

```
interface X
{ attribute String A;
  property Y B}
```

becomes in O_2:

```
class X
   type tuple ( A: string, B: Y )
```

O_2 method interfaces for the class can be listed following the keyword **method**, although, as they can be added at any time, it is not unusual to create the class without methods and later to add each method one by one. The methods are similar to ODMG operations, except that in O_2 it is not necessary to indicate whether each parameter is an input or output parameter, some of the scalar type names change and the syntactic order is changed. Thus the ODL operation interfaces:

```
void op1( in Boolean X, out B Y );
Unsigned Short op2( out String Z );
```

becomes the O_2 method signatures:

```
method op1( X: boolean, Y: B ),
method op2( Z: string ): integer;
```

The extents of the types are persistent sets of values, but O_2 does not provide any mechanism for the automatic maintenance of extents. Instead, if it is required to maintain an extent, it must be created as a named persistent root object in O_2. However, O_2 is more flexible in that other values, for instance individual objects, literal values or collections which are not extents, can also be made persistent roots – and this flexibility will be used in Section 8.3.5.

■ 8.3 Creation of an O_2 schema

This section describes how the schema is entered in O_2. The schema object is first created along with a database. Then classes are added to the schema with their properties and methods. Finally the persistent roots are identified.

■ 8.3.1 Setting up the environment

The start point is the creation of a schema. This is achieved by issuing the command:

```
create schema Email
```

The schema, *Email*, now becomes the current schema and all changes made will be to this schema. When restarting or after working with a different schema, it is always possible to return to the *Email* schema by using the command:

```
set schema Email
```

The schema at the outset consists of the single class, *Object*, since no user-defined classes have yet been added.

To test the schema, there must also be a database defined to hold data. No code can be executed without the presence of a database. The following command creates a first database called *MailDB*:

```
create base MailDB
```

To change to another database, the **set base** command is used, as in:

```
set base MailDB2
```

The environment has now been constructed with a schema and a database. The next step is to start adding some user-defined types and classes.

■ 8.3.2 Adding classes

There are four classes to add and all of these require the use of the **create class** command. In this subsection, only the structural aspects of the class will be discussed – the method interfaces will be added in Sections 8.3.3 and 8.3.4.

For the *User* class, the structural description looks as follows:

```
create class User
  private type tuple (
     name: string,
     login: string,
     password: string,
     incoming: Mailbox,
     storage: set(Mailbox)
  )
end
```

Some points to be noticed here are that the application has been coded using the most rigorous form of encapsulation. All of the properties are private and the methods to be added in the next section will be public. No superclass has been indicated, so *User* is a subclass of *Object*, by default. The class *Mailbox* has not yet been defined and this makes the definition of *User* incomplete. Even so, this specification will not be rejected. O₂ does not require the kind of artificial means so often met in some systems which prevent the use of forward references and so require a dummy definition for the name *Mailbox* before *User* is defined.

However, the system does keep track of which definitions are not complete and reminds the programmer of this (see below).

The class hierarchy can be displayed at any time with the command

```
display classes
```

and if this were requested now, the response would be:

```
Object
   User*
```

in which the * next to *User* indicates that the definition is incomplete. A complete definition is required at run-time since, before code can be run, every class in the schema must be made complete.

The next step is to put in the *Superuser* class. This requires no extra properties to be defined – there will of course be extra methods, but these will be discussed in Section 8.3.3. At present, all that needs to be specified is that it is a subclass of *User*:

```
create class Superuser inherit User
end
```

The mapping into O₂ of the *Mailbox* class is equally straightforward:

```
create class Mailbox
   private type tuple (
      name: string,
      holds: list(Message)
   )
end
```

Finally, here is the structure of the message class:

```
create class Message
   private type tuple (
      subject: string,
      dateSent: Date,
      body: Text,
      heldin : set(Mailbox)
      sender: User,
      recipients: set(User)
   )
end
```

Now if the class hierarchy is requested, the following would appear:

```
Object
   User
      Superuser
   Mailbox
   Message
```

Notice that the * that previously appeared after *User* has disappeared – the definition now being complete since *Mailbox* has also been defined.

This completes the class structure, although new classes and new properties of classes may be added later if the need arises.

8.3.3 Adding operations

The operations required are those discussed in Section 6.3.2. At first, the incremental addition of operations one by one will be described, but the text for providing a single complete specification of each class will be given when the incremental specification is complete in Section 8.3.5. This subsection discusses most of the operations required, but there is a special set of methods which are used to initialize objects and these will be discussed in the Section 8.3.4.

The operations required for the *User* class were those to test a user's details, to send, receive and read mail, summarize the user details, create and flush a mailbox and display the mail. There is also a method to create a user, but this is left to the next subsection.

The operation to test a user takes in a potential user name and password and returns the value true if the current user matches those data. The interface for such a method can be added with the command:

```
create method public testUser(  testLogin: string;
                                 testPassword: string ): boolean
                                 in class User
```

The operation to send a mail message has no parameters and so is a little simpler:

```
create method public sendMail in class User
```

The other operations are similarly defined:

```
create method public receive( theMessage: Message ) in class User
create method public summarize in class User
create method public readMail in class User
create method public flushMbox in class User
create method public createMbox in class User
create method public displayName in class User
```

There were three operations to add for the *Superuser* class and these are added by:

```
create method public makeUser in class Superuser
create method public deleteUser in class Superuser
create method public statistics in class Superuser
```

Similarly the *Mailbox* class requires the following additions:

```
create method public insert( newMessage: Message ) in class Mailbox
create method public testMbox( testName: string ) in class Mailbox
create method public showHeaders in class Mailbox
create method public getMessage( number: integer): Message in class
                                                              Mailbox
create method public delete( theMessage: Message ) in class Mailbox
create method public flush in class Mailbox
create method public display in class Mailbox
```

Finally, the *Message* class also has a list of methods to be added, thus:

```
create method public summarize( number: integer ) in class Message
create method public display in class Message
create method public reply( sender: User ; replier: User ; oldSubject:
                                          string ) in class Message
```

■ 8.3.4 Constructor operations

As has already been mentioned, there is a special kind of operation whose task it is to carry out any activities that should accompany the creation of an object. These initializing operations are called **constructor** operations. In O₂C, these are named *init* and there is one for each class. The methods are never explicitly called. Instead, they are called when a *new* operation is executed.

Roughly speaking, *init* is used to accomplish two types of task. It can replace the default values of the fields of the new object and it can make the object persistent. In the current case, the *init* operation of the *User* class must make the user object persistent by adding it into the extent of the class, which is a persistent root as described in Section 8.3.5. The *init* operations of the *Superuser* class needs to store the information that there is a new superuser. The *init* operations of the other two classes do not need to make the objects persistent since they are made persistent by reachability.

The other task for *init* is to set the initial values of fields. For example, a string field will usually be initialized to the empty string, by default. It might be useful in a particular circumstance to use something else – for instance, the comments field of a document class might better be initialized to "Newly created document" than to the empty string. Alternatively, the initial value of the field might be sought at run-time. This can be achieved in two ways – by holding a dialog with the user or by parameterizing the operation.

Looking at the *User* class, there are therefore at least four different ways that the initialization might be managed:

- Use the default *init* – the three string fields will all be set to the empty string, the mailbox fields will be set to a null pointer and an empty set, respectively.

- Replace the string fields with other defaults, such as "DummyUser", "DummyLogin" and "DummyPassword". Replace, the *incoming* field with a new (empty) mailbox, and make *storage* hold an empty set of mailboxes as before.
- Include in the *init* operation, a dialog to request the values of the string fields from the terminal.
- Parameterize the operation so that the fields are determined in the calling program and passed into *init* using the *new* command.

Of these, the first option requires that some other program change the fields at a later date and this will require field setting operations to be added to the class, and so this option is rejected. Changing the string fields to a dummy value has no merit at all in this case, since the dummy value must immediately be replaced by the appropriate instance specific value. However, making the *incoming* field be a new mailbox is precisely what is required, so this will be done.

Holding a dialog is a reasonable way to proceed, but so is parameterizing the operation. To illustrate the process of parameterizing the *init* operation, this will be the method chosen. So the following command is issued:

```
create method public init( userName: string; userLogin: string;
                          userPassword: string )in class User
```

This means that any attempt to create a new *User* object must be parameterized with actual values, such as:

```
new User( "Jane Brown", "jbrown", "r4t5y6u7" )
```

The initializing methods of *Mailbox* and *Message* can similarly be parameterized – the *Mailbox init* with the name and the *Message init* with the user sending the message. These are therefore added with:

```
create method public init( theName: string) in class Mailbox
create method public init( sendingUser: User) in class Message
```

The *init* for the class *Superuser* must set the value of the persistent root. It has no parameters :

```
create method public init in class Superuser
```

8.3.5 The completed class specifications

Sections 8.3.3 and 8.3.4 have shown how the class methods can be added incrementally. Now, the schema is summed up by listing the completed class definitions using the syntax that could have been used to define each class in one command.

```
create class User
  private type tuple (
    name: string,
    login: string,
    password: string,
    incoming: Mailbox,  ! NB Mailbox need not be defined yet
    storage: set(Mailbox)
  )
  method
    public init( userName: string; userLogin: string; userPassword: string ),
    public testUser( testLogin: string; testPassword: string ): boolean,
    public sendMail,
    public receive( theMessage: Message ),
    public summarize,
    public readMail,
    public deleteMsg,
    public createMbox,
    public removeMbox,
    public flushMbox,
    public displayName
end
create class Superuser inherit User
  method
    public init,
    public makeUser,
    public deleteUser,
    public statistics
end
create class Mailbox
  private type tuple (
    name: string,
    holds: list(Message)
  )
  method
    public init( theName: string ),
    public insert( newMessage: Message ),
    public testMbox( testName: string ),
    public showHeaders,
    public getMessage( number: integer): Message,
    public delete( theMessage: Message ),
    public flush,
    public display
end
create class Message
  private type tuple (
    subject: string,
    dateSent: Date,
    body: string,
    sender: User,
    recipients: set(User)
    heldin : set(Mailbox),
  )
  method
    public init( sendingUser: User ),
    public summarize( number: integer ),
    public display,
    public reply( sender: User ; replier: User ; oldSubject: string )
end
```

■ 8.3.6 Creating persistent roots

Now, it is vital to ensure that the data is stored. Mostly, the reachability criterion will ensure that any data which is accessible will be stored. However, in order to achieve this, some initial data items must be explicitly marked as persistent roots – these are the *names* of the O₂ schema. Figure 8.2 illustrates the kind of data that must be stored.

The figure shows three of the users, Jane's incoming mailbox (which has no name), her three storage mailboxes ("Archive", "Current" and "ToDo") and one message in her incoming mailbox. This message has been sent by John and has also been sent to Fiona. In the present application, all of the messages, mailboxes and users must be stored. To do this, which persistent roots are needed and which data can be expected to be stored by reachability?

Consider first of all the messages. It is only necessary to store messages which are in mailboxes. However, if a message is in a mailbox, then there will be a reference from the mailbox to the message – it will be a component of the *holds* property. Therefore, if every mailbox is stored then all of the messages will also be stored since they are reachable from at least one mailbox. Therefore it is not necessary to store the messages explicitly.

Now consider the mailboxes. All of the mailboxes belong to a user and are

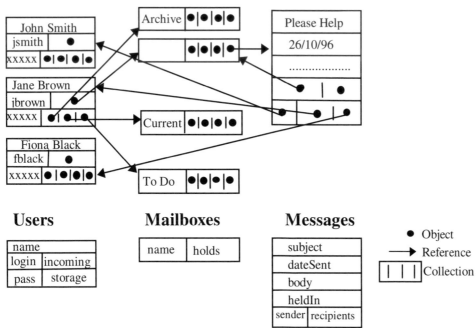

Figure 8.2   The electronic mail data.

either the value of the *incoming* property of that user or a component of the *storage* set of mailboxes. Therefore, it is also true that a mailbox will be stored if its user is. This means that mailboxes also do not need to be stored explicitly.

The users on the other hand are not referred to by anything except the mailboxes and messages and so, as these are not explicitly stored, the users must be. This was the reason that in ODL, the *User* type had its extent explicitly mentioned. To store the users, the extent must be named in O_2 as follows:

```
name theUsers: set(User);
```

This means that an explicitly persistent set of users exists in the database. It does not mean that this set will automatically be maintained. When the coding of the application is considered in a later chapter, it is going to be necessary to ensure that users are added to this set as they are created and removed from the set as they are removed from the mail system. However, if this is carried out, then no further action needs to be taken to store the messages and the mailboxes.

Turning to the superuser, it is clear that this user will already be stored in *theUsers*. However, there is no way of identifying which of those users is the superuser. This could have been done by adding a boolean property which is set to true only for the superuser. However, an alternative approach will be taken here, by making the superuser separately identifiable as a root in its own right. Therefore the following will also be indicated:

```
name superUser: Superuser;
```

and this will ensure that the superuser object is available globally across the application code.

The resulting database is shown as Figure 8.3. Notice that everything in the database is accessible via one of the root objects, so no data will be lost.

■ 8.4 Creation of an O_2 application

This section will show how an O_2 application can be developed to accomplish the tasks described in Sections 6.1 and 6.3. Each of the facilities in the application will become one of the programs or transactions in the application. In this description, the overall structure of the application will be discussed together with the interfaces to the programs and transactions. At the interface level, these can all be considered programs. Later chapters will discuss how the programs are implemented in a programming language.

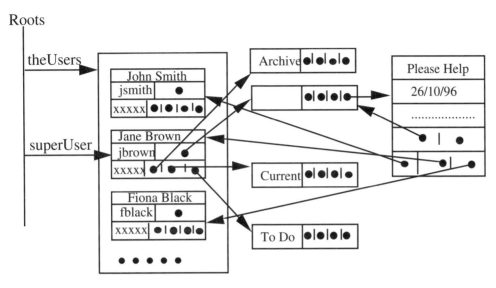

Figure 8.3 The electronic mail database.

■ 8.4.1 The application framework

The application is created quite simply with the command:

```
create application mailControl
end
```

This creates a new application which runs against the schema which is currently open – in this case the *Email* schema. This becomes the current application in the same way that *Email* is the current schema. This means that the "in application mailControl" clause can be omitted from the create variable and create program commands discussed in Sections 8.4.2 and 8.4.3.

To run the application, the following command is used:

```
run application mailControl
```

and the following appears:

```
The programs available: (<RETURN> to exit application)
mailControl>
```

The first line is the heading of a menu, which is currently empty as no programs have yet been added. The line also indicates the only thing that can be done – pressing the return key to exit the application. The second line is a prompt using the application name.

■ 8.4.2 Global variables

As an application is really a suite of programs, it is not surprising that the programs should want to communicate data between themselves whilst running, even though the data need not be stored. To achieve this, an application may contain some global variables.

In the mail example, many of the programs need to have access to the user who is currently logged on. The current user can therefore usefully be made a global variable, which will be set by the login facility, cleared by logout and consulted by several of the other facilities.

A global variable can be defined either in the **create application** command which, in this case, would be extended to be:

```
create application mailControl
User currentUser
end
```

or using an incremental style, it can be added at any time with the command:

```
create variable User currentUser in application mailControl
```

Note that there is a clear difference between a global variable, such as *currentUser*, and a named root, such as *superUser*. The difference lies in the persistence of the two objects. The application is intended to be run repeatedly and it is vital that an indication of who is the superuser is retained between application runs. It is not the same for the current user and it will be assumed that when the application is halted, the current user will automatically be logged out. Thus the current user need not be persistent and this is the difference between the two.

A named root is persistent, whereas as a global variable is transient.

■ 8.4.3 Application programs

Now the application needs to be extended with some programs. In this section, each of the facilities in Chapter 6 will be turned into programs in the application. This can be specified in two ways, either incrementally, by use of a command which adds a program to a previously existing application or in a single "create application" command. Each program will be introduced using the incremental style, but the section will end with a full specification of the application.

The critical part of a program specification is the choice of the arguments that it requires. Some of the programs do not require arguments, while others do. Given two programs, one called *P*, which requires no arguments, while the other, *Q*, requires an integer, called *I*. These will appear as:

```
create program public P in application mailControl;
create program public Q( I: integer ) in application mailControl;
```

Sometimes it is a design decision whether to provide the program with arguments or not. Take, for instance, the login facility. There are several options here: make the program for logging in have no parameters and instead query the user for login name and password by putting interaction code into the body of the method; make login name and password parameters; or make the login a parameter, but request the password. The final option is the one chosen, since the password needs to be kept hidden, and so this program will be specified as:

```
create program public login( userLogin: string ) in application
                                                      mailControl;
```

The addition of the keyword **public** means that this program will automatically be added to the menu. The specification means that to use the program, a string must be given with the user's login. After the addition of this one program, the call "run application mailControl" will result in:

```
The programs available: (<RETURN> to exit application)
   login( params )
mailControl>
```

to which the response could now be:

```
mailControl> login( "jbrown" )
```

The logout facility needs no parameters and so it can be added with:

```
create program public logout in application mailControl;
```

which will add "logout" to the menu resulting from the "run application" command.

Sending a message will similarly need no parameters:

```
create program public sendMessage in application mailControl;
```

Checking the mailbox, reading a message and flushing a mailbox could all best be achieved by providing the mailbox name as a parameter, whose actual value should be the null string if the incoming mailbox is required. Therefore, the following are required:

```
create program public checkMailBox( name: string ) in application
                                                      mailControl;
create program public readMessage( name: string ) in application
                                                      mailControl;
create program public flushMailBox( name: string ) in application
                                                      mailControl;
```

Of the superuser functions, creating a user is probably best carried out with a dialog and so requires no parameters, deleting a user would be most easily achieved by including the user login as a parameter, while getting the statistics is parameterless. The last three programs are therefore:

```
create program public createUser in application mailControl;
create program public deleteUser( userLogin: string ) in application
                                                  mailControl;
create program public statistics in application mailControl;
```

There is a need for one more program – one to set up the *superUser* variable. This will be a privileged operation protected by a password. It takes two parameters – the user login and the password for the operation, both strings.

Clearly, it is in many ways much better to design the whole application and to input it in one command – the "create application" command. To provide a summary, here is the create application command which achieves the same effect as the incremental method that has been used above.

```
create application mailControl
    User currentUser
  program
    public login( userLogin: string),
    public logout ,
    public sendMessage ,
    public checkMailBox( name: string),
    public readMessage( name: string),
    public flushMailBox( name: string)
    public createUser,
    public deleteUser( userLogin: string),
    public statistics,
    public changeSuperUser( userLogin: string, password: string )
  end
```

■ 8.4.4 Running the application

Having defined the behavior of the application as a set of programs, there is still a little more that can be specified in terms of how the execution of the programs in the application will be managed. In particular, there are four other programs which implicitly exist in the application and each of these has a default version which can be modified. To introduce these, here is a flow of how an application session.

1. The *run application* command is executed and this calls the application's *init* program.
2. This is followed by an execution of the application's *dashboard* program, which will provide the menu, from which the user will choose one the programs in the application, or indicate that the application is to be quit.

3. The selected program is executed. If the program executes a commit or abort operation or there is deadlock or a fatal error, then the application calls the *restart* program. In any case, it then returns to (2) – the dashboard program.

4. When the quit option in (2) is requested, the **exit** program is called.

So there are four implicit programs which may be modified:

- *init* carries out any initial set up work that might be required;
- *dashboard* provides a menu of operations which can be requested;
- *restart* deals with transaction boundaries and exceptional situations, ensuring that the system is always in a consistent state; and
- *exit* clears up before the application is quit.

These need no further specification in the current application. However, a modification of the *init* program will be used to illustrate the value of changing one of these default versions. This can be parameterized so that when the application is launched, specific data can be used to help initialize the environment. Imagine that the mail system is augmented with a feature which sends a set of statistics to the superuser after a certain number of users have logged in. This number could be a parameter to the system, in which case the following might be specified:

```
create public program init( Nusers: integer) in application mailControl
```

and now to run the application, an actual value for the parameter must be given, as in:

```
run application mailControl( 100)
```

to get the statistics after every 100th login.

■ 8.5 Summary

This chapter has shown how the structure of a database can be defined and how an application to run against that database can be set up. A schema has been created with four classes. A database has been installed and an application comprising 10 programs has been set up.

Here are some of the important points in the chapter:

- Instead of providing an ODL interface, an ODMG compliant system will provide its own data definition interface.
- The ODMG proposal gives no detail on how application and schema structure should be organized, so each OODBMS has to provide its own.

- The ODMG does specify named values, but whereas they are only start points for programmer access in ODMG, they are also roots of persistence in O_2.

There is, however, as yet no data and no code to make use of data. Neither is there any code in the application. The next two parts of the book deal with how to implement the code and how to fit it in with the schema and application structures. Part Three deals with how to query an ODMG database and Part Four with how to program against ODMG data.

Part Three

Querying object-oriented databases

The ability to query the data relatively easily is one of the trademarks of a good database management system. The user must be able to retrieve particular parts of the database by issuing a command which has a simple structure and can untangle the various relationships between the data quickly.

For an OODBMS to be taken seriously, this querying capability must be supplied. Indeed, it is one of the continual criticisms of OODBMS by relational devotees that they do not provide this facility, that their implementors are not really interested in querying, and indeed cannot provide a decent query language because of the nature of an object-oriented data model. The criticism centers around the claim that an OODBMS is little more than a souped-up network DBMS and that these are notably poor at supporting querying.

The debate starts from the division of all queries into two kinds – navigational queries, in which the user moves from datum to datum by following relationships, and *ad hoc* querying, in which a single command, expressed declaratively, retrieves part of a database. It is the generally accepted viewpoint that network DBMS are much better for navigational querying, while relational DBMS are much better at *ad hoc* querying. It is also generally accepted that OODBMS will also be good for navigational querying.

The discussion in this part of the book is entirely concerned with *ad hoc* querying. In relational DBMS, the languages QUEL and SQL have been developed for this purpose, and SQL is now the standard language for querying a relational database. The existence of such a standard is one of the great strengths of relational systems and enables them, for instance, to communicate data between a heterogeneous network of relational DBMS. SQL has, of course, a lot more than a querying capability. It has features for data definition and data manipulation as well as for data retrieval. The database creation described in the previous chapter would probably, in a relational environment, have been achieved by using SQL. However, this part of the book concentrates entirely on querying, leaving until the next part discussion of more complete interfaces for data description and manipulation.

This part of the book comprises two chapters. Chapter 9 describes the role of a query language in an OODBMS. Chapter 10 describes the ODMG query language, OQL, with some examples and a description of how to use OQL in the O_2 system.

9 Query languages and object systems

This chapter discusses the role of a query language in an OODBMS. The first section looks at the nature of query languages and how they might fit with an object-oriented system. The second section looks at SQL and how it is being developed. The third section surveys some early object query languages.

9.1 Query languages

This section considers the nature of query languages in the context of an OODBMS. To do so it looks at the following questions: what is a query language?; how is it used?; is there any need to have a query language which is separate from the object programming language?; what are the desirable features of a query language?; and what are the problems with providing a query language for an OODBMS?

9.1.1 What is a query language?

A query language provides a mechanism by which a user can request a subset of the data from a database, such a request being called an *ad hoc* query. The query identifies a part of the data either explicitly by naming the parts to be returned or implicitly by specifying conditions which must be met by any data being returned. A typical query might be "Return the names of the mailboxes of the user named Jane Brown". In this query, the data returned is determined by (i) only the names of mailboxes will be returned; and (ii) only those mailboxes will be considered that meet the condition that they are owned by the user with the name "Jane Brown".

A query therefore is built out of a number of schema names and one or more constraining predicates. An interface to support querying must allow the user to specify both of these. A variety of styles of querying interface have been proposed, including graphical interfaces in which a schema diagram is used as a basis for framing the query; form-based interfaces such as query by example (QBE); and textual interfaces. Whereas graphical selection of schema names works well, graphical input of constraints has been found to be too clumsy to be usable. QBE works well for simple queries, but quickly becomes less useful as queries get more complex.

A textual language, on the other hand, can provide full generality with a syntax in which the data model constructs are used as the basis for slots in the syntax of query formulations. Moreover, the syntax can include sections for predicates using standard boolean expression parsers. For these reasons, the standard mechanism for inputing user queries is a textual language, called a query language.

■ 9.1.2 Uses of query languages

Although responding to *ad hoc* queries is the core function that query languages were designed to provide, there are at least four ways in which query languages have used this ability:

(a) To produce an immediate return of the results of a query to the user. Thus the query language processor will take in a query and display or print the results obtained.

(b) To control all access to the data. Many relational systems make the query the primary means of retrieving data, with all other access being mapped into a form that the query processor can deal with. Even access via programming languages is usually achieved by embedding the query language within it.

(c) As a simple programming language. In some systems, it is possible to write the whole of an application in the query language, as long as the data manipulation required is fairly simple.

(d) To supply application programming shortcuts. Even if full database access is provided to a programming language, some program modules can be coded in the query language, since this may well be easier to achieve and will be optimizable.

Furthermore, query languages have been extended to support two more tasks:

(e) Data definition. The syntax of the query language is extended to allow the schema to be defined uniformly with the specification of queries.
(f) Data manipulation. The syntax of updating can be made to look very like querying with an assignment added to it. Thus "print the names of mailboxes of the user called 'Jane Brown'" is very similar to "flush all of the mailboxes of the user called 'Jane Brown'". Therefore a uniform language can be created which performs all database access.

For object-oriented databases, these last two activities need not be supported. Data definition is implicit in the construction of an object-oriented application. At the same time, a key concept of the object-oriented approach is that data manipulation, if achieved wholly through the type operations, will be in a coherent and tightly integrated structure and will consequently be more easy to program correctly and to maintain.

9.1.3 A single language interface for OODBMS

One issue which needs careful examination is whether a DBMS needs, any longer, to have separate programming and querying languages. Clearly the presence of two interfaces is costly to maintain and also requires users to learn two languages. The pressure to unify querying and programming comes from two directions:

- The scope of query languages is being extended to encompass more activities. The languages are consequently becoming richer with more complex constructs (see Section 9.2).
- The tight integration of a programming language with a database seems to offer the possibility of writing queries in a programming language which is well tuned to the specification of schema components and constraints.

It may indeed eventually be possible that there will be a single database language which is equally usable by a variety of users for a variety of purposes, but at the present time, language design is an insufficiently well understood art for this to be achieved. What actually occurs in the move away from a simple query language is that writing queries becomes significantly more difficult to master. Chapter 11 discusses database programming languages. In that chapter, it will be seen that one goal is the design of a language which combines simplicity of expression with the power of constructs, by allowing those constructs to be mixed freely. This helps since the programmer need not remember and program around limitations. Even with such languages, however, there is no possibility of a user without programming skills learning the language.

It therefore seems that a simple query language is a necessary component of a DBMS, in order to permit non-programming staff to be able to access their data easily. OQL is the query language proposed for OODBMS by the ODMG.

One of the consequences of having two separate languages, each with different capabilities has been that sometimes both are needed. This has resulted in an "embedded" query language, whose use has been problematic, for instance, when embedding SQL in a language such as C (see Section 11.3.1). Embedded languages are again proposed for OODBMS, but now there is a difference which makes them a much more attractive proposition.

The problem with linking C and SQL is that they each have very different models of data. This is the so-called "impedance mismatch" problem. Combining a programing language which is based on an object data model with a query language based on the same model is much less problematic, since the query is directly using values from the language type system and is returning values in that same model. Therefore, it should prove to be true that crossing the boundary between the two languages causes much less difficulty.

■ 9.1.4 Desirable properties of query languages

A query language should have the following properties:

- It should be easy to use. The user should be able to frame the query in a natural and concise style.
- It should be high level. A query should describe the data required and not refer to details of the way in which it is stored. This is one of the main supports for the data independence that database systems provide.
- It should be declarative. The language must allow the specification of the data required in a manner which does not control how the data is retrieved.
- It should be algebraic in the sense that every query will return data described in the data model of the DBMS and not by using any other structures.
- It should execute the queries efficiently. The declarative and algebraic nature will make available a variety of equivalent strategies for executing

the query. The query processor can then use the one which is the most efficient.

- It should be application independent. The language should allow queries to be framed against any database which the DBMS can manage.
- The main task of the query language is to support data retrieval, not data manipulation or data definition.

The query languages SQL and QUEL are two relational query languages which have all of these properties (except the last) and they have been impressively successful. The adoption of SQL as the standard relational query language may not have been to the liking of every database expert, but the fact that there is a standard is to everyone's advantage.

Turning to OODBMS, there is a need to provide a similar level of support for *ad hoc* querying. The lack of such support has been a leading criticism of OODBMS, but it is a need that OODBMS vendors have paid heed to. The first effort at approaching an OODBMS standard, "The Object-Oriented Database Systems Manifesto" of 1988 states as guideline 2.13:

Thou shalt have a simple way of querying data.

9.1.5 The tension between object orientation and querying

However, it is one thing to have a goal and another to reach it. In this case, there is a body of opinion that claims that OODBMS and querying cannot mix, since the fit of querying with relations depends on the simplicity of the relational model. The criticisms of relational advocates center around two potential problems.

- Because data is often encapsulated in such a way that properties are hidden, the query language cannot have access to enough of the data and metadata to allow any query to be executed.
- Queries cannot be executed efficiently.

These two problems will be considered in this section.

The first criticism starts from the strong notion of information hiding discussed in Section 2.4, which is found in some object-oriented systems. In these systems, the data structures installed by one piece of program development become completely inaccessible to future developments, thus ensuring that no problematic dependencies between the two are created. This might mean that in an OODBMS, it becomes infeasible to write queries which access private properties. However, OODBMS can, and must, be designed so that this is not a problem.

This can be done for two reasons:

- The query processor, since it is a system element programmed by the OODBMS vendor, can be made a privileged "user" of the system. It can be given access to metadata which is kept hidden from ordinary programmers and users.
- A query is intended only to retrieve data and not to update it. Therefore, the integrity of the data cannot be compromised by the query processor. This is one of the key reasons why it is a good idea to restrict the activities of the query processor to querying.

It therefore becomes feasible to provide users with a querying capability which is not restricted by encapsulation.

There are at least two reasons why it might prove difficult to create an efficient OODBMS. The first reason is that the "network-like" structures seem to imply a significant amount of costly "pointer chasing", worsened by object table lookup. The second reason is that a query might include the execution of operations with hidden updates (or "side effects") in them, so it is no longer possible to re-order data accesses to make execution more efficient.

The first point really brings to prominence the underlying architecture of the OODBMS. It is going to be necessary to separate out a logical architecture – how the user believes the data are organized – from a physical architecture – how they actually are organized. One of the cornerstones of DBMS architecture has been that it is possible to layer the system so that user access is at a logical level, using a single logical model, while physical data organization can take any form that seems appropriate from an efficiency point of view.

This argument carries right over to OODBMS architecture. $O_2Engine$, for instance, is specifically layered in such a way that the physical representation is as a set of records and the upper layers surround this with an object wrapper. One of the important aspects of this method of layering is that many of the efficient structures from relational systems can be re-used.

The problem of hidden updates is more relevant to the query processing issues, since much query optimization relies on the equivalence of different orderings of the component parts of the query. If any of the operations involved includes some updates then it may not be correct to assume that different orderings are equivalent.

Again, the important issue here is to restrict our attention to queries, i.e. code fragments which only retrieve data. It would be useful if queries and updates were clearly distinguished. Although it may be possible to design a system in which this is automatically detected, it may be better from a documentation point of view to provide some kind of protocol which distinguishes which parts of the schema involve updates and which do not. In such a system, the programmer would be required to distinguish updating operations from non-updating ones. This however has still to be effectively implemented.

■ 9.2 SQL and object querying

SQL is the standard query language for relational systems. Since network databases do not usually have a query language, it is fair to say that for most users the terms "query language" and "SQL" are synonymous. The object-oriented community have recognized this and have worked towards the goal of producing an SQL-like query language for OODBMS. In this section, however, the various standards for SQL itself will be discussed.

■ 9.2.1 The development of SQL

SQL emerged through a sequence of precursors – SQUARE, SEQUEL (1974), etc. SQL86 was the first attempt to standardize the language, and is consequently often called SQL1. Standardization is carried out under the auspices of the International Standards Organization (ISO) and the American National Standards Institute (ANSI). These have set up committees for standardizing in the database area: ISO JTC1/SC21/WG3 – Information Processing/Open Systems Interconnection/ Database Working Group, and X3H2 – ANSI Accredited Standards Committee X3/Database.

There is a problem with trying to improve standards in this area. The goal is to produce a language which will be supported by all major relational systems and so permit the development of multi-platform applications. At the same time, that standard must be made sufficiently powerful to support application development effectively. The reality is that any system that is currently available will support SQL1 plus other features which will vary from system to system. The problem is that to increase the core set of constructs across all platforms is very ambitious, so that third-party manufacturers are averse to basing their work on anything that is not available everywhere. It will be noted that this is exactly the same problem that the ODMG sets out to achieve for OODBMS. However, ODMG has the edge in that most object-oriented vendors are clear about the need to adhere to standards to sell any of the products at all. This contrasts with relational vendors who are already selling their products successfully and may find it hard to justify further development.

Despite this, various working groups are developing SQL and they came up with a small revision in 1989. This included referential integrity and generalized constraint features. Then followed SQL2 (or SQL-92) which is intended to be the standard to which relational manufacturers will be committed from now on. Here are some of the features which SQL2 adds to the standard:

- dynamic SQL;
- extra operations such as outer join, and the set operations union, intersection and difference;
- integrity enforcement through cascaded update and delete;
- an improved set of built-in data types, including date, time, timestamp, interval, national and varchar, and improved support for character strings;
- the ability to define additional domains in the schema;
- the ability to define different levels of isolation between transactions;
- other facilities such as temporary tables, deferred constraint checking, scrolled cursors and better diagnostics.

Essentially, the 1989 and 1992 revisions of SQL produced a number of useful but small increments on SQL1, filling in noticeable gaps in the original specification, but not attempting anything too radical. However, a new revision to the standard is in the process of being created which will be a substantial increment to SQL as it is currently known. This will be SQL3.

■ 9.2.2 SQL3

Although upwardly compatible with SQL2, SQL3 introduces a radically enhanced data model as its basis, one that encompasses objects. Furthermore SQL is a computationally complete language and it is seen as a sufficient language for the whole of database application development.

The SQL initiative came out of a sub-committee of ANSI X3, the X3/SPARC/ DBSSG/OODB Task Group, set up in 1989. In 1991, their first contribution was a report with a glossary of object-oriented terms, a reference model characterizing OODBMS and a set of recommendations for standardization. They fell short of specifying actual interfaces, however, recognizing that object orientation is arising in areas other than DBMS and that integration of all usage may thus be difficult. They recommend a set of composable standards rather than one monolithic standard. This has led on to further ANSI efforts in the formation of the X3H7 Object Information Committee in January 1993. This committee is considering how to accommodate application-specific differences in object data models and how to manage the reality of a multiplicity of object models.

Much more ambitious is the move to SQL3 and the attempts to bring objects into SQL. SQL3 is a massive increase in the scope of SQL. It has the following new features:

- triggers – which can be defined on insertions, deletions and updates to particular tables;
- roles – which allow privileges to be granted more abstractly than to individual users;
- recursion in queries, for example a recursive union operator – both linear and non-linear recursion is permitted, together with the ability to specify the search strategy and stop conditions to be used;
- many more built-in data types including:
  - booleans and new character sets;
  - enumerated and collection types;
  - large object types – binary large objects and character large objects (i.e. text);
- user-defined types – including the ability to define parameterized type templates;
- user-defined operators and functions;
- asynchronous query execution – to speed up database usage;
- access to routines, externally programmed in other languages – allowing code libraries to be re-used;
- sub-tables – so that collection hierarchies can be maintained more efficiently;
- savepoints;
- a variety of extensions to assertions, predicates, null values, integrity, view updateability and joins;
- a call-level interface with over 40 procedures for accessing the database capability;

and, most ambitiously,

- full programming language capability, through a block-structured procedural language with the usual computational constructs for sequential, conditional and repeated execution, for variable declaration and assignment, and for procedure definition and execution;
- abstract data types (ADTs).

The provision of an ADT mechanism in the language puts SQL3 into the object-oriented framework. ADTs have the following features:

- they may define either a value type or an object type;
- a set of attributes, each of any type, and each of which may be made immutable, non-null or read-only;
- a set of operations to manipulate these including, for each attribute, two automatically generated operations which update (the *Mutator* operation) and access (the *Observer* operation) the attribute;
- strict encapsulation in that only the operations can be accessed;
- multiple inheritance;
- privileges to allow access control to a type or to its operations.

Instances of object types have object identifiers, as usual, and these are unique system-wide. The extents of types are not automatically maintained. In fact, the persistence mechanism has, in all of this, not been changed at all. Only tables are persistent, but a table can hold any object or value type, and so anything can be stored. This does not seem to have the same automatic support for integrity as the reachability model. It is not clear what would happen if an object, *O*, which is in a table has as a property value an object, *P*, which is not in a table. Does *P* persist or not?

The SQL design effort is now so enormous that it has been split up into seven parts. SQL3 is intended to be finalised in 1997 or 1998. The wealth of extensions is not seen as the end of the road by any means. SQL4 is in the pipeline, at first as a catch-all for useful features which DBMS vendors could not reasonably be expected to implement in the near future. At the same time, certain user groups are augmenting SQL in other ways, to support particular application areas. The provision of spatial data types and temporal data types are two examples of this.

■ 9.3 Early object query languages

Returning to the OODBMS community, there have been a number of attempts to come up with a query language for objects, mostly based on SQL. These include Object SQL – this was developed as part of the IRIS system by Hewlett-Packard, and ReLoop – an early O_2 experiment.

■ 9.3.1 Object SQL

Object SQL is a computationally complete language which is based on a functional model. Objects are instances of types situated in a multiple inheritance hierarchy. The top of this hierarchy includes types for: types, surrogates (objects with an oid), aggregates (values with components), literals and transients. Transients are objects which never need to be stored – system examples of this include transactions, savepoints, sessions and cursors. The properties of a type are all modeled as functions – including stored and derived attributes, relationships and other computations. The definition and implementation(s) of a type are kept separate.

The language allows the following kinds of command:

- data definition such as **create type** and **create function**. Here are some examples:

```
create type part functions
   ( name Char (var 128 ) )

create type complexPart subtype of part;
create function subparts(complexPart) -> bagtype(part)

create function price(part) -> Real;
create function price( complexPart p ) -> Real as osql
   sum( select atomic price(q) forEach part q
      where q occurs in subparts(p) );
```

- querying is similar to the familiar **select … from … where …** structure with some extension so that the whole syntax looks like:

```
select <restrictions> <result list>
   forEach <declarations>
      where <boolean expression>
         groupBy <group>
            having <expr>
               orderBy <order>
```

The restrictions include the ability to assert that the result is a single value, is made atomic, etc.

■ 9.3.2 ReLoop

This is also an SQL-like language, but one which uses a functional approach, produced in an early O_2 experiment. An example from the mail application can illustrate how a query appears in ReLoop. To return the names of all of the mailboxes used by "jbrown", the query is:

```
select     name(M)
from U in USER
           M in storage(U)
where      U(login) = "jbrown"
```

while the following query lists the subject and sender's name of all messages in Jane Brown's incoming mailbox:

```
select     [ subject(M), name(sender(M)) ]
from U in USER
           M in holds(incoming( (U) )
where      U(login) = "jbrown"
```

All queries return sets, as usual, but the sets may be values, as in the first instance; objects, dropping *name* from the first query would return the set of mailboxes, for instance; or constructed records, as in the second query. The **select** clause determines what kind of set is returned. The **from** clause is used to list any selection of items from sets, while the **where** clause holds a boolean expression relating constants with objects and values in the database.

The various object query languages are all fairly similar, using an SQL-like syntax, but extending this by permitting methods, properties and path expressions built by these to be used whereas field names are in SQL. Creating a standard for an object query language is therefore not just a desirable goal but one which is attainable. One such language is OQL, which is the subject of the next chapter.

■ 9.4 Summary

This chapter has discussed the need for a query language in an OODBMS. In doing so, it has restricted the role of the query language to the support of querying, rather than including data definition and manipulation as well. In an object-oriented context, these are seen as being best carried out in the object-oriented programming languages, which the DBMS supports. However, an alternative view is that taken by the SQL3 committees, who are bringing the object-oriented language constructs into SQL and attempting to provide complete database support in one language. The main danger in doing this is that the result is a language which is so large that potential users will be frightened away. However, it can always be argued that since each development is a strict superset of the previous version, SQL1 users can continue unchanged.

The main points argued in the discussion were:

- OODBMS need a query language as much as do relational DBMS.
- The query language is used to support optimizable access to the data, which is simpler to code than using a programming language.

- To provide such a language the OODBMS manufacturer has to overcome potential problems caused by information hiding, which might result in restricting data access, and by the more complex structure, which might result in inefficient access.
- SQL is the basis of object query languages and is also being developed into a full programming language with objects.

The provision of a separate and small query language is the viewpoint taken by ODMG. They propose a language called OQL, which will be supported by OODBMS vendors. In the next chapter, OQL is described as well as its use in O_2.

However, the last point that needs to be made in this chapter concerns the relationship between SQL3 and OQL. This is covered in the discussion paper "Accommodating SQL3 and ODMG". This discusses a meeting between SQL3 and ODMG participants and lists some of the main differences between the data models involved. The most interesting part of this is the potential relationship between the two:

- the SQL model will be a subset of the ODMG model, since SQL is never intending to support a richer object model, nor to provide persistence to anything other than a table;
- the SQL language will be a superset of OQL since OQL is only for queries;
- OQL queries should be able to access SQL databases; and
- SQL programs should be able to access ODMG databases.

10 | The object query language OQL

This chapter describes OQL, which is the query language proposed by ODMG. OQL has been designed to be the language for writing queries which access a database organized according to the ODMG data model which was described in Chapter 5.

The chapter has six sections. The first introduces OQL by describing some general features that it possesses. Section 10.2 gives some simple examples to demonstrate the features of OQL. Section 10.3 describes the syntax of these features in depth and can be omitted if the reader does not wish to master the fine detail of constructing OQL queries. Sections 10.4 and 10.5 describe how O_2 supports the language and how the mail application might make use of OQL. The chapter ends with a summary.

10.1 Principal features of OQL

OQL is a member of the SQL family of languages and so the most common kind of query written in OQL has the familiar **select ... from ... where ...** structure. OQL is designed to have the following features:

- It is a superset of the **select** query syntax of SQL.
- It is purely for writing queries and has no facilities for supporting data definition, constraint specification, data manipulation or any other data management tasks.
- It is not computationally complete.
- The result of a query is usually a collection of ODMG values, but a query may instead produce any single ODMG value as its result. Thus a query can return a list, a record, an integer or a single object.
- It is designed to support two kinds of usage:

  - When used in an OQL interpreter, the querying facility is provided interactively to the user and the results are displayed immediately.
  - When embedded in a program, the queries are written as part of the program and the results returned to the program. Execution of a query now takes the form of a function call with the results being used by the calling program in whatever way is required.

- OQL is declarative and hence optimizable.
- The operators in the language can be freely composed. There are operators for creating collections, arithmetical and logical operators, quantifying operators, aggregating operators, and sorting and grouping operators. Each of these operators can make use of the results of any of the others.
- Although OQL does not provide generic update statements, a query can invoke an operation on an object and this operation can cause an update to occur.
- OQL is defined as an abstract language, albeit one with a well-defined syntax. Each OODBMS implementing the ODMG proposal may well provide a slight variant of this basic syntax.

A query in OQL starts from the denotable objects which have an available name. The names available include those of: root persistent objects, extents of classes declared in the schema, and (when run in the context of a programming language) object and value identifiers declared in the current scope of the program. From these, the query can iterate over collections and access parts of the data objects by use of path expressions which permit the operations and properties of any object to be used to retrieve components.

Queries can take several forms:

- The simplest form is a single literal value, for instance:

5

- Alternatively, a reference to a single object can be query, as in:

  ```
  superUser
  ```

- Given that an object can be referenced, a path expression can retrieve characteristics:

  ```
  superUser . name
  ```

  or

  ```
  aMailbox -> size
  ```

- These can be combined into expressions, such as:

  ```
  aPerson . age + 25
  men union women
  for all U in Users: U . login
  ```

- New constructed values can be returned as the result of a query:

  ```
  struct( name: "John"; age: 25 )
  ```

- Finally, the **select** expressions can be used as usual:

  ```
  select U . name from U in theUsers where U . login = "jbrown"
  ```

All of these can be combined freely as long as the type system is respected. This means that although a select query which returns a bag of items is the most common, it is possible to write queries which return any type of value that is permissable in the ODMG data model.

Queries can be given names for later re-use. These named queries become part of the schema. The name given can then be used to stand for the whole of the query, which will be executed whenever the name is provided as a query or part-query. In this way, the frequent re-entry of useful queries can be avoided. Named queries can be parameterized.

To sum up, OQL provides an SQL-like language for the querying aspect of object database access. The next two sections will describe OQL and how it is used. Section 10.2 informally introduces some of the main facilities in the language, while Section 10.3 gives a more detailed account.

■ 10.2 Some examples of OQL queries

In this section the various features of OQL will be introduced using small examples of increasing complexity which query a mail database.

■ 10.2.1 Simple queries

The first example shows how simple expressions are valid OQL queries:

```
5 + 23 * 10
```

which, of course, returns the integer 235.

The second example shows a path expression. This starts from the persistent root, *superUser* and accesses a property, which is a mailbox, and an operation defined on mailboxes.

```
superUser . incoming->size
```

returns the number of messages in the incoming mailbox of the superuser. In the queries presented here, the dot operator dereferences properties and the arrow operator invokes methods. This style has been adopted to inform of the reader of when operations are being invoked and when properties are being dereferenced, although it is in the nature of object-oriented programming to blur the distinction.

It is also possible to create new constructed values as the result of a query. For instance:

```
struct( name: superUser . name, unreadMessages:
                  superUser . incoming->size )
```

constructs a pair containing the user's name and the number of messages in that user's incoming mailbox.

Similarly, it is possible to construct collections as the result of a query, as in:

```
list( 'A', 'b', 'c' )
```

and

```
set( 2, 3, 5, 7, 11, 13 )
```

A query can return an object instead of a value. Thus, the query:

```
superUser
```

returns the superuser object. A query can also construct an object as its result. For instance, given a class, *UserDetails*, whose only properties are string fields called *userName* and *userLogin*, the following query would return the details of the superuser as an object of that class:

```
UserDetails( userName: superUser . name, userLogin: superUser . login )
```

Notice the difference between this and creating a record – the class must have previously been defined, while the record structure is created on the fly.

10.2.2 Manipulating collections

Ad hoc query processing is largely about retrieving collections of values. OQL permits the explicit construction of collections as shown above, but most queries return collections as the result of **select** commands. In fact, collections can be returned by a query in the following ways:

- explicit creation – as shown in the previous subsection;
- the result of a select query;
- the result of accessing a multi-valued property of an object;
- the value of a persistent root – very often this will be the extent of a type and hence be a collection.

Thus the following queries all return sets:

```
set( 7, 5, 23 )
select distinct U from U in theUsers
superUser . storage
```

and

```
theUsers
```

Having generated collections in this way, there are a number of ways they can be used in queries:

- Unordered collections can be combined by the usual union, intersection and difference operators. Thus

```
superUser . storage union set( superUser . incoming )
```

creates the set of all of the mailboxes owned by the superuser as the union of the storage mailboxes with the set just holding the incoming mailbox.
- Collections can be iterated over to determine quantification operations. The query:

```
for all U in theUsers : U . incoming -> size > 0
```

returns the boolean value **true** if every user has mail in their incoming mailbox, while

```
exists U in theUsers : U . incoming -> size > 0
```

returns the boolean value **true** if any user has mail in their incoming mailbox.
- Collections can be iterated over in select queries. The example

```
select U . name from U in theUsers
```

iterates over the set of users and creates an equivalent sized bag to hold their names.

- Individual elements can be extracted from collections by using the **element** operator. Here is an example:

```
element( list( 3 ) )
```

returns the number 3. It is important, when using the element operator, to ensure that the collection has just a single member. If the collection had no members or more than one member, then a run-time error would occur.

- Given an ordered collection, i.e. an array or a list, it is possible to extract a particular element by its position. For instance:

```
list( 23.1, 44.2, 39.7, 12.4 ) [ 2 ]
```

returns 39.7. The operator is written by placing the index in square brackets after the collection. Notice that as the index of ordered collections starts from 0, the 23.1 has index 0, the 44.2 has index 1 and so on.

Since strings are in many respects just lists of characters, the same operator works for them, thus:

```
"123456789"[5]
```

returns the character '6' – again '1' is the 0th character of the string.

- Portions of ordered collections can also be retrieved. For instance:

```
list( 5, 7, 9, 11, 13 ) [2:3]
```

retrieves the list from the second to the third element, i.e.

```
list( 9, 11 )
```

and again the same operator is available for strings and so:

```
"123456789"[5:7]
```

returns "678".

- There is an operator which tests whether or not a value is to be found as an element of a collection. Two examples of this are:

```
6 in list( 5, 7, 9, 11, 13 )
```

and

```
'6' in "123456789"
```

which return **false** and **true** respectively.

- Collections can be reduced to single values by aggregation operations:

```
count( superUser . storage )
```

returns the number of storage mailboxes that the superuser has. As usual, there are aggregate operators to create maxima, minima, sums and averages of numerical collections.

• In some cases, collections can be turned from one form to another. Thus, the ordering can be removed from a list, as in:

```
listtoset( superUser . incoming . holds )
```

while a bag can also be turned into a set. For example:

```
distinct( select U . name from U in theUsers )
```

is no longer a bag but a set, since the operation removes all duplicates.

One last operator is **flatten**. This takes a collection of collections and returns the collection which is the union of sub-collections. For example:

```
flatten( set( set( 1, 2, 3 ), set( 4, 5 ), set( 6, 7, 8, 9 ) ) )
```

returns

```
set( 1, 2, 3, 4, 5, 6, 7, 8, 9 )
```

10.2.3 Select queries

Select queries return collections, which will usually be bags. Thus:

```
select U from U in theUsers where U . incoming -> size > 0
```

returns the bag of users with incoming mail, while

```
select U from U in theUsers where U . login = "jbrown"
```

returns a bag containing just one user – the one whose login is "jbrown". It is possible to reduce this result so that the object itself is returned by use of the **element** operator, already discussed. Thus, to retrieve the user object instead of the set, the previous query is extended to:

```
element( select U from U in theUsers where U . login = "jbrown" )
```

The next query returns the bag of sizes of incoming mailboxes:

```
select U . incoming -> size from U in theUsers
```

but if instead duplicates are to be removed, then the keyword **distinct** should be added:

```
select distinct U . incoming -> size from U in theUsers
```

and the result is no longer a bag, but a set – one which contains all the different sizes of existing incoming boxes.

The other collection type which may be returned is a list. This occurs either if a list property is returned or if a **select** query is augmented with an **order by** clause. For instance:

```
select U . incoming -> size from U in theUsers order by U . name
```

returns the sizes arranged into alphabetical order of the user name.

The other feature that may be added to a select query is to group the results by partitioning them according to characteristics of the properties of the data. For instance,

```
select U . name from U in theUsers group by inBoxSize: U . incoming -> size
```

groups the names of users by the size of their incoming mailbox. The result of a grouped query is somewhat different. It is a set of records, each of which has two fields – a field called *inBoxSize* which holds the incoming mailbox size of a group of users, and a field called *partition* which is a bag of the names of those users. Thus the result would be of the form:

```
( inBoxSize: 0, partition: bag( "Jill", "Joe", "Pan", "Shaheen" ) ),
( inBoxSize: 5, partition: bag( "John", "Kwame", "Ruth" ) ), etc.
```

Finally, the results of this last query can be filtered by constraining which records are returned. For instance, to return only those mailbox sizes with less than four users, the following query would be used:

```
select U . name from U in theUsers group by inBoxSize: U . incoming -> size
having count( select N from partition ) < 4
```

This works by generating each of the records of the result, as above, but then testing the cardinality of the *partition* field, returning only those which meet the criterion provided. Thus the record with *inBoxSize* = 0 would be excluded as it has four members, whereas the size 5 record would be returned.

■ 10.2.4 Miscellaneous features

Creating named queries

One useful facility in OQL is the ability to name queries for later re-use. Queries are added to the schema by the use of the **define** command and persist until they are removed explicitly by using the **delete definition** command.

For instance, a user might wish to retrieve the number of messages in a mailbox called *TODO* and define a query for that purpose:

```
define TODOsize as
  select M->size from U in theUsers, M in U . storage
       where M . name = "TODO" and U . login = "jbrown"
```

At any point later in the session it becomes possible to run the query:

```
TODOsize
```

to get the current size of the *TODO* mailbox of user *jbrown*.

Named queries can be parameterized as in the example:

```
define IncomingSize( loginName ) as
    select U . incoming. size from U in theUsers
          where U . login = $loginName
```

which could be used as follows:

```
IncomingSize( "jbrown" )
```

Query names cannot be overloaded. That is, the same query name cannot be used for different queries, each having a different number of parameters. There could not, for instance, be one version of *incomingSize* with a parameter and one without.

Stored queries are removed as in the following example:

```
delete definition IncomingSize( loginName )
```

Type coercion

Sometimes, it is necessary to access an object as an instance of one of its supertypes, but then to use the characteristics of the object's actual type – for instance, the object might be located by searching the extent of a supertype. This causes a potential problem in that only the characteristics defined on the supertype can be used. In this case, it is necessary to move the object down the hierarchy, a process of coercion often called **downcasting**.

Consider the following small schema:

```
interface Vehicle            interface Car : Vehicle        interface Boat : Vehicle
( extent theVehicles         ( attribute Integer wheels      ( attribute Integer draught
   attribute String registration  )                              ... )
... )
```

In this case, it is straightforward to retrieve the set of registration numbers:

```
select V. registration from V in theVehicles
```

since this property is available in the supertype.

However, to retrieve the number of wheels of a car or the draught of a boat proves difficult, since there is no explicitly maintained set of boats or cars. Using a query like the one above does not work either since *V* is of type *Vehicle* and this does not have the requisite attributes (*wheels* or *draught*). What is really wanted here is to make *V* have, as its type, one of the subtypes. This can be achieved in OQL by asserting the sub-type, as in:

```
select ( (Car) V ). wheels from V in theVehicles
                          where V . registration = "KLS 504D"
```

The "((Car) V)" part retrieves a car object instead of a vehicle, by coercing the object down the type hierarchy.

However, an important component of this query is the **where** part, since this has been used to ensure that *V* actually refers to a car, since boats do not have this kind of registration number. The following, on the other hand, would not be guaranteed to work:

```
select ( (Car) V ). wheels from V in theVehicles
```

This cannot be used to retrieve the wheels of all the cars, since the query would attempt to retrieve the *wheels* property of the boats as well and these do not have this attribute. This would therefore cause a run-time error if there were any boats in *theVehicles*. In order to achieve this, the type *Vehicle* would have to be enhanced with a boolean operation, *isCar* say, which returns true if the vehicle is a car. The query can then be completed as in:

```
select ( (Car) V ). wheels from V in theVehicles where V -> isCar
```

■ 10.2.5 Discussion

These then are the main kinds of query which can be specified in OQL. All produce values in the ODMG data model and are combinable in any way which respects the type system. The query language is therefore, as usual, algebraic and this algebraic nature of the language enables equivalences between different query forms to be used as the basis for query optimization.

This section has been informal in nature. The next section puts more precision on the definition of the components of the language.

■ 10.3 Queries in OQL

OQL is an expression based language. Each query must be an expression which is well formed according to the rules of the language. This section lays out those rules. One of the strengths of OQL is that the rules are completely orthogonal. Most of the kinds of expression permitted have components which are themselves queries.

After discussing how queries can be named, the section builds up the various kinds of expression from the simplest query which consists of the extraction of a single value by name. The discussion then builds on this by describing the ways in which single values can be combined, how complex values can be returned, how objects are manipulated and how collections can be used. The last parts of this section discuss queries which iterate over collections, first quantified queries and then **select** queries.

10.3.1 Named queries

The most general and complex form of a query is achieved by creating a program which defines a number of named queries and ends with a single unnamed query. The general form is:

```
define Q₁( p₁₁, p₁₂, …) as <query>
define Q₂( p₂₁, p₂₂, …) as <query which can use Q1 as an atomic component>
...
define Qₙ( pₙ₁, pₙ₂, …) as <query which can use Q₁, Q₂, .. Qₙ₋₁
                                        as atomic components>
```

The named queries are stored in the schema and can be used as part of any subsequent queries.

10.3.2 Atomic queries

The most primitive form of query in OQL is an atomic query. There are three kinds of atomic query:

- An atomic literal, i.e. a literal constant value, of which there are:
    integer literals – such as 25;
    real literals – such as 4.56 or 456e 015 – 2;
    character literals – such as 'A' (note the single quotes for characters);
    string literals – such as "Jane Brown" – note the double quotes for strings;
    boolean literals – **true** or **false**;
    object literals – the null value **nil**.
- A named object. This is an object whose name is in scope, either by being a named root object or by being a variable in scope in a calling program.
- A named query.

10.3.3 Atomically typed expression queries

These comprise the usual kinds of expression provided in programming languages, which include:

- unary numerical expressions of the form:

```
<op> <query>
```

where query is a numerically valued query and op is one of "+", "-" or "abs" or query is a boolean expression and op is "not".

- binary expressions of the form

```
<query₁> <op> <query₂>
```

where both queries have the same type and op is one of:

integer operators – "+", "-", "*", "/", and "mod";
floating point operators – "+", "-", "*", and "/";
boolean operators – "and" and "or";
string operators – "| |" and "+" – both of which mean concatenate the two strings;

- binary relational expressions on values, which return a boolean value and are of the form:

```
<query₁> <op> <query₂>
```

where both queries have the same type and *op* is one of: "=", "!=", "<", "<=", ">", and ">="

10.3.4 Construction queries

OQL permits the construction of new objects and complex values as the result of a query. There are several different constructors available.

Object construction

Given a type, *T*, it is possible to return an object of type *T* as the result of a query by writing:

```
T( prop₁: query₁, prop₂: query₂, ..., propₙ: queryₙ )
```

where the *propᵢ* are the previously defined names of the properties of *T* and the *queryᵢ* return results of the appropriate types.

Structure construction

It is possible to create a record dynamically and return it as the result of the query by an expression of the form:

```
struct( prop₁: query₁, prop₂: query₂, ..., propₙ: queryₙ )
```

in which the *propᵢ* are field names for the record structure which are introduced as part of the query.

Collection construction

Collections can be formed and returned by queries by using the following expressions:

```
set( query₁, query₂, ..., queryₙ )
list( query₁, query₂, ..., queryₙ )
bag( query₁, query₂, ..., queryₙ )
array( query₁, query₂, ..., queryₙ )
```

in each of which all of the queries must have a common type.

10.3.5 Object expressions

Given an object returned as the result of the query, it is possible to dereference the properties, to execute the operations or to return the value of the object. It is also possible to test if two queries have returned the same object. Finally, it is possible to assert that the type of an object is actually a subtype of the type that the expression would normally return.

Dereferencing object properties

If *query* returns an object whose type has a property, *prop*, then either of

```
<query> . <prop>
```

or

```
<query> -> <prop>
```

will return the value of the property. In all examples, the dot operator will be preferred to distinguish property dereferencing from operation invocation, but either are equally acceptable in OQL.

Invoking an object operation

If *query* returns an object whose type has an operation, *oper*, which has no parameters then either of

```
<query> . <oper>
```

or

```
<query> -> <oper>
```

returns the result of the operation.

If the operation has *n* parameters, then the forms must be extended to

```
<query> . <oper>( <query₁>, <query₂>, ..., <queryₙ>,)
```

or

```
<query> -> <oper>( <query₁>, <query₂>, ..., <queryₙ>,)
```

In all of the examples presented here, the arrow operator will be used for operation invocation to distinguish it from dereferencing a property.

Path expressions

A path expression is created by chaining together a number of property references and operation invocations. The general form is therefore:

```
<object query> <op> <char₁> <op> <char₂> ... <op> <charₙ>
```

in which *op* can either be "." or "->" and the *char*$_i$ are the characteristics (i.e. either property names or operation names with actual parameter values supplied if required).

Accessing the value of an object

If *query* returns an object, then the query:

```
* <query>
```

returns the value of the object. This is a literal which holds the same information as the object. Usually this will be a record literal whose fields have the same values as the properties of the object.

Binary relational expressions on objects

These test whether two object names refer to the same object. There are two of these:

```
<object query> = <object query>
<object query> != <object query>
```

which return **true** if the two queries return the same objects and different objects, respectively. The two queries must return values of the same type. Note that neither of these test whether the properties of two objects are the same. That would be tested by:

```
*<object query> = *<object query>
```

which constitutes a shallow test of equality.

Asserting the type of an object

Usually the type of an object will be inferred automatically from the context. Thus

```
select U from U in theUsers
```

will return the bag of users and *U* will have type *User*. Sometimes it is necessary for the programmer to ensure that the object, although retrieved from a collection of one type, is returned as an object of one of the subtypes of this type.

Thus the following might be required:

```
select (Superuser) U from U in theUsers where U . login = "jbrown"
```

which returns a single element set containing the superuser object. Should *jbrown* not be the superuser, then an exception will be raised.

10.3.6 Expressions which manipulate collections

The ODMG data model has a number of collection types – sets, bags, lists and arrays, together with strings which are treated mostly as lists of characters. There are a number of kinds of query which are specific to collections. These provide the normal set operators for unordered collections, membership tests, pattern matching on strings, selection operators from ordered collections, operators which convert from one kind of collection to another and aggregating operations.

Binary set expressions

These are of the form:

```
<collectionQuery₁> <op> <collectionQuery₂>
```

both collections must be either bags or sets and the operator must be one of:

- **union** to create the union of the two collections – removing duplicates in the case of sets and retaining them in the case of bags;
- **intersect** to create the intersection – which, in the case of bags, means retaining the minimum number of duplicates of each value;
- **except**, to create the difference, i.e. the collection containing all of the members of *collectionQuery₁* but not *collectionQuery₂* – in the case of bags, this means iterating over the second bag and, for each value found, removing one matching value out of the first bag if there is one.

If the collections are both sets then the result is a set. If either or both are bags then the result is a bag.

Containment test expressions

These test whether a character is to be found in a string or an element is to be found in a collection – these tests are carried by:

```
<character query> in <string query>
<query> in <collection query>
```

(In the latter case, the query must be the same type as the elements of the collection.)

The result of these tests is a boolean value.

Pattern matching expressions

These use the **like** operator and are of the form:

```
<string query> like <string literal>
```

which returns the value **true** if the string matches the literal, where the latter may include the following wild-card characters:

"?" or "_" match any character;
"*" or "%" match any string including the empty string;

Selection expressions from ordered collections

It is possible to extract either a single element or a sub-sequence of elements from an ordered collection (i.e. a list, an array or a string). It is important to note that the indexes of all ordered collections number the first element as 0.

Selecting single elements uses square brackets to contain the index of the element required. Thus:

<string>[i] returns the ith character of the string;

while

<orderedCollection>[i] returns the ith element of an array or list.

Selecting a sub-sequence requires the first and last index of the sub-sequence to be given, as in:

<string>[i:j] returns the substring of the string from the ith to the jth character;

while

<orderedCollection>[i:j] returns the sub-collection of an array or list starting at the ith element and ending with the jth element;

Converting collections

Given a collection which has only a single member, it is possible to extract that member using:

```
element ( <collectionQuery> )
```

Should the collection hold more or less than a single member, then an exception will be raised.

It is also possible to turn lists and bags into sets by use of:

```
listtoset ( <listQuery> )
```

and

```
distinct ( <bagQuery> )
```

The **distinct** operator can also be used to remove duplicates from ordered collections, thus

distinct(`<listQuery>`)

returns a list with all of its duplicates removed.

Finally it is possible to turn a collection whose elements are themselves collections into a collection which is the union of the elements. This is done by:

flatten(`collectionOfCollectionsQuery`)

The result of this operation depends on the kind of collections involved in the input as follows:

Input Type	Output Type
Any collection of bags	Bag
Any collection of sets	Set
Ordered collection of lists	List
Ordered collection of arrays	Array
Unordered collection of ordered collections	Set

Aggregate expressions

If *query* returns a collection value of any kind then

`<op>(<query>)`

returns a value derived from the collection by use of one of the operators: *min*, *max*, *count*, *sum* and *avg*. The elements of the collection must be numerical for each of these except *count* which can be used to count the number of elements in any collection.

■ 10.3.7 Quantifying expressions

There are three kinds of expression which iterate over collections – the familiar **select ... from ... where** expressions which will be covered in the next subsection and the quantification expressions, **for all** and **exists**.

Both of these construct boolean valued queries out of a collection and a predicate which tests members of the collection. The form of the two expression types is similar:

`for all <iteration-variable> in <collection query> : <boolean query>`

and

`exists <iteration-variable> in <collection query> : <boolean query>`

in which *iteration-variable* introduces a variable which will take as its value each member of the collection in turn. The boolean query will usually include the iteration variable as an atomic element.

The first of these returns **true** if the boolean query evaluates to **true** for every member of the collection. An **exists** expression returns **true** if the boolean query evaluates to **true** for any member of the collection.

■ 10.3.8 The select expression

A select expression returns a collection of values or objects and has the form:

```
select [distinct] <query>
   from <iter₁> in <coll₁>, <iter₂> in <coll₂>, ... , <iterₙ> in <collₙ>
      [where <boolean query>
         [ group by <label₁> : <partitionQuery₁>, ...,
                     <labelₚ> :<partitionQueryₚ> [having <boolean query>] ]
            [ order by <orderQuery₁> [<dir₁>], ..., <orderQueryᵣ> [<dirᵣ>] ]
```

The meanings of the various parts of the query will be described starting with the **from** clause, since this introduces much of the context for the other clauses. Note that the last four clauses in the expression are optional.

The *from* clause

The **from** clause lists the collections, *collᵢ*, which will be searched for candidate data to be returned. In doing so, it introduces iteration variables, *iterᵢ*, which may be used in either of the other two parts. As with the quantification expressions, such a variable takes each member of the collection in turn as its value.

In fact the author has seen three different versions of the syntax of the **from** clause:

```
<iter> in <coll>        e.g. U in theUsers
<coll> as <iter>        e.g. theUsers as U
```

and

```
<coll> <iter>           e.g. theUsers U
```

In this text, the first of these will be used throughout.

The result of the **from** clause is, as usual, to create a Cartesian product of the collections involved. The query will iterate over the "rows" of this product.

The *where* clause

The role of the **where** clause is to filter this Cartesian product in order to focus the data returned by the query. The boolean query which is used may use any of the iteration variables, available names and named queries which have been defined (as described in Section 10.3.2). The usual kinds of query optimization will be employed to reduce the amount of the Cartesian product actually generated.

The *select* clause

The **select** clause determines which parts of the filtered data are actually returned. If the keyword **distinct** is included this will be a set of filtered items, if not then a bag will be returned (unless an **order by** clause is given). In either case the clause determines what type of item will populate the collection that is returned. This may be constructed using any data which is dereferencable by available names, defined queries or iterator variables. Furthermore any of the other expression types described here can be used. In particular, it possible to construct a new type of value or object as the result.

To illustrate the kinds of item which can be returned, here are some of the more familiar kinds of query expression used in a **select** clause:

- an atomic query of the kinds described in Sections 10.3.2 and 10.3.3 – in which case a collection of such values is returned;
- * – which returns the whole of the elements of the Cartesian product;
- $<iter_i>$. $<prop>$, ..., $<iter_j>$ -> $<oper>$ which returns a collection of implicitly created record structures;
- **struct**($prop_1$: $query_1$, $prop_2$: $query_2$, ..., $prop_n$: $query_n$) which returns a collection of explicitly created record structures;
- $<type>$($prop_1$: $query_1$, $prop_2$: $query_2$, ..., $prop_n$: $query_n$) which returns a collection of objects of a previously created type.

Thus the collection can contain values or objects and these can be either implicitly created or explicitly created.

The *group by* clause

The **group by** clause causes the query to partition the data returned into p bags. The clause consists of partitioning expressions which are labeled. The labels provide names for the partitions and the partitioning expressions provide tests for membership of the predicates.

The result of a grouped expression is a set of record structures, which has one field for each of the partitioning expressions and one field, called *partition*, holding the bag that constitutes that partition. There is one such record for each distinct set of values of the partitioning expressions.

Here are two examples:

1. The first example partitions a set of people on the first letter of their name:

    ```
    select * from U in theUsers group by initial: U . name[0]
    ```

    The result of this query would be the set including:

    ```
    struct( initial: 'A', partition: bag of users starting with 'A' )
    struct( initial: 'B', partition: bag of users starting with 'B' )
    ```

    and so on, in which there is one record for each different initial value found.

2. The second example shows the common occurrence of partitioning by use of predicates. Here the storage mailboxes for a user are divided into empty, small and large mailboxes.

    ```
    select M from U in theUsers, M in Mailboxes where M in U . storage
    group by empty: M -> size =0,
       small: M -> size > 0 and M -> size < 100,
       large: M -> size >= 100
    ```

    The result of this query is the following set of structures:

    ```
    struct( empty: true, small: false, large: false,
                                partition: bag of empty mailboxes )
    struct( empty: false, small: true, large: false,
                                partition: bag of small mailboxes )
    struct( empty: false, small: false, large: true,
                                partition: bag of large mailboxes )
    ```

    in which there is one record for each different combination of values for the three partitioning expressions, *empty*, *small* and *large*. Since these are mutually exclusive, there can only be the three records shown.

The *having* subclause

The **group by** clause can be extended with a subclause which can filter out the set of partitions returned. The **having** subclause consists of a boolean query which determines whether or not this partition is returned.

For instance the first of the two queries above can be extended to:

```
select * from U in theUsers group by initial: U . name[0]
                   having count( select * from partition ) > 1
```

The effect of this is that the partition is checked and if there is only one user in the partition, it will not be returned as part of the query. Thus, if there is just one user whose name begins with 'B' then the B partition shown above will be omitted from the answer.

The *order by* clause

The **order by** clause causes the query to return a list instead of a set or bag. The order of the list is determined by the values of the queries given, the list is ordered first by the result of *orderQuery₁*, then where these are the same, on *orderQuery₂*, and so on. The direction of the ordering can also be given as "asc" or "desc" for ascending or descending order. If omitted, the previous direction is used and ascending order is used if no other directions are given.

■ 10.4 OQL in O₂

O₂ provides OQL as an integrated component of the OODBMS. That is, there is not just a single interface which provides access to an OQL interpreter, augmented with an embedded language processor. Instead, there is a query processor component in O₂, which is accessible from any other tool as required. Figure 10.1 demonstrates the structure of the interaction between OQL and the other components.

OQL can be used in the following ways:

- In the textual interface, the OQL interpreter can be summoned. Textual queries are submitted interactively and the results are displayed directly.
- Using O₂Tools, a query window can be opened using the shell facility, from which queries can be executed and into which results can be returned.
- In an O₂C program, there is a system function which takes the query as an argument and returns the query results as a result of the function. The calling program can then use the data in whatever way it sees fit.

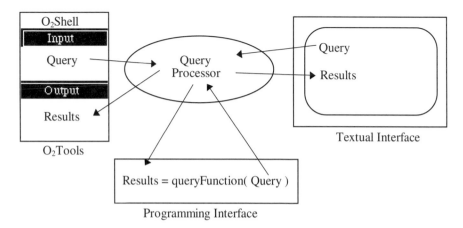

Figure 10.1   OQL in O₂.

- In a C++ program, there is class of queries and members of this class are built from strings using one system function and executed using another.
- In a Smalltalk program, the system class *Database* has an operation which accepts an OQL query as a parameter and which returns the query result.

Each of these will now be discussed.

10.4.1 Interactive use of OQL in O_2

The OQL query processor can be run interactively both in the alphanumeric interface and in the graphical interface, O_2Tools.

Textual interactive use of OQL

The command:

```
query
```

calls the query processor and prompts with:

```
Query Interpreter
type in your query and end with ^D
```

From now on, until an empty line is input, all input should be in OQL. Results will be displayed textually. Literals are displayed using their printable form as usual. Objects are displayed in an HTML-like form, which mixes their structure and the values of their components.

Graphical interactive use of OQL

OQL is used from O_2Tools via the O_2Shell Editor. This is summoned from the dashboard described in Chapter 7 and shown again as Figure 10.2. The O_2Shell Editor is a window with three components – a menu bar at the top, a text input window underneath the menu bar, and a textual output window at the bottom.

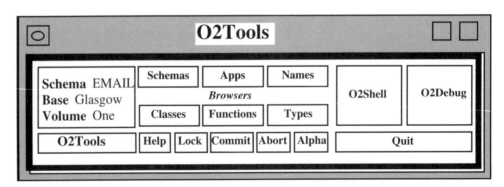

Figure 10.2 The O_2Tools dashboard.

The lower two windows are used similarly to the alphanumeric interface except that input and output are separated.

One of the menus in the menu bar is labeled "Query" and this is used to summon the query processor.

To run a query session, the following should be carried out:

1. Summon the O₂Shell Editor from the dashboard.
2. Enter a query into the input window.
3. From the *Query* menu, select the option *Query* to execute the query and display the results in the output window.
4. If the results are required to be viewed graphically in an O₂Look window, then there is an option in the menu, *Graphic Query*, which should used.

In this way it is possible to write and execute a sequence of queries. There is another way of running the session which is more flexible. The input window can be used to hold a number of queries which can be edited by the user. At any time one of the queries can be selected and then a menu option can be requested which will execute the query composed of the selected text. One such option displays the result in the output window, while another displays the result graphically. Figure 10.3 shows a typical session snapshot using OQL through O₂Tools.

10.4.2 Embedded use of OQL in O₂

Each of the languages which are implemented in O₂ have a method of calling an OQL query during program execution. The basic method used in all cases is to create a query from a string and to pass this to a system function which returns its result to the calling program. The mechanism will be described for each of the languages O₂C, C++ and Smalltalk.

Using OQL from O₂C

In O₂C, there is a system function, called *o2query*, which executes a query. This function can take a variable number of arguments of which the first two are mandatory. The arguments are, in order:

- a variable name to hold the result of the query;
- a string holding the query, possibly including placeholders for parameters of the query;
- (optionally) one expression for each query parameter, which evaluates to the actual value of the parameter.

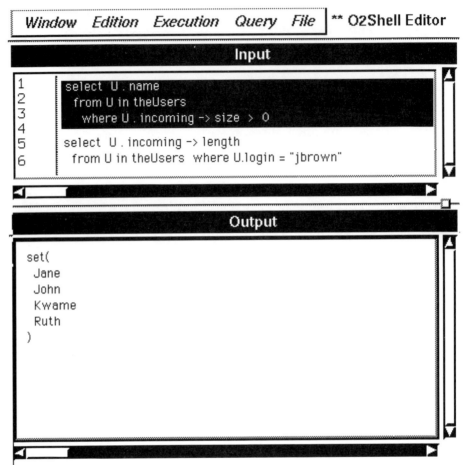

Figure 10.3 Using OQL in O₂ Tools.

For instance, if *aUser* is a variable of type *User*, then the following query returns the user with the login, "jbrown":

```
o2query( aUser, "element( select U from U in theUsers where
                          U . login = \"jbrown\" )" )
```

Alternatively, given another O₂C variable – a string variable called *userLogin* – this query could be generalized to:

```
o2query( aUser, "element( select U from U in theUsers where
                          U . login = $1 )", userLogin )
```

When this second query is executed, the placeholder $1 is replaced by the value of the variable, *userLogin*.

There may be as many placeholders in the query as required, and they must be called $1, $2, $3 and so on. There must then be as many parameter expressions in the call as there are placeholders.

Using OQL from C++

To use OQL in a C++ fragment, the free standing function *d_oql_execute* is used. Unlike O₂C, the C++ binding contains a class whose members are queries – this class is called *d_OQL_Query*. The class *d_OQL_Query* interface contains the following:

- four constructors, for creating a null query, a query from a C++ string (i.e. of type *char); an ODMG string (of class *d_String*) or as a copy of another query;
- a destructor;
- an equality test operator – to test if two references refer to the same query;
- an overloaded operator "<<" for setting the actual value of each query parameter.

To show how these are used, the same two queries will be shown:

```
d_OQL_Query jbQuery(
    "element(select U from U in theUsers where U . login = \"jbrown\" )");
d_oql_execute( jbQuery, aUser );
```

The first line creates the query and the second one executes it.
To use a placeholder, the query becomes:

```
d_OQL_Query genQuery( "element( select U from U in theUsers where
                                 U . login = $1 )" );
genQuery << userLogin;
d_oql_execute( genQuery, aUser );
```

The second line provides the actual value for the parameter *$1*. The general form of the line to provide actual parameter values is:

```
query << ActualValue₁ << ActualValue₂ << ... << ActualValueₙ
```

which takes the original query and adds each actual value in turn.
Chapter 12 has more on the use of OQL from C++.

Using OQL from Smalltalk

Access to OQL within a Smalltalk program is provided via a method defined on the *Database* class.

The *Database* class has a special operation, *query : withArguments*, which executes a query. The second of the two queries above would appear as follows in Smalltalk:

```
aUser := aConnection query: 'element( select U from U in theUsers where
                                                  U . login = $1 )'
                        withArguments (Array with: userLogin )
```

Chapter 13 has more on the use of OQL from Smalltalk.

10.5 OQL queries for the mail application

The chapter finishes by returning to the mail application and determining some queries which might be useful. First, some more complex *ad hoc* queries will be shown to illustrate the language features as they work together. Finally, some queries will be integrated into the application that was developed in Chapter 8.

10.5.1 Further OQL queries

Using the mail schema, here are some more queries that can be defined:

1. Return the names of all mailboxes in the system, together with their user's login and their size.

   ```
   select MB . name, U . name, MB -> size
      from U in theUsers, MB in U . storage
         order by U . name, MB . name
   ```

2. Return the subjects of messages that John has sent to Jane and that she has not discarded, ordered by their date.

   ```
   define john as select U from U in theUsers where U . name = "john"
   define jane as select U from U in theUsers where U . name = "jane"
   define janesBoxes as ( jane . storage ) union set ( jane . incoming )
   define janesHolds as select MB . holds from MB in janesBoxes
   define janesHeldMessages as flatten( janesHolds )
   select MS . subject
       from MS in janesHeldMessages
           where MS . from = john
   ```

3. Return the name of the sender and the recipients of any messages containing the word "secret" in the subject line.

   ```
   select MS . sender . name, ( select R . name from R in
                                                MS . recipients )
       from U in theUsers, MB in ( set( U . incoming ) union U . storage ),
                                                MS in (MB . holds)
          where "secret" in MS . subject
   ```

■ 10.5.2 Queries in the O₂ application

Recall the application as developed in Chapter 8:

```
create application mailControl
    USER currentUser
  program
  public login( userLogin: string);
  public logout ;
  public sendMessage ;
  public checkMailBox( name: string);
  public readMessage( name: string);
  public flushMailBox( name: string)
  public createUser;
  public deleteUser( userLogin: string);
  public statistics;
  public changeSuperUser( userLogin: string; password: string );
end
```

Some of these programs would best be implemented largely in OQL. The advantage of this is that more query optimization will be available than would be the case if all of the programming was done in a programming language.

Of these programs, many are updates for which it is not worth using OQL, but the statistics program needs to retrieve a lot of information and an OQL program may be useful. Also several of the programs depend on finding a user by name. In this section, the *login* and statistics programs will be built in OQL. The queries will use O₂C in this section. The later chapters on C++ and Smalltalk will include versions which are used with those languages.

The *login* program

This program has the user login as a parameter and must return its result into the global variable *currentUser*. The command is therefore:

```
o2query( currentUser,
   "element( select U from theUsers as U where U . login = $1 )",
                                          userLogin )
```

Section 12.5.3 describes how this fits into a C++ application.

The *statistics* program

This has not been fully determined but the definition taken here is that the program is meant to retrieve the following for each user: the number of mailboxes, the number of messages and the name of each mailbox; and the average message size for each mailbox and for the user in total.

It will be necessary to define a type for these statistics:

```
interface STATS
( attribute String userName;
  attribute Integer nBoxes;
  attribute Float overallAveLength;
  attribute struct BOXDETAILS
      { String boxName, Integer nMessages, Float aveLength } boxDetails )
```

Now the program will need a local variable to hold the statistics:

```
o2 STATS theStats
```

and it can be populated with:

```
o2query( theStats,
  "select STATS(
    userName: U . name, nBoxes: count( U . storage ),
    overallAveLength: avg(
      select MS . body -> length
      from MB in ( (U.storage) union set( U.incoming ) ), MS inMB.holds),
    boxDetails : ( select BOXDETAILS(
                      boxName: MB . name,
                      nMessages: MB -> size,
                      aveLength: avg( select MS . body -> length
                                          from MS in MB . holds ) )
                  from MB in ( (U . storage) union set( U . incoming ) ) )
  from U in theUsers" )
```

■ 10.6 Summary

This chapter has described the query language OQL, which was developed by the ODMG for use with ODMG databases. The main points covered were:

- OQL is one of the SQL family of languages.
- OQL only provides querying capability. It has no features for defining data or for updating data (although updating methods can be called inside an OQL query).
- The familiarity of the SQL syntax should enable a user acquainted with SQL to master OQL quickly. Indeed, in so far as the classes resemble tables, querying an ODMG database can be identical to querying a relational database.
- OQL as implemented in O$_2$ is not just a query interface, but may be used as part of the textual, graphical or programming interfaces.

Although this part of the book has emphasized the value of query languages to an OODBMS, such a language is insufficient for expressing a large amount of the computation required for a database supporting a complex application. Instead, there will necessarily be recourse to a programming interface to implement the class operations and to build the applications. Part Four describes programming interfaces for OODBMS.

Part Four

Programming an OODBMS

This part of the book examines the role of the programming language in the use of OODBMS. The increased importance of the programming interface is one of the principal differences between traditional DBMS and OODBMS. This part of the book examines this difference and the kinds of language being proposed. However, providing a programming interface to a database is not a simple matter. Merely extending the scope of the context of a programming language to incorporate a database is not enough. The language has to be the right kind of language and some of the criteria for judging the quality of a programming language change dramatically when long-term storage is seriously considered. Chapter 11 surveys database programming languages with this in mind.

This is followed by chapters which discuss the use of the two principal object-oriented languages, C++ and Smalltalk, for database programming. These two languages have been chosen by the ODMG as important languages which it is vital that an OODBMS should support. A large part of the ODMG standard consists of guidelines for how the languages should be used in the context of a DBMS which complies with the ODMG model.

11 | Database programming languages

Programming with a computationally complete language and manipulating data in a database have traditionally made uneasy bedfellows. The ways in which each of these represent data are significantly different – a difference which can be difficult to resolve. This difficulty has been given the name the *impedance mismatch problem*, the solution to which is the creation of a language which integrates storage mechanisms with facilities for complex data manipulation. Such a language is called a database programming language (DBPL).

DBPLs have been the subject of a great deal of research. Early research was surveyed by Atkinson and Buneman in 1987, a paper which still provides the most appropriate start point, since it clarifies some of the fundamental issues involved. Since then the field has grown, not least due to two interleaved biannual series of workshops concentrating respectively on the implementation of persistent object systems and the design of DBPLs. In this chapter, work up to the present time will be surveyed. Many of the examples described here are not object-oriented languages. The examples chosen are included either because they have historical interest or because they support features which object-oriented database languages either do already possess or would ideally possess to give the greatest possible assistance to the programmer. The following two chapters will then examine mechanisms for using C++ and Smalltalk as database programming languages.

The chapter starts with a section motivating the need for DBPLs. Then follow sections on: the important features which a DBPL should have, a survey of DBPLs, the role of object-oriented programming languages, and a summary.

■ 11.1 Why integrate programming languages with DBMS?

Traditionally, the use of the data in a database is carried out with relatively simple interfaces: parametric interfaces reduce access to minimal complexity by providing a consistent structure within which a few query parameters are entered; graphical interfaces provide an intuitive, if simple, view of the databases; form-based interfaces map very well onto the tabular nature of relational (and indeed much object-oriented) data; and query languages such as SQL provide a stripped-down textual command language for achieving the most commonly needed kinds of data manipulation. Sooner or later, however, there is the need for data manipulation which is sufficiently complex to require the facilities of a full programming language.

One of the major changes when moving from traditional database applications to the advanced applications considered in Chapter 1 is that this point is reached much sooner and that consequently a programming interface is much more important. This section contrasts the two kinds of language interface: a querying interface is one which uses a language like SQL; while a programming interface uses a language which is computationally complete.

In a relational DBMS, all of the data is kept in very simple structures. This makes possible the provision of simple access mechanisms such as SQL. SQL is built around constructs which allow parts of tables to be systematically retrieved and pairs of tables to be combined to form larger tables. The operations provided by SQL are simple and can be systematically combined.

Even in this restricted world, SQL is insufficient in at least two ways:

- the expression of complex queries quickly becomes very difficult;
- there are a range of computations involving recursive iteration which SQL cannot express at all.

The kinds of SQL query which test for the existence of data in one table leading to the extraction of data from others, involving quantifiers, set tests and so on, are already beyond the range of most database users. Queries which use recursive iteration over tables, for instance finding all of the ancestors of a person in a genealogical database, cannot be expressed at all. Thus, on the one hand, programming with SQL becomes, in some cases, at least as difficult as managing a well-designed programming language, and, on the other hand, programming language functionality has, in any case, become a necessity.

Moving to an object-oriented data model exacerbates this situation. Traversing the data structures is now a much more complex task involving much more variety, since objects, literals and different kinds of data structure all take part. Chapters 9 and 10 have demonstrated that a query language for objects can be developed and does continue to be a vital aspect of an OODBMS, but the increased complexity of the data model means that there are many tasks involved in the use of the DBMS that are easier to carry out using a programming language.

Furthermore, the object-oriented model encapsulates operations with the data, and these operations require implementation, which, in general, must be done by programming. In addition, there is an increased need to integrate derived data and to include values with components which are program code. Again, a programming language will provide a superior mechanism for this.

In summary, although a query language will continue to be useful in providing a relatively simple and optimizable means of achieving data access, recourse to programming becomes much more important in an OODBMS, since then both simple and complex forms of data access can be carried out in the same language. For all of these reasons, a programming language moves to center stage. However, this means a language which has appropriate mechanisms for describing and manipulating data that is to be held in a database. The next section will look at what such a language should provide.

▨ 11.2 The important features required of a persistent language

A database programming language must support the expression of two activities: access to data held in long-term storage, and the implementation of algorithms. Unfortunately, the data structures suitable for these two activities have traditionally been different in important ways. Data storage has involved the use of simple collections, with facilities to edit their membership and to iterate over them. Algorithms on the other hand, have been implemented in terms of structures which interrelate data in more complex ways. The computational structures of database languages are, typically, quite minimal, consisting of controlled iteration over collections. On the other hand, the computational structures of a programming language provide looping and conditional constructs as well as mechanisms for modularizing the code, since "programming in the large" becomes an important issue.

In bringing these two aspects together, it is important to keep clear what are the crucial properties that a combination must contain. In particular, the following issues are vital:

- the type system and how appropriate it is for data modeling;
- the management of collections;
- the provision of types which a DBMS can use to specify domains – temporal, spatial and monetary types for instance;
- the provision of other kinds of DBMS object – databases, locks, transactions and so on;
- the ways in which the code is integrated with the database;
- the computational constructs provided.

In the next section these properties will be discussed, but first approaches to combining a DBMS and a programming language will be examined.

11.2.1 Integrating DBMS facilities into a programming language

In the discussion and the survey that follows it, two ideas should be kept in mind: the way in which the DBMS facilities and the programming language have been brought together, and the way new features have been made available in the language.

There are three approaches to combining DBMS and programming facilities:

1. combining a DBMS with a language by integrating the DBMS data model into the language type system and by adding computational constructs which manipulate the data model;
2. extending the support for a programming language from a purely run-time system to a persistent system;
3. starting from scratch and designing a language which has all of the programming and database characteristics needed.

In practice, the first two of these approaches dominate, since familiarity with much of the resulting language is felt to be important. Completely novel languages do not, in general, thrive.

In extending a language to encompass DBMS capabilities, there are two ways to proceed:

- The additional facilities can be *built-into* the language by extending the syntax.
- The language can be left alone but already existing generic features, such as the function library or the class hierarchy, can be used to hold the new facilities, which are thus *added-onto* the language.

The two approaches can be illustrated by using the example of adding transactions to a language – transaction support being a vital feature that a language must provide if it is to be a **database** programming language. This could be achieved by providing extra syntax, as in:

```
open transaction TX1;
... updates;
commit transaction TX1;
```

or by providing a class for transactions:

```
TX1 = new Transaction;
TX1 -> open();
... updates;
TX1 -> commit();
```

The advantage of the former method is to permit the language implementors to produce some efficiency gains by fine tuning the requirements of the particular construct. In addition, older languages may not have suitable generic features for the alternative approach. The advantage of the latter method is that the language is kept small and simple, requiring less for the new programmer to learn.

■ 11.2.2 Atkinson and Buneman's four main principles

In their landmark paper, Atkinson and Buneman produce a number of guidelines on the design of a DBPL and then survey a number of early DBPLs with regard to the these guidelines. The guidelines are the consequence of four main principles: persistence, an adequate type system, data type completeness and expressive power.

Persistence

The concept of persistence has been described in Chapter 3. A DBPL must include some mechanism for controlling the transfer of data to and from the database and this can be more or less confined to particular kinds of data; and can also be more or less explicitly indicated by the programmer. In the context of a DBPL, therefore, a number of desirable features arise, which can be restated here:

- If a value can be described in the language, it should be able to be stored, no matter what type it is.
- When data is stored, it should not lose its type or be accessible by operations other than those provided for this type.
- Explicit storage commands are unnecessary and distracting. "The required transfers between stores can, and should, be inferred from the operations on the data."
- On the other hand, the type descriptions of the data should not determine the organization of the data on the disk. In particular, it is not a good idea to restrict the organization of stored objects to the extents of their classes.

Types for data definition

One of the key areas in combining programming and data management is the mechanism for describing the data. Combining a type system with a data model is extremely tricky since low-level programming concepts and high-level data modeling constructs may not fit well together. Indeed, one approach is to continue to separate the two by providing a data modeling tool which maps down to the programming language.

However, to provide full DBPL functionality, an adequate type system will be required. This means at least two things:

- The type system must be suitably expressive. It must provide specific types for the most useful kinds of basic data, type constructors for the most common kinds of compound data and generic and polymorphic types to enable flexibility in data and application definition.
- The type system must be secure. It must ensure that data is not misused, which it can achieve by checking that the operations invoked on them are appropriate for their types. Preferably this will occur as the program is constructed (static type checking), but sometimes necessarily when it is run (dynamic type checking).

Sections 11.2.3 and 11.2.4 examine each of these in detail.

Data type completeness

Having provided an appropriate type system, it is important that all general-purpose system facilities be available to data of all types. Here are some of the ways in which data of every type should be able to be used:

- There may be variables in the program whose value is of that type.
- Values of that type may be the arguments or results of functions or procedures.
- Values of that type may be the components of bulk objects.
- Values of that type may be stored in the database.

A programming system in which facilities of these kinds are available to all types is called *data type complete*. In fact, most programming languages are not data type complete, but place restrictions on some types of data. A type which has all of these facilities is said to be a *first-class* type. A data type complete language is one in which all types are first-class.

A related term which is used to describe a particular feature as being *orthogonal* to the others. This means that there is no interaction between features and no restriction on how they can be combined. For instance, if there can be collections of one kind of value but not of others then the provision of collections is not orthogonal. If all features are added orthogonally then a language will be data type complete.

The reason why this is an important issue is that a data type complete language is both simpler to use and more powerful than a non-data type complete language. Every departure from the complete provision of a facility has to be remembered by programmers, who in some cases will need to program around the gap. This double improvement is, of course, bought at the price of complicating the implementation of the language, which is why most languages are not complete.

In the following, one issue is whether or not functions or procedures are provided with the same power as other kinds of data. In the section on PS-algol, it will be argued that this is a desirable feature, although not one found in commercial systems so far.

Expressive power

Atkinson and Buneman's final point is an argument for the value of a computationally complete language in much the same way as that carried out in Section 11.1.

■ 11.2.3 Type systems for database management

The first goal in designing a DBPL is to create a type system which is appropriate for data modeling. This will involve appropriate base types, a set of type constructors and possibly generic and polymorphic types of some kind. This section will look at each of these.

In the process of examining the different categories of types, two issues should be kept in mind – expressivity and implementation. Each of the categories of type described here are undeniably useful and to do without any one of them will force the programmer, in some circumstances, to achieve the same effect by less desirable and more indirect means. However, to have all of them is a daunting implementation effort (in some cases leading to undecidable type checking) and will also complicate the language for novice users. All languages choose a trade-off of some kind.

Base types

These are the fundamental building blocks of any development system for data manipulating software. There should be types for numbers, character strings, booleans and also multimedia data. For this latter purpose, some DBPLs include the bit-string as a base data type. The semantics of various kinds of multimedia type can then be built on top of this. PS-algol and Napier88 provide the multiplane pixel as a base type and a type constructor to create bitmapped images out of pixels.

The main use for base types in traditional DBMS is to provide types for *domains*. However, the set of domain types used in database work tends to be different from the set of base types typically provided in a programming language. Databases rarely use booleans, but they often provide currency types or temporal types.

It is therefore necessary for a DBPL to have a fairly extensive set of base types – including programming language base types, multimedia types and database domain types.

User-defined types and recursion

At first, programming languages such as Fortran presented the programmer only with a pre-defined set of types. Quickly, however, languages such as Pascal introduced the ability to declare new type names in the language and then to use them as if they were built-into the language. Thus, for instance, for documentary purposes, it might be valuable to create a numerical type as a synonym for the integer types as in:

```
Let catalogNumber = integer
```

Clearly, the ability to introduce new types is a necessary feature for any DBPL if the type system is to be used to describe schemata. All DBPLs have this feature therefore. Type declarations may be separated from other parts of the language by specialized keywords, such as "class", or they may be introduced in the same way as other data. For instance, some DBPLs follow ML in allowing declarations anywhere in the program by use of the keyword **let**. Some languages (Tycoon and Fibonacci) are adopting a standard in which type manipulating operations use keywords starting with a capital letter, while the equivalent keyword starting with a lower-case letter introduces the equivalent operation on instances. Thus a value in Tycoon or Fibonacci would be introduced with the keyword **let**, while a type is introduced by the keyword **Let**, as above.

Most, if not all, schemata of any complexity will have recursive references between the types. In the electronic mail example, *Message* and *Mailbox* refer to each other. It is vital therefore to be able to define types with mutual references and this means that the system must accept the definition of a type in which components have types which have yet to be defined. From the programmer's point of view the best way to achieve this is to allow forward references and let the compiler sort out at the end what has not been defined properly. Unfortunately, most languages prohibit this and instead provide one of the following mechanisms:

- force the programmer to make dummy definitions as in:
  ```
  Let typeTwo = nulldef;
  Let typeOne = ... uses typeTwo ... ;
  Let typeTwo = ... proper definition which uses typeOne ... ;
  ```

- provide a special syntax for recursive definition:
  ```
  Let typeOne = ... uses typeTwo ... ;
    & typeTwo = ... uses typeOne ... ;
  ```

in which the "&" means define all of the linked types simultaneously.

Type constructors

Any database system or programming language will need to support the creation of data structures. To this end, programming languages provide type constructors with which it is possible to create new types of data as needed. A type constructor is a partially defined type, the rest of which is parameterized, often by other types. Programming languages usually provide the record constructor and the array in this way. For instance, an array is parameterized in terms of its bounds and the type of its elements, so to create an array of 100 *User* values, the type *SomeUsers* would be defined (abstractly) as Array[1, 100, User].

Database systems require other bulk types for precision of modeling and type constructors are the way in which these are provided. Here are some of the ones which might be provided:

- collection types such as set, list, sequence, bag, fixed length array and variable length array;
- union or variant types which create types with more than one form – for instance, the type *Number* might be created as a variant of integers and reals;
- record types;
- table, dictionary or map types, which provided associative access by pairing key and result values.

A DBPL may well build in the use of a type constructor. For instance, Fibonacci has syntax for defining sequences, while records, variants and arrays are built into most languages. In this case, there is a syntactic unit in the language for declaring and using a bulk type, such as (in Pascal):

```
SomeUsers = array[1::100] User;
```

Often, however, at least some type constructors will be provided as add-ons, by specializing one of the general purpose facilities in the language – for instance, generic type constructors.

Generic type constructors

A generic type constructor provides a way of describing new type constructors and thus adding to the power of the language. For instance, if the language does not include a list type, this can be added as a specialization of the generic type, by a declaration similar to:

```
Let List[T] = record( value: T; next: List[T] )
```

which states that, for any type *T*, a list element is a record which pairs a value of that type with a pointer to another list element of the same type. It is then possible, to use this later in the program to declare new types, such as:

```
Let UserList = List[ User];
```

Generic constructors are increasingly provided in languages – an example is the template class mechanism which has been added to C++. A language without such a mechanism forces the programmer to use more indirect means to achieve the same purpose.

Polymorphic functions

Just as type constructors can be parameterized, so too can code modules, such as functions or procedures. In order to express operations which ignore part of the type of their parameters, some languages provide polymorphic functions.

For instance to count the length of the list, the following function might be declared:

```
let length = fun[T]: List[T] -> integer;
```

in which *length* is parameterized by the element type of the list. It is important to note a subtle difference between generic types and polymorphic functions. The former are not fully specified, so *List[T]* cannot have any instances – it must be completed by providing a concrete type for *T*. On the other hand, *length* is fully specified since it is possible to write code which iterates over any list, ignoring the element type, and thus implement the specification.

Both generic types and polymorphic functions can be described as being *universally quantified*. The definitions of *List* and *length* can be read as being prefaced by "for any type *T*". Some languages, notably Tycoon, provide a generalization of this called *bounded quantification*. In such a language it is possible to write:

```
let countMen = fun [T ≤ Person ] : List[T] -> integer;
```

meaning only define *countMen* on lists of types which are subtypes of *Person*, because the implementation is going to make use of a *sex* property which will only be defined in the class *Person*.

Abstract data types

An abstract data type (ADT) is one in which some part of the type has been hidden. Unfortunately, there are two flavors of ADT provided in programming languages:

- An *algebraic ADT* hides at least part of the representation and exports the operations associated with it – classes in OOPLs are abstract data type in that sense.
- A *logical ADT* provides a common interface to a number of representation types, called *witness types*. This kind of ADT – also called an *existentially quantified type* – is beyond the scope of this book.

Algebraic ADTs are the backbone of object-oriented systems. Bertrand Meyer states that all object-oriented programming is the creation of ADTs. Most modern DBPLs will provide some way of providing ADTs.

Object types and pointers

Much of the foregoing has been about the ability to describe particular kinds of structure. There remains to be discussed the semantics of accessing values with those structures. One important distinction which has been maintained throughout this book has been the one between objects and literal values. In general, it can be said that instances of base classes are literals (even if the language hides the difference for programming simplicity), while instances of ADTs are objects. There is, however, no uniformity in the semantics of constructed types.

There are two possible semantics for the ways in which constructed values are used:

- They are literal values in which case making a copy creates a new value, which includes new copies of all of its components and testing equality means testing the equality of the components. This is called a *value semantics*.
- They are objects in which case copying means copying a reference to the same object which is now shared, while equality testing means checking whether or not two references refer to the same object. This is called a *pointer semantics*.

The ODMG model provides both kinds of constructed type as discussed in Chapter 5. The DBPLs discussed here vary in their approach. In Pascal/R, for instance, all constructed types produce literals. In Napier88, on the other hand, records and arrays are objects with pointer semantics.

Even when it is clear that objects are being constructed, the treatment of the references to them tend to differ between languages. C++ for instance, being a superset of C, provides operators for distinguishing addresses and values pointed at and even provides pointer arithmetic. Other languages have cleaned this up considerably and most of the languages discussed here provide a sharing pointer semantics. In such a language, an object variable holds a pointer to the object and dereferencing the "value" of the object is achieved via the characteristics of the class of the object. The address of the object is not manipulable by the programmer.

Dynamic types

Another useful way of providing polymorphism is via the use of a type which essentially represents the unwillingness of the programmer to make any restriction at this point on the type of the schema component being defined. Such a type is called a dynamic type and will usually have the property of being a supertype of all other types – it is often referred to as *top* in type theory for that reason.

In programming languages, such as Amber and Napier88, this type is called **any** and it is used anywhere where a more precise specification would be unnecessarily restrictive or where no restriction is, in fact, possible. For instance, there might be a need for a list whose members are not all of the same type.

Here is a declaration of such a list:

```
Let heterogeneousList = List[ any ]
```

Another way of thinking about dynamic types is that they generalize union types to be infinite union types, i.e. unions of all possible types. One place in which dynamic types are profoundly useful in database systems is where some kind of extension is envisaged which has not yet been determined. For instance, in creating the electronic mail system, it is clear that the schema so far produced is not exhaustive of all of the data structures which might prove useful. One way of producing a schema, which is securely described for immediate use and yet leaves a place for subsequent extension, is to add to each of the classes a property, called *extension* say, which is of type **any**. It would then be possible to create new classes – *User2*, *Mailbox2*, etc. – which describe the new properties and to which the *extension* properties will refer. Unfortunately, C++ provides no dynamic types. Even more unfortunately, Smalltalk provides only a dynamic type and nothing else.

The main problem with dynamic types is that they prevent static type checking which will be discussed in the next section.

Environments

An environment is a set of bindings which pair identifiers with typed values. Environments are also a kind of dynamic type which can be thought of in at least three ways: as extensible records, as typed directories, or as manipulable symbol tables. Languages, such as Galileo, Fibonacci and Napier88, which have environments, use them to organize the database in much the same way as the directory structure is used to organize a file system.

The mail database could be organized as an environment containing two bindings:

- *theUsers* which is bound to a set of user objects; and
- *superUser* which is bound to the superuser object.

Environments have operations to add and remove bindings at run-time and also to bring bindings out of the environment into the current scope of the program. However, using these facilities prevents static type checking of the bindings used in this way, since it is no more possible for the compiler to check which bindings are held in an environment than it is to check the contents of an array. Thus if a program specifies that it will use a particular binding from an environment, failure of the existence or the correct typing of that binding can only be discovered when the program is run.

Null and bottom types

Finally, there is the need to consider null values. Most object systems provide a value, usually called **nil**, which can be used wherever an object reference is required, but no object is available. The semantics of null values is itself an interesting area of research and a range of null values with different properties would be useful to cover cases like "not known", "not needed" and "not applicable". However, all systems known to the author only provide at most one null value.

Ideally, **nil** should be sole member of the type, often called **null,** which is the subtype of every other type. This is the inverse of **any** discussed above and so is called *bottom* in type theory. However, some languages (for instance Napier88) do not implement it in this way, since then all of the implementation software of the system must be prepared to look out for **nil** wherever it expects any object and this can be costly in efficiency. Instead Napier88 makes **null** a base type, unrelated to any other type.

■ 11.2.4 Type security for database management

The type security requirement centers on the issue of **type checking**. A declaration associates an identifier with a type, either implicitly or explicitly, creating a binding. In the design of programming languages, it has come to be recognized that the enforcement of declarations is vital for supporting the creation of correct software. When managing long-lived data, this issue becomes even more important.

Here is an example of the problem in a nutshell:

```
identifier I is declared to be of type T
operation O is invoked on identifier I
```

but does type *T* have the operation *O*? There are a number of ways that a language can deal with this problem:

- Use a compiler, which checks all uses of all identifiers to ensure that each operation is valid. If it is invalid, give an error message. This is called *static type checking*.
- Check the operation when the program is running, but before the operation is invoked. If the operation is invalid, abort the program. This is called *dynamic type checking*.

In general, static type checking is to be preferred, especially in the database context. Static type checking verifies the correctness of the code as soon as possible and assists the debugging process. Leaving the check to run-time delays, the correctness check and, in the context of a large database application, raises the possibility of bugs buried deep inside rarely executed code, which are not encountered until years after the software is installed.

Unfortunately, static type checking has the negative effect of restricting the kind of code which can be written, since it removes the possibility of using dynamic types or environments. Many languages, such as Eiffel, therefore do not provide these. For full flexibility, however, dynamic types are useful and so a mixture of dynamic and static type checking is desirable, although the emphasis should always be on the latter.

Another issue is the way in which type checking is carried out. In general there are two techniques used:

- *Structural type checking* examines the inner structure of the two types and is satisfied only if they have the same structure – for instance if they are both record types, do they have the same number of fields, with the name and type of each being the same.
- *Nominal type checking* accepts that two types are the same only if they have been declared to have the same name.

For instance, consider two record types, both consisting of two integers named *x* and *y*, but one, *Point*, intended to be used for points in x, y space and the other, *Size*, to be used for the sizes of rectangular areas. A structural type check will accept them as being the same, while a nominal type check will not. There are even some differences between different structural type checking strategies. In some systems *Point* and *Size* would be considered the same type, even if the names of the fields are different, just as long as the types are the same. Which is required varies from situation to situation, but most languages use one strategy for consistency.

A slightly different facility is the ability of some systems to discover whether the type of one value is a subtype of a particular type. This is necessary, for instance, if inheritance is used and an object can be used wherever an object or one of its supertypes is expected.

Subtype checking uses two techniques – explicit or implicit checking. Explicit subtype checking is similar to nominal equivalence because it uses programmer declarations to test which types are subtypes of each – using inheritance assertions for instance. Implicit subtype checking examines the structure of the types and uses a set of rules to determine whether one is a subtype of another. One typical rule is that if the system finds two record types, *A* and *B*, then *A* is a subtype of *B* if it has all of the fields that *B* has together with some additional ones.

Finally, many of the languages discussed here follow ML and use *type inferencing* to determine the type of a value rather than rely on declaration. In such systems, which are usually interactive, the user types "1" and the system works out that this is an integer. Similarly if "[1, 5.3]" is entered this must be a record with an integer field and a real field. Even quite complex type systems, such as those underlying Fibonacci and Tycoon, can make use of type inferencing in this way.

■ 11.2.5 Domain types

Database systems usually provide the user with a set of atomic types for describing useful kinds of data. Typical examples include strings, monetary values, spatial locations, dates and times. Programming languages rarely provide types such as these. Even strings are provided as arrays of characters as often as not, rather than as atomic values in their own right. A DBPL will be expected to support domain types of this kind or, at least, some means of creating them.

■ 11.2.6 Collections

Database work centers around the use of collections, such as sets and lists. Programming languages, on the other hand, usually provide indexable arrays. Database collection elements are usually identified by their values, while programming language collections are identified by position.

Resolving the difference in this case is relatively straightforward – provide everything from both environments. Even within a particular collection type, it is possible to provide facilities from both worlds – for instance, it would be useful to allow arrays to be queried over, and lists to be accessed by position. Given a language with generic types, this is relatively easily achieved by providing type constructors. The template class of C++, for instance, is an ideal mechanism for expressing novel collection types. Given the wide range of bulk types which might be required – there are many different kinds of lists and trees as well as stacks, queues and so on – it is important to have an extensible environment so that these can be added. Moreover, for any collection type, there is a potentially large number of operations which might be provided (Napier88, for instance, comes with a library containing over 100 operations on bulk types), so the ability to extend the operations available on any particular type is valuable.

As well as the collection types themselves, one useful way of controlling the iteration process is to provide an *iterator type*. An iterator is not specific to the type of the elements of the collection, but can be attached to any collection. The role of the iterator is to act as a reference to each element of the collection in turn. The order used will be meaningful only if the collection is itself ordered, such as a list or sequence, while an arbitrary order has to be imposed for notionally unordered collections such as bags or sets. The only important feature of the arbitrary ordering is that it is consistent.

The iterator type will be provided with operations which:

- set the iterator to refer to the "first" member of the collection;
- step the iterator onto the "next" member;
- test whether it is at the "end" of the collection;

and one or more operations which manipulate the member to which the iterator is currently pointing.

Iterators are usually created by invoking an operation on the collection object and will be used as follows:

```
iterator := collection -> createIterator();
iterator -> first();
repeat
    begin
        value := iterator -> getValue()
        ... make use of value referred to by the iterator
    end
  while not iterator -> last()
    do iterator -> next()
```

11.2.7 DBMS objects

Quite separate from the issue of object persistence is the issue of how to support DBMS style access to the data. This is a matter of providing some structuring mechanisms for data, metadata and application code. To this end, a DBPL will usually provide a number of built-in types for a selection of the following:

- *Databases* – A database object will hold a coherent set of data arising in the context of an application. The type should provide mechanisms for creating, opening and closing the database, as well as a means of inserting, retrieving and deleting data. The database access may well have modes for read-only or write-enabled access. The insertion operation may only be needed for root objects, with reachable data being inserted automatically.
- *Schemata* – These hold the description of a database structure, in terms of a collection of types. A schema type will require operations to add and remove types named objects and queries to and from the schema.

- *Transactions* – A transaction is used to build a number of updates into an atomic change to the database. A transaction type should be provided with operations to start the transaction, to abort the transaction and to complete it successfully saving any changes securely in the database – called committing the transaction. There may well also be an operation to save the data part-way through the transaction – usually called a checkpoint. Several systems restrict all access to persistent data to lie within transactions. Transactions may be nested or not.
- *Locks* – Many systems handle locking automatically, but others permit the programmer to lock the data they are using. In which case, there may be a number of kinds of lock and an operation for attaching a lock to a value.
- *Sessions* – Some systems provide a surrounding structure for access to the DBMS server, called a session. A session type will provide operations to connect to a server and to break the connection.

As already noted, access to these structures may be via syntactic extensions to the language or by using, for instance, the class hierarchy to hold classes with the required operations.

11.2.8 Code integration

As discussed in Section 1.1.5, one increasingly important issue is the degree to which the code is integrated into the DBMS. Figure 11.1 gives a historical perspective on the development in this area.

The figure shows five organizational structures for data (boxes) and code (circles). In pre-DBMS times, all code and data were held in the file system, with unstructured references connecting the different code and data items. The DBMS (the rounded box) brought clarity to the data, organizing them and shielding them from misuse. Extensions to relational systems, such as POSTGRES, make a start at managing code as well, since schemata can now include references to code bodies, although these are still held in the file system. Object orientation brings the code into the database in the form of user-defined operations attached to types. An alternative is provided by persistent programming languages in which the code is held in the database, but not in a rigid form. In a persistent programming language, the differences in the data storage facilities provided for code and data disappear completely.

Why should storage of code matter? This is a consequence of the increased importance of code. Much more of the specification of data integrity and even of the values of data are held as code, in which case, keeping the code "out in the cold" is no longer supportable.

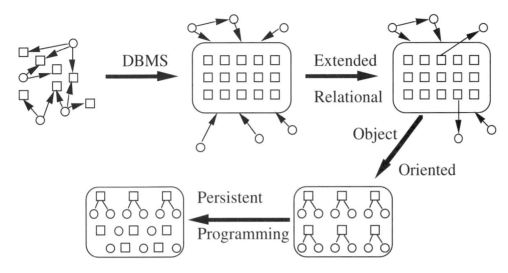

Figure 11.1 The management of code and data.

11.3 Some important database programming languages

In this section, some of the more important attempts to create a database programming language will be considered. The survey is broken into different approaches. It starts with a brief discussion of embedding query languages and then continues with: database extensions to existing languages, programming languages built on data models, polymorphic languages, and finally persistent programming languages. The survey will concentrate on the ways in which the languages provide the features so far discussed.

11.3.1 Embedded query languages

The most primitive attempt to provide a language with database access and programming capability is to embed a database query language inside a programming language. The programming language syntax is extended with a construct which permits a query to be embedded within the code in a way which gives the query a means of accessing both the database and the variable space of the program. Here is an example:

```
string aName = "Jim";          // variable declared in the PL
user = $select U from theUsers  // query delimited by $...;
       where U . name = $aName;
```

As can be seen this is not the most elegant of way of accessing the database. The combination of two languages joined by an ugly seam is unnecessarily complex. The programmer has to create a language representation which corresponds to the database description and to keep these two representations consistent. Moreover the connecting channel is quite constrained – the data has to be reduced to the lowest common denominator of the two systems – and this usually means scalar literal values. The critical problem, however, is that the programmer has to manage two languages at once.

On the other hand, the ability to continue to use querying to achieve simple kinds of access to the data does have two important advantages. In some cases, it can be easier to write the query than to write a program fragment and, more importantly, it is likely that the system will be able to optimize a query, but not a program fragment.

For these reasons, the embedded query language continues to be a feature of modern DBMS, as discussed in the previous two chapters. Notice however, that in the ODMG proposal both the programming language and the query language are built around a common object model. The ODMG data model becomes "the lowest common denominator", but this is one in which much more of the semantics of the application can be maintained across the seam between the two languages, since objects can be transmitted between the two components.

■ 11.3.2 Merging a data model with an existing programming language

One approach to the problem of creating a DBPL is to start with a programming language and extend it to encompass a data model and database facilities. In this section, three such attempts are considered: Pascal/R, DBPL and Adaplex. Pascal/R extends Pascal with first-normal form relations. DBPL extends Modula2 with nested relations. Adaplex extends Ada with a functional data model including complex entities and inheritance. DBPL and Adaplex also add a transaction mechanism.

Pascal/R

The first attempt to produce a seamless database programming language was Pascal/R designed and implemented by Joachim Schmidt and his group. In this language, the type system of Pascal was extended to include constructors for databases and relations and the computational model was extended to support iteration and selection over relations.

In Pascal/R, the electronic mail database would look like:

```
User = relation login of          Message = relation MSid of
   record name: string;              record MSid: integer;
          login: string;                   subject: string;
          password: string;                body: string;
          incoming: integer;               sender: string;
   end;                              end;

Mailbox = relation MBid of         HeldIn = relation message, mailbox of
   record MBid: integer;              record message: integer;
          name: string;                     mailbox: integer;
          owner: string;             end;
   end;

Recipients = relation message, receiver of
   record message: integer;
          receiver: string;
   end;

Email = database
   theUsers: User;
   theMailboxes: Mailbox;
   theMessages: Message;
   theStorageBoxes: StorageBoxes;
   theRecipients: Recipients;
  end
```

Notice that the Pascal record type has been used as the basis for defining a relation type (with a key given after the keyword **relation**), although only atomically valued fields are allowed, so foreign keys must be provided (*MSid* and *MBid*). The schema is further complicated by the need to provide intersection relations for message recipients and mailboxes containing messages. The database then consists of relational instances of each of the five relational types that were defined. The dot operator is then available to select fields from relations and to select relations from records.

The computational additions include the following:

- a **for each** command to iterate over the records in a relation – for instance:

  ```
  for each U in Email . theUsers do writeLn( U . name );
  ```

- a selection operator, **each**, which returns some of the records in a relation – for instance:

  ```
  unreadMailUsers := each U in Email . theUsers U, Email . theMailboxes MB:
               U . incoming = MB . MBid and MB . number > 0;
  ```

- an **in** operator to test if a particular record is in a relation.

Pascal/R constitutes an elegant extension of Pascal's syntax to provide access to relational databases. However, there is the considerable drawback that the database constructs cannot be orthogonally used with the other features of the language. A relation may not be based on a nested record structure, for instance.

Following Pascal/R, there were a number of other proposals for embedding the relational model in a programming language of which Rigel, built on top of Ingres, and Plain were the most important. The Pascal/R group continued their work in the same direction as the developers of Pascal, by moving on to add relations to Modula, firstly in the form of Modula/R and then DBPL.

DBPL

As a follow-up to the work on Pascal/R, the language DBPL was designed as an extension to Modula2. Some of the features of DBPL are:

- A relational type constructor, but one in which the fields need not be atomic (although keys must be). Relations have the following facilities available:

  - the ability to create instances by listing the records in the relation;
  - the quantifiers, **SOME** and **ALL** which range over relations;
  - the operator **EACH** as in Pascal/R and also operators for creating cartesian products;
  - relational operators for set insertion and deletion.

- Transactions which are code modules that access persistent data and are managed by a serializing transaction manager. Transactions can be named and parameterized.
- Selectors, which constrain the records which may be held in a relation.
- Constructors, which create derived relations, i.e. views.
- A database constructor, which creates modules which can contain type definitions, variable declarations and transaction definitions. All of the declarations in a database module create persistent values which can be accessed concurrently by many processes.

The DBPL system also provides gateways to external relational systems, such as INGRES, by providing a tool which permits a DBPL relational variable to be attached to a table managed by the DBMS.

Adaplex

DAPLEX is the language which Shipman designed as a data definition and manipulation language for the functional data model, FDM. In FDM, all data is modeled by functions. There are functions which represent entity types (organized into an inheritance hierarchy), functions which retrieve stored attributes and functions which calculate derived data. DAPLEX permits the declaration of these functions and it also provides querying commands.

Adaplex is a DBPL which brings together FDM and the programming language, Ada. Adaplex uses the same functional style as DAPLEX, but in the context of Ada's syntax. A database is declared in a similar way to DBPL, except that inheritance between types is permitted. A more important difference is the limitation that the declaration creates a single database, rather than a schema with multiple coexisting databases. Transactions are provided as fragments of Ada code delimited by the keywords **atomic** and **end atomic**.

Discussion

Designing a language which brings together a data model and a programming language is a difficult undertaking because of the differences in the features of the two components being integrated. Inevitably, the designer is forced down to the lowest common denominator. It is instructive from these three examples that the quality of the resulting DBPL depends largely on the sophistication of the data model being integrated – DBPL is much more expressive than is Pascal/R for instance, since it is not restricted to first normal form. One problematic feature is that many of the best features of the language become unusable in the proximity of the database components, so attention is now turned to an approach which starts from the data model and then only adds those programming features which are appropriate for managing data describable in that data model.

■ 11.3.3 Persistent data models

The next approach is to start with a data model and to extend this with persistence. The most notable work in this area is carried out by the group led by Antonio Albano at the University of Pisa leading to the two languages, Galileo and Fibonacci. The Pascal/R group have also taken this route with their most recent work, which has designed an object-based system and language called Tycoon. This section will look at these three languages.

It should be noted first that all of these languages and the ones in the next section are strongly influenced by the functional language ML and the way it is used. ML is usually described as "an interactive language of expressions". Access to the system is achieved by the user entering expressions, which the system then checks and evaluates. ML uses type inferencing to deduce the type of the expression and then evaluates it accordingly, while the languages in this section depend upon the programmer explicitly providing definitions of the types involved. This is a more suitable approach for languages which include features for data definition. The languages in Section 11.3.4 use type inferencing as well.

Galileo

Galileo was designed to be a language which tries to combine the best of semantic data modeling (classification, aggregation and specialization) with a rich type system and a modularization mechanism. Galileo is in the style of ML, but is statically typed. All interaction with Galileo takes place in the context of an environment.

As discussed in Section 11.2.3, an environment is a set of bindings, which pair a name with storage space for a particular type of value. The environment and its bindings are created by the **use** command. In Galileo, an environment can be used to hold type definitions or classes, which are extents of types. Environments can also hold bindings which name sub-environments in much the same way as a directory can hold subdirectories. In Galileo, there is a global environment which will be used by default. It is also possible to create user-defined environments, which in database terms can act as a combination schema–database. An environment for electronic mail would be created in the following way:

```
use Email := (
  rec theUsers class
    User <-> ( name: string
      login: string;
      password: var string;
      incoming: Mailbox
      stored: var optional seq Mailbox)
    key (login)
  and theSuperusers class
    Superuser <-> (is User)
  and theMailboxes class
    ...
  )
```

In this example, the environment *Email* is introduced by the **use** command and is defined as a set of recursively interrelated classes. Each class is an extent of an abstract type (thus *theUsers* is the collection of all instances of *User*) and may have a key. Each property has associated options – it may be modifiable (**var**) or not; optional or not; and it may be a literal, object or collection (**seq**). Inheritance is available to create subtypes (**is**) or subclasses. Subclasses may be created as restrictions of other classes, as partitions or as potentially overlapping subsets.

The class *theUsers* primarily refers to a modifiable sequence of values of type *User*. In order to populate this sequence, the system generates a function, *mkUser*, which when called creates a new *User* value and adds it to *theUsers*, i.e. it takes the role of *new* in object-oriented systems. There is also a command to remove an instance from a class.

The environment *Email* has been created as a component of the global environment and may have subsidiary environments defined within it. To access the contents of an environment, the user must **enter** the environment whereupon all of the definitions in the environment become usable. There are also a number of operators for combining environments.

Environments are a very powerful mechanism in the database context, since it is possible to create environments which combine the data from other environments and to create environments which contain a subset of the values in an environment. Thus they can be used for information hiding, by producing a restricted environment which only makes limited data available, and they can be used as a view mechanism.

Galileo has a wealth of other interesting features – first-class function values, transactions and a rich type system. Use of the system is strongly typed, but literal types are checked with structural equivalence (since, in the designers' minds, the identity of a record type depends entirely on its components), while abstract types are checked by nominal equivalence (since their identity rests primarily on the name the programmer has given them).

Fibonacci

Fibonacci was also developed at the University of Pisa and is a development of Galileo with the following improvements: a richer type system, in which types themselves are first-class; polymorphic functions; exceptions; associations; and roles. Of these, the last two are the most novel and it is these that will be discussed here.

An *association* is a relationship, which explicitly contains references to related objects. It is equivalent to the intersection relation which represents an *m–n* relationship in a relational schema. In the electronic mail database, the relationship between messages and mailboxes might best be represented as an association.

A *role* is one of a number of representations of the same object. In Fibonacci, an object type defines a distinct category of objects, while a role type defines one of a number of variations on that object type. For instance, in a company database, there might be object types representing people, departments and projects, and role types for employees, dependents, managers, secretaries, production departments, marketing departments, research projects, development projects and so on. An object has only one object type, which can never change, but may have more than one role type and may gain or lose roles during its lifetime. Operations are defined on role types not on object types – the only operations on object types are system defined and carry out tasks like testing for equality and checking which roles an object has.

To illustrate Fibonacci, here is part of the electronic mail schema again:

```
(*Object Types*)
Let UserObjectType = newobject;        (* This introduces an object type *)
Let MailboxObjectType = newobject;
Let MessageObjectType = newobject;

(* Role Types *)
Let User = isa UserObjectType with     (*Role types inherits from an object
                                           type*)
   name: string;
   login: string;
   password: string;
End;

Let SuperUser = isa User    (* Note this role type inherits from another
                                role type *)
End;

Let Mailbox = isa MailboxObjectType with ... (* Definition omitted *)
Let Message = isa MessageObjectType with ... (* Definition omitted *)

(* Classes *)
let theUsers = emptyClass of User
   key login
   elsefail "A user login must be unique"
end;

(* Associations *)
let incoming = emptyAssoc of
   [ theUser: User; theBox: Mailbox ]
end;
let storage = emptyAssoc of ...
let holds = emptyAssoc of ...

(* Functions *)
let createUser = fun( aName, aLogin, aPass: String ) : User is
   begin
     let newUser = role User
        private
          pass = aPass;
        methods
          login = aLogin;
          name = aName;
     end;
     insert newUser into theUsers;
     let newBox = role Mailbox
          ...
     insert [newUser; newBox] into incoming;
   end;
```

In the code above, the style of the language is seen as a mixture of an object
model and first-class functions in an imperative setting. The first part introduces
the three object types for users, mailboxes and messages (superuser is just one
of the roles a user may take and so does not need to have a separate object type).
Then the role types are defined and their definitions include the specification of
all of the attributes of the type. The relationships, on the other hand, are specified

as associations. Finally, the functions which make up the application are coded.

It is one of the unsolved problems of object orientation to maintain the appearance of a one-to-one relationship between a changing real-world object and its computer representation in the context of a strongly typed system. It is quite normal for real-world objects to change their "types" during their existence – people change jobs, companies become international, and so on. The inclusion of the role type in Fibonacci is an interesting attempt to allow the type of an object to evolve during its lifetime in a way that mirrors the change to the real-world object.

Tycoon

Tycoon is an open persistent polymorphic programming environment, which includes as its primary programming interface the Tycoon language, T_L. This language is developed from DBPL and has a similar syntax, which is in the style of Modula, but is presented to the user, like Fibonacci, more in the style of ML.

T_L is built on a type system which includes the usual set of base types, a top type, records, unions, abstract data types and functions, all of which are first class and have recursive and bounded parametric forms. T_L is designed so that any mixture of functional, imperative or object-oriented programming can be supported. As well as the usual computational structures, T_L provides exceptions and a modular structure in which modules, interfaces and libraries can be explicitly organized.

Persistence is provided in the form of a globally persistent environment which is accessed by the **import** command, as in:

```
import store;
```

This provides access to two things: the top environment of a persistent store; and a function, called *stabilise*, which can be used to make changes to the store permanent. Values at the top level are automatically added to the store, when the *stabilise* command is called or at the successful completion of the program. Functions are stored in the same way as other kinds of data and reachability is used to make any component data of bulk structures persistent.

Tycoon incorporates more than just a persistent language. It also includes a number of support tools of which the *Style workbench* is the most interesting. Style provides a data modeling interface to the Tycoon system and constitutes a significant experiment into the interrelation of data models and programming languages. Using style, a data model diagram is created and this is automatically transformed into a T_L schema, which is then extended by programming in T_L. The system takes great care that the data model and programming version of the schema are kept synchronized by mechanisms which raise and lower the semantic level of the description. Style is described in more detail in Section 15.4.4.

Discussion

The languages presented here have shown how a programming language can be built around a data model. The syntax of the language is specifically organized to enable the programmer to manipulate instances of categories defined in the data model. As long as the data model is sufficiently powerful, it creates a coherent access mechanism for complex data. However, the languages described would be novel to most potential users and so will meet strong user resistance.

■ 11.3.4 Polymorphic database languages

The problem with most statically typed languages, illustrated clearly in the language Pascal/R, is their inability to express code which uses data types which have yet to be defined. The next group of languages has been designed with this in mind. They have been influenced even more strongly by ML, taking from it not just an interaction style, but also the use of type inferencing. The other languages which have influenced the design of these languages were Russel and Poly, both of which provided generic types. Taken together these allow the creation of code which is not tied to a single type. Machiavelli, a language designed by Peter Buneman's group at the University of Pennsylvania, brings these ideas into the database context.

Machiavelli

Machiavelli's design starts from the desire to provide the following kind of polymorphic code:

> Given any relation which has an age and a salary field, produce the salaries of persons aged 28.

This query must be expressible in a statically typed environment, with no run-time type checking. It would be expressed as:

```
fun salary28( X ) = select x.salary where x <-  X with x.age = 28;
```

which means that the function takes a set of values, X, and iterates over this set, using x as the iteration variable, retrieving the salary field of those whose age field holds the value 28.

The type of this function is inferred to be:

```
{ [ ("T) salary: "U;age: int ]} -> { "U }
```

which means that the function will take a set of values ("{}") which are records ("[]") which have at least a *salary* field of some unknown type, *U*, and an integer *age* field. The values may have other fields, which taken together, are of type *T*, and return a set of objects which are the same type as the *salary* field. The key part of the preceding sentence was the "at least" – any other fields may appear and are irrelevant to the type checking.

Machiavelli can use this kind of technique to represent not only relational operations, but also object-oriented or semantic data modeling operations.

Amber and Quest

Luca Cardelli, of DEC's SRC laboratory, has contributed many of the most valuable ideas in the categorization of types for database programming. As a basis for experimenting with these ideas, he has produced a number of languages which have been extremely influential, including Amber and Quest.

Amber provides polymorphism with a universal union type, **dynamic**, out of which types may be projected or coerced. Rather confusingly, it ties this mechanism to persistence since only objects of type **dynamic** may persist. This design decision was taken because this was a simple way of ensuring that the actual type information was stored with persistent objects, since dynamic types must store the actual type so that the value can eventually be safely coerced back into a usable static form. The language is rich in type constructors, having tuple, record, variant, array, function and channel (for concurrency communication) constructors.

The coercion strategy, which is essentially the same as used by the persistent languages, permits objects of as yet unknown type to be assigned the temporary type **dynamic**. Objects of this type may be passed around, but in order to use them, they must be forced into a concrete type, at which point the operations for that type become available. These operations can be statically type checked because the coercion operation must appear in the code before the operations and so the concrete type of the operand is known. Objects are made persistent by converting them from concrete types to type **dynamic**, at which point the concrete type is stored alongside the object's value, and then exporting them from the current module.

The types are arranged into an inheritance hierarchy by an automatic type inclusion algorithm which asserts, for instance, that a record with a set of fields is a subtype of a type which includes only a sub-set of these fields. Similar inclusion rules are developed for variant, array, channel, tuple and functions. This is similar in every respect to the type inference of Machiavelli (which was developed from it) and means that Amber, too, can supply the basic functionality of object-oriented systems in a properly typed environment.

The ideas in Amber are developed further in a landmark paper written with Peter Wegner of Brown University. This paper puts the type systems of DBPLs onto a firm basis within a single type calculus, with a basic set of types, some type constructors and universal and existential quantification. The type system of any of the languages referred to here is describable in terms of this calculus. This work starts to supply the kind of basic theory to type systems of database programming languages which Codd provided for relational systems.

In the language Quest, Cardelli adds a new concept for polymorphism, the *kind*. A kind is a set of types in much the same way as a metaclass is a set of classes. There will in general be a kind called *type*, for instance, which is the set of all types, and there could be a kind which is the set of all tuples having an integer field called *age*. Thus, the parameters of functions can have either their type or the kind of their type specified. Quest provides mechanisms within which it is convenient to describe everything known about the types in the database. One drawback is that it is not clear whether or not languages of this kind can be implemented or type-checked.

■ 11.3.5 Persistent programming languages

The languages described in this section were developed at the universities of St. Andrews and Glasgow by groups led by Ron Morrison and Malcolm Atkinson. They aim to provide uniform support both for database and for system programming. As such, they do not provide a single DBMS, but rather lower level functions out of which different styles of DBMS can be developed.

PS-algol

PS-algol was the first implemented system which provided orthogonal persistence, built on a persistent object store. The language S-algol was chosen as a basis for the development work, since it was felt necessary to start from a language which was already simple and regular. In both languages, the fundamental design principle is to provide data type completeness as described above.

PS-algol provides the usual kind of algol computational structures over a type system which includes a set of base types, arrays, bitmapped images, procedures and objects. The last two of these are the two most important features of the language, since they are provided in a different manner from the other languages discussed here. As a data type complete language, all of the facilities of the language, including data storage, are provided. Data of any type can be stored without losing its type.

Objects are provided as non-first normal form records with object identity and sharing pointer semantics – literal records are not available in the language. An object class structure is defined as a list of properties, each of which can have any type, including images, arrays, objects or procedures. PS-algol is not object oriented since the classes are not linked by inheritance. Unfortunately, in PS-algol, all objects have the same type, **pntr**, which makes data modeling very imprecise, but does permit a similar kind of polymorphic programming to Amber, since **pntr** is a dynamic type.

To illustrate this, here is the electronic mail schema in PS-algol:

```
structure User( name, login, password: string; incoming pntr; storage:
                                                            *pntr)
structure Mailbox( name: string; holds: *pntr )
structure Message(subject, body, date: string; heldIn: pntr; sender:
                                        pntr; recipients: *pntr)
```

in which it is possible to detect that *incoming*, *heldIn* and *sender* are object properties, but not what kind they are. *storage*, *holds* and *recipients* are arrays of objects (the "*" means that *recipients* is an array). In fact, the **pntr** type has been overburdened with the dual roles of being both a dynamic type and a pointer type.

In PS-algol, a procedure is a first-class value which consists of one or more named and typed arguments, either one or no typed result, and the code body which implements it. Creating procedures as first-class values is of considerable value, since they then have the four properties described in Section 11.2.2: being values of variables, parameters of other procedures, components of bulk objects or items stored in the database.

These last two properties are particularly important since they provide the basis for a number of benefits:

- Derived data can be freely mixed with other data.
- Properties which are inherently procedural can be modeled easily. For instance, it might be useful for every user to have a signature property, but for this property to be a piece of code, not just a text string, thus making it much more flexible.
- Information hiding can be implemented by the creation of packages of procedures (see below).
- The database can be used as the basis for modular programming and, by suitable use of different structures, can support a variety of methodologies, including object-oriented design.

- The compiler can be added as a system procedure. This means that programs can generate components at run-time, compile them and integrate them into their structure. This facility, called *linguistic reflection*, is an extremely valuable component of a database programming language, since it means that applications can be written which generate efficient components to deal with new types of data which are yet to be defined.

To illustrate the information hiding aspect, here is an outline of the way in which the electronic mail application would be created in PS-algol:

1. Declare four structures, each containing the operations of one of the four classes.
2. Declare *theUsers* to be a set of users.
3. Declare one creation procedure for each of the four classes, each of which encapsulates the properties and the methods but exports only the methods via one of the method structures declared in 1.
4. Create an application structure built in a menu and consisting of calls to the methods.

For instance, the operation structure for users would look like:

```
structure UserOps( testUser: proc( string, string );
                   readMail: proc( );
                   ... )
```

and the user creation procedure would then look like:

```
let createUser = proc( -> pntr )    // the procedure returns a UserOps object
  begin
      ...get the user's name, login and password from the terminal
      let incoming = createMailbox( "" ) // Create a mailbox with no name
      let storage = createMailboxSet( ) // Create an empty set of mailboxes
      let theUser = User( userName, userLogin, userPass, incoming, storage )
      let testUser = proc( userLogin, userPassword: string )
        code to implement the testUser procedure
      let readMail = proc( t )
        code to implement the readMail procedure
      ... the operations
      UserOps( testUser, readMail, ... ) // Export the package of procedures
  end
```

in which the procedure has three parts: the construction of a data structure of class *User* to hold the object properties, the implementation of the set of operations to be provided, and the construction of an abstract data type just holding these operations, which is returned as a result of the procedure.

Now the user properties are completely hidden from the outside world – the variables *incoming*, *storage* and *theUser*, for instance, cannot be referred to anywhere else in the code – all that is accessible are the operations in *UserOps*.

The application would be programmed as a single procedure, parameterized on the persistent roots (*theUsers* and *superUser*), which calls a menu of the main options and these in turn call the operations coded in the create object procedures.

Persistence in PS-algol is provided via the database construct. A database is a particular kind of structure which is a persistent root object and is only accessible via a set of system procedures – to open the database, close it, and so on. Databases can be opened in read or write mode, permitting many readers or a single writer at any time. The data structure underlying a database is called a table, which is a lookup mechanism which holds pairs of strings and objects.

The electronic mail application could be developed in a completely non-persistent manner as described above. To make the application persistent, it would be necessary to add the following to the application:

```
let emailDB = createDatabase( "Email", "Password" )
enter( emailDB, "The Users", theUsers )
enter( emailDB, "Super User", superUser )
enter( emailDB, "The Application", application )
commit()
```

after which the two persistent roots and all of their component data will be stored as well as the application code (which is thus kept well connected to the data). Subsequent uses of the application will require this short program:

```
let emailDB = openDatabase( "Email", "Password", "write" )
let theUsers := lookup( emailDB, "The Users" )
let superUser := lookup( emailDB, "Super User" )
let application := lookup( emailDB, "The Application" )
application( theUsers, superUser )
commit()
```

which opens the database in write mode, retrieves the root objects and the application and then starts it off, committing any changes during the application run.

PS-algol has some nice features, but falls a long way short of being a usable database programming language. It has very few of the features required in Chapter 1 and moreover has deficiencies in data modeling that have been discussed. Most of these deficiencies have been dealt with in the successor language to PS-algol – Napier88.

Napier88

The design of Napier88 was based on the experience of using PS-algol. The principal additions of Napier88 are a much richer type system, an environment mechanism similar to that of Galileo, a thread mechanism and support for concurrency and distribution. Napier88 is provided as a programming language with a very simple computational model that provides orthogonal support for a rich type system. The breadth of the language has been created by including additional components which are programmed in the language itself. In this way, collection types, events, windows, fonts, editors, compilers, semaphores and remote access mechanisms are values in the language, whose operations are available by loading suitable libraries.

The type system of Napier88 includes base types, constructors for array types, union types and (logical) abstract data types. It also permits parameterized types and polymorphic functions and includes a **null** type (but one that is unfortunately not a bottom type), the dynamic type **any** and a type for environments. An environment in Napier88 is similar to the environment structure of Galileo and Fibonacci, being a set of bindings, which can be added to or removed from during the run of a program, although in Napier88 a program must explicitly indicate the bindings that it is going to use. Environments are the structure underpinning persistent storage. The only persistent root object in Napier88 is the top-level environment, inside which are subsidiary environments organized in a hierarchical structure. On delivery, the Napier88 system comes with sets of environments which contain system functions, one somewhat unusual feature of Napier88 being that system functions are not implicitly available to the programmer, but must be explicitly retrieved from library environments in the persistent store (some examples are shown in the browser window in Figure 11.2).

Here is the electronic mail schema in Napier88:

```
rec type Mailbox = structure( name: string; holds: List[Message] )
   & Message = structure(subject, body, date: string; heldIn: Mailbox;
             sender: User; recipients: List[User] )
type User = structure( name, login, password: string;
             incoming: Mailbox; storage: Set[Mailbox] )
```

Creating a database in Napier88 uses a mixture of the methods of PS-algol and Galileo. An electronic mail environment would be installed in the persistent store (under the *User* environment where user databases are placed as shown in Figure 11.2) and this would be populated with the application, the superuser object and a set of users. Objects would be accessed using the record of operations style of ADT discussed in PS-algol.

Napier88 has been the basis of a number of user interface and software engineering experiments. In particular, a complete window management system, called WIN, has been implemented and forms the basis of most interaction with the Napier88 system. In WIN, interaction objects such as sliders, menus, windows and so on are Napier88 objects and may be stored inside the database.

Another significant body of work has produced the hyper-programming interface. Hyper-programming is a completely different kind of database programming from

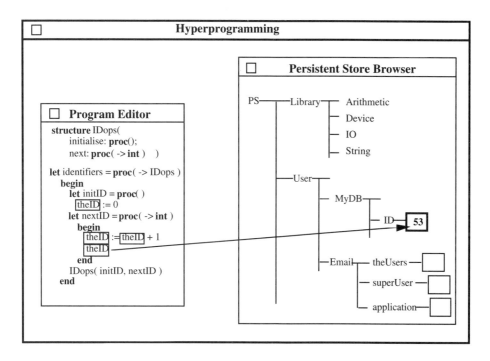

Figure 11.2 Napier88 and hyper-programming.

anything else discussed in this book. In the hyper-programming environment, it is possible to program directly against the database. Most database programming, including using query languages, uses path expressions which retrieve the data to be used from their database location. In the hyper-programming system, the programmer can embed direct database references into the code.

The way this is achieved is shown in Figure 11.2. This shows the hyper-programming interface to Napier88, which contains a set of windows including a browser for the persistent store and a program editor. The programmer uses the editing window mostly to type in program source code as usual. However, at various points the programmer can embed a direct reference to the database object, which is found using a store browser. Database objects may be dragged from the browser window into the programming window, as has been done for the persistent object, called *ID*. The example shows the component of a database application which issues identifying numbers in order. This is provided as two operations, one which resets the value to zero and one which increments and returns the value.

In most systems, access to data is either by direct reference to a memory value or by a path to a stored value. Recompiling a program causes any variables referring to memory to be reset and, if *ID* were such a variable, it would be reset to zero. Accessing a stored value essentially involves a query and so is slow. In the hyper-program, however, recompilation will not cause the value to be reset since it is not declared in the program and so will not be re-allocated. Therefore, if the program is recompiled, the value in the database will remain at 53 and so the system will not start re-issuing the numbers from 1. On the other hand, the reference is a direct link, not a query. Moreover since the system procedures are in the database, they can be accessed by hyper-programming and this means that applications can be written using system functions and these will continue to run using the latest versions without any effort when these functions are updated. The ability to modify database locations directly is an unusual feature of Napier88 and one which permits novel styles of programming, whose value is yet to be determined.

The powerful type system has enabled a wide range of experimentation into appropriate application development techniques for database system, concurrency mechanisms (built on a thread package and semaphores), user interfaces and distributed systems (using remote procedure calls). In each of these lies of the promise of configurable control over DBMS functionality for which a single strategy may not be appropriate for all uses.

Napier88 is a powerful language which integrates low-level and high-level abstractions of data processing. It has yet to be seen whether there is a market for a language such as this with undeniable strengths, yet possessing features with which most programmers will be unfamiliar.

11.4 Object-oriented programming languages and persistence

None of the languages discussed in the previous section are properly object oriented. Either they lack one or more of the critical properties of an object-oriented system – object identity, inheritance or encapsulation – or they provide additional constructs such as first-class code values. In this section, the focus is entirely on object-oriented languages and what it means to make them the primary interface to a DBMS.

To start with, here is a restatement of some of the important features that a persistent OOPL will possess:

- The schema will be structured in the form of a class hierarchy.

- The application will be coded largely as the operations of the classes.

- The database will be an object.

- The database will be accessible either via language constructs which "open" it or preferably by means of the operations of a class for database objects.

- There will be additional classes for collections, domain types, transactions and other DBMS objects.

- It is desirable that as few extensions to the basic language as possible are required.

The primary mechanism for adding persistence to a programming language is by creating what is called a *language binding*, which brings support mechanisms for persistence into the run-time environment of the language. This might be achieved by adding new syntactic features to the language, new system functions or new system classes. In order to exploit these, the system will usually provide additional language processing components. This may take the form of a pre-processor or a transparent change to the compiler or run-time system. For instance, many OODBMS maintain dual representations of data in the form of a language version and a DBMS version of any class which may have persistent instances, although the programmer may well have no need to refer to both of these explicitly.

In the following, some of the main OOPLs will be surveyed briefly and attempts to make them persist are listed. Each language has built in some way on others, but some (C++, CLOS) are attempts to add object orientation to non-object languages, while others (Smalltalk, Eiffel) have a novel syntax with which to use the object model.

C++

C++ is the most commonly used object-oriented language. It is estimated that more than 50% of all object-oriented programs are written in C++. C++ is an extension of C to include a class mechanism with multiple inheritance and static (but unsafe) type checking. C++ is also the most common language to build an OODBMS around. It is therefore an important aspect of a standard for OODBMS to discuss how best to integrate the language with a database. The next chapter discusses the ODMG proposal for C++ bindings, as well as the way that O_2 implements this.

Smalltalk

Smalltalk is the second most popular OOPL and, in the form of GemStone, was one of the first to be made persistent. It provides multiple inheritance, but uses dynamic type checking. The ODMG is also producing a standard binding to Smalltalk and this is discussed in Chapter 13.

Eiffel

Eiffel is a statically typed OOPL, designed by Bertrand Meyer, and marketed through his company, Interactive Software Engineering, among others. It has exceptions, generic classes and constraints in the form of assertions, such as pre- and post-conditions of operations and invariants specifiable on classes. Since it is a type-safe language and uses garbage collection rather than destructors, Eiffel would seem to be an extremely suitable language for DBMS work, but the author is not aware of any persistent Eiffel implementations.

Common Lisp Object System

Common Lisp Object System (CLOS) is an object-oriented extension to Lisp. It provides the usual class and instance structures, but adds to these generic functions (i.e. functions with a common interface, but with potentially many class-specific implementations) and genuine metaclasses, which can be used to customize system behavior. Itasca (see Section 16.4), Statice and Allegro are among the commercially available persistent versions of Lisp.

Modula-3

Modula-3 is the latest member of the Modula family and is being developed at Digital Equipment Corporation's SRC research lab. Modula-3 is a single-inheritance language with dynamic typing, generic classes, exceptions and support for multiple threads. Like C++, Modula-3 permits programming at the machine language level, but clarifies this by marking modules which use machine level as "unsafe". Modula-3 has been used as the basis for the development of the graphical and forms-based interfaces, Trestle and FormsVBT. It has also been used for implementing the scripting language, Obliq. Although Modula-3 is not itself a persistent language, work is being carried out by Eliot Moss and Tony Hocking at the University of Massachussetts to add persistence by reachability to the language.

Beta

Beta is a descendant of Simula67 and was developed in Denmark and Norway by the Mjøllner group led by Ole Lehrmann Madsen. Beta is rather different from the other languages described here. Instead of being built around a class hierarchy, Beta programs are built using patterns. A pattern is a description from which an object can be created. However, the term "object" in the previous sentence includes procedure or function activations, exception occurrences or concurrent processes. Beta is mostly statically checked, has single inheritance, exceptions and generics. It also provides libraries which support concurrency, distribution and orthogonal persistence. Beta claims to be inherently persistent.

Java

Java is an OOPL designed by Sun Microsystems to create small, reliable, portable, distributed, real-time embedded systems. It was designed as a development of C++, but one which removed some of the more problematic features of that language, such as pointer arithmetic and indefinite parameter types. Java is a single inheritance, statically type checked language. It has multi-threading and distribution support.

There are a number of groups working on creating persistent versions of Java and the first workshop in this area was held in 1996. Since the World Wide Web access mechanisms are increasingly being created in Java, the importance of this language in the future would be hard to over-estimate. Because of this, Java is the next language for which the ODMG is intending to create a standard binding.

■ 11.5 Summary

This chapter has discussed the work in the area of database programming languages. There have been a wide variety of proposals and implementations for DBPLs – both object oriented and not – but there is a recognizable set of the most important issues:

- A DBPL must integrate the usual programming language capabilities with the ability to access values in the database.
- A DBPL should provide a seamless mechanism for combining these two sets of features.
- A DBPL must provide a type system which is suitably expressive both for data modeling and data manipulation purposes. The type system should be rich enough for the direct and succinct representation of the schema, but not so complex as to be obscure or to make type checking undecidable.
- The type system should be enforced to ensure programming safety. As far as possible, the checking should be carried out as soon as possible, i.e. statically at compile-time.

- However, some desirable features, such as dynamic types and environments, necessitate the use of dynamic type checking, i.e. the checks are carried out as the program is run.
- A DBPL must integrate the description of DBMS objects, such as collections, databases, transactions and so on.
- Explicit transfer to and from memory and explicit memory allocation and de-allocation complicate the coding task unnecessarily and permit the development of potentially unsafe programs.
- Providing functions or procedures as first-class values is useful since this permits direct representation of behavioral values, permits succinct functional kinds of programming, supports run-time reflection and provides the basis for the creation of application development tools, which use the database to store software components.
- Object-oriented languages provide suitable candidates for database work since the object-oriented model is appropriate for data modeling and DBMS objects can easily be represented as objects.

The next two chapters turn to the creation of DBPLs out of the non-persistent languages C++ and Smalltalk.

12 C++ as a database programming language

C++ is the most pervasive object-oriented programming language. Surveys estimate that C++ usage accounts for at least 50% of all object-oriented programming and C++ is certainly the most likely object-oriented language to be used as an initial teaching language for computer science courses. It is therefore to be expected that when potential customers hear about a DBMS which is "object oriented", they will expect to be able to use it with C++ programs.

Part of the motivation for a customer moving to a database approach is to take existing non-persistent software, which has developed heavy data management requirements, and to use DBMS technology to fulfil these requirements. In order to do this, the customer does not wish to completely re-program what may be a substantial body of code. The growing appreciation of object-oriented principles led to the desire to use an object-oriented language. The widespread use of C led to the conviction that C++ was the most practical language to embody those principles. Therefore, there is an increasingly large body of critical software written in C++, much of which now requires the addition of persistence.

This chapter describes what it takes to make C++ persistent, with examples of different approaches. The chapter starts with a critique of the suitability of C++ for database use and then continues with a discussion of some of the different ways in which C++ can be tied to a database system. Then follows a section in which the ODMG C++ binding proposals are described, before the chapter ends with sections describing how O_2 embodies this methodology, and how the electronic mail application can be built using C++ in O_2.

■ 12.1 C++ and database management

This chapter introduces the language and discusses its suitability for database work. This is not the place to provide a complete description of C++. There are many excellent texts which achieve this. Instead, Section 12.1.1 will review the main features of the language, Section 12.1.2 will provide an example, while Section 12.1.3 discusses how the features of C++ fit with the various requirements for object-oriented data management introduced in previous chapters.

■ 12.1.1 The language C++

C++ was developed in the early 1980s at AT&T Bell Labs by Bjarne Stroustrup. The motivation for the language was to provide a more secure method of writing C programs by augmenting that language with new components which enable the use of object-oriented programming.

When one language is developed from another, there is a common requirement that all programs written in the first language continue to work unchanged in the second. The new language is described as being a *superset* of the old one. C++ is a superset of C and so any C program should run in a C++ system. In this case the extensions were designed in order to facilitate the development of event-driven simulation programs. These would have been easier to write in Simula67, which was a language designed for such tasks, but the code produced by Simula would have been too inefficient. Therefore, the appropriate parts of Simula were imported to extend C, thus combining the programmer efficiency of Simula with the execution efficiency of C.

As well as providing some cleaner equivalents to parts of the C syntax, the primary extensions involve the addition of a class construct in the language. Classes in C++ have the following features:

- A class encapsulates properties, called data members, and operations called member functions.

- Member functions may be overloaded – that is, the same operation name can be used to refer to several different operations. The alternatives are distinguished by the number and type of the parameters that they have.
- A class can also describe operators which can be used instead of member functions to permit computations to be invoked on members of the class.
- A class can also describe static members which are properties and operations which are specific to the class as a whole rather than to individual instances.
- The system variable name **this** is used to indicate the object currently being manipulated – it plays the same role as **self** in other object-oriented languages.
- Constructors are member functions which are called when an object is created.
- Destructors are member functions which are called when an object is deleted and one of the tasks they must implement is the de-allocation of the memory which the object has been using.
- The set of characteristics are divided into private, public and protected sections, in which the last of these means that the characteristic is accessible from within the operation of the class and any of its subclasses, but not elsewhere.
- Friends are classes and operations defined on one class which are permitted to access the private characteristics of another class.
- Classes take part in a subclass with multiple inheritance.
- Some of the member functions can be indicated to be virtual functions, i.e. only to be implemented in subclasses.
- There is the ability to describe template classes – classes which are parameterized, usually by a parameter whose value is another class.
- There is a promise to extend the language further to include an exception mechanism but this has yet to become part of the standard language.

■ 12.1.2 An example – the O_2 template class *d_Collection*

Here is the definition of the class which implements collections in the O_2 implementation of the ODMG proposal.

```
1   template < class T >   class  d_Collection : public o2_col_root {
2   public
3                           d_Collection();
4                           d_Collection( const d_Collection<T>& copy );
5                           ~d_Collection;

6   d_Collection<T> operator = ( const d_Collection<T>& copy );
7   d_Collection<T> operator = ( const d_Ref_Any& copy );

8   friend int operator == ( const d_Collection<T>& cL, const
                                                    d_Collection<T>&cR )
9   friend int operator == ( const d_Collection<T>& cL, const d_Ref_Any& cR )
10  friend int operator == ( const d_Ref_Any& cL, const d_Collection<T>& cR )
11  friend int operator != ( const d_Collection<T>& cL, const
                                                    d_Collection<T>& cR )
12  friend int operator != ( const d_Collection<T>& cL, const d_Ref_Any& cR )
13  friend int operator != ( const d_Ref_Any& cL, const d_Collection<T>& cR)
14  unsigned long  cardinality() const;
15  int            is_empty() const;
16  int            is_ordered() const;
17  int            allows_duplicates() const;
18  int            contains_element( const T& elem ) const;

19  void           insert_element( const T& elem );
20  void           remove_element( const T& elem );
21  void           remove_all( );

22  d_Iterator<T>  create_iterator( ) const;
23  d_Iterator<T>  select( const char* predicate ) const;
24  T              select_element( const char* predicate ) const;
25  int            query( d_Collection<T>& subcol, const char* predicate )
                       const;
26  int            exists_element( const char* predicate ) const;
    };
```

Each component of this definition will be examined in turn:

Line 1 introduces the template class and places it in the class hierarchy as a subclass of *o2_col_root*. The line names it as *d_Collection* and also specifies that it has a parameter, *T*, which is a class – this is the type of the elements of the collection.

Line 2 asserts that all of the characteristics which are listed are public – available to all programs using the class.

Lines 3–5 describe two constructors and one destructor (*~Collection*) for the class. The first constructor creates a new empty collection, while the second one creates a new collection which is a copy of another collection. The collection to be copied is passed as a parameter called *copy*. Notice that this is typed *d_Collection<T>*, meaning that it is a collection of the same type, *T*, as the one being created.

Lines 6 and 7 define the assignment operators. There are two of these, both using the same symbol ("="), i.e. the operator is overloaded. One of them assigns the variable to another collection of element type T, while the other downcasts the value of a *d_Ref_Any* object, since instances of this class may be dynamically typed versions of collections (see Section 12.4.4 for details).

Lines 8–13 define operators to test the equality and inequality of two collections. They allow expressions of the form

C1 == C2 and C1 != C2

to be used in the program. Again both are overloaded, each having three versions – one for the case in which both of C_i are instances of *d_Collection<T>* and one for each case in which one of the C_i is an instance of *d_Ref_Any*.

Lines 14–18 define operations which test the collection. *cardinality* returns the number of elements in the collection. Lines 15–17 define operations which return boolean values which test which kind of collection it is. The operation defined in line 18 takes in a value of type T and tests if it is in the collection.

Lines 19–21 define the operations which add and remove elements from the collection – the first two taking an object of type T as a parameter.

Lines 22–26 define operations which create iterators over the collection and query the collection.

12.1.3 A critique of C++ as a database programming language

C++ has a great many features, some of which are valuable in the database context and some of which are extremely problematic. The valuable features include the class mechanism, information hiding and template classes. The problematic features include the unsafeness of the language, pointer arithmetic, explicit destruction of objects, the lack of a mechanism for an object to change type and a lack of domain classes.

As has been discussed, an object-oriented class hierarchy is an entirely suitable repository for structuring schemata and this is what C++ provides. It also provides multiple inheritance which improves its expressiveness for data description. The information hiding of implementation detail is another positive feature. Perhaps the strongest feature of all is the recent addition of template classes to the language, since these provide an invaluable mechanism for adding new data definition features, such as collections. Template classes are heavily used in the ODMG binding, of which the previous subsection contained one example.

The principal problem with C++ is that it includes explicit memory allocation and de-allocation primitives. This is extremely beneficial for the production of real-time non-persistent software which must exploit memory to the full and which must be as fast as possible. In a database context, it is also valuable for the implementation of the components of the DBMS. However, a DBMS is supposed to take control of all data and metadata manipulation to ensure that they are used in a consistent manner. For the DBMS to provide an interface which supports direct memory operations is extremely dangerous, since the programmer can undermine the system at any time.

A similar problem is that of data integrity. Unlike some other languages, C++ provides for the explicit deletion of objects through the use of destructors. The unconstrained use of C++ can therefore lead to the removal of objects to which there are references. Attempting to access those objects by following references to them can therefore cause severe run-time problems. Another way in which C++ supports the violation of database integrity is through the provision of pointer arithmetic facilities. Indeed the syntax surrounding the use of pointers is extremely confusing and is only there to support activities which are redundant in a database context.

Friend classes have been widely criticized and they can be used to violate the information hiding aspect of the schema. This is reasonably supportable in a non-persistent environment, since at least the programmer can expect to have all of the class descriptions to hand and so any friend references can be clearly determined. In a persistent environment, in which classes coexist which have a variety of sources and ages, the programmer is unlikely to have enough information to make safe use of friends.

Another aspect of this is that the type system of C and therefore of C++ is quite insecure. Whereas, for large parts of the program, the programmer can rely on the type checking, in some cases this is not safe. Furthermore, the type system is not appropriately expressive, having few of the advanced type categories described in the last chapter. Indeed, the language shows its antiquity most clearly in the failure to provide boolean or string types. Having to remember which integer value means which boolean value is just the kind of indirectness which can cause programs to be costly to write and to be incorrect.

To summarize, from a database perspective, what is valuable about C++ is the set of object-oriented features and what is problematic is the cluster of features left over from C. C is an inappropriate start point on which to build an object-oriented language. By insisting on being a superset of C, C++ is one of the poorer attempts at designing an object-oriented language.

■ 12.2 Techniques for making C++ persistent

The previous chapter discussed the constituents of a database programming language. This could be built by: adding database features to a language, adding computational features to a data model, or building a new language from scratch. In this section, the first of these approaches is considered where the language being extended is C++.

In extending a language, there are always two techniques which can be used. Either the syntax can be extended or the working environment can be extended. In the case of an object-oriented language, the latter means the provision of system-supplied classes. There is a strong argument for preferring the second of these alternatives wherever possible, since this means that pre-existing code is not perturbed. In the ODMG proposal, a mixture of the two techniques is used.

Creating a persistent form of C++ consists of making the following additions to the language:

- a means of referring to databases;
- a means of describing schemata;
- a means of indicating that some of the values are to persist;
- a means of referring to other DBMS values such as transactions, queries and so on;

and, in the context of the ODMG:

- a means of referring to ODMG specific constructs such as relationships and names.

Each of these will now be examined in turn.

■ 12.2.1 Databases in C++

A database is a repository for data and in the context of C++, this means a repository for C++ values and objects. In an object-oriented representation, a database should be an object – one which supports the insertion and retrieval of objects. The operations of creating, opening and closing a database must also be supported with the options of opening the database in read-only or write modes.

To achieve this, it would be possible to extend C++ with extra syntax such as:

```
open database <Dbname>
```

and so on, but this is unnecessary since object orientation shows its power in that it is possible to create a class, *Database*, with all of the these operations supplied as member functions. This is the path that all OODBMS manufacturers have taken and it is the route followed by the ODMG.

■ 12.2.2 Schemata in C++

A schema in the object-oriented context is mainly made up of a set of class definitions. It would be desirable if a standard C++ header file could be used as the schema. However, several problems arise in implementing this:

- Persistent objects and transient objects may well be managed by different system components – transient objects by the language run-time system and persistent objects by the storage manager. It may therefore be necessary to distinguish persistent objects from non-persistent ones.
- There is a strong DBMS tradition of holding the metadata inside the database.
- There are other aspects to a schema such as named root objects, keys, extents, queries and so on.

It would therefore be useful to construct a class of schemata which includes not just the class definitions in C++, but also the various other aspects required. However, the ODMG make no attempt to propose this and the management of schemata and applications remain product specific.

■ 12.2.3 Persistent classes, objects and properties in C++

Methods of indicating persistence

In adding persistence to C++, it is usually considered necessary to have some way of indicating which objects are persistent and which classes can have persistent members. As was seen in Chapter 3, there are several different ways in which it might be possible to indicate which objects persist:

- by a persistent form of the *new* operation;
- by attaching the ability to persist to one particular class, so that the instances of this class (and any of its subclasses) can potentially be persistent while all other objects must be transient;
- by indicating that a class has potentially persistent members as part of its description;
- orthogonally by reachability from named persistent roots.

Persistence capable classes

All four of these mechanisms are in use in current products, so to achieve a consensus for a standard would be difficult. In order to support all of these, it is necessary to distinguish two kinds of class – ones which have only transient members and ones whose members might be stored. The latter are called in ODMG terminology, *persistence capable classes*.

Now the options become:

- Force the programmer to determine which classes are persistence capable at creation time.
- Maintain two versions of each class, one which is transient and one which is persistence capable.
- Maintain only persistence capable classes.

The second of these has been the route taken by the ODMG, with one of the versions being automatically created from the other. When an application is programmed in the DBMS, a set of persistence capable classes is specified and transient classes automatically created if needed. When an application is programmed in C++, the transient classes are created and when an object is created in C++, a persistence capable version of the class is automatically created so that the object can be stored.

Creating persistent and transient objects

Given a set of classes and a database, the means of creating a persistent object may be any of:

- using a persistent form of *new* or indicating that it is a member of a persistent class;
- inserting the object explicitly into a database;
- attaching it to a persistent root object.

In fact these can all be used in concert to give the programmer a wide range of means of storing objects. In the ODMG proposal, *new* is overloaded so that it can be used to create:

- a transient object of either a transient or persistence-capable class;
- an object which is held in a particular database;
- an object which is clustered "close to" another object.

Furthermore, named objects can be used as persistent roots to a database. Products are free to determine the degree to which reachability is used to bring data which has not been explicitly stored into the database as well.

References to persistent objects

References in C++ use the "*" and "&" notations. In the 1993 version of ODMG's specification, it was felt necessary to distinguish references to persistent objects from references to transient objects. This has been done not by extending the syntax with yet another confusing punctuation mark, but by using a template class, called *Ref*. Thus, if a non-persistent program has a pointer data member, then this must be turned into a *Ref* reference if the property is persistent. Thus:

```
*Department dept;
```

becomes

```
Ref<Department> dept;
```

In general, the description of a class can mix persistent and transient attributes, distinguishing them by use of *Ref* and "*". The persistent attributes will be stored when a transaction commits, whereas the transient attributes will be discarded and will need to be re-initialized when the object is brought back into memory.

■ 12.2.4 DBMS objects in C++

An OODBMS must be more than just an object store. It must manage a range of DBMS activities such as concurrent access, security and querying. How can these be incorporated into a C++ interface?

One of the fundamental components of database use is the **transaction**. DBMS make so much use of transactions that these must be made available in an OODBMS. A transaction is capable of being started and successfully or unsuccessfully completed. It may also be useful to be able to commit modified data in the middle of a transaction.

Transactions could be incorporated into C++ in one of four ways:

- transparently, by making every operation execution have the qualities of a transaction;
- by making a language extension with commands like "begin transaction" and so on;
- by providing additional operations on the class *Database* to manage transactions;
- by providing a transaction class with the appropriate properties.

The first of these is too inflexible and costly, while, as discussed for databases, the second is unnecessary. The third seems to overburden the *Database* class, although this is the choice made for the Smalltalk proposal (see next chapter). A class of transactions is the appropriate mechanism and the proposed ODMG C++ class has operations to start the transaction, commit data in the middle of the transaction (*checkpoint*), to abort the transaction and to complete the transaction by committing the changes. ODMG transactions are essentially short. No progress has been made in designing a distinct long-transaction component.

An OODBMS could also usefully include a class for **locks**. In the ODMG standard, locks are not explicitly defined, but individual systems may very well include one or more classes to cover different kinds of lock.

Part Three covered queries, but these are often embedded in a language, as discussed in Section 11.3.1. In the context of a program, a query consists of collection to be searched, a filtering predicate, a target object or collection for the result and, possibly, a projecting component which chooses part of the objects to return. There are a number of ways in which this can be done:

- by an extension to the language syntax;
- by use of a free-standing function;
- by providing a class for queries.

A language extension is unnecessary, but both of the other options are good solutions. ODMG specifies a free-standing function with arguments which hold the result, a parameterized OQL query as a string, and actual parameter values. An alternative option is to provide a class with operations for specifying the various components of a query and for executing it, not dissimilar to the way in which O_2 accesses legacy data (see Section 7.5.3) and this is, in fact, what O_2 does.

■ 12.2.5 ODMG specific constructs

The ODMG model includes a number of specific features which the binding must cater for: the class hierarchy, relationships, names, extents and keys.

The ODMG class hierarchy was shown in Figure 5.2 and this must be supported by C++. This means, in particular, support for the ODMG collection classes. The ODMG binding specifically asserts that a compliant system must support collection and its subtypes *Array, Varray, Set, Bag* and *List*.

Relationships provide a more difficult extension to manage without perturbing the language. C++ must now distinguish data members which are attributes from data members which are relationships. Moreover, the specification of a relationship must also include its inverse. ODMG proposes a language extension to cope with this. Here is an example:

```
Ref<Department> dept inverse Department :: employees;
```

Names provide a way for the programmer to refer to objects which is distinct from their value. In order to provide a scope for this naming, ODMG attaches names to databases, in which case they become a potential means for describing persistent roots. Whereas providing a class of names is one potential design alternative and extending the language another, the most attractive alternative is to manage names in the context of databases. Therefore the class, *Database*, has commands for inserting and retrieving named objects.

Extents could be managed by a language extension in which a name for a class extent is optionally added to the class description (as happens in ODL). Alternatively, extents could be transparently managed and the system provide a name for the extent, such as *AllPersons* for the class *Person* and so on. In fact, ODMG adopts no policy on this issue, since flexibility of implementation is required given the range of efficiency concerns involved.

Keys are another issue for which the ODMG has no recommendation. They could have recommended a language extension or a system function for specifying a key of a class, but they just say "Key declarations are not supported by C++".

■ 12.3 The ODMG C++ binding

This section provides detail on the decisions made by the ODMG on the issues discussed above. It starts by describing how user-defined classes differ from their standard C++ equivalents. It then describes the domain and collection classes from the ODMG hierarchy. The next subsection describes the way in which persistent objects are managed. Then the classes *Database* and *Transaction* will be described. Finally access to OQL is discussed.

It should be noted at the outset that a number of the features of the ODMG model are not found in the C++ standard binding. This does not mean that such features will not be supported by C++ in an ODMG-compliant system, merely that there is no standard recommendation for how to achieve this. Among the aspects of the model which do not appear in the binding are:

- Multiple implementations of a specification are not supported since C++ itself does not permit this.
- Extents are not directly supported, although any system is certain to have a standard way of managing a class extent.
- Keys are not directly supported.
- Exceptions will not be supported until they become a regular feature of C++.

Furthermore, the C++ binding does not provide facilities for creating databases or indexes. These must be created in some other way or by using implementation-specific extensions. The standard does provide features for using databases once they have been created and for defining queries.

■ 12.3.1 User-defined classes

A schema in C++ is a set of persistence capable classes. These appear as normal C++ classes with five main extensions, only one of which (the third in the list) uses a syntactic extension to the language:

1. A persistence capable class must inherit from *Persistent_Object*, the class which holds all of the behavior associated with storing objects. This class is described in Section 12.3.4.
2. References to properties whose values are instances of persistence capable classes must use the *Ref* template class.
3. Relationships must have an inverse specification added to their definition.
4. There are a number of system-supplied domain classes – *String*, *Interval*, *Date*, *Time* and *Timestamp* – which may be used as property or parameter types. These are described in Section 12.3.2.
5. There are also a number of system-provided template classes for collections. These are described in Section 12.3.3.

To give an example, in ODMG C++, the *User* class definition would be written:

```
class Message : public Persistent_Object {
private
    String subject,
    Date dateSent;
    String body;
    Ref<Mailbox> heldin inverse Mailbox :: holds;
    Ref<User> sender;
    Set< Ref<User> > recipients;
public
    void Message( const Ref<User> &sendingUser );
    void summarize( const int number );
    void display;
    void reply( const Ref<User> &sender, const Ref<User> &replier;
                                  const *char oldSubject );
};
```

In this example, all of the five extensions are used:

1. In the first line, *Message* is defined as being a subclass of *Persistent_Object*. Notice that this is required even though the extent of *Message* will not be stored. As messages will be stored as components of mailboxes, they must be instances of a persistence capable class.
2. The *heldin*, *sender* and *recipients* properties use *Ref*, as do the parameters of the constructor operation *Message* and the operation *reply*.
3. The property *heldin* has an inverse.
4. The *String* class is used instead of **char* and the *Date* class is also used.
5. The *Set<T>* template class is used to define the set of recipients.

The template class, *Ref*, is used to represent references to persistent objects. It is the intention of ODMG that this is a temporary measure and that ultimately there should be no syntactic difference between the representations of transient object references and persistent object references. However, many of the current OODBMS rely on the system maintaining the difference between objects managed by the run-time system and objects managed by the DBMS. These systems require the programmer to tell them when persistence is to be expected. In the previous example, *Ref<User>* is placed where **User* might have been expected. The implication is that the sender of a message, for instance, may well be stored in the database, whereas if **User* had been used, the reference must be to a transient object.

The use of inverses is a straightforward extension of C++ syntax. Any property which is a relationship should have its inverse specified as shown in the example, after which the integrity of the relationship will be maintained by the system. If the property value of one side of the relationship is changed, there will be a compensating change to the property on the other side of the relationship. As in the ODMG model (described in Section 5.3.2), the mechanism covers one-to-one, many-to-one, one-to-many and many-to-many relationships. To illustrate this, if classes *A* and *B* have one relationship between each other of each of these kinds, then this will appear in the two classes:

```
class A ...
   Ref<B> A1to1 inverse B :: B1to1
   Ref<B> ANto1 inverse B :: B1toN
   Set< Ref<B> > A1toN inverse B :: BNto1
   Set< Ref<B> > AMtoN inverse B :: BMtoN
...

class B ...
   Ref<A> B1to1 inverse A :: A1to1
   Set< Ref<B> > B1toN inverse A :: ANto1
   Ref<A> B1to1 inverse A :: A1toN
   Set< Ref<A> > BMtoN inverse A :: AMtoN
...
```

Note however, there can still be object-valued attributes, i.e. properties without inverses. For instance, to have an attribute in class *A*, whose name is *Attribute* and whose type is *B*, the following can be written:

```
class A ...
   Ref<B> Attribute
...
```

In summary, the schema is a nearly vanilla C++ set of class descriptions. The only syntactic extension can be avoided altogether – given a pre-existing program which already maintains the integrity of any relationship, then the relationships can be represented unchanged (in ODMG terms as apparently unrelated attributes) since the automatic work to maintain the integrity of the relationship has already been coded.

The modifications to a non-persistent C++ program are fairly modest. To use an ODMG database, it will be necessary to put in the inheritance relationships from *Persistent_Object*. If the application uses collection classes, strings, dates and so on, their performance would be improved by switching to the ODMG classes, but otherwise nothing else needs to change in the program.

12.3.2 Domain classes

The system supplies a number of classes which provide support for some common kinds of data. These would be the same kinds of data for which a relational database might provide domain types. In the current version, ODMG provides the following classes.

- *String* is a class of persistent strings. This does not replace the normal C++ *char** string, which is still required for string manipulation. It is instead intended to be a representation of strings which eases their storage in databases. The class supports copying to and from *char** strings, comparison operators, an indexing operator and a length function.
- *Interval* is a class whose members represent time durations. An interval has components for days, hours, minutes and seconds and the class has functions for retrieving these as well as a constructor function and operators for arithmetic and comparison.
- *Date* instances represent a time value, with components for years, months and days. The class provides a wide range of functions and operators which support arithmetic, comparison, and the generation of names of months and days of the week. It also supports the testing of whether or not two time periods overlap, taking four dates as parameters – the start and end points of two time intervals.
- *Time* is a class of time values in hours, minutes and seconds. It also supports overlapping tests and arithmetical and comparison operators and, although it works in terms of GMT, there is support for different time zones.
- *Timestamp* is another class of time values, but one which incorporates both date and time, having year, month, day, hour, minute and second components. It supports the same kinds of operation as do *Date* and *Time*.

■ 12.3.3 Collection classes

The ODMG data model contains constructors for defining collections of different kinds – sets, bags, lists and arrays. In fact, the normal C++ array facility is used for fixed length arrays, but the model also supports variable length arrays and so provides a class for these. The model uses inheritance to partition the behavior between that which is general to collections of all of these kinds and that which is specific to each kind. The generic virtual class, *Collection*, is defined with subclasses *Set*, *Bag*, *List* and *Varray*. The behavior of a *List*, for instance, is described partly as operations of *Collection* (such as the test of whether a value is a member of the collection) and partly as operations of *List* (such as the operation which removes the first element from the list). There are also subtypes of *List* which represent strings and bitmaps. Finally, there is a template class, *Iterator*, which manages the traversal of collections.

All of these constructs are generic, and are specified using type generators. Thus the construct for sets defines the behavior of sets of elements all of which have the same type, but the construct is generic over the element type. The generator is described as *Set<T>* and it describes instances such as *Set<integer>*, *Set<Person>* or *Set< Set<Address> >*.

This maps very nicely into C++ template classes with element types being a type parameter of the class. Thus, the definition of *Set* begins:

```
template <class T> class Set : public Collection<T>
```

in which *Set* is described as being parameterized and of inheriting from *Collection* (also a template class).

The template class, *Collection*, is virtual since all of its members must be members of one of its subclasses. The interface to *Collection* was given in Section 12.1.2. As well as two constructors and a destructor, the definition of *Collection* includes operations which: return the cardinality of the collection; test if it is empty, if it is ordered, or if it allows duplicates; insert and remove elements; test if it contains a particular element; remove all elements; create and use iterators; and query the collection. The iterator operations are dealt with in the discussion of the *Iterator* class. The querying operations are discussed in Section 12.3.6.

The subclasses of *Collection* are:

- *Set* contains a number of operators and operations for computing set unions, differences and intersections. It also has subset and superset tests.
- *Bag* has equivalent union, intersection and difference operators and operations as *Set*, but does not support subset and superset testing.

- *List* has operators and operations for inserting new elements at the beginning or the end of the list or at a specific position. It also supports the removal of elements, retrieval of elements by position and concatenation of lists.
- *Varray* is the class of variable length arrays. It has operators to retrieve and change the upper bound (the lower bound of all arrays and lists is zero, following the convention of C and C++).

The template class, *Iterator*, is used to provide a consistent mechanism for iterating over the members of a collection. An iterator is an object which takes as its value a reference to each element of a collection in turn. For the ordered collection kinds, *List* and *Varray*, the iterator will assume the values in the specified order. For the unordered collection kinds, *Bag* and *Set*, there will be a fixed but meaningless order. The functionality of iterators is provided partly by the *Iterator* class and partly by the *Collection* class:

- In the *Iterator* class, there are operations to create an iterator for a collection, or as a copy of another iterator. There are also: a destructor, an operation to reset the iterator to the beginning, an operation to move on to the next element, and an operation to retrieve the element at the current position.
- In the *Collection* class, there is an operation to create an iterator for the collection, and operations to retrieve, remove and replace the element at the current position.

To give an example, here is a piece of code which takes a message and replaces user *jbrown* with user *jblack* in the list of recipients:

```
Set<Ref<User>> receivers = theMessage . recipients;
Iterator<Ref<User>> receiver =            // create the iterator
    receivers . create_iterator();
while (receiver . not_done() ) {          // iterate until none left
if (receiver . get_element() == jbrown   // test the element
receivers . replace_element              // replace at the iterator
    ( jblack, receiver );
receiver . advance();                     // move on to next element
}
```

In this code, *receivers* is a variable holding a set of users and *receiver* is an iterator over this set. The loop iterates over every member of *receivers*, testing to find the one which is referred to by the variable *jbrown*. If it finds this, it replaces *jbrown* with user object *jblack*. This makes use of the *replace_element* operation defined on *Collection*. This takes two parameters: the replacement value and the iterator.

There is also an equivalent form for using a **for** loop:

```
for (   Iterator<Ref<User>> receiver = receivers . create_iterator();
        receiver . not_done();
        receiver ++ )
            if (receiver . get_element() == jbrown )
                receivers . replace_element( jblack, receiver );
```

in which the **for** loop constructor takes three arguments: an iterator, a test for the end of the loop and an instruction to advance the iterator (using the operator "++" rather than the alternative operation *advance*).

12.3.4 Persistence and data manipulation

Data manipulation is mostly carried out by the use of the normal C++ programming constructs, whose semantics continue unchanged. The goal is that transient and persistent objects are subject to the same facilities, although transactions and querying are only available on persistent objects. The principal changes are in the areas of creation, update and deletion of persistent objects. These are changed by the addition of operations on the classes *Persistent_Object* and *Ref* . *Persistent_Object* contains the facilities for creating objects and for the behavior which should occur when an object is moved between memory and disk. *Ref* contains the facilities for managing the relationships between persistent objects.

The *Persistent_Object* class

The class *Persistent_Object* holds the operations which are concerned with storing objects. These are:

- three new forms of the operation *new*;
- an operation, *mark_modified*, which must be called when an object is updated;
- two operations one of which, *odb_activate*, is automatically called when an object is brought into memory, while the other, *odb_deactivate*, is called when the object is swapped out again.

The operation *new* creates objects. In standard C++, this allocates memory appropriately. In a persistent system, the operation must also prepare the object to be stored. The ODMG binding supplies three versions of *new* which can be used:

- The first version requires a parameter which specifies a database in which the object is to be placed.
- The second form omits this parameter and assigns the database to a substitute value, *transient_memory*, and so creates a transient instance of a persistence capable class.

- The third form specifies another persistent object "near" which this one is to be clustered The exact meaning of "near" is implementation dependent, but may mean on the same disk page if at all possible.

Here are three examples:

```
Ref<User> jbrown = new( EmailDB ) User; // Put this user in the Email
                                                    database
Ref<User> currentUser = new User;        // This is a transient application
                                                    variable
Ref<User> jblack = new( jbrown ) User;   // Put this user near jbrown
```

The *mark_modified* operation is called whenever the object is changed. For instance, in the operation to delete a message from a mailbox, the process must call *mark_modified* on the mailbox object. The point of this is, once more, to give the system implementors programmer assistance so that application data can be committed efficiently.

The *odb_activate* and *odb_deactivate* operations are provided as a place in which the programmer can determine what should happen about transient components of persistent objects when the objects get swapped between memory and disk. The programmer can re-program these for each class to achieve the behavior desired. One standard kind of transient component is the display representation of the object, which need not be stored with the object. For instance, in a window-based display system such as O_2Look, the presentation associated with an object need not be stored. In this case, *odb_activate* might create and bring up the presentation of a retrieved object, while *odb_deactivate* might clear the screen area used by the presentation.

The *Ref* class

The *Ref* template class provides persistent references between objects. The operations and operators provided in this class largely duplicate the facilities of transient C++ pointers in the persistent environment.

Ref has the following operations:

- four constructors, which create references which are uninitialized or are copies of pointers, other references or instances of *Ref_Any* (see below);
- a destructor;
- an operation, *clear*, which nullifies the value of the reference;
- an operation to delete the object from memory and from the database;
- an operation to test if the reference is set to a null value.

There are also operators to dereference the value and to test for equality and inequality.

The *Ref_Any* class

The class *Ref_Any* is provided to support references of any type and so is a dynamic type in the terms discussed in the previous chapter. This is a useful addition since it is possible to create code which is generic over any object type. *Ref_Any* is also used to cast objects as copies down the inheritance where the application knows that this is safe (see Section 12.4.4 for more on this). There are operations defined on the class to create a *Ref_Any* version of any object and to convert it back to its more specific form.

For instance, the lookup operation of the database class described in the next section returns a *Ref_Any* value. The operation takes a C++ string and retrieves the object that is named by that string. Providing a type for the object returned is tricky since it could be anything and so the implementor of the operation cannot be specific. Therefore, the operation is made general by returning a dynamically typed value. This can then be cast to the correct type since the programmer using the operation should know the expected type of the returned object.

Here is an example of the use of the operation:

```
Ref_Any result =  EmailDB -> lookup_object( "SuperUser" );
Ref<Superuser> superuser = result;
```

in which the result is returned as a *Ref_Any* and this is then cast to be a *Superuser* object. More usually these two lines would be collapsed to:

```
Ref<Superuser> superuser =  EmailDB -> lookup_object( "Super User" );
```

so that the coercion is immediately performed.

■ 12.3.5 DBMS classes

There are two system-supplied classes which are provided in order to support a DBMS environment. These classes are *Database* and *Transaction*.

The *Database* class

Database objects provide mechanisms for managing the coherent storage of data from different applications. A database object is created as a transient reference to an area of persistent store called a database, which must already exist – databases cannot be created through C++. The database class has the following operations:

- *open* links the database object to a named database and makes it available for data access;
- *close* cleans up the database, writing committed updates to disk and then prevents further updates via this database object until another *open* operation is carried out;

- *set_object_name* creates a persistent named root object in the database;
- *get_object_name* retrieves the name of a root object;
- *rename_object* changes the name of a root object;
- *lookup_object* retrieves a root object by name (as discussed above).

Here is an example of the code which populates the Email database.

```
Database DBref;
Database * EmailDB = &DBref
EmailDB -> open( "Email" )
Ref<User> SuperUser = new( EmailDB ) User
Set<Ref<User>> theUsers = new( EmailDB ) Set<Ref<User>>
EmailDB -> set_object_name( SuperUser, "SuperUser" )
EmailDB -> set_object_name( theUsers, "theUsers" )
EmailDB -> close();
```

In this code, a database called *Email* has already been created. *EmailDB* is a transient objects which refers to this database. The next two lines create potentially persistent objects in memory – *SuperUser* and *theUsers*. The two lines following these make them persistent by naming them in the database and the *close* operation completes the database interaction.

The *Transaction* class

Any change to an ODMG database must take place in the context of a transaction. The boundaries of the transaction delimit a sequence of C++ instructions which contain an atomic change to a database and the *Transaction* class provides operations for starting, checkpointing, aborting and committing changes. Transactions are not automatically started when a database is opened, but must be explicitly started.

The class supports the following operations.

- The *begin* operation starts a transaction.
- The *abort* operation aborts all changes and releases all locks. The transaction object is not deleted.
- The *checkpoint* operation makes all changes to persistent data permanent. It does not release locks or affect any pointers or references. Therefore updates can continue.
- The *commit* operations also makes all changes permanent but completes the transaction, releasing all of the locks. As part of this operation, transient references in persistent objects are set to a null value.

An update operation should be implemented in terms of a transaction. Thus the operation to flush a mailbox looks like:

```
void Mailbox :: flush()
{    Transaction TXflush;
     TXflush . begin();
     for (   Iterator<Ref<Message>> messageIter = holds . create_iterator();
                  messageIter . not_done();
                  messageIter ++ )
           { holds -> remove_element_at( messageIter );
             messageIter . get_element() . mark_modified();
           };
     mark_modified();
     TXflush. commit();
}
```

This operation starts by creating a transaction object, *TXflush*, and starting it. It then iterates through the messages held in the mailbox and removes them one at a time from the set of held messages (thus unlinking them from the mailbox as well); it marks each message as having been modified; and finally marks the mailbox as being modified. The two uses of *mark_modified* ensure that all of the changed messages and the changed mailbox have their updated versions written back to store.

■ 12.3.6 OQL in C++

There are two ways of including OQL queries in the ODMG standard C++ binding:

- by use of query operations definitions defined on class *Collection*; and
- by using one of a family of free-standing functions, collected together as the overloaded function *oql*.

The querying operations in the *Collection* class

There are four of these:

- *query* is an operation which retrieves the results of an OQL query into a C++ collection;
- *select_element* is an operation which retrieves the single element which is the result of the query;
- *exists_element* takes an OQL query and tests if there are any results to this query;
- *select* takes an OQL query and returns an iterator over the collection of results.

Here are some examples:

```
Set<Ref<User>> usersWithMail;
theUsers -> query( usersWithMail, "this . incoming . number() > 0" );
```

in which the set of all users, *theUsers*, is queried and those with a non-empty mailbox are placed in the collection, *usersWithMail*;

```
jbrown = theUsers -> select_element( "login == \"jbrown\"" );
```

in which the single user with that login is returned. Finding no such user or more than one user results in an error;

```
mailFromJane? = incoming . holds ->
   exists_element( "this . sender . login == \"jbrown\"" );
```

which queries the incoming mailbox and returns a positive integer if there is a message sent by "jbrown"; and

```
Iterator< Ref<User> > userIter = theUsers ->
   select( "this . incoming . number() > 0" );
for ( userIter, userIter->not_done(), userIter++ )
   cout << userIter->get_element() . login << endl;
```

in which an iterator is created for the set of users with mail and these are then iterated over and their login names are printed.

The function *oql*

oql is a family of overloaded functions which provide full access to OQL by passing a query to OQL as a string parameter. Besides the query, the function takes a result identifier and query parameters as arguments. All versions of *oql* have an indefinite number of arguments for this purpose since the number of parameters varies from query to query. The varieties of *oql* differ in the kind of result returned – there is one function for collection results, one for object results and one for each type of atomic literal value. All versions return an integer, which is zero if the query is correctly formed.

The queries can be parameterized. The actual parameters appear as the third and subsequent parameters to *oql*. The formal values appear in the query in the form $<p><t> in which <p> is a number indicating its order in the actual parameter list and <t> indicates its type. <t> may be any of: "o" (object of <Ref> class); "k" (collection), "s" (string), "r" (real), "c" (character), or "i" (integer).

Here are some examples of each of these:

```
int ok?;
Ref<User> jbrown;
ok? = oql( jbrown, "element(select U from U in theUsers
   where U . login == \"jbrown\")" );

Ref<User> theUser;
         *char userName;
ok? = oql(theUser, "element(select U from U in theUsers
   where U . login == $1s)",userName)
```

```
Set<Ref<User>> usersWithMail;
ok? = oql( usersWithMail, "select U from U in theUsers
    where U. incoming . number() > 0" );

int howMany;
ok? = oql( howMany,
        "element(select M . number from M in $1o . storage
    where M . name = $2s)", theUser, "Archive" );
```

In the first of these queries, the query has no parameters. It finds the user with the login "jbrown" and refers to it by the variable *jbrown*. The second query has a single string parameter for the user name and refers to its result by *theUser*. The third query returns a collection – the users with incoming mail. The fourth query returns the number of messages in somebody's "Archive" mailbox. The query has two parameters – the first being the user object being queried and the second being the name of the stored mailbox.

■ 12.3.7 Summary

The ODMG proposal for the way in which C++ should be bound to an ODMG-compliant DBMS includes system-supplied classes for domain types, collections, databases and transactions; a general class supporting persistence capability; a generic class for persistence object references; a syntactic extension for relationship inverses; and two means to access OQL from within the language. Unfortunately, there are some differences in the ways in which persistent and non-persistent data are referred to, since the former must use the *Ref* template class rather than the usual pointer notation. This would heavily impact on porting existing applications to an ODMG-compliant system, but it is expected that this distinction will be removed in later versions of the standard.

There is still a great deal of flexibility in the standard and each compliant system will provide the features described in its own individual way. In order to consider how this works out in practice, the next section discusses how O_2 implements the proposal.

■ 12.4 C++ in O_2

The previous section described the design of the C++ language binding produced by the ODMG. This section demonstrates the implementation of this binding produced as a component of the O_2 system. In this section, the differences between O_2 and the ODMG standard will be described. Firstly, an overview of the C++ component will be given. Then the class library which supports ODMG concepts is described. Finally, some of the techniques for using this class library are discussed. In Section 12.5, the electronic mail application will be used to describe how the database schema is input, how the operations are programmed and how the application is completed.

■ 12.4.1 Overview of the facilities

The ODMG standard is intended to provide a baseline for the use of C++ in OODBMS. O_2, in common with other ODMG-compliant products, provides more than this baseline and some of the facilities appear in a slightly different form than that described in ODMG-93. Furthermore, C++ is just one of the interfaces which a programmer can use to manipulate O_2, so many of the facilities are equivalent to mechanisms in the system administration tools.

Here are some of the extensions and differences:

- O_2 does not force the programmer to create classes as subclasses of a class called *Persistent_Object* in order to attach storage facilities to objects. Instead, it provides a system tool, *O2import*, which takes class definitions from a header file and creates O_2 versions of those classes. It then uses the *d_Ref* template class to distinguish instances of the O_2 class from instances of the standard C++ class. There is also another tool, *O2export*, which produces plain C++ from O_2 classes.
- O_2 provides persistence in exactly the way ODMG specifies with versions of **new** which place persistent objects in a database or close to other stored objects. However, it also provides persistence by reachability from roots which are the named values in databases.
- O_2 provides an extra DBMS class for sessions, which are the controlling structure for database server access.
- There is also a class for locks, so that lock management can be explicitly managed in O_2.
- There are facilities for using the graphical interface generator, O_2Look, within C++.
- O_2 provides the free-standing query function in a different way, by making a query be an object and providing a class of queries. It also removes the requirement that the query parameters be typed.
- Some of the class names used have changed, usually by the addition of the prefix, "d_", to distinguish ODMG classes from similar classes which existed in previous versions of O_2. For instance, the database string class is called *d_String*.

In the rest of this section, the classes which O_2 supplies for database management will be described and then techniques for their use will be demonstrated.

■ 12.4.2 O_2 specific classes

The O_2 implementation of C++ provides its own class library to support the activities promised in the ODMG standard.

The Persistent object classes

When the *o2import* program is run, it places the user-defined classes in the context of a set of system-supplied classes which are shown in Figure 12.1. *d_Object* and *o2_root* between them implement the *Persistent_Object* class defined by ODMG and described in Section 12.3.4. *mark_modified, d_activate* and *d_deactivate* have the same uses as defined in the ODMG section – indicating that an object has been changed, preparing an object for use once it has been swapped into memory, and preparing the object to be swapped out again. The O_2Look operations will be discussed later in this section. The *copy* operation provides for shallow copying of an object, while *deep_copy* performs a deep copy (see Section 2.1.3 for the differences). Similarly *equal* and *deep_equal* perform shallow and deep equality tests.

The template class, *d_Ref*, is used for references to persistent pointers. It implements the ODMG proposal described in Section 12.3.4. The class provides the operations specified there together with an operation to lock the object within a transaction, as described below. *d_Ref_Any* implements the *Ref_Any* proposal in the same way.

Domain classes

The classes *d_String, d_Date, d_Time, d_Timestamp* and *d_Interval* implement the ODMG classes described in Section 12.3.2. Apart from the change of name these classes implement the proposals as specified.

The Collection classes

The template classes *d_Collection, d_Set, d_Bag, d_List, d_Array, d_Varray* and *d_Iterator* implement the ODMG proposals described in Section 12.2.3. *d_Collection* is the generalization of *d_Set, d_Bag, d_List* and *d_Varray*. *d_Array* is supplied to provide a uniform access method for C++ non-persistent arrays. Once more, apart from naming, these classes implement the proposal very closely.

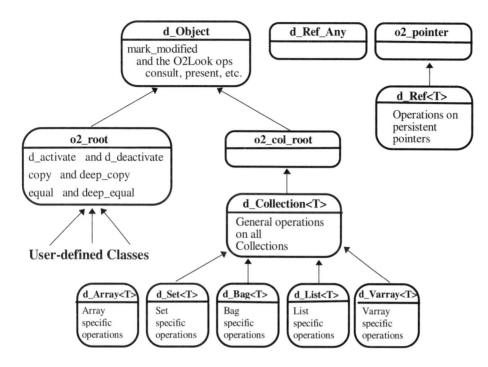

Figure 12.1 The persistent object class hierarchy.

The DBMS object classes

As well as classes for databases and transactions, O₂ also provides a class for sessions. The class *d_Session* defines objects for managing a session which connects to the DBMS. The class has a constructor which creates a session variable, which is then used with member functions which begin and end the session. The *begin* operation connects the client process with a server, while the *end* operation disconnects the session and commits any uncommitted changes. The *begin* operation can take parameters which give the system name, the server name and the home directory of the O₂ system to be used. It is also possible to identify libraries which will be used, to pass the command line parameters from the system command which invoked the application and to determine the interaction mode (textual or graphical).

The class *d_Database* implements the ODMG proposal for a database class described in Secton 12.3.5. As well as the operations to open and close the database and to manipulate named objects, the class is extended with the following operations:

- operations to create the database either in the context of a schema, or in the context of a schema and a disk volume;

- an operation to destroy the database;
- an operation to garbage collect the database, i.e. to free up the disk space used by unreachable data (garbage collection will be described in Section 14.7);
- operations to create and destroy persistent roots;
- operations to access and change the volume used by the database.

The class *d_Transaction* implements the ODMG proposal for a transaction class, described in Section 12.3.5. It has the begin, abort, commit and checkpoint operations defined in the proposal and there is an extra operation called *validate*. This operation increases the range of commit behavior, by providing a half-way point between *commit* and *checkpoint*. The *checkpoint* operation makes all changes permanent, but otherwise continues the transaction. The *commit* operation not only does this but also cancels all locks held, frees up memory and terminates the write access to the database. The problem with *commit* is that in order to continue, it is necessary to reconstruct the program's references to data, since all of these will have been de-allocated. The operation *validate* makes the changes permanent, releases all locks and returns to read-only mode, but does not free up memory or remove all current references, so that, after invoking *validate*, it is easier to continue.

The other change to the transaction mechanism is that there is explicit support for locking. O_2 provides two-phase locking with deadlock detection. To support this, a transaction holds a list of locked items, which is normally managed transparently, i.e. locks are set when attempts are made to read and write objects. However, the programmer also has access to this list and can use it to generate "intention" locks. There are three ways in which locks can be set:

- by providing a list of objects to be locked when starting the transaction;
- by accessing an object inside the transaction, in which case a lock is set automatically;
- by invoking the lock operation on any object inside the transaction.

For example, in the transaction, *T*, that follows, locks on five objects are built up:

```
d_Transaction  T;
T . begin( [O1, O2, O3] );    // Three objects are locked from the outset
O4 = ...                       // Now O4 is locked as well
O5 . lock( OL_WRITE )          //  and so is O5 (in write-mode)
```

Deadlock is one of a number of system events which are handled automatically in the system, but in a way which allows the programmer to alter the consequences of their occurrence. Other events are: waiting on a locked object, fatal errors from *O₂Store*, and fatal errors from *O₂Engine*. To give an example of how the programmer might make use of this, consider the following code:

```
void waitReactor( O2_event eventKind, .... ) {
   switch (eventKind) {
      case O2_WAIT: message( "Waiting" );
      case O2_DEADLOCK: { T . abort(); message( "Aborting due to deadlock") };
      }
   }
O2_handler myEventHandler;
myEventHandler = o2_event( O2_WAIT, waitReactor )
```

The code defines an event handler, *waitReactor*, which tests the kind of event and reacts differently. If it is waiting for a lock, it prints "waiting", although the code here could be extended to give the user a chance to abort the transaction. If the event is a deadlock, the transaction is aborted. The system-provided *o2_event* function associates the handler with the event.

Access to OQL

Queries are objects in O₂. There is a class called *d_OQL_Query*, whose instances are constructed from strings or as copies of other queries and which has an overloaded operator, "<<", with which the actual parameters are given. The function, *d_oql_execute* is then used to execute the query.

Thus the way in which a query is written and used is:

```
d_OQL_Query  aQuery( "select ... $1 ...  $2 ... $3 ... " );
aQuery << actualValue₁ << actualValue₂ << actualValue₃;
int ok? = d_oql_execute( aQuery, result );
```

which illustrates a query with three parameters. The first line creates the query object. The second line assigns the actual parameters by repeated use of the "<<" operator. The third line executes the query, returning zero if the query was successful. In this case, the result value is assigned to the variable given as the second parameter to *d_oql_execute*. After the execution of the query the list of actual parameter settings is flushed, so that the same query can be re-used subsequently with different parameter settings.

Another change to the way in which OQL is used is that O₂ does not require that the parameters of a query be typed – thus parameters are written, as shown above, as "$1" rather than as, for example, "$1k" to indicate that the parameter is a collection.

Access to O₂Look

The facilities of *O₂Look* (described in Section 7.5.4) are provided in two ways: as a set of free-standing functions; or as a set of member functions defined on all objects in the class *d_Object* (see above). Recall that in *O₂Look* a presentation is a screen window displaying all or (if a mask is used) part of the contents of an object. Presentations can be used to create a non-editable display or an editor for the object. In the latter case, editing changes a copy of the data which is local to the presentation and must be explicitly written back into the objects.

There are six free standing functions which manipulate the data presentations currently displayed: create a presentation from an object, return the data currently presented into an object, refresh a presentation, return all the presentations defined in the application, return all the currently displayed presentations, and return the current presentation.

The member functions defined on *d_Object* provide these same facilities, but also permit: the presentation associated with the object to be displayed (either in an editable or non-editable form), the erasure of one or all of the presentations of the object, and the ability to enable or disable each of the methods of the object's class (i.e. to add or remove them from the menu of operations in the presentation).

To illustrate this, here are three methods which might be added to class *User*, to manage the display. The first one creates a display presentation and puts it on the screen. The second invokes an editor presentation and copies the data back if the pencil icon is used to quit the editor, since this is used to indicate that changes should be retained. The third one removes all presentations associated with an object.

```
void show( ) {
    Lk_Presentation userPresentation = present( 0 ); // Use a default mask
    display( userPresentation );                      // A non-editable display
}

void modify( ) {
    Lk_Presentation userPresentation = present( 0 ); // Use a default mask
    int result = edit( userPresentation );            // An editable display
    if (result == LK_SAVE)                            // Was exit via the
                                                      //     save button?
        { int saved = consult( userPresentation );   // Copy the changes
          if (saved == 0)                             //    back to the object
              message( "User object modified successfully" );
          else message( "Failed to save changes" );
        };
}

void remove( ) {
    if (erase_all() != 0)                            // Remove the presentation
        message( "Error removing the object from the display" )
}
```

■ 12.4.3 Making C++ objects persistent in O_2

O_2 provides two ways of making objects persistent – by the use of persistent roots plus reachability (as described in Section 3.3.2), and by explicit storage in the database. To illustrate the difference, here are two ways to set up the extent of class *User* and to add a user to this extent.

The reachability method is coded as follows (assuming an open database referred to by the variable, *emailDB*):

```
d_Set< d_Ref< User > > theUsers;
d_Ref< User > jbrown;
emailDB . create_persistence_root( "The Users", theUsers )
theUsers . insert_element( jbrown );
```

in which *theUsers* is explicitly stored by making it a persistent root, while *jbrown* becomes persistent by reachability from *theUsers*.

The explicit method looks like:

```
d_Set< d_Ref< User > > theUsers = new( emailDB ) d_Set< d_Ref< User > >;
d_Ref< User > jbrown = new( emailDB ) d_Ref< User >;
emailDB . set_object_name( "The Users", theUsers )
theUsers . insert_element( jbrown );
```

in which the two objects are attached to the database as they are created and *theUsers* is given a name in the database, which makes it accessible by a program. *jbrown* is then accessible since it is an element of *theUsers*.

Given the existence of these two objects, it is possible to add a second user object which is to be clustered near the first by:

```
d_Ref< User > jblack = new( jbrown ) d_Ref< User >;
theUsers . insert_element( jblack );
```

The difference between the two versions seems slight. In the first version, *jbrown* has been created in memory and only gets stored because it has been inserted into a persistent set and is therefore reachable. In the second version, the use of **new** has explicitly placed it into the database. The difference between a named object and a persistent root is quite subtle. The former is to allow the programmer to access a value, while a root is used to ensure that its components are stored. From a named object, there are only reference links, i.e. a means for the programmer to access one object from another. From a root object, there are reachability links, in which case if the first object is stored, the second will be as well.

■ 12.4.4 Manipulating persistent and transient objects

Accessing and managing the data held in both persistent and transient objects makes use of both normal C++ references and O₂ object references via the template class *d_Ref*. Storing objects in the database and retrieving them later makes use of the operations, *d_deactivate, d_activate* and *mark_modified*. The *d_Ref_Any* class is used to change the types of object. The use of each of these will now be described.

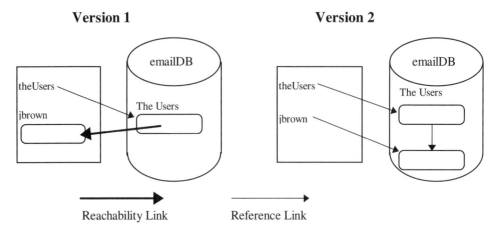

Figure 12.2 Persistence and object creation.

The class *d_Ref*

All references to objects which might become persistent must use the template class *d_Ref*. The *o2import* tool automatically transforms normal C++ pointers from the star notation to instantiations of *d_Ref*. *d_Ref* has constructors which create instances from a C++ pointer, from another *d_Ref*, from a *d_Ref_Any* or from a root in the database. All of these create transient object references which could become persistent. There is also another version of the **new** operator which also creates transient objects which could become persistent.

Thus all of the following four commands create transient references (i.e. in-memory references, which if nothing else affects them, will be discarded at the end of the transaction):

- ```
  d_Ref<SuperUser> superUser( "Super User", OL_READ );
  ```

  superUser is an in-memory reference to a value which is already persistent, being a root in the database. The syntax of the line specifies the type of the object and a variable name, as usual. The two parameters in brackets are a name for the object in the database and an indication that this is to be opened in read-only mode. This means that it will not be assigned an exclusive lock as yet. If an assignment which modifies one of its properties is encountered subsequently, the access mode will be changed and the object will be exclusively locked.

- ```
  *User mustBeTransient;
  ```

  mustBeTransient, being a normal C++ pointer, can never be used to refer to an object in the database.

•
```
d_Ref<User> couldBePersistent1( dummy1 );
```

couldBePersistent1 is created as an in-memory reference. It could become persistent either by being named in the database or by being made reachable from a persistent root.

•
```
d_Ref<User>couldBePersistent2 = new( transient_memory );
```

couldBePersistent2 is also created as an in memory reference rather than as a component of a database. However, it too could become persistent by being named in the database at a later date or by being made reachable from a persistent root.

The different effects are shown in Figure 12.3.

It is also possible to create normal C++ references to persistent objects, thus:

```
User* transientUser = jbrown . ptr;
```

which provides a normal C++ reference, which might be necessary, for instance to use as a parameter to an external library.

The critical feature of transient references is that they hold on to areas of memory. It is important, from an efficiency point of view, to get rid of them as soon as they are no longer needed. This could be when an object is removed altogether or it could be when an object is put back into the database since it is no longer needed by the current process. In either case, the reference should be deleted. Thus:

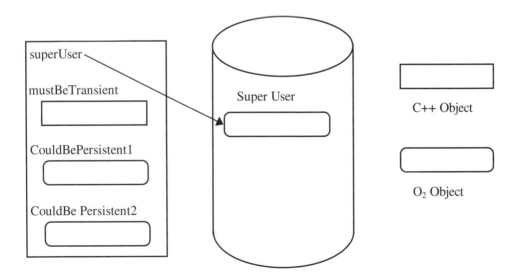

Figure 12.3 Persistent and transient references.

```
theUsers . insert_element( jblack );
```

should be followed by:

```
jblack . destroy( );
```

if this object is no longer to be manipulated by the code. If this is not done, then the object will be removed only when no more in-memory space remains. Furthermore, when the data structure contains cycles, these can only be removed from memory by using the *destroy* method.

d_deactivate, d_activate and *mark_modified*

Removing an object from memory (which might happen because of the *destroy* operation, when no in-memory references to the object remain, or when the data is committed) results in the *d_deactivate* function being called. Its main purpose is to tidy up memory. The function, which is defined on class *o2_root*, can be overridden in any user-defined class to carry out any other changes which should accompany the removal of an object of that class.

Similarly, when an object is swapped into memory, the *d_activate* function is called. This is vital if a persistent object holds transient properties, i.e. ones which are not to be stored in the database. For example, it might be useful to enhance the mail application with a memo pad. Each user object could be given the ability to manage a list of strings which can be consulted while they are logged in, but which are removed when they log out. The property might be programmed as a property:

```
stringList memoPad;
```

where stringList is a C++ list of strings, programmed using normal C++ pointers. In this case, the *d_activate* function must be used to initialize the list when the user object is swapped in.

After a persistent object is modified, it is important to call the *mark_modified* operation. In:

```
jblack . password = "NewPassword";
jblack . mark_modified( );
TX . commit();
```

failure to include the second line will mean that the update will not be committed. Essentially *mark_modified* ensures that the updates to the in-memory object are passed back to its persistent version.

d_Ref_Any and downcasting

One last issue concerning the manipulation of object references concerns changing the type of an object reference and the use of the *d_Ref_Any* class.

Suppose that the following have been created:

```
d_Ref<SuperUser> superUser( "Super User", OL_READ );
d_Ref<User> jbrown;
```

then it is all right to do:

```
jbrown = superUser;
```

but not:

```
superUser = jbrown;
```

since the latter makes *superUser* refer to an object which may not have all of the required operations defined on it. However, if it is known that *jbrown* is the superuser, then the latter would, in fact, be fine. The fact that is not in general acceptable prevents it being used in specific instances. Downcasting, as this process is called, is achieved instead by commands such as:

```
superUser = d_Ref<SuperUser> ( d_Ref_Any( jbrown ) );
```

in which the user object has been turned into a dynamically typed object (i.e. of class *d_Ref_Any*) and then the constructor for *d_Ref* is used which takes a *d_Ref_Any* object as its argument.

■ 12.4.5 Database management

The fundamental way in which an application accesses a database is to open a session and then a database as in:

```
d_Session theSession;
d_Database emailDB;
if (session . begin( argc, argv, "mailServer", "mailSystem",
                                "/sys/lib/o2home" ) )
   { message( "Application cannot reach the server" );   exit(1) };
emailDB . open( "emailDB" );
... accesses
emailDB . close();
theSession . end();
```

In this code, session and database variables are declared in the first two lines. Then the *begin* operation of the *Session* class is used to connect the client to the server and then the database can be opened. After the program is finished the database is closed and the session finished.

Usually, the database will be held in one particular volume (as described in Section 7.3.1), which is specified when it is created (note, however, that this does not happen within C++). However, it is possible to make the database span multiple volumes and for the application to span multiple databases. In the following:

```
emailDB extend( "emailDB", "SecondVolume" );
```

adds a second volume to the database, while:

```
d_Database emailDB, emailDB2;
emailDB . open( "emailDB" );
d_Set< d_Ref<User> > firstUserSet( "The Users" );
emailDB2 . open( "EMAIL2db" );
d_Set< d_Ref<User> > secondUserSet( "The Users" );
```

would be used in which the data had been split into two databases. Only one database can be open for the explicit retrieval of objects at any one time. The third line retrieves the user set from the first database (since that is the one that is open), while the fifth line uses the second database. Now both sets are available for use in the program, since both the variables *firstUserSet* and *secondUserSet* remain in scope.

■ 12.5 The electronic mail application in O₂ C++

This section uses the facilities just described to create a complete electronic mail application in O₂'s C++ implementation. Firstly, the schema will be created. Then the application structure will be created. Finally, the operations will be implemented. The whole application is listed as Appendix A.

■ 12.5.1 Database definition

All use of O₂ takes place in the context of a schema and a database instance of that schema. Neither of these can be created from within C++ and so must be set up using one of the system interfaces. As shown in Section 8.3.1 these are created with:

```
create schema Email
```

and

```
create base EmailDB
```

C++ can then be used for the schema and application development by creating C++ files and then using *o2import* to bring these into the database context. The example calls for the creation of files containing the four classes: header files *User.hxx*, *Superuser.hxx*, *Mailbox.hxx* and *Message.hxx*; and code files *User.cc*, etc. In this subsection, the header files will be described and then how they are used.

C++ header files for the mail application

The structure of the schema was described in Section 8.3. Now this structure is revisited in terms of C++. The following code is derived directly from the schema found at the end of Section 8.3, being rewritten in C++ syntax with reference to the O₂ versions of the ODMG classes: *d_String*, *d_Ref*, *d_Set*, *d_List* and *d_Short*.

Here is the first class description:

```
class User {
  private:
     d_String name,
     d_String login,
     d_String password,
     Mailbox incoming;
     d_Set<Mailbox> storage;
  public:
     User(const char* userName; const char* userLogin,
        const char* userPassword);
     void sendmail(),
     void receive( d_Ref<Message> theMessage );
     void summarize();
     void readMail();
     void deleteMsg();
     void createMbox();
     void removeMbox();
     void flushMbox();
     void displayName();
     static d_Set< d_Ref<User> > theUsers;
     static void restart(int);
     static void clear();
};
```

This class is mostly straightforward except for the introduction of the static members. As before, *theUsers* is the extent of the class and this is managed by the two operations, *restart* and *clear*. *restart* is needed to refresh the set after transaction commits and aborts, while *clear* flushes the set of users. Section 12.5.3 will provide more details on these and how they are implemented.

The other three header files hold no surprises:

```
class Superuser : User {
  public:
     Superuser();
     void makeUser();
     void deleteUser();
     void statistics();
};

class Mailbox {
  private:
     d_String name,
     d_List<d_Ref<Message>> holds;
  public:
     Mailbox( const char* theName );
     Unsigned Long number();
     void insert( d_Ref<Message> newMessage );
     void showHeaders();
     d_Ref<Message> getMessage( Unsigned Long number );
     void delete( d_Ref<Message> theMessage );
     void flush();
     void display();
};
```

```
class Message {
  private:
    d_String subject,
    d_Timestamp timeSent;
    d_String body,
    d_Set< d_Ref<Mailbox> > heldin;
    d_Ref<User > sender,
    d_Set< d_Ref<User> > recipients;
  public:
    Message( d_Ref<User > sendingUser );
    void summarize( d_Short number );
    void display();
    void reply( d_Ref<User > sender, d_Ref<User > replier,
                      const char* oldSubject);
};
```

Using the header files

Having written the header files in pure C++ as listed above, the classes described are added to the schema by use of the *o2import* tool. This is an operating system level command and in the *User* case would look like:

```
o2import ... -schema Email -class User User.hxx
```

in which the dots hide options which identify the server and machine names. The result of this is that the file, *User.hxx*, is changed and a new file, *User_code.cc* is created.

The new version of *User.hxx* includes the original file contents but extends these with some additional operations. The structure of the new file is:

```
#ifndef __ODMG_93__
class User {
  ... old contents
};
#else
#include "o2_root_defs.hxx"
class User : public virtual O2_root {
  ... old contents repeated
protected:
  virtual void o2_new();
  ... some more virtual functions
public:
  User( o2_Shadow shad, Handle hd );
};
#endif
```

The new version is controlled by a switch (*_ODMG_93_*) which permits the code to be used unchanged if an ODMG database is not being used. The database version is extended with system functions which O$_2$ uses to manage access to persistent data.

There are three other system commands which are similar to *o2import*. These
are:

- *o2unimport*, which takes a modified header file and returns it to its original
state;
- *o2export*, which takes a file containing an O$_2$C class and creates a C++
version including the O$_2$ virtual functions for database access;
- *o2unexport*, which reverses the effect of *o2export*.

■ 12.5.2 Setting up the database

The database cannot be created from within C++. Instead the system commands
described in Section 8.3.1 are used, as discussed above.

The persistent roots, however, can be set up from within C++ and this is
done with the following program:

```
main() {
  d_Session theSession;
  d_Database theDatabase;
  if (theSession. begin( .... ) )      // parameters select the server, etc.
      { showSnl( "Connection error" );   exit(1);   }
  *char databaseName = getString( "Which database do you want to set up? " );

  d_Transaction TXcreateRoots;
  TXcreateRoots . begin();
    theDatabase . open( databaseName );
    theDatabase . create_persistence_root( "The Users",
      "d_Set< d_Ref<User> >" );
    theDatabase . create_persistence_root( "Super User",
       "d_Ref<SuperUser>" );
    d_Ref<SuperUser> superUser( "Super User" );
    superUser = User( "Jane Brown", "jbrown", "????" );
    d_Set< d_Ref<User> > theUsers( "The Users" );
    theUsers . insert_element( superUser );
  TXcreateRoots . commit();

  theDatabase . close();
  theSession . end();
}
```

The program uses some interaction functions (*showSnl* and *getString*) which
will be described in the next subsection. The code begins with three lines which
connect to the server and then it requests the database name from the user.
Inside the transaction, *TXcreateRoots*, the database is opened, the persistent roots
are created and the superuser object is also created and inserted into the set of
users. The program ends by committing the transaction, closing the database
and ending the session.

■ 12.5.3 Application implementation

Unfortunately, the O_2 application structure described in Section 7.4.2 is not available with C++. This means that the application needs a main program which provides the ability to choose between a set of transactions equivalent to each of the facilities required.

The application is built around a menu. The CD-Rom which accompanies this book will illustrate how this would be built on top of O_2*Look*. In the text of the book, a simple textual interface will be used. This will present the user with an indexed menu which begins:

```
1: Login
2: Logout
```

etc. If the superuser is logged in, then the *Superuser* operations will be added to the menu. The menu ends with the quit option:

```
0: Quit
```

To achieve this, the application will be coded as:

- a number of free-standing functions which interact with the user;
- 12 parameterless functions which implement the facilities;
- query functions which retrieve a user by login and a mailbox by name;
- one function which prints the menu;
- a menu function which requests a choice and distributes control according to that choice; and
- the main function.

The *interaction* functions

The interaction functions display scalar values, request confirmation from the user and request scalar values from the user. The request functions print a prompt and request the input of a particular scalar value. Here is a list of the functions required:

- *showS* prints a string provided as a parameter;
- *showI* prints an integer provided as a parameter;
- *showSnl* prints a string provided as a parameter and follows it with a new line;
- *showInl* prints an integer provided as a parameter and follows it with a new line;
- *yesNo* prints a question and returns an indication of whether the answer was "yes" or "no";
- *getInteger* prints a prompt and awaits the input of an integer;
- *getString* prints a prompt and awaits the input of a string.

The *main* function

The *main* function must connect to the database and control the menu. To achieve this, the program starts a session and then opens the database chosen by the user. The heart of the function is a loop which iterates around calls to the menu function. This is implemented to return the user's choice. As soon as the choice is zero (which is the "quit" option), the program quits, closing the database and the session.

The function looks like:

```
main() {
   d_Session theSession;
   d_Database theDatabase;
   if (theSession. begin( .... ) )      // parameters select the server, etc.
      { showSnl( "Connection error" );   exit(1);  }
   *char databaseName = getString( "Which database do you want to open? " );
   theDatabase . open( databaseName );
   printMenu();
   while ( menu() > 0 )  {};            // call the menu until quit is chosen
   theDatabase . close();
   theSession . end();
}
```

The *menu* functions

printMenu is a simple function which prints the list of options. An outline of the code to achieve this now follows:

```
void printMenu( ) {
   showSnl( "Choose one of the following:" );
   showSnl( "1: Log In" );
   if (currentUser != NULL)              // Options 2-9 only appear
      { showSnl( "2: Log Out" );         //  if someone is logged on
         ...
         showSnl( "9: Flush a mailbox" );
      };
   if (currentUser == superUser)         // Options 10-12 only appear
      { showSnl( "10: Create a User" );  //  if the superuser is logged on
         showSnl( "11: Delete a User" );
         showSnl( "12: Statistics of Usage" );
      };
   showSnl( "0 : quit" );
}
```

The menu function is also very simple. It requests a number between 0 and 9 (or between 0 and 12 if the superuser is logged in) and then uses a case statement to distribute control to the appropriate facility functions. Finally it returns the choice so that *main* can test for the quit option.

\

```
int menu( ) {
  int choice = -1;
  int top = 9;
  if (currentUser == NULL) top = 1;
  if (currentUser == superUser) top = 12;
  while ( choice < 0 or choice > top)
        choice = getInt( "Choose an option between 0 and " + top + ": " );
  switch  (choice) {
    case 1: loginFacility(); break;
    case 2: logoutFacility(); break;
  ...
    case 12: statisticsFacility(); break;
    default {};                             // Do nothing if quit is requested
  }
  return choice;
}
```

The *query* functions

At several points in the program, there is the need to retrieve a member of *theUsers* by the login name of the user – for instance, in the login facility. In the application design, this was coped with by a test operation in *User*. However, as OQL is available, it would be far better to make use of that.

The basic query is of the form:

```
element ( select U from U in theUsers where U . login = $1 )
```

where $1 represents a formal parameter whose value must be supplied before the query can be executed. An O_2 query object to hold this can be created as follows:

```
d_OQL_Query findUser ( "element( select U from U in theUsers where U.
                                                  login = $1 )" );
```

Rather than embed calls like this directly into the code, the query will be turned into a C++ free standing function which calls the query and returns a user. This looks like:

```
d_Ref<User>  getUser( const *char aLogin ) {
  d_Ref<User> aUser;
  findUser<< aLogin;
  if ( d_oql_execute( findUser, aUser ) )
    return NULL;
    else return aUser;
}
```

The function takes the login as a parameter, which it passes to the query in the third line. It then executes the query and returns the user object found.

Similarly, the program must find a storage mailbox by name. There is a similar query for this purpose:

```
d_OQL_Query findMbox( "element( select M from M in $1 where M.name = $2 )" );
```

in which the first parameter is the set of mailboxes and the second is the name sought. Again this is turned into a function which is given in Appendix A.

The *facility* functions

These functions implement the 12 facilities introduced in Section 6.1. Those facilities which change the database will contain transactions, while read-only facilities will not. The facilities make use of a transient object holding a pointer to the current user. This will therefore be declared at the top of the application file as:

```
User *currentUser = NULL;
```

The login facility requires that the user inputs a login (*uLogin*) and password (*uPassword*), queries the user set on the login and checks the password. The code for this is:

```
void loginFacility( ) {
  Ref<User> theUser;
  d_String uLogin = getString( "Give the login name: " );
  d_String uPassword = getString( "Give the password: " );
  theUser = findUser( uLogin );
  if ( theUser != NULL && theUser . password == uPassword )
          currentUser = theUser;
          else showSnl( "Login incorrect" );
  printMenu();
}
```

The logout facility is even simpler:

```
void logoutFacility( ) {
currentUser = NULL;
}
```

Notice that neither of these use transactions since they do not change the database – they only modify the transient variable, *currentUser*.

The other facilities consist almost entirely of calls on the *User* or *Superuser* class operations. The only way they are distinguished is whether or not they change the database and are therefore transactions. The summarize and statistics operations do not change the database and so are not transactions. Here is the statistics facility (the summarize facility is similar):

```
void statisticsFacility( ) {
  superUser -> statistics();
}
```

The sendmail, readmail, delete message, create mailbox, delete mailbox, flush mailbox, create user and remove user facilities must all contain transactions since each of these potentially changes the database. The transaction commands could either be embedded in the class member functions or within these facility functions. Placing them in the member functions is superior, since then any locks that the transaction requires will be held for as little time as possible. Here is the way the *sendmail* facility is implemented:

```
void summarizeFacility( ) {
    if (currentUser != NULL)          // redundant guard since the operation
        currentUser . sendMail;       //    cannot be requested anyway
}
```

■ 12.5.4 Member function implementation

This section considers the contents of the code files which implement the operations described in the header files. In this chapter, there is only room for the development of a few of the operations – the rest can be seen in Appendix A.

Creating and deleting users

In order to demonstrate the way in which persistent objects are created and deleted, the first member functions to be dealt will be the ones which create and remove users. These are operations on class *Superuser* and look as follows:

```
void Superuser :: makeUser( ) {
    if ( currentUser == superUser ) {
        d_String uLogin = getString( "Give login name for new user: " );
        Ref<User> aUser = findUser( uLogin );
        if ( aUser == NULL )
                showSnl( "User already exists" );
        else { d_String uPass = getString( "Give password for new user: " );
                d_String uName = getString( "Give real name for new user: "
);
                Ref<User> newUser( uName, uLogin, uPass );
                d_Transaction TXcreateUser;
                TXcreateUser . begin();
                   theUsers . insert_element( newUser );
                   theUsers . mark_modified( );
                TXcreateUser . validate(); }
    }
}
```

This is relatively straightforward. The login for the user is requested and the OQL query, *findUser*, is used to check if the user exists, and, if it does, this would be reported as an error. If not, the password and name of the user are requested and a user is created. Then the transaction is created and this inserts the new user into *theUsers* (thus making it persistent). Notice that the transaction is started as late as possible to avoid locking *theUsers* too long. The function depends on an appropriate constructor for *User*. This is as usual:

```
User :: User( const char* userName; const char* userLogin,
                                    const char* userPassword)
   { name = userName; login = userLogin; password = userPassword; }
```

Deleting a user proceeds similarly:

```
void Superuser :: deleteUser( ) {
   if (currentUser == superUser ) {          // extra guard just in case
      *char uLogin = getString( "Give login name for user to delete: " );
      Ref<User> theUser = findUser( uLogin );
      if ( theUser == NULL )
         showSnl( "User does not exist" );
      else { d_Transaction TXdeleteUser;
            TXdeleteUser . begin();
                theUsers . remove_element( theUser );
                theUsers . mark_modified( );
            TXdeleteUser . validate(); }
   }
}
```

Again the user login is requested and *findUser* is used to look the user up in *theUsers*. This time failure to find the user would be an error, which would be reported by the sixth line. If the user does exist, the user object is removed from *theUsers* within the transaction.

The static members of class *User*

The static members of the class *User* provide globally available ways of clearing the database and of restarting. A restart function is required to read the root values from the database after a transaction commit. The restart functions looks as follows:

```
static void User :: restart(int) {
   theUsers = new d_Set< d_Ref<User> >( "The Users", OL_WRITE );
   superUser = new d_Ref<superUser>( "Super User", OL_WRITE );
}
```

in which the two objects are retrieved from the database by the appropriate use of **new**.

The database clearing function can also be used as part of the initialization of the system. It looks like:

```
static void User :: clear() {
   superUser = User("Jane Brown", "jbrown", "????" );
   d_Set< d_Ref<User> > emptySet;
   theUsers = emptySet;
   theUsers . insert_element( superUser );
}
```

in which *theUsers* is re-assigned to a freshly created empty set and the superuser object is created (from the user's name, login and password) and put in as the first object.

Sending mail

The process of sending mail starts with a call on the *sendMail* member function of the class *User*. Here is that function:

```
void User :: sendmail() {
   d_Ref<Message> theMessage( this );
}
```

i.e. the function merely calls a member function on *Message* providing the sending user as an argument.

The required constructor for message is:

```
void Message :: Message( Ref<User> theSender ) {
   sender = theSender;
   subject = getString( "Subject: " );
   recipients = d_Set< d_Ref<User> >( );
   *char uLogin = getString( "Give first recipient: " );
   while (uLogin == "")
      { Ref<User> receiver = findUser( uLogin );
        if ( receiver == NULL )
              showSnl( "Cannot find that user" );
        else recipients . insert_element( receiver );
        uLogin = getString(
              "Give next recipient (or empty string to quit): " );
      }

   heldIn = d_Set< d_Ref<Mailbox> >( );
   body = getString( "Body of message: " );
   timeSent = d_Timestamp :: current();
   for (U in recipients) U . receive( this );
}
```

The constructor puts together a message and then sends it to its recipients. The sender of the message and the subject are given values in the first two lines. The next section requests the login names of the users who are to receive the message. Again, *findUser* is used to retrieve the appropriate user objects which are built up as the set, *recipients*. The *heldIn* property is initialized to an empty set. This will be populated automatically by calls to the *insert* operation on mailboxes since *heldIn* has been defined to be the inverse of *holds*. The *body* and *timeSent* properties are provided with values in the next two lines. Then the message is disseminated by sending the message ("this") to the *receive* operation of user class.

Note that the message has not yet been made persistent. This will happen in the *insert* operation of the *Mailbox* class, which is called through the *receive* operation of the *User* class. These two operations are therefore:

```
void User :: receive( Ref<Message> theMessage ); {
      incoming . insert( theMessage );
}
```

and

```
void Mailbox :: insert( Ref<Message> theMessage ); {
    d_Transaction TXinsertMessage;
    TXinsertMessage . begin();
      holds . insert_element( theMessage );
      mark_modified( );
    TXinsertMessage . validate();
}
```

Note again that the transaction mechanism has been used to localize the change and to lock the mailbox for as short a time as possible.

Reading mail

Reading mail is primarily the responsibility of a function in the *User* class. It must allow the user to choose a mailbox and then a message from that mailbox. The message is displayed and then it may be replied to and it may be stored or deleted. This is one of the longest of the operations and looks as follows:

```
void User :: readMail() {
// Part 1 - get the mailbox and the message and display the message
    d_Ref<Mailbox> readBox = chooseBox
                          ( "Give name of mailbox with message in: " );
    if ( readBox != NULL ) {
          readBox . showHeaders();
          int messageNum = getInt( "Which message do you want to see? ");
          while (messageNum < 1 or messageNum > readBox . number() )
             messageNum = getInt( "Incorrect Message Number, Try Again: " );
          d_Ref<Message> theMessage = readBox . getMessage( messageNum );
          theMessage . display();

// Part 2 - If the message is to be replied to call the reply operation
//    on the message.
    if ( yesNo( "Do you wish to reply to this message? " ) )
             theMessage . reply( this );

// Part 3 - If the message is to be stored, request a storage mailbox
//    and insert the message.
    if ( yesNo( "Do you wish to store this message? " ) )
      if ( storage . is_empty() )
             showSnl( "But you do not have any storage boxes - sorry!" )
      else {
         d_Ref<Mailbox> storeBox = chooseBox( ;
                "Give name of mailbox to store the message in: " );
         if ( storeBox != NULL ) storeBox . insert( theMessage );
           };

// Part 4 - Optionally delete the message from its current mailbox.
      if ( yesNo( "Delete this message? " ) )  readBox . delete( theMessage );
    };
}
```

In part 1, the name of a mailbox is requested, the headers of the messages in that mailbox are shown and the user is asked to identify the one to display. The first part ends with the display of the chosen message. The user is then allowed to respond to the message, which is achieved by a call to the *reply* operation of the message class. This is an alternative constructor for messages, which uses the current message to build the values of its properties. For instance, the subject is "Re:" concatenated with the title of the original message, while the recipient of the reply is the sender of the original message. Part 3 manages the storage of the message. If the message is to be stored, a storage mailbox is chosen and the message is inserted into it. If it is to be removed from the original mailbox, part 4 achieves this by a call to the mailbox operation *delete.*

Again none of this function touches the database directly, only through the insert and delete operations of the mailbox class.

The other operations can be found in Appendix A.

■ 12.6 Summary

This chapter has shown how C++ can be used to manage an OODBMS. Although it is by no means an ideal language for database work, it can be bound into a database environment in the manner shown. Some of the important points which came out in the chapter were:

- There must be some way of referring to databases inside C++. A database class is used for this, although instances of this class cannot be created inside C++, merely opened, used to access data and closed.
- Other DBMS objects such as transactions, queries, sessions and locks must be available. These may also have system classes defined for them. In ODMG, there is a transaction class. In O_2 there are session, lock and query classes.
- Calls to OQL can be embedded in a C++ program either by collection member functions or via a free standing function.
- There need to be collection classes since a DBMS relies on these. Furthermore, there should also be some domain classes. Since C++ does not provide enough of either of these, they will be added as system-provided classes.
- There must then be ways of making objects persist. There are two aspects to this:

  - The values must be linked through to the database in a programmer-accessible way. This is done by naming some root values from which the programmer can retrieve all of the values by access paths which start from the named values. O_2 also provides persistent roots, from which all reachable data is automatically stored.

- Each object needs to be created either as an ordinary C++ object in which case it cannot be stored, or as a potentially persistent object, in which case it can. In ODMG and O$_2$, transient objects can be referred to using the C++ pointer operators, while persistent operators must be referred to by use of the *Ref<T>* template class.

The next chapter considers Smalltalk in a similar light.

13 Smalltalk as a database programming language

Smalltalk is probably the second most widely used object-oriented programming language. It was the first language to bring widespread use to object-oriented programming and, although subsequently overtaken by C++ in popularity, would seem by some estimates to be gaining ground on that language once more.

This chapter parallels Chapter 12 and considers Smalltalk in the context of database programming. Following a critique of the language, there will be a description of what has to be achieved to create a Smalltalk environment suitable for database work. Then the ODMG proposals (limited as they are) will be outlined and the O$_2$ implementation of those proposals will be described. Finally, the electronic mail application will be developed in Smalltalk.

The chapter is much shorter than the previous one for two reasons. First, the ODMG proposals have been less completely worked out for Smalltalk. Second, much of the development process from the last chapter is repeated.

■ 13.1 Smalltalk and database management

Smalltalk as a language has many enthusiastic adherents, who believe that by avoiding the insecure features of C and by promoting the strong form of encapsulation, Smalltalk is inherently a safer and more productive language in which to construct robust software than is C++. However, in the database context, the lack of a strong type system seems to be a strong drawback. This section will consist of a discussion of the major features of Smalltalk and an examination of how well these features fit with the requirements of database programming.

■ 13.1.1 The language Smalltalk

Smalltalk was developed in the 1970s by the Software Concepts Group of Xerox Palo Alto Research Center and emerged in the form of Smalltalk-80. This is much more than a language, in that programming is achieved by the use of a sophisticated development environment, which includes a windowing system with menus for program editing together with browsers and debuggers.

The original group of Smalltalk developers evolved into ParcPlace Systems, who are one of the main vendors of Smalltalk systems. They provide the VisualWorks programming environment, which is the evolved form of the visual environment of Smalltalk-80. Other vendors include Gemstone, who provide support for non-persistent Smalltalk, as well as for their Smalltalk-based OODBMS; IBM, who also provide the VisualAge visual environment; and Object Technology who provide ENVY, an environment which supports cooperative working among other facilities.

The language can be distinguished from C++ in several important ways:

- All values in Smalltalk are objects.
- The language is completely dynamically type checked.
- Most implementations of the language only support single inheritance, although there are experimental versions which provide multiple inheritance.
- It is a vital design feature that only operations can be public, i.e. all properties must be private.
- The language is typically used in an interpretative workspace environment.
- The language is accessed via a "graphical" user interface which is continuously supportive of the class and method structure.

Each of these will now be discussed.

In Smalltalk, literals and objects are not distinguished. The basic atomic classes take their part in the class hierarchy alongside user defined abstract classes. The operations on the basic classes, such as addition and string concatenation, are all provided as methods. Moreover classes, symbols and code blocks are themselves objects. One consequence of this is that programming the metadata is possible, since the metadata is held in the class descriptions and these are available for manipulation.

The usual way in which Smalltalk programming is described involves phrases like "everything is an object" and "data is typed but variables are not". In fact, all variables in a program are all of the single dynamic type *Object*. What this means is that code fragments like the following are allowed:

```
V := 1.
...
V := 'ABC'.
```

since *V* is not specified to have any particular type. Type checking happens at run time, at which point a check is made that the value to which a variable name is bound may be used in that particular way. Thus the program fragment:

```
V := 1.
...
V := 'ABC'.
W:= 1 + V.
```

will only fail at run-time at which point it will be noticed that *V* currently holds a string and in addition is not a permissible method. Indeed, it is debatable whether Smalltalk does type checking at all in the conventional sense, since all that happens is that the program fails because the required method is not found.

The object model is also different from that provided in C++ in two ways. First, only single inheritance is normally provided. Second, the strict form of encapsulation is enforced. It is not possible to access properties outside of the object's own class, only operations are exported.

Programming in Smalltalk is carried out in a rather different way from C++. C++ is used with the source program editing–compilation–object code linking and loading cycle typical of imperative programming in the algol family. Smalltalk, on the other hand, is usually accessed by entering code into a working visual environment and summoning an on-line interpreter in the manner introduced in the early Basic systems. This means of access is backed up by an architecture which partitions the working environment into two parts:

- a virtual machine which is general to all users and contains the system functions and the interpreter;
- a workspace called the image, in which the dynamic part of the class hierarchy, specific to a particular user, is held, i.e. the image holds the user's classes and instances and any libraries which are used.

Accessing Smalltalk consists of loading the virtual machine and image and inputting and executing new code interactively. The source code entered is held in the Smalltalk image and is not necessarily copied out to the file system. The manner of interaction when developing software is almost always via the use of a visual environment. Indeed, Smalltalk systems were among the first to be widely available which provided adequate graphical support for software engineering. This was important since at the time (i.e. the early 1980s), the object-oriented style of programming being popularized by Smalltalk was entirely unfamiliar. It was therefore important that the user could interact with a direct representation of the unfamiliar class hierarchy rather than have to manage linearly organized source code files. The Smalltalk interactive environment is shown in Figure 13.1. It has been extremely influential in object-oriented systems – for instance, the *O₂Tools* interface is clearly similar in important respects.

The figure shows the Smalltalk interface in action. There are several windows: a system workspace so that the system can communicate to the programmer, a scratch window which the programmer can use as a workspace for entering text (in this case the programmer has entered the implementation of *newName* here first) and the system browser. There may be other windows, but the system browser is the most important.

The system browser is split into five panes: four lists of system components and a text pane underneath these. From left to right, the lists contain: categories

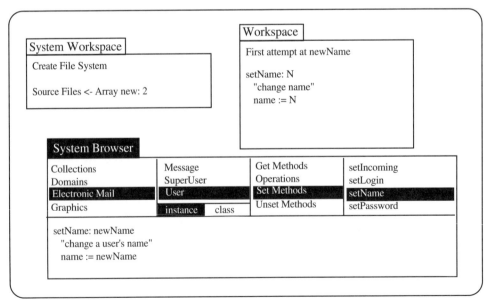

Figure 13.1 The Smalltalk-80 interactive programming environment.

of classes, classes within a chosen category, categories of methods and methods within the chosen category. In this case, the *setName* method of the *User* class has been chosen and the most recent version of the source code for this method is shown. The text window contains the implementation of a chosen class or method and may be used to bring up an editor. The browser can therefore be used to manage the entry of code in a systematic manner.

Another important feature added on top of the language was an extensive library of system classes, which any Smalltalk programmer could expect to find in a Smalltalk system. This included support for different kinds of collection and scalar values. Continuing in this spirit, each of the currently available commercial systems, Gemstone, VisualWorks, VisualAge and ENVY come with a substantial number of useful classes.

Smalltalk-80, as the first heavily used object-oriented language, deserves much of the credit for popularizing the paradigm. Its consistent application of object-oriented concepts and its extremely usable interface make it a suitable choice for programming many kinds of application. The next section examines to what extent it is suitable for database programming.

■ 13.1.2 A critique of Smalltalk as a database programming language

The features of Smalltalk just described include some beneficial and some problematic features in the context of a database system. The beneficial features include the visual environment and the support for collections, code objects and metadata. The problematic features are the use of dynamic typing, the less expressive object model and the workspace mechanism.

The availability of a visual programming environment is extremely important for database systems. All OODBMS users expect to have visual tools for browsing, data definition and program construction. The fact that Smalltalk systems traditionally provide this kind of environment means that appropriate DBMS interfaces can more easily be provided, since they can be adapted from standard Smalltalk components.

The need for a range of collection types has already been mentioned and Smalltalk has these in abundance. A typical Smalltalk collection hierarchy contains the following:

```
Collection
  Bag
  Set
  Dictionary                         "Collections of key, value pairs"
  SequencableCollection
    AdditiveSequencableCollection    "variable length lists"
      OrderedCollection              "sorted by insertion position"
      SortedCollection               "sorted by content"
    ArrayedCollection                "Fixed size ordered collections"
      Array                          "Fixed size, numbered from 1"
      ByteArray                      "Arrays of values in the range 0-255"
      String                         "Arrays of characters"
        Symbol                       "Strings used for names (e.g. of
                                       methods)"
      Interval                       "Computed arrays of regularly spaced
                                       values"
                                     " e.g. 1 to: 4 is the array {1, 2, 3, 4]"
```

and this provides good support for database work. There are two provisos to this. First, database collections are likely to grow rather larger than a Smalltalk system might expect to have to deal with. The DBMS must therefore provide their own implementations for persistent collections. Second, Smalltalk collections are potentially heterogeneous, since there is no way of the programmer specifying that a particular collection is, say, a bag of integers, or of the language checking whether inserted values are of the appropriate type.

Having classes as objects in the system is extremely valuable for a database language, as explained in Section 2.8. In Smalltalk, it is possible to retrieve the class of any object by use of the *class* operation defined on the *Object* class. This returns an object which can be accessed using operations which return the class name, superclass, subclasses, instance variable names, etc. Using the *Object* class means that metadata management can be provided in a DBMS. Moreover as the system provides classes for symbols and for blocks of code, there is at least the potential for the reflective programming of generic features and for the maintenance of code-valued properties.

Less positively, the lack of static type checking seems like a serious drawback when using Smalltalk to manage long-term data, for reasons described in Section 11.2.4 – particularly the delay in providing the programmer with feedback. Waiting until run-time to discover programming errors can seriously complicate application development. Moreover, this means that a schema written in Smalltalk is a less complete specification than one written in C++, since none of the properties or operations are typed.

The restrictions in the object model also seem negative in a database context. The choice between multiple and single inheritance is still hotly debated and, in the programming context, there are clearly pros and cons. However, in the data modeling context, single inheritance means that the structure of the data involved in some applications cannot be directly represented. Instead indirect means must be used and the schema becomes significantly more complicated and unwieldy.

Access to properties is another hotly debated subject. Smalltalk is the most draconian language on this count. Whereas access to properties can always be provided via operations, this can greatly reduce the directness of expression in the application code.

Finally, the workspace methodology is difficult to resolve with DBMS organization. The arguments against "session persistence" were given in Chapter 3 – failure to distinguish transient and persistent data, lack of concurrent access, problems in making the system resilient against crashes, and difficulties in providing distributed systems. In order to use Smalltalk, the DBMS implementors have to find some way of creating the effect of merging multiple workspaces and creating a resilient and efficiently accessible database out of these.

■ 13.2 Techniques for making Smalltalk persistent

Much of the discussion in this section repeats that found in Section 12.2 and so the arguments will be truncated.

Databases will be objects in Smalltalk, just as they are in C++. There will be a class with operations to open and close a database. The normal Smalltalk method of application and schema development is used to build up the application in the workspace and when it is completed, to strip out the development environment, and to store the workspace as an executable file. This mechanism requires some high-level tools for the DBMS to have access to the metadata, which otherwise is hidden. Fortunately, the metaclass functionality means that any particular system should be able to implement this straightforwardly.

Support for persistence can be supplied by the same kinds of techniques that are available as for C++ – altering and overloading the *new* operator, providing explicit insertion operations on class *Database*, and using reachability from named roots. The first of these alternatives is not really in the spirit of Smalltalk. On the other hand, the existence of the *Dictionary* collection class provides an appropriate structure within which to store explicitly named values and reachability is a technique that non-persistent Smalltalk makes heavy use of. The difficulty for DBMS implementors will be in safely supporting the transfer of objects between the image and the persistent store.

The same options exist as were described in the context of C++ for representing transactions – making every operation be a transaction, extending the syntax, providing a class for transactions or providing operations on the database class. However, the fact that blocks are objects in Smalltalk raises the possibility of creating a transaction class as a subclass of the block class, thus confirming its role as a kind of code value. Locks could also be objects in a Smalltalk DBMS. Queries could also be objects or querying capability could be provided in the form of operations on collection classes or the database class.

As for the ODMG-specific constructs, the distinction between attributes and relationships would seem to require a language extension, while names could make use of the *Dictionary* class as a namespace mechanism. Extents and keys could be provided as system-supported class variables. The *allInstances* method provide by some Smalltalk implementations might seem suitable for the management of extents, but this would have to be modified to make the extent persistent.

■ 13.3 The ODMG Smalltalk binding

The ODMG-93 recommendations for a Smalltalk binding were far from complete. They are of interest here since there are a number of ways in which the recommended Smalltalk binding differs significantly from the C++ binding. The recommendations also lay the basis for the O_2 implementation.

■ 13.3.1 User-defined classes

The ODMG data model is mapped into a Smalltalk class hierarchy, but with the loss of some of the distinctions found in the ODMG model:

- The distinction between objects and literals is lost. Even integers are mutable objects in Smalltalk.
- Relationships are not supported by Smalltalk either. ODMG-93 does not suggest a language extension (as they do for C++).

Otherwise, Smalltalk classes can be derived simply from ODL. Here is the start of a class description for messages in the electronic mail database:

```
Object subclass: #Message
    instanceVariableNames: 'subject dateSent body heldin sender recipients'
    classsVariableNames: ''
    poolDictionaries: ''
    category: 'Electronic Mail'
```

In the description, the new class, *Message* is introduced as a subclass of the most general class, *Object*. It has six properties – called instance variables since there will be one value of each for each instance of the class. It has no class variables – properties which have only one instance for the whole class. It does not use any pool dictionaries (dictionaries which are used to share constants between classes) and the class will be grouped with the other mail classes into a category called *Electronic Mail*.

This is probably the least complete description of the properties of this class found using any of the various languages discussed in this book. There are no property types, no distinction between attributes and relationships and no keys or extents.

Instead attributes and relationships are distinguished by the kinds of operation that must be provided to support them. Attributes are represented by simple get and set methods, for instance:

```
subject: newValue
  "set the subject attribute"
  subject := newValue.

subject
  "return the subject"
  ^subject.
```

The first of these two fragments describes an operation which takes a parameter (*newValue*) and sets the *subject* property to the value of that parameter. The second fragment takes no parameters and returns the value of the *subject* property. (The second lines of each of these are documentary comments.)

Relationships are more complex and their implementation depends on the cardinality of the relationship. Consider three kinds of relationship between classes *A* and *B*:

- A one-to-one relationship requires methods to set, destroy and return the relationship – with the setting operation calling its equivalent in the related class. The relationship would be coded as:

```
Object subclass: #A                     Object subclass: #B
   instanceVariableNames: 'A1to1'          instanceVariableNames: 'B1to1'
getA1to1                                getB1to1
  "Return the related object"             "Return the related object"
  ^A1to1.                                 ^B1to1.
setA1to1: Bvalue                        B1to1: Avalue
  "Set the relationship"                  "Set the relationship"
  A1to1 == Bvalue                         B1to1 == Avalue
     ifFalse [                               ifFalse [
       A1to1 notNil                           B1to1 notNil
         ifTrue: [self unsetA1to1].             ifTrue: [self unsetB1to1].
       A1to1 := Bvalue.                        B1to1 := Avalue.
       Bvalue setB1to1: self. ]               Avalue setA1to1: self. ]
```

```
unsetA1to1:                              unsetB1to1:
  "Remove the relationship"                "Remove the relationship"
  | temp |                                 | temp |
  A1to1 notNil                             B1to1 notNil.
    ifTrue: [                                ifTrue: [
       temp := A1to1.                           temp := B1to1.
       A1to1 := nil.                            B1to1 := nil.
       temp unsetB1to1 ].                       temp unsetA1to1 ].
```

The left-hand side includes the description of a property of class *A* called *A1to1* and the get, set and destroy (unset) methods to manipulate this property. The right-hand side provides the parallel set of methods for the inverse relationship.

The get methods return the value of the property.

The set method of *A* takes a parameter called *Bvalue* and only takes effect if this is different from the value *A1to1* already has. In this case, each set method unsets the original value (thus breaking the reverse link), sets the new value of *A1to1* and calls *B*'s set method to create the reverse link.

The unset method of *A* sets the value of *A1to1* to nil and then breaks the reverse link by calling *B*'s unset method.

The methods of class *B* are equivalent to those of *A*.

- A one-to-many relationship also requires a method to remove the relationship from the set. The three methods would be coded as:

```
Object subclass: #A                      Object subclass: #B
  instanceVariableNames: 'A1toN'           instanceVariableNames: 'BNto1'
getA1toN                                 getBNto1
  "Return the related set of objects"      "Return the related object"
  ^A1toN.                                  ^BNto1.
setA1toN: Bvalue                         setBNto1: Avalue
  "Add B to the relationship"              "Set the relationship"
                                         BNto1 == Avalue
    ifFalse [                                ifFalse [
       self A1toN add: Bvalue.                 BNto1 notNil
       Bvalue setBNto1: self. ]                   ifTrue: [self unsetBNto1].
                                                BNto1 := Avalue.
                                                Avalue setA1toN: self.  ]

unsetA1toN: Bvalue                       unsetBNto1:
  "Remove B from the relationship"         "Remove the relationship"
                                           | temp |
  A1toN includes: Bvalue                   BNto1 notNil.
    ifTrue: [                                ifTrue: [
       self A1toN remove: Bvalue.              temp := BNto1.
       Bvalue unsetBNto1.  ]                   BNto1 := nil.
                                               temp unsetA1toN: self ].
```

The class *A* has an instance variable, *A1toN*, which holds a set of *B* objects, while *B* has a single valued property called *B1toN*.

The get methods just return the property values.

The set method on *A* checks to see if *A* is already related to the *B* object and if not, adds the *B* value to the set of related objects and then sets the reverse relationship.

The unset method of *A* checks to see if *A* is related to the *B* object and, if so, removes the *B* object from the relationship and calls the unset method of *B*.

The methods of *B* are exactly equivalent to those given above for the one-to-one case.

* A many-to-many relationship would be coded with methods for the *A* and *B* class which are the same as those for the *A* class in the one-to-many relationship given above.

User-defined operations of the class are also coded as Smalltalk methods and are added to the classes, for instance the receive operation on class *User* would appear as:

```
receive: aMessage
  "Insert a message in the incoming mailbox"
  incoming insert: aMessage.
```

Extents and keys can be considered as class variables. Extents will not be automatically managed, the programmer is responsible for managing these. On the other hand, there is a specification for managing keys, which relies on the addition of a method *addKey* to the class *Behavior*. This method accepts a symbol or an array (for a compound key) and can be called repeatedly to create multiple keys. To create the key for class *User*, it would then be possible to write:

```
User addKey: login.
```

■ 13.3.2 Domain classes

ODMG-93 has nothing to say about the domain classes, *Date*, *Time* and so on. However, there is no reason why they cannot be coded in Smalltalk and added to the system-provided classes in exactly the same way as has been done for C++.

■ 13.3.3 Collection classes

ODMG-93 asserts that the built-in Smalltalk classes will be adequate, although warns about the heterogeneous nature of the sets.

■ 13.3.4 Persistence and data manipulation

Persistence in Smalltalk is achieved by reachability – anything reachable in the workspace continues to exist, anything that is no longer referred to is garbage collected. This is naturally extensible to persistence by reachability in the database. The ODMG recommend that persistent classes are not distinguished (unlike their proposal for C++). Rather they state that all classes can have persistent instances. The OODBMS must create database versions of all classes and these will hold the code which manages the transfer of objects to and from store.

The creation of persistent roots is to be achieved by use of a global dictionary called *DatabaseGlobals*. Creating, accessing and removing root objects are then achieved by the commands:

```
DatabaseGlobals add: #name -> anObject.
anObject := DatabaseGlobals at: #name.
DatabaseGlobals remove: #name.
```

Updating objects is achieved using normal Smalltalk since the values are transferred into the workspace whenever they are accessed. Updated objects are sent back to the database when transactions commit, an activity that will require the use of a *markModified* method. This distinguishes the updated objects, so that the system can efficiently identify all of the objects which need to be stored.

■ 13.3.5 DBMS classes

ODMG-93 describes a *Session* class, which is used to connect to a database. Sessions are created by use of *new* and there are further methods to login, connect to a specific database, and to logout. This class takes the place of the *Database* class in the C++ proposal.

There is no suggestion of a *Transaction* class. Instead methods to begin, commit, checkpoint and abort a transaction are provided in the *Session* class. Locks are held on objects which have been swapped into the workspace, but there is a proposed method, *acquireLock*, which can lock an object ahead of its use.

■ 13.3.6 OQL in Smalltalk

OQL is implemented as methods on the *Collection* class. A typical use of it would be:

```
theUsers select: [ :U | U incoming number > 0 ].
```

which returns the users with incoming messages.

13.4 Smalltalk in O₂

As with C++, the O₂ implementation of Smalltalk integrates the language with the O₂ model of database structure and interaction, extending the ODMG proposal in several ways. In doing so it needs to overcome a number of problems:

- the O₂ model is strongly typed – all stored data has a type which it retains while being stored;
- O₂ supports multiple inheritance, but Smalltalk has single inheritance;

and, of course,

- Smalltalk data must be indicated to be persistent in some way.

On the other hand, as has already been mentioned, the O₂ model of persistence by reachability fits well with the normal memory management methodology of Smalltalk.

The primary design decision made in integrating Smalltalk into O₂ is that the language is perturbed by forcing the programmer to provide typing information for the instance variables of any class whose instances may become persistent. This requires a syntactic extension to the language.

The O₂ system is designed to run in the context of ParcPlace Smalltalk and VisualWorks. The O₂ version comes as a specially extended version of the Smalltalk virtual machine and a source file which must be used to extend the image with the appropriate DBMS classes.

13.4.1 Persistence in O₂ Smalltalk

The O₂ system provides an implementation of the ODMG proposed *Session* class, but in O₂ it is called *Database*. A connection to a server is created by:

```
aConnection := Database new.
```

after which there are methods which can be called to set the system name, server name, library location path, etc. After these are established, the connection is started with:

```
aConnection open.
```

Having opened a connection to a server, the next step is to access the database. There are methods available to create, open and garbage collect databases. To control persistence, there is a class of persistent roots, *O2Root*, which can be added to the database, although these are usually used transparently via methods of class *Database*. In the context of an open database, the method *bind* creates a persistent root, while *resolve* retrieves a root value. Here are examples of their use:

```
theUsers: = aConnection resolve: 'The Users' ifAbsent: [nil].
aConnection bind: 'Super User' to: superUser.
```

where the names of roots can be strings, as shown here, or symbols.

Transactions are provided as per the ODMG recommendation, i.e. methods on the session class. There are methods to begin a transaction (optionally locking objects), to validate, checkpoint, commit and abort the transaction. Thus a simple database accessing program would be structured as follows:

```
| aConnection |                        "Declare the variable"
aConnection := Database new.            "Create a Database object"
aConnection sysDir: 'theSystem'.        "Set the O2 system to which to connect"
aConnection open.                       "Connect to the system"
aConnection setBase: 'EmailDB'.         "Open the database"
aConnection beginTransaction.           "Start a transaction"
... update commands
aConnection commitTransaction.          "Successfully complete the transaction"
aConnection close.                      "Drop the connection to the system"
```

13.4.2 Persistent classes

O_2 does not provide support for the persistence of all Smalltalk objects. Of the predefined classes, O_2 can only store objects from a number of atomic classes – Integer, LimitedPrecisionReal, Boolean, Character, String, Symbol and ByteArray – and also on the collection classes Bag, Set and OrderedCollection. Each of these maps into equivalent O_2 classes. For instance, Character becomes the O_2 class *char*, while OrderedCollection becomes *list*.

The only other persistent objects allowed are the instances of any user-defined class. However, in order to store values from a class, the definition of the class must have been changed to provide types for the instance variables. These are included in angle brackets following the property name. For instance, the *Message* class defined earlier must be changed by the programmer to:

```
Object subclass: #Message
  instanceVariableNames: '
     subject <String>
     dateSent <String>
     body <String>
     heldin <Set of: Mailbox>
     sender <Person>
     recipients <OrderedCollection of: User> '
  classsVariableNames: ''
  poolDictionaries: ''
  category: 'Electronic Mail'
```

and in this code any of the instance variables can be marked as non-persistent, in which case those properties will not be saved.

There exist import and export tools which are used to manage the translation between O₂ versions of the class and Smalltalk versions:

- Import takes class definitions and creates O₂ versions of them. It can also create callback links to Smalltalk methods from within the O₂ class.
- Export takes a set of classes defined in an O₂ schema and creates Smalltalk versions of these. This only works if multiple inheritance is avoided in the O₂ schema.

13.4.3 Querying the data and the metadata

OQL is accessed via a method on class *Database*. Here is an example:

```
usersWithMail := aConnection query: 'select U from U in theUsers
    where U.login = $1'
        with: 'jbrown'.
```

in which the query is provided as a parameter to the *query* method of the *Database* class. As for C++, the query may be parameterized – parameters being denoted by "$" followed by an integer. Actual values are then passed as parameters to the *with* method.

In fact, the actual parameters can be specified by repeated use of the *with:* method or by the single method *withArguments* which takes an array as its message:

```
usersWithMail := aConnection query: 'select U from U in theUsers
    where U.login = $1'
        withArguments: (Array with: 'jbrown').
```

In Smalltalk, metadata is equally accessible. The class of an object can be retrieved and there are methods which return: the name of the class, the superclass, the subclasses, the comment line, the instance variable names and so on.

13.4.4 The programming interface

Figure 13.2 shows the visual interface which is used in addition to the usual features of the main Smalltalk window. As can be seen, the window contains three main menus and three scrollable windows. The menus offer the following facilities:

- The *Connect* menu provides three options which set up the configuration properties such as the server name, connect to the server, and disconnect.

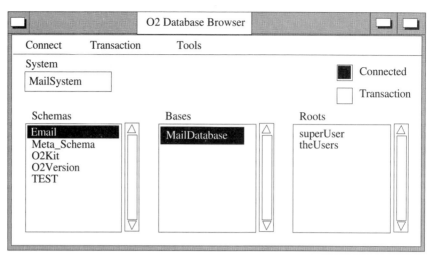

Figure 13.2   The O₂ Smalltalk visual environment.

- The *Transaction* menu provides options to begin, abort, checkpoint, validate and commit a transaction. Any change to the data or metadata must occur while a transaction is open.
- The *Tools* menu supports the import and export facilities, checking the consistency between the Smalltalk classes and the O₂ schema and bringing up a Smalltalk inspector.

The three scrollable windows hold the system objects and also support pop-up menus. They provide the following:

- The *Schemas* window lists the schemata available on the server and supports an operation to create a new schema.
- The *Bases* window lists the databases available with that schema and supports an operation to create a new database.
- The *Roots* window lists the persistent roots in the database and supports a menu with options to print the roots, summon a Smalltalk inspector on the root objects, re-assign the values of the roots, and to create a new root.

These features and the normal Smalltalk programming techniques provide a supportive environment for the creation of database applications.

■ 13.5 The electronic mail application in O₂ Smalltalk

The structure of the application should be very familiar by now, and so this section will be kept short.

13.5.1 Database definition

The four classes will be defined as follows:

```
Object subclass: #User                    User subclass: #Superuser
   instanceVariableNames: '                  instanceVariableNames: "
      name <String>                            classsVariableNames: "
      login <String>                           poolDictionaries: "
      password <String>                        category:' Electronic Mail'
      incoming <Mailbox>
      stored <Set of: Mailbox> '        Object subclass: #Message
   classsVariableNames: "                     instanceVariableNames: '
   poolDictionaries: "                           subject <String>
   category: 'Electronic Mail'                   dateSent <String>
                                                 body <String>
Object subclass: #Mailbox                        heldin <Set of: Mailbox>
   instanceVariableNames: '                      sender <Person>
      name <String>                              recipients<OrderedCollection of:User>'
      holds <OrderedCollection of: Message> '    classsVariableNames: "
   classsVariableNames: "                     poolDictionaries: "
   poolDictionaries: "                        category: ' Electronic Mail'
   category: ' Electronic Mail'
```

Set and get methods will be added for each of the attributes and relationships as specified above in Section 13.3.1.

13.5.2 Setting up the database

The following piece of code will create the appropriate database and roots:

```
"Declare the variables, create a Database object and connect to theSystem"
| aConnection theUsers superUser |
aConnection := Database new.
aConnection sysDir: 'theSystem'.
aConnection open.

"Create a database in the context of a schema and a volume"
| aConnection createBase: 'EmailDB' schema: 'Email' volume: 'Vol1'.

"Create the superuser object and the set of users, adding the superuser as
the first user"
superUser := Person new( 'jbrown', '   ', 'Jane Brown' ).
theUsers := Set new.
theUsers add: superUser.

"Add theUsers and superUser as roots of the database and close the connection"
aConnection beginTransaction.
   aConnection bind ''The Users' to: theUsers.
   aConnection bind ''The Users' to: superUser.
aConnection commitTransaction.
aConnection close.
```

13.5.3 Application implementation

Since Smalltalk does not have free standing functions, the application will be implemented as a class with the facilities as methods. The shared global variable, *currentUser*, can be made a class variable of this class. Thus there will be:

```
Object subclass: #MailApplication
   instanceVariableNames: ''
   classsVariableNames: 'currrentUser'
   poolDictionaries: ''
   category: 'Electronic Mail'
```

This will be followed by the method definitions, including:

```
login
   "Login a user"
   | uLogin uPassword theUser |
   uLogin := System prompt: 'Give the User Login: '.
   uPassword := System prompt: 'Give the User Password: '.
   theUser := aConnection query 'element( select U from theUsers U
        where x.login = $1)'
     with uLogin.
   theUser password = uPassword
     ifFalse: [ System message: 'Login incorrect' ].
     ifTrue: [ currentUser := theUser ].
```

which requests a login and a password and then searches for a user with that login, checks the password and sets *currentUser* if all is correct.

The logout operation is less complex:

```
logout
   "Logout the current user"
   currentUser := nil.
```

The statistics operation only works if the current user is the superuser and then calls the method which summarizes usage:

```
statistics
   "Statistics summary"
   currentUser = superUser
     ifFalse: [ superUser statistics ].
```

13.6 Summary

Smalltalk is a rather different language to C++, with complementary strengths and weaknesses. The value of providing both bindings is that there are very good reasons why a particular programmer might strongly prefer one of the languages (and therefore be more productive, if allowed to use it).

The main points were:

- Smalltalk supports a different style of programming than does C++. In Smalltalk, the programmer interacts with a visual interface to a workspace which is organized as a single inheritance class hierarchy.
- Smalltalk represents all data as an object and only permits access through the methods of the class of the object.
- Smalltalk only supports dynamic type checking.
- Binding the language to a DBMS involves creating some method of moving data between the workspace and the DBMS.
- The ODMG proposal, although incomplete, describes a class with which it is possible to access databases and run transactions. Persistence by reachability is proposed, with each database having a dictionary of named roots.
- The O_2 implementation demonstrates one way in which these proposals can be made concrete.

Part Five discusses some of the implementation and user interface issues which arise in the context of a DBMS.

Part Five

Implementing OODBMS

The final part of the book considers some of the issues in the practical implementation of OODBMS. An OODBMS has to provide database functionality to manage data which has a more complex structure and to do so in a usable way. Although abstractly the database facilities will remain the same, practically they will need different implementation techniques which are likely to be more complex in nature – to match the complexity of the data. At the same time, the usability of the data will be more of an issue since it will be more important to provide direct representations of data if the user is to overcome the conceptual difficulty of manipulating complex data.

This part of the book comprises four chapters. Chapter 14 discusses some of the main issues in implementing an OODBMS. Chapter 15 discusses the various kinds of user interface – both for the end user and for the application developer. Chapter 16 surveys some of the more important OODBMS currently available. Finally, Chapter 17 summarizes the main ideas in this book and discusses likely future developments.

14 Aspects of OODBMS implementation

This chapter provides a brief overview of some of the principal issues underlying the implementation of an OODBMS. Of course, this is a large topic, which requires a book in its own right, and here there is only room to touch on some of the more important aspects.

The chapter will contain sections on OODBMS architectures, mechanisms for managing persistent objects, efficiency concerns, transaction management, ensuring reliability, security and garbage collection.

14.1 OODBMS architecture

Any DBMS is a very large and complex piece of software. An OODBMS must provide a way of using the bits held in the memory and backing store of a network of computers to hold objects and to provide secure, concurrent and efficient access to those objects. Like any other complex piece of software, a layering approach is often used to manage the safe construction and integration of the components. Section 14.1.1 describes ways in which OODBMS functionality might be layered.

In a distributed system, the OODBMS is almost certain to use some kind of client/server architecture. When this is used, the layers of functionality are divided into two (or sometimes three) tiers. The upper tier runs the process with which the user interacts, the lower tier(s) perform(s) low-level tasks, including retrieval of data from the database. Section 14.1.2 will describe the various kinds of client/server architecture.

■ 14.1.1 Layering OODBMS functionality

The ways in which an OODBMS can be built up from the bare machine vary considerably. The first decision that needs to be made is what to use as the basis on which to construct the OODBMS. Some of the choices are:

- A bare machine. This promises the ability to maximize the potential of the hardware in the context of the particular needs of an OODBMS. However, the work required to achieve this is extensive, necessitating a considerable amount of measurement and analysis before any gains will be made. Furthermore, the bottom layer will have to be re-implemented for each hardware platform and, in any case, suggests that other software cannot easily coexist with the DBMS since the operating system on which they run has been stripped away.

- A full networked operating system, such as UNIX or Windows. This will make it easier for the DBMS to operate with other software but may slow down the OODBMS somewhat. Providing versions for different platforms is somewhat simplified since there are fewer standard operating systems than there are hardware platforms.

- A distributed kernel operating system, such as Mach or Chorus. Such a system is likely to be more efficient since it will provide low-level functionality which was designed to support distribution in heterogeneous environments. Such systems also show the influences of object orientation in their design. Thus the creation of an OODBMS on top of a system such as these may well be simplified, firstly because they provide one multi-platform target against which to implement, and secondly because they are likely to provide some measure of object support already built in.

On top of this platform, the OODBMS must provide DBMS support for objects. This immediately raises two possibilities: build the object system on top of the DBMS facilities, or build the DBMS on top of an object server. In the former case, the OODBMS replaces the upper layers of a traditional DBMS – O_2, for instance building on top of a record server. In the latter case, support for transmitting objects about the network forms the core, while resilience, transaction management and efficiency mechanisms are built on top of this.

14.1.2 Client/server architecture

A survey of commercial OODBMS, such as that given as Chapter 16, reveals that one of the few common features of the system implementations is that they all used a client/server architecture of some kind. In a client/server architecture, the DBMS is partitioned into two or three process types, each of which can be replicated throughout the network. The two principal process types are:

- the client, which is responsible for the upper layers of the use of the DBMS – certainly user interaction and probably most of the application processing as well;
- the server, which is responsible for the lower layers of the use of the DBMS – certainly disk management and concurrency control and maybe some of the data intensive processing.

Sometimes there may be an intermediate process, which partitions the workload still further into three tiers. Client processes usually run on the machine that the user is using, while the server process usually runs on the machine that the disk holding the databases is connected to. The intermediate processes, where they exist, migrate to whichever machine achieves the better performance.

Traditional DBMS are often built around a client/server architecture, but they use a particular instance of this, with a single server, attached to the disk, and running on a powerful mainframe, while multiple clients run on less powerful terminals or workstations. OODBMS usually provide a more flexible structure which has several servers and in which the difference in power between the client and server machines is much less pronounced. In fact, many OODBMS permit the processes to migrate in order to balance the load between machines.

There is a great deal of variability between systems in the matter of which process is responsible for which DBMS activity. Each manufacturer makes a particular choice in that area, usually backed up by convincing arguments including impressive benchmark results. The primary consideration is between loading the client with the bulk of the work as against making heavy use of the server. Here are some of the arguments:

- The server should be kept small and simple since there will probably be very many clients to each server and so the server will be kept busy.
- The server should do most of the data processing since then fewer objects need to be transmitted across the network and so the system will be faster.

- Any complex computation should happen on the client, since if the server were to be involved, it would block its ability to service other clients' needs.

GemStone has a very flexible mechanism in this regard. Server processes are kept small, but the client layer can be split with client processes both on the user machine and on the database machine. The client process on the database machine carries out data-intensive work, while the client process on the user machine carries out computationally intensive and user-involved work. Figure 14.1 shows two- and three-tier architectures.

One other benefit which accrues from the provision of a multi-client/multi-server system is that it becomes possible to create a heterogeneous DBMS. There is no reason why some of the servers should not be to different OODBMS or even RDBMS, provided that an object interface is programmed on top of it.

14.2 Managing persistent objects

Managing an object system for non-persistent programming mainly involves the creation of a mapping between object identifiers and a memory location. In fact, in a virtual memory system with a sufficiently large address space, the address can be the object identifier. In a persistent system, there will be two kinds of address – a memory address and a disk address. If the system is distributed, there will be more than one set of memory addresses and probably more than one set of disk addresses. In this section, techniques are described for managing that complexity.

The section starts with ways in which object identity might be represented, continues with what happens when objects move between disk and memory and concludes with a short discussion of managing objects in a distributed system.

14.2.1 Object identifiers

Recall that each object must be uniquely identified by a value called an object identifier (oid) which is system created, hidden from the user and invariant for the lifetime of the object. How will an object identifier be structured? There are basically two choices – to make use of an address where the object can be found or to use a purely logical identifier which is mapped into an address. Each of these choices has several flavors.

A DBMS is very likely to run in a paged virtual memory environment, in which software is written against an address space that is very much bigger than memory. At any time, only part of the address space will be held in physical memory, attempts to access pages which are not in memory will result in a page

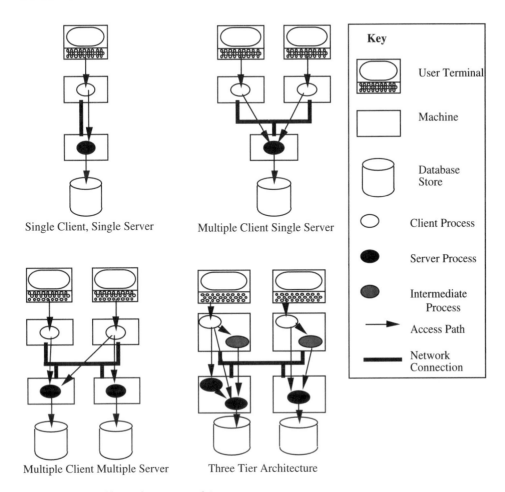

Figure 14.1 Client/server architectures.

fault. This causes the requisite page to be brought into memory, replacing another, hopefully unneeded page.

Therefore, one choice which can be taken is to use the virtual memory address as the oid, which is what ObjectStore does with its virtual memory mapping architecture. This greatly simplifies the use of the system and means, for one thing, that the difference between persistent and transient data is done away with altogether. This should produce a performance gain in that it eliminates the need to transform data and/or references when persistent data is brought into memory. Implementing a distributed virtual memory system is a daunting task, however, and potentially suffers from the drawback that data integrity may be compromised. If an unsafe language such as C++ is used, then the programmer, in modifying the currently available memory representation of a persistent page, can have the effect of directly programming against the physical database. Thus, if the program modifies memory locations or destroys objects which are referred to, then database corruption will occur.

There are various kinds of semi-logical structures for oids. Section 7.3 described how O_2 manages objects by identifying the records which provide the concrete implementation for objects. The record identifier will lead to a disk address and when the record is retrieved an in-memory reference for the record, called a handle, is created. One advantage of this system is that although logically an object is atomic, practically it is a collection of records. In using an object, typically only some of the records required need to be fetched and so a saving is made. Another advantage is that finely tuned relational and network techniques for record management can be re-used.

The classical description of an object identifier, however, is of a logical value which is completely independent of where (in memory or on the disk) an object resides. Such an identifier is often called a *surrogate*, following the name established for extended relational databases by Codd in the design of RM/T. In some cases, a surrogate includes, as part of its identification, the class the object belongs to, in which case it is called a *typed surrogate*.

The obvious problem for a system which uses surrogates is to find out where the object is and to do so quickly. In this regard, the OODBMS implementor will make heavy use of the mechanisms provided in traditional DBMS for indexing records. That is, there will be a hash function which produces the location from the identifier or, more likely, there will be an index which pairs the oid with its location. Such an index is called an *object table*.

One further problem that relational systems typically do not attempt to deal with is the management of large objects. These are often bitstrings representing pictorial, aural or video data and have the feature that they span multiple memory pages. In managing large objects, a structure must be developed which logically keeps together pages which might become physically separated. Usually either a tree structure or a directory will be used to break the object down into smaller components and to keep a coherent record of where those components are.

■ 14.2.2 Object movement

Each access to an object in the client process potentially requires the following steps:

1. Search the object table to find an address.
2. If it is not in memory, request the server to provide either the object or the

page on which the object is known to be. When it has been brought into memory, replace the address in the object table with the physical address.

3. Retrieve the object from the address.

To use this cycle every time an object is accessed would clearly slow the DBMS considerably and make it practically unusable. It is vital that the OODBMS avoids the indirection seen in step (1) and reduces the likelihood of having to access the disk in step (2). To avoid the indirection, a technique that is known as pointer swizzling is used to replace the oid by the address when the object is first accessed. Subsequent object accesses then become as fast as for transient objects. As usual, however, there is a pay-off. The cost of replacing the oid must be less than the saving, so if objects are accessed only a few times, it may be better not to swizzle.

A secondary point, which is hotly debated among the OODBMS vendors, is what the server supplies to the client – objects or pages? Convincing arguments are made on both sides. If the server supplies pages, then it can find them and send them quickly and the client can locate the objects on the pages. If the server supplies objects, then the network traffic should be less and this will help performance. One way that a page server can be made more efficient is to use clustering (see below). Another technique which can speed access is to add all objects in a retrieved page (whether requested or not) to the object table immediately (instead of one by one).

Eventually, when memory fills up, bringing in a new page means that one of the pages that is currently in memory must be replaced. One difficult task is to identify which page is least likely to be used again. This will usually be the least recently accessed page. A second problem then arises – whether or not to write it out again. Only pages which have been updated need to be written out, so there has to be a means of indicating which pages these are. Usually a page has associated with it a dirty bit which, if set, means that it contains an update and must be written out. How and when the dirty bit gets set is another aspect that varies between systems. The ODMG-proposed function *mark_modified* is one commonly used technique. This permits the programmer to indicate which pages need to be copied out, by marking each object that has been changed. Alternatively, the system could automatically set the dirty bit when it detects that a value has been changed.

One additional aspect of data management is the use of tertiary storage. If this system is to manage large databases and to keep previous data, the disks which make up secondary storage will be insufficient. Tertiary storage such as magnetic tapes and optical disks will be required. These have the feature that they can be taken off-line and so are likely to require human intervention to access. None of these issues are different for OODBMS than they are for other kinds of DBMS, but they are an important requirement that some OODBMS vendors are trying to address.

■ 14.2.3 Distributed object management

The arguments above were developed in the context of a single-server system. As was seen in the previous section, an OODBMS is more likely to be used with multiple servers cooperating. Now there is an additional problem in that an object may be anywhere on the network. Each server process must have some way of locating not just data in its local store, but also data being managed by other servers.

There are at least two ways in which this can be achieved. Every server could hold a copy of a universal object table, so that the actual location of every object could easily be found. Alternatively, each server could provide a table of just those objects which it was managing, in which case other servers would have to examine each of these to locate an object. The first of these options would be quick to use but hard to maintain. The second would be easy to maintain but slow to use.

A second problem with any distributed system is to cope with the occasional failure of some of the servers. For a system to be truly resilient it is likely that each server should be replicated at least once. Providing replications results in a form of reliability called *fault tolerance*. However, if all of the replications of a server are simultaneously unavailable, then the system must cope with the inaccessibility of some of its data gracefully.

Yet another issue concerns the movement of data between servers. For efficiency reasons, it may sometimes be beneficial to move objects between servers, for instance, to balance the load on the servers or because the data is moving geographically closer to where it is most frequently used. To move an object from one server to another raises three problems: how much of the object should be moved, when should the components move, and are there not components of the object that the other server already has?

An object is typically related (transitively) to much of the rest of the database. It is therefore an important policy matter to determine when one object moves, which of the objects that it refers to should follow it. In the electronic mail database, if a *User* object moves, then it is probably sensible to move the user's mailboxes as well, but what about the messages in those mailboxes? These may well be held in other mailboxes as well – should those mailboxes be copied as well? … and so on. It is very easy to "move the world" when moving one object, if the system is not sensibly implemented.

If the components of the object are to be moved, should they all be moved at the same time or not? If the system uses *eager fetching*, then the components of an object will all be moved when the object is retrieved. If *lazy fetching* is used, the components will only be moved as they are actually required. The former has the benefit that it avoids the overhead of breaking down the retrieval of an object into several parts. The latter avoids fetching components which will not, in fact, be used.

When an object is moved, (copies of) some of the objects it refers to will already be held by the server to which it is going. For instance, the objects are likely to make reference to system classes which are duplicated on every machine. Clearly it would be inefficient to keep multiple copies of such objects by bringing them along with every object which refers to them. It is, in general, wasteful to move objects which are already there. A mechanism is needed which removes references to such objects before movement and rebinds them to the local copies when the movement is complete.

For all of these reasons, the final word has yet to be said on the management of objects in a distributed object system.

■ 14.3 Efficiency mechanisms

The movement of data between the permanent store, the server and the client is the most time consuming part of object management. It is therefore very important that all means should be taken to make this process as efficient as possible. The twin goals are to reduce the number of disk accesses and the amount of network traffic generated. Three techniques for this will be discussed here: retaining objects on the node of which they are being used so that they need not be repeatedly retrieved (*caching*), putting objects together which are likely to be retrieved together therefore reducing the overall time to retrieve them (*clustering*), and splitting an object up so that every part of it is not retrieved, thus once again reducing the amount of data being transmitted (*fragmentation*).

One general question in this discussion is "Who controls use of the efficiency mechanisms?" Is it the programmer, the DBA or the DBMS? It may be presumed that the programmer knows certain application-specific details which indicate that, for instance, a group of objects should be clustered together. In the ODMG binding to C++, one of the versions of **new** allows the programmer to store an object "near" another. Conversely, there is a strong argument that specifying efficiency details distracts the programmer from the main task of clearly expressing the computation required and that, anyway, the system should know better than the programmer where to place the data for optimally efficient access. However, it is extremely difficult to design a system which monitors usage patterns continuously and relocates data efficiently (without the relocation itself causing delays). Most systems provide administration tools which allow the DBA to tune the system to create a set-up which is efficient for the particular activities which the users are involved in. It seems that features which allow the programmer to assist the system are still valuable, but that these can be expected to fall into disuse as systems are increasingly effectively designed.

14.3.1 Caching

Each process (client or server) will be managing a certain number of objects, which are reachable from the variables in the code. As the process continues, it will access more objects and eventually run out of memory to hold them. At this point, the process must replace some of the objects it currently has with the new ones. Which ones should it replace? If the decision is made randomly, then it is very likely that the process will be forced to re-read some objects many times. A better bet is to replace the objects least recently used, since these are least likely to be used again.

Even this algorithm sometimes falls down and what is actually required is a mechanism which explicitly retains some objects which are known to be of continual use to the process. A *cache* is a collection of data which are to be held accessibly for as long as required. This usually takes the form of a memory buffer or a disk file, which is quick to access. An object which is held in a cache is said to be *pinned*.

There are two kinds of cache in use – object caches and page caches. As the name suggests an *object cache* will hold objects, the objects being copied from whichever page they reside on into the cache area. A *page cache*, on the other hand, holds the pages intact. The usual kinds of pay-off distinguish the two approaches – object caches are smaller but require processing to construct them since the objects need to be retrieved from pages; page caches may waste memory and hold a lot of unwanted data, but are quick to build since they can be quickly mapped into the cache area.

The design issues surrounding caching include "How big should they be?" and "Which processes should be supplied with caches?" The former is a finely balanced question between keeping many objects, which are known to be useful, as against having a large amount of memory for new objects. The second question concerns whether only clients should have caches or is there a use for server caches.

A server cache is valuable because it cuts down on disk accesses. The server can usefully hold onto a number of objects if these are frequently requested by clients and thus avoid the need to fetch them from disk every time. A server for the mail application could hold the superuser object in a cache for instance. A client cache is valuable for reducing network traffic. A client process for the electronic mail application could usefully maintain continual access to the user object of the currently logged-in user and all of the user's mailboxes and messages. Some systems provide both kinds of cache to achieve both kinds of gain.

14.3.2 Clustering

The second mechanism for reducing access time is to place together objects that are frequently used. Disk accesses always operate on a page basis. Therefore, if the server process, in retrieving one particular object, is bringing in the page which holds that object, it would be extremely valuable if other objects that the process needs are also on that page. If objects that are required together are stored on the same disk pages, then the number of disk accesses per required object would diminish considerably.

The client/server interaction could also benefit from the use of clustering. Network traffic is also sometimes organized in terms of pages and if so, those pages should be as full as possible of useful data. Even if data transfer is on an object-by-object basis, it may be slower for the overall network to have lots of small messages (one per object) than to send fewer bigger messages (several objects at a time). In this case it is up to the server to bring together the objects suitably. ObjectStore servers, for instance, bring pages in from disk and build up clusters of the objects required, rather than send the whole pages.

As well as programmer-determined clustering, the system could provide a number of ways in which the logical organization is used to determine clustering. For instance an object and its properties could be clustered, as could the extent of a class that is frequently traversed. Most systems use some aspect of the data structure to control object placement.

14.3.3 Fragmentation

Finally, when a process requires an object, it may very well not require the whole of that object. Moreover, there is the possibility that the same parts of some large objects are much more frequently accessed than others. In the electronic mail example, the incoming mailbox may be much more frequently used than the storage mailboxes. In this case, it may be useful to separate the representation of the objects into fragments.

This is a technique that carries over from relational systems and as for RDMS, there are two possibilities:

- vertical fragmentation splits an object into a number of components – thus *User* could be split into (*name, login, password, incoming*) and (*storage*);
- horizontal fragmentation splits a collection into sub-collections – *theUsers* could be fragmented into groups determined by the last time they logged in – thus users who have recently logged in will be sought first by the *login* facility.

In both of these cases, the goal is to cut down the amount of data which needs to be transferred and searched, thus reducing the time for the overall process.

■ 14.4 Transaction management

Transaction management underpins concurrency control, recovery and integrity checking in a DBMS. This important component of DBMS functionality was described in Section 1.1. In this section, attention is focused on two concerns – how the system uses locks to enable multi-user data access, and how the system supports multiple versions of data. This section also includes a discussion of a related activity – event management – the reaction of the application to various changes in the database.

■ 14.4.1 Locking protocols

Transaction management in OODBMS is intended to support both short competitive transactions in the similar ways to traditional DBMS and also to support long cooperative transactions. Most of the OODBMS currently available concentrate on the former, providing transaction management using pessimistic two-phase locking. This means that data is locked as it is accessed and the locks are released only when a transaction commits. In this case, it is also vital that the transaction manager provides a means of deadlock detection, so that conflicts on data access do not result in the non-termination of waiting transactions. Some systems, including O_2, permit the programmer to provide exception handlers to customize the response to problems in transaction management.

Some OODBMS support optimistic locking, in which the copies of the data are modified, but the data is not locked. Instead, when the transaction commits the transaction manager checks to see if any other transaction has attempted to change the data and, if not, the changes are committed. Locks are usually supported on single objects or collections. It is the ability to lock at the individual object level that allows optimistic protocols to work effectively.

The same kinds of locks are used as in traditional DBMS, shared locks for reading and exclusive locks for writing. However, some systems also provide intention locks, which lock a particular object ahead of its use. By doing this, the transaction gains immediate access to the objects it will use and thus avoids the possibility of deadlock.

Support for long cooperative transactions is more patchy. Most systems support a check-out, check-in form of access, in which the process takes a copy of the data into local store, modifies it there and writes it back. In a cooperative system this can be used as the basis of a mechanism for cooperatively changing the data. The other two components required for this are notify locks and transaction groups. *Notify locks* held on an object do not prevent other transactions from using the object, but instead force such transactions to send back an alert that changes to the object may be being made. *Transaction groups* permit a group of users (and therefore transactions) to jointly access data. Thus an exclusive lock held by one member of the group may not lock out the other members of the group but would lock out non-members.

The scope of a lock can vary widely in granularity. Locks can be held on databases, classes, objects or properties. Finally, VERSANT supports a number of different locking protocols which allow continued working without checks and even supports "a flexible ability for users to extend the model to define their own locking rules".

14.4.2 Version management

Some OODBMS support the maintenance of concurrently available versions of objects. In Chapter 1, it was argued that version management is an important requirement of design applications. It is the intention of OODBMS vendors to support version management, but the mechanisms provided vary considerably.

One of the simplest schemes is that provided by O_2. A version graph, as described in Section 7.5.8, is a data structure which enables different versions of the same set of objects to be held in a collection in which derivation paths link the versions. In such a system, no attempt is made to manage the differences in the contents of the versions. All that can be interpreted from the graph is that the nodes all represent the same data and that each link represents the fact that one version is derived from another.

Another requirement is to be able to build configurations of the versions of groups of objects. A configuration of a group of objects is a set of versions, one for each object in the set. For instance, a document might be constructed as a set of objects (maybe one for each chapter), each having multiple versions. Any document made out of exactly one version of each component would constitute a configuration of the document.

In the O_2 scheme, a version graph has nodes, each of which hold values for the same set of data. The only configurations available in this design are the sets of versions which are nodes in the graph. Another approach is to hold versions only of single objects and to build all of the combinations of versions of versioned objects. However, this has the twin drawbacks that an enormous number of configurations might be created and that many of these are meaningless. A more flexible approach, semantically determined configurations, would be to permit the ability to store versions of individual objects and to be able to represent constraints that limit how they can be combined. This reduces the number of configurations by removing inappropriate ones. For instance, the document might have versions of each chapter in a number of languages. A correct configuration would have all chapters written in the same language. No system implementing this is known to the author.

Another question that arises when configuration creation is provided, is at what point are the configurations created? Even using a semantic approach, there may be many configurations generated if they are created at the same time as versions. A better approach would be the separation of version creation from configuration creation – the latter being achieved on demand as a kind of query.

■ 14.4.3 Event management

One of the benefits that OODBMS have brought by including code in the database is the ability to program the effect of some kinds of changes which happen to the data. For instance, it may be useful to accomplish another task every time an instance of a particular class is created. An event management system ties a particular program module to an event and is similar to exception handling.

The kinds of event which may be managed include: object creation, object deletion, operation invocation, property update, or, more generally, any change which causes a specified predicate to become true. Event management allows these kinds of events to trigger a piece of code and this may perform tasks such as informing a user or making a compensating change to other data. For instance, removing a *User* object may be programmed to remove all of the messages that user has stored.

14.5 Ensuring reliability

There are two aspects to reliability. One is ensuring that the DBMS continues to run even if some machines are unavailable. The other is ensuring that if the DBMS crashes, it returns with the data still held in a consistent form. The next two subsections consider these issues.

14.5.1 Fault tolerance and replication

One aspect of support from a DBMS that users expect is the so-called "24 × 7 availability", meaning twenty-four hours a day, seven days a week. Users get this from traditional DBMS and must also have it from OODBMS. Each OODBMS vendor emphasizes some aspect of the ability to continue even if a machine running the server breaks down.

To achieve this, the OODBMS will typically replicate each server so that all information is at least doubly available. Of course, replication brings its own problem – the requirement that all replications are the same. Each system has its own method for keeping the multiple copies consistent.

14.5.2 Crash recovery

All OODBMS expect to recover consistently from system crashes. In doing this, they make use of the same kinds of technique as traditional DBMS – logging and shadow paging. All database textbooks contain detailed descriptions of recovery techniques, here they are briefly reviewed in the context of a database of objects.

In the middle of a transaction an OODBMS will store changes in a copy of the database, in a log of changes, or in both of these. In order to recover from system crashes, the OODBMS can use these in one of three ways:

- *Deferred update* – changes are written not to the database but to a log and then transferred to the database at a later date. In this case, on system restart, the changes involved in successfully completed transactions are written from the log to the database, while updates arising from half-completed or aborted transactions are ignored.
- *Immediate update* – changes are recorded both in the database and in the log and on recovery, the log is used to undo the updates in any half-completed transaction.
- *Shadow paging* – multiple copies of the database are kept and changes are made to only one, so that when the system is restarted the old or new versions can be used as required.

In an OODBMS, the need to maintain a network of objects complicates the implementation of any of these mechanisms.

■ 14.6 Protection

Maintaining a secure environment for data management has two aspects:

- a system is *safe* if inadvertent behavior by processes cannot compromise data integrity;
- a system is *secure* if the data cannot be accessed by unauthorized users.

Each of these will now be considered.

■ 14.6.1 Safety

A system is safe if any use of the data manipulation facilities is guaranteed to maintain the structure of the data. The DBMS approach attempts to provide safety by having the DBMS control all data access. There are therefore two aspects of safety – the degree to which the data can be tampered with outside the DBMS, and the degree to which the DBMS permits unsafe access. The former is really outside of the scope of this book and depends upon the operating system within which the DBMS is housed and also the physical management of the computer equipment.

Within the DBMS, safety is a matter of the power of the user interaction tools which the DBMS provides and the degree to which they respect data organization. User interaction tools will be described in the next chapter, but here it is noted that simple-to-use interfaces such as parametric and graphical interfaces usually severely constrain the user's ability to modify the data and its structure, so that they prevent the misuse of data. Query languages are more powerful but still are relatively constrained. The principal culprit in data misuse is most likely to be a programming interface, which will provide powerful ways to manipulate the data.

Chapter 11 included some discussion of the kinds of support that a programming language can bring to the maintenance of data integrity. These include a secure type system, type checking to prevent data misuse and information hiding through the use of abstract data types and inheritance. In Chapter 12, the critique of C++ was most trenchant in the failure of C++ to provide a safe environment. Pointer arithmetic, programmer-instigated object destruction and weaknesses of the type system mean that the use of C++ renders the data open to misuse. The critique of Smalltalk in Chapter 13 was similarly concerned about the universal use of dynamic type checking, which delays safety checking unnecessarily.

Despite the historical use of these languages, OODBMS are in a good position to provide safe database environments. A well-designed language with an appropriate mix of dynamic and static type checking, in which the latter dominates, can ensure that applications respect their schemata. Furthermore, the pervasive use of abstract data types can secure the representation of the data against the possibility of access by unauthorized users. Therefore, the protection of data is reduced to a matter of security.

14.6.2 Security

The security of a system is provided by mechanisms which authorize users to have access to the different facilities. Most multi-user DBMS require password authorization as a top-level method of restricting access. Traditional DBMS then provide means of establishing privileges to gain access to different parts of the data – usually, in relational DBMS, to whole tables or views.

OODBMS can provide the same kind of security methods as traditional DBMS, but on a much wider range of data granularity. An OODBMS can provide the ability to restrict access to volumes, to databases, to classes, to different properties and operations of classes and even to individual objects. The range of options means that the authorization sub-system of an OODBMS is likely to be more complex than for a relational DBMS.

The system maintains an access list which matches resources with individual users and/or groups of users. Each use of the data can be checked against this access list before it is allowed to proceed. One way of managing this, which fits well with the object mentality, is the use of capabilities. A capability is an object which gives access to some resource (hardware or software) in the system. In order to use that resource, the user must be granted access to a copy of the capability which controls it.

To summarize the protection issues, the increased complexity of an OODBMS brings both the benefit of an increased range of ways of securing data and the drawback that the increased complexity will make the implementation and management of security mechanisms more difficult.

14.7 Garbage collection

The storage capacity of computers, although growing in size, is limited. It is therefore vital to re-use that storage whose content is no longer useful whether it be memory or disk space – a process known as *reclamation*. To do so means that redundant data must be replaced and to achieve this the redundant data must be identified. The redundant data is referred to as garbage.

There are three ways in which garbage can be identified:

- by the run-time system managing the processes, which can, in some languages, distinguish data which is no longer manipulable, for instance having gone out of scope;
- by the programmer issuing explicit destruction commands;
- by the underlying system providing an operation which examines all data to see which are still useful and automatically removing the data which are not useful.

The last of these three alternatives is called *garbage collection* and this operates by distinguishing as garbage those data which are no longer accessible by any process. Garbage collection is heavily used by OODBMS because the integrity of the object store can be violated by programmer-specified destruction, while language run-time reclamation is confined to memory.

An OODBMS has to reclaim both memory and disk space and often provides different processes for the two tasks. Memory garbage collection is vital to stop the process running out of memory and to prevent it from needlessly swapping disk pages in and out when much of the space is wasted. Disk garbage collection is vital to stop the disk filling up.

Both kinds of garbage collection are built upon the idea of holding onto accessible data and reclaiming everything else. Objects in memory are accessible if they are reachable from one of the objects currently in scope. Disk objects are accessible if they are reachable from persistent roots or from a currently running process.

Given these definitions of accessibility, there are two main kinds of garbage collector in use: ones which use *reference counting*, in which the number of references to each object is maintained, and ones which use *tracing*, in which the store is traversed starting from the roots, marking all accessible data and identifying unmarked data as garbage. Tracing itself comes in two flavors: *mark-and-sweep*, in which non-garbage is marked and then garbage is removed in two separate phases; and *copying*, in which non-garbage in moved to a new copy of the store. Each of these will now be considered in turn.

■ 14.7.1 Reference counting

The idea behind a reference counting garbage collector is very simple. For every object, the system maintains a count of how many other objects currently refer to it. Every time a new reference is made to the object, the count is increased by one. Every time a reference is removed, the count is decreased. Thus if a property of object *A* currently points to object *B*, but is re-assigned to object *C*, then the reference count of *B* is decremented and the count of *C* is incremented.

If this value is available for all objects, then objects which are not roots and whose count is reduced to zero are identified as garbage as nothing refers to them and so they are inaccessible. The garbage collector searches for and reclaims the space used by such objects.

Although reference counting is an intuitively appealing and simple approach, there are at least three drawbacks to it, the last of which fatally reduces its usefulness:

- The reference counts use up space. If the system is to be absolutely sure that it has correctly maintained the counts, it must use a large integer for the purpose.
- Maintaining the reference counts takes valuable processing time. Two more data updates are required every time a reference is changed from one object to another.
- Cycles of inaccessible data can never be identified as garbage.

To see why this last point is true, consider the situation in which root object *A* refers to *B*, *B* refers to *C*, *C* refers to *D* and *D* refers back to *B*. In this case, *B*, *C* and *D* form a cycle which is only reachable via *A*, *B* having a reference count of 2, *C* and *D* both having a count of 1. Now suppose that the property of *A* that points to *B* is re-assigned to *E*, say, in which case *B*'s count goes down to 1. *B*, *C* and *D* are now unreachable and yet all have non-zero reference counts. Moreover being unreachable, these counts will never change and they can never be thrown away.

This means that reference counting can never be used alone, since ultimately the store will fill up with unwanted cycles of data. If reference counting is used then it is up to the programmer to break the cycle by explicitly removing one of the objects or one of the links. As this is a needless distraction to the programmer, reference counting is not much used in production quality software.

■ 14.7.2 Mark and sweep

A mark-and-sweep garbage collector works by identifying all accessible data and then throwing away the rest since this must be garbage. The collector starts by marking all root objects as non-garbage, then visiting the objects which the roots point to. As these are reachable from the roots they are not garbage either, so they are marked. The process is repeated, marking any objects referred to by newly marked objects until no more are found. Anything left is unreachable. Therefore such collectors have two phases: the mark phase identifies non-garbage, while the sweep phase removes the garbage. Each of these phases has potential problems.

The mark phase

The mark phase of a tracing garbage collector is obviously guaranteed to identify garbage correctly, as long as the contents of the store do not change. Unfortunately, the contents are being changed all the time that the DBMS is running. There are two choices therefore:

- *stop-the-world collection* – the DBMS is temporarily halted so that the garbage collection process can be executed satisfactorily;
- *incremental collection* – the DBMS continues to run and the collector interleaves its work with the DBMS, identifying garbage and freeing up space a little at a time.

For a large object store, a DBMS which is supposed to be providing 24 × 7 availability cannot take the first of these options, since the collection process will take a significant time during which the DBMS is unusable. Therefore the second approach is required, but this brings other problems. In garbage collection parlance, the DBMS which is coexisting with the collector is called the *mutator*, since it has the annoying habit of changing the state of the store, while the collector is trying to analyze reachability.

In an incremental mark phase, the collector is traversing the store in the same kind of way as it would for a stop-the-world collection. It visits each object that it finds and marks all referenced objects. However, the activity of the mutator might cause two kinds of problem:

- The mutator breaks a link that the collector has used, therefore making some objects which the collector has marked into garbage.
- The mutator creates a link from a marked object to an unmarked one and then breaks the link from a yet-to-be-visited object. In this case the object will never be marked and will be erroneously thrown away.

The two problems are illustrated in Figure 14.2. Diagram (a) shows the situation in the mail database when the mark phase is in progress. The collector is busily marking the data associated with the *jbrown* object. It has completed marking the stored mailboxes (they are marked with a black dot to indicate this) and is currently working its way through marking the messages in the

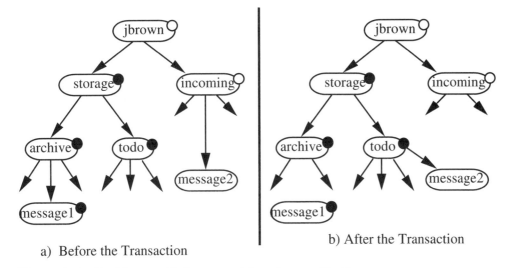

a) Before the Transaction

b) After the Transaction

Figure 14.2 Problems with incremental garbage collection.

incoming mailbox (shown with a white dot to indicate marking from an object has begun but is not yet complete). At this point, a transaction comes along which does two things. It removes *message1* from the archive and it moves *message2* from the *incoming* mailbox to the *todo* mailbox. The result of this is shown as diagram (b).

The first of the problems is exhibited by *message1*, which is now garbage, but has been marked and so will not be thrown away. This is not really an important problem since it will be found to be garbage during the next iteration of the garbage collection process. The second problem is more serious and is illustrated by what has happened to *message2*. This has been moved from a position that the collector has not reached, to a section which the collector has completed. This means that *message1* will never be marked and so will be thrown away. There are several methods of overcoming this problem, of which the simplest is for the mutator to inform the collector whenever it makes a reference from a marked object – ensuring that the collector visits it.

The sweep phase

There are two basic ways in which garbage can be reclaimed from the marked store:

- maintaining a free list; or
- compacting the non-garbage.

Maintaining a free list is a technique which has been used for computer systems since the early 1960s. The free list holds a list of addresses of locations which can be re-used. The store is traversed and the locations of all non-marked objects are placed on the list. The result is an easily accessed collection of re-usable space. The main problem is that the store gets fragmented, with an increasing number of increasingly small holes, which cannot be used for larger objects. The technique also fits poorly with clustering, since, if objects are assigned to the next free location, clustered objects can become separated.

Compacting is achieved by sliding all of the non-garbage down over the gaps left by the garbage. This results in a large block of re-usable store, which is much more useful. To achieve this, the compaction phase can be very slow, since objects are now being moved about the store. Furthermore, it can result in a great deal of recalculation of addresses.

14.7.3 Copying

Copying collectors use a single phase to gather together non-garbage in a process known as *scavenging*. These traverse the store much like the mark phase of the mark-and-trace collectors. Instead of marking the data, they copy the reachable data found to build up a new copy of the store. This process usually involves the use of *semi-spaces*, in which the whole store is split into two equal halves which are used alternately. When one fills up, the garbage collector copies live data to the other and further processing occurs using the second semi-space. The obvious problem with this is that only half the store is usable at any time. Additionally, interleaving the mutator is even more difficult to manage since at any time, the objects may be in one or other of the two versions of the store.

One improvement on the basic semi-space mechanism is the *generational garbage collector*. This makes use of the commonly found observation that the more recently an object was created, the more likely it is to be garbage. The whole store is divided into a number of generations. New or modified objects are held in the most recent generation and, at intervals, objects are "aged" into the next generation. Each generation can be separately scavenged using a semi-space algorithm, with the more recent generations being scavenged more regularly. Each scavenging process will be quicker to run since it is only working on a fraction of the store and the space needed to be made available for the new copy will be smaller as well. However, a generational collector is much more complex to design and implement. Among the decisions which need to be taken are: how many generations should there be and how much space to use for each; how often are objects aged; how often are the different generations scavenged; and, most importantly, how is the reachability of objects between generations managed?

Garbage collection is an important process for OODBMS, since the data is organized in a graph and reclamation should be based on a technique which maintains integrity and frees the programmer from the tasks of store allocation, which will be both difficult to achieve correctly and distracting from the description of the application. Appropriate and efficient techniques, of the kind discussed here are still evolving to satisfy the needs of OODBMS.

14.8 Summary

OODBMS must provide a similar set of facilities to those provided by traditional DBMS. However, the increased complexity of the object model has two offsetting effects. First, the added power of the model provides increased flexibility and allows a great range of ways in which each feature is provided. Second, to implement any of the facilities for an OODBMS is intrinsically more challenging.

Here are the main points:

- An OODBMS is implemented in layers, although the precise nature of the layers varies from system to system.
- Most OODBMS support a distributed multi-server, multi-client architecture. The clients provide the upper layers of the functionality, while the servers provide the lower layers.
- All OODBMS support some way of uniquely identifying each object and each manages this within a persistent environment in which the object might sometimes be on a disk managed by a server process and sometimes in memory managed by a client process.
- A variety of efficiency-producing techniques are used including clustering, caching and fragmentation.
- The usual kind of two-phase locking transaction management is common among OODBMS, but they add a variety of other techniques for transaction support.
- Crash recovery and protection mechanisms are provided in a similar manner to traditional DBMS, although both are more complex and more flexible.
- Garbage collection is the main technique for store reclamation in OODBMS, since the integrity of the object graph can be better ensured than by forcing the programmer to free up space.

In the next chapter, attention is turned to the user level and techniques for user interaction are surveyed.

15 User interfaces to object-oriented database systems

The ANSI-SPARC three-level architecture promises much in terms of multiple user interfaces to the **same** internal data model. DBMS as delivered have traditionally been quite deficient in this area, particular as compared with the variety and excellence of the storage structures and database facilities which they offer. In contrast, the user interfaces provided are usually few in number, difficult to use and constrained in their power. As described in Section 1.1, the advanced applications place a much greater emphasis on the quality of the user interface. The increased complexity of the data means that they can only feasibly be manipulable if the data and the operations are provided using appropriate visualizations and metaphors.

Even the notion of what a user is, is no longer so clear cut. Previously, two broad classes of user could be distinguished. End users, such as bank staff, booking clerks or research scientists, are those who wish to gain access to data whose containing structure has been set up for them. They have typically interacted wholly within the confines of the DBMS using whichever interfaces it provided. Database administrators, programmers and data processing staff are responsible for setting up the structure of the database and the applications which make use of the database. They have typically interacted partly with the DBMS and partly with the file system and with programming interfaces which were tacked on to the DBMS in a clumsy way. An OODBMS provides a wider range of interfaces which support not just the needs of end users, but most of the needs of database professionals as well. The distinction between the two classes of users is increasingly blurred, not least because end users are increasingly used (through access to spreadsheets, word processors and drawing packages) to taking more control of the context in which they use their data.

This chapter takes as its starting point a deeper discussion of the kinds of user that the DBMS must support and the kinds of task for which a user interface is required to support one or both of these two broad classes of user. Following this, a survey of interface styles is presented, from which some basic issues are discussed. Some interesting systems are examined, both drawn from the commercial world and from research, before a summary is given.

■ 15.1 The interfaces required

In considering the kinds of user interface which are required, it is important to keep in mind two things: the classes of user being supported, and the kinds of task which they will be involved in.

■ 15.1.1 Categories of user

It is important to consider all of the categories of DBMS user. This means not just the end user and how they will interact with their data, but also the users whose job it is to create applications and set up databases. Each come with a different set of requirements.

The end users are only interested in interacting with their data as directly and easily as possible. The user interface should support their various data-manipulation and querying activities in a framework which is appropriate to their notions of the data, which is familiar from the real-world context which the application is modeling, and which affords the actions which invoke the operations that they wish to carry out. Form-based interfaces achieve this admirably for relational data, since they are appropriate for tables, are familiar from paper versions and provide an appearance which makes data entry, editing and presentation simple. When the user is managing data which represents a more complex information structure, appropriate interfaces will be even more important.

Application developers are another important class of user. In an OODBMS, the application is more tightly integrated with the DBMS and so support tools should be integrated also. Since the emphasis is increasingly on code inside the database, user interfaces for software development must be provided and must be of reasonable quality. To provide good end-user interfaces and not bother with facilitating programmer interfaces would be somewhat like expecting furniture to be smoothly finished off and comfortable, but for carpenters to be provided with broken hammers, inaccurate rules and blunt chisels.

Similarly, database administrators require interfaces for setting up the DBMS, managing databases and support structures, such as indices, and tuning the system for performance. In a distributed system, their activities will be more complex and require better support from the interface.

Furthermore, in a well-designed OODBMS, the distinction between end-users and system users becomes increasingly blurred. Whereas there will continue to be many users who will never get involved with setting up their environment, object orientation should permit a wider range of users to be involved in schema design and database management. This is another reason why the user interface needs of all users should be considered together.

▨ 15.1.2 Kinds of task

It is necessary to keep in mind the kinds of task which a DBMS must support, since a different kind of interface might be appropriate for each. Traditionally, a DBMS has had to support the following three kinds of task:

- data definition – the specification of the structures which will hold the data;
- data manipulation – the tasks involved with entering and editing data;
- querying – the extraction of data from the database, which is usually sub-divided into:
  - *ad hoc* querying – extracting a subset of the data by posing a general question; and
  - navigational querying and browsing – the activity (usually interactive) of selectively viewing data by moving from one value to another related value.

However, in the context of the increased complexity of the data, some additional kinds of task are required.

- data visualization – the ability to render appropriate representations of the data onto the terminal;

- imprecise querying by content – providing approximate values which the DBMS attempts to match as well as it can;
- application and user-interface development – building the application inside the DBMS.

Each of these types of task is now discussed.

Data definition of an object database requires a more complex interface than those provided for relational systems. Schema design should be somewhat easier with an object model than it is for relations since the data model has higher level constructs. Conversely, entering the schema once it has been designed takes more effort and so an interface which improves support for this task is important. The interface can be improved either by becoming more visual, for instance by showing the class hierarchy graphically, or by using the syntactic structures involved to determine the visual structure. The O_2Tools window shown in Figure 7.7 shows both of these at work. The class hierarchy is seen graphically, while the classes, properties, methods and so on, all have their specific window area in which they are manipulated. Moreover the different representations of the item being manipulated are all highlighted and so it is difficult for the programmer to become confused when managing the complexity of the structure.

Data manipulation is also more complicated and the consequent importance of programming interfaces has already been emphasized. Data entry by forms will continue to be important and there is likely to be a growing use of direct manipulation for creating and removing objects and for changing relationships. Furthermore, the manipulation will increasingly take place in the context of a background or visual metaphor which resembles the real-world situation in which the data is used.

Ad hoc querying has been discussed at length in Part Three. The query processor will continue to be a vital DBMS component in OODBMS. Navigational querying in object databases is just about as important. The fact that the object database is logically a graph implies tools which work against the graph, for instance by following links between objects. Graphical and textual means of navigating the graph will be increasingly valuable.

The term data visualization means the production of human-detectable representations of the data. Visualization, despite its name, is not necessarily restricted to visual representations, but may include the production of sounds. It might also involve the presentation of video clips. The visualization of data is much more important for object databases than for relational ones. The simplicity of the relational model meant that a tabular visualization is usually sufficient. The only additional visualization tools expected of a relational DBMS are report generators and a means of generating graphical diagrams, particularly of statistics drawn from the data. Object databases support spatial, pictorial, aural and video data and so they must be capable of providing user-detectable versions of these. Furthermore, the complexity of the data also makes direct methods of visualization vital if the user is to continue to make sense of the data. One of the effects of this may be an increasing use of three-dimensional visualization techniques. There is also a need for a DBMS component which permits the user to customize the way in which the data is visualized.

The complexity of the data also increases the need to support querying based on imprecise specifications. In multimedia databases, the user will often wish to find a particular text or image by providing samples of data that are similar to or descriptive of the information that is to be retrieved. The retrieval of data in this way is the subject matter of information retrieval (IR). Techniques for retrieving data from complex texts is increasingly well understood. Similar techniques are also required for the other kinds of data.

Finally, application development is not a novel task for a DBMS. Application development tools are available with most relational systems. The novel feature is that the applications will (mostly) live inside the DBMS with the databases that they use. Integrated application development environments have been developed for object-oriented languages and these have been extended to act as front ends to OODBMS. A further aspect of application development is the quality of the programming language which the programmer has to use and how suitable this is for database work.

The outcome of this development is that the environment for using a DBMS of any kind must increasingly become a multi-window environment, in which application development, schema design, data manipulation and querying appear in different windows, alongside windows showing visualized data, all of which are kept in a mutually consistent state by the DBMS.

■ 15.2 Kinds of interface

There follows a list of the main kinds of user interface found in DBMS. The strengths and weaknesses of each as related to OODBMS will be presented.

Database query languages

These were dealt with extensively in Part Three. They are textual languages which typically provide facilities for data definition and data manipulation, as well as for *ad hoc* querying. Navigational querying is less often supported by textual languages, but note that languages associated with network databases provide textual means for navigational querying. Query languages are particularly suitable for *ad hoc* querying, for which they are relatively easy to learn and, usefully, they map queries down into an algebraic form which can be optimized. On the other hand, they lack computational completeness and become difficult to use for complex queries. Given their familiarity for many database users, an object query language such as OQL is an essential component of an OODBMS.

Database programming languages

These were dealt with in Part Four. They are languages which try to integrate the rather different worlds of values manipulated by a program and values which are stored in a database. Typically different data structures are used in the two environments and these are hard to keep consistent. This "impedance mismatch" problem is tackled either by adding database structures to a programming language or by adding persistence to database structures.

A DBPL provides computational completeness and, if well designed, a seamless integration of the database with transient data. A DBPL also promises a tighter integration of the application and user-interface code with the data that is being manipulated. If the DBPL supports first-class code values then it will be an appropriate mechanism for describing active data of various kinds. On the other hand, programming is difficult to learn and most languages are poorly designed for database work, neither providing a suitably abstract means of describing data nor an equal amount of support for transient and persistent data – nor do they provide support for transactions.

However, in the context of the kinds of complex data inherent in the advanced applications, a database programming language must be the most important interface to the database and its quality will affect both the cost and the reliability of the applications provided to end users.

Form-based interfaces

These are interfaces which are used to display records of information and also used to capture such information. They are very commonly used with traditional applications. For example, banks, travel agents and car hire firms all make heavy use of form interfaces.

In their favor, forms are a familiar representation of data and directly present record structures. Even when moving to object databases, the record remains one of the core data structures which a database will contain. Using a form to represent an object structure, which is essentially a nested record is somewhat more difficult. However, provided that there is some mechanism for controlling the depth of nesting, it is not difficult to generate forms for nested records. In *O₂Look*, the *Presentation* object is a nested form controlled by a mask. Forms will continue to be a heavily used interface for data visualization and entry.

Graphical interfaces

A graphical representation of information, usually in the form of a labeled node-and-arc graph which links icons with various kinds of line, is familiar in the context of schema design. Most DBMS provide a graphical data modeling design tool to help in constructing database structures. Graphical manipulation of the data itself (for instance to support querying) has been proposed, but visual graphs have not yet been found to be as useful a metaphor for data manipulation as they have been for schema design.

Given the logically graphical nature of an object database, visual graphical interfaces will continue to become more prevalent. With better design of visual graph structures, better line styles and icons, and the occasional use of 3D, increasingly impressive and affording interfaces can be expected.

Menu and window interfaces

The Macintosh interface, X-windows, Smalltalk and Windows have made multi-window, menu driven interfaces an essential tool for any substantial software development. All kinds of DBMS have revitalized the user's involvement with the database by moving to this kind of interface, at first in the context of portable computers, but increasingly with more powerful machines.

The user can expect to access an OODBMS primarily through this kind of interface and to be able to bring up windows for browsing the data, schema design, application building, querying and programming. *O₂Tools* is just one example of this kind of interface. The important feature that such a system must possess is to ensure that the differing views are kept consistent. Furthermore, they must be built on top of the transaction mechanism so that any changes that are made using them are atomic.

Direct manipulation interfaces

Direct manipulation interfaces permit the user to interact with iconic representations of the data, moving them about the window in such a way that the movement invokes operations against the database. Direct manipulation has been popularized by the Macintosh interface and has been very successful since most users quickly build up a close connection between what they do with the mouse and the effect this has in the computer.

In an OODBMS, direct manipulation has a clear role in improving the directness of user interaction with the data and the metadata. Direct manipulation techniques can be used for any of the following: the creation of schema elements and data, by dragging new elements out of a "factory" icon; the creation of relationships between objects by "drawing" lines between them; the deletion of objects by use of trash can; and the movement of data between databases and the movement of databases between nodes on a network by using drag-and-drop.

Three-dimensional and virtual reality interfaces

One kind of setting for direct manipulation is the use of techniques for simulating a third dimension on the screen. Such techniques provide a context in which the data can be viewed and operations to navigate around this context. At its best, the third dimension can considerably enhance the user's understanding of the structure of the data they are using. The ultimate form of this is the virtual reality interface in which the notion of data is pushed far into the background as the user seems to be interacting directly with information.

Three-dimensional interfaces are not yet widespread. This is partly because they are extremely processor intensive and partly because an understanding of when and how they are appropriate is only slowly being achieved. Not everyone finds them usable. In a poorly designed system, users experience feelings of nausea and easily become lost in the virtual world that the interface is presenting. However, users who are familiar with 3D modeling, for instance those using molecular databases, can adapt quickly to these interfaces for other tasks, such as data definition. It is clear that, in general, the important criterion is the suitability of the metaphor being presented to the user. Rendering bank account data into 3D by randomly selecting three properties as the dimensions is unlikely to add much understanding to the user. Another important finding is that the use of color, shading and texture is essential to underpin notions of reality that the third dimension is encouraging. All of this implies fast and expensive hardware and so may not be generally available for some while.

Natural language and text retrieval interfaces

The term "natural language interface" should imply some kind of semantic analysis of the content and structure of sentences written in a language such as French, English or Japanese. In fact, this is still beyond the range of under-standing of cognitive scientists, so what it usually means is content-based querying of textual data. A natural language instruction is entered, its structure is mostly ignored and words whose value is largely syntactic (such as "the") are eliminated. The remaining words are stripped to their stems and these are sought in the database. Thus "tell me about all the messages sent to Jane about football" is stripped to "message sent Jane football" and the data and metadata is searched for these words.

In the complex mixture of numerical, textual, pictorial, video and aural data that databases increasingly contain, mechanisms of this kind will gradually become available in all media. Methods are being researched for extracting the essential physical and even æsthetic characteristics of data and indexing the data on those characteristics. This will mean that users who are unfamiliar with the database structure and contents can still find what they need. The search engines of the World Wide Web demonstrate one kind of example of such interfaces.

Other kinds of interface

Canned or parametric queries are highly constrained interfaces which are tuned to a single task, which is to be accomplished by entering a few parameter values. These are the kinds of interface given to a frequent user who is not necessarily computer literate. Examples are those for the functions available to a bank teller or to a librarian. The most common example in general use is the cash point where the parameters are the PIN number, function selected and cash required. Given the need for users of all kinds to access data, the ability to create this kind of interface will remain a vital aspect of an OODBMS.

Cooperative interfaces permit users on different machines to collaborate in the way in which they are using the data. One way of providing this is to provide each user with windows which show what each of the other users is doing. Another tool would be a collaborative notepad window in which each user can write. This could be used for resolving differences in committing conflicting changes to the database. The interface depends on the availability of DBMS features intended for cooperative work – such as locks which cause the user to be notified of any changes to the data and cooperative workgroup management. Virtual reality interfaces are appearing which support cooperative work. In such interfaces, the user becomes a visible object inside the virtual world and can interact with other users as well as with the data.

■ 15.3 Issues

This section touches briefly on some of the general issues which become important when moving to an OODBMS. One considerable improvement that OODBMS provide over previous systems is the potential to provide many more kinds of user interface and to give the user control not just of selecting which ones to use, but also to configure their own interfaces as required. The word "potential" dominates the previous sentence, since this has not yet been much exploited. This section analyzes the components of user interaction and shows what is possible.

Control of the interface is partly made available by classes of interaction objects (also called interactors or widgets). These make it possible to build more powerful generic interfaces. They also permit the building of multiple coexisting interfaces. Control of visualization is another possibility. Given an appropriate architecture for visualization, it becomes possible to allow the user to customize the way the data is rendered. Each of these aspects will now be discussed.

15.3.1 Interactors as data

One considerable advantage conveyed by an OODBMS is the ability to assist in building the interface by including interaction object classes. This means that the database application can be built in such a way that it uses the interactors seamlessly, rather than by making calls out into the operating system. Although interaction objects are usually transient, some systems permit the storage of interaction objects as well. In order to support user design of interfaces, therefore, the DBMS should have access to a library of interactor classes. Some companies specialize in such libraries and one example, shown in Figure 15.1, is the class hierarchy of the View library available from RogueWave.

As can be seen the library includes a wide variety of interaction objects, including menus, dialog boxes, windows and buttons. The application will be built with calls to the operations of these classes. The library is available for multiple platforms, the value of this being that the same interface can easily be constructed for multiple platforms.

15.3.2 Generic interfaces

One way in which this kind of library can be used is in the creation of generic interfaces. A generic interface is one that is parameterized on the type of data being interacted with. Given data of a particular type, an appropriately structured instance of the generic interface will be generated and used. Most relational DBMS have a generic forms interface for example. This is a component which, given a table, automatically generates a form structure, with one entry for each of the columns of the table, which can be used for editing or for data display.

The same technique can be used in an OODBMS, although the more complex structure may make building the interface constructor somewhat more difficult.

Figure 15.1 The RogueWave user interface class library.

The *O₂Look Presentation* is one example of such a generic interface. The interface generator can take an object, discover its class and build the appropriate interface by embedding sub-interfaces for each property and labeling them with the property names.

■ 15.3.3 Coordinating the interaction

Interaction must occur in a framework which permits all data access to use coherent representations whose contents are mutually consistent. Any change in one representation should automatically propagate to any other rendering of the same data. This also fits well with the object-oriented paradigm since it implies the use of call-backs which are a cornerstone of object-oriented design.

Similar mechanisms would be used for collaborative working, as this amounts to keeping multiple representations on multiple machines synchronized.

15.3.4 The elements of visualization

The visualization of a set of data is built on two components:

- a set of *visualization primitives*, each specific to a particular type of data or type constructor;
- a set of *presentation frameworks*, each appropriate to different sets of data.

Each primitive takes a particular aspect of the type system and produces a rendering of it. Thus there will be primitives specific to integers, primitives for collections, primitives for images, primitives for objects etc. An integer may be represented as a list of digits ("11"), a textual string ("eleven"), a line of a particular length, a note of a given frequency and so on. Each primitive may itself be parameterized. A line is parameterized by its length, thickness, color, angle and these parameters can be used to convey several properties at once. Object orientation provides the means for new primitives to be added to user-defined classes. Thus, the mailbox class can be enhanced with a primitive which displays a picture of a mailbox colored differently for each class of user.

The framework provides a context in which the user can make sense of the individual representations. The framework provides a means in which to visualize a set of data by organizing the various representations produced by the primitives. This may be fairly abstract – a graph or a scattergram, for instance – or it can be concrete – placing a mailbox object in a room. The importance of the framework is that it must reinforce the understanding that the user has of the relationships between the data. It is an important design issue that the framework is meaningful in this way.

Furthermore, the WIN component of the Napier88 system demonstrates how windows, menus and other interaction objects can be provided as objects in the database. Given interactor classes and appropriate primitives and frameworks of this kind, an OODBMS provides a very powerful setting in which the user interface can be fine tuned. Furthermore, it allows the building of tools with which the user can customize visualizations.

15.3.5 Customizing the interaction

In order to support a wide variety of users, the DBMS could usefully provide a tool which allows the user to select among the interactors, the primitives and the frameworks and to associate these with the data. Each of the components described in the last section are provided separately and the tool allows a user to choose a framework and in this framework, to connect visualization primitives with database retrieval functions. When a function is called, the associated visualization technique displays the values in the manner required. Section 15.4.6 shows one system which provides this.

Customizing the interaction is more complex. This means that the tool gives the user the ability to determine the specific sequence of user actions which are required to invoke each aspect of database functionality. Providing this kind of feature in a usable manner has still to be achieved.

15.4 Some examples of interfaces

This section looks at a few user interfaces which have been developed both commercially and by research groups in order to survey the kinds of feature which are either already available or are imminent.

15.4.1 VisualWorks

VisualWorks is the visual programming environment created for Smalltalk by ParcPlace-Digitalk. It is one of a number of such environments for object-oriented languages, including VisualAge for IBM Smalltalk, and Visual C++. The existence of such environments gives the OODBMS vendors a big advantage in producing a usable interface. Since the environments are built using the object-oriented language itself and since class hierarchies can easily be integrated, it is relatively simple to combine a user-friendly environment, supplied by a specialist third-party vendor, with a database manager.

VisualWorks provides a wide range of tools running under a common interface. From the launcher window which appears at start-up time, it is possible to integrate the use of the following:

- a graphical user interface painter;
- a database application development environment;
- a set of object-oriented development tools;
- a tool to preview the application as it would appear on different visual environments, such as the Mac Interface, Windows and Motif;
- access to external relational database systems such as DB2, Oracle7 and SYBASE, and to OODBMS such as ObjectStore.

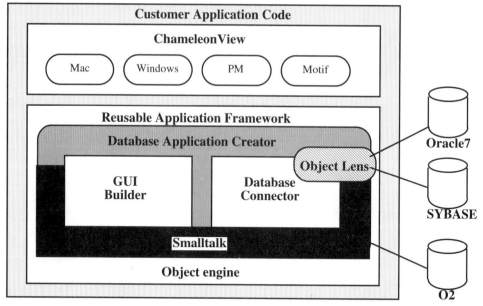

Figure 15.2 The organization of VisualWorks.

Figure 15.2 shows the architecture in which this is combined. The graphical user interface builder is coded in Smalltalk and includes tools for icon, palette and menu editing, customizing windows, creating applications and implementing frameworks from the properties in the schema. The database connector provides tools which access relational databases as if they contained objects, a visual data modeler, a forms package, an application template, an SQL interface, a query editor and a class editor. All of this is provided with an application framework to act as a start point for application building.

With such a tool, all control of the data, metadata and application code can be provided in a single coherent form. In Section 13.4.4, the way in which O_2 builds on VisualWorks was demonstrated, adding the database functionality as additional components to the controlling window.

15.4.2 The Starfield Viewer

The Starfield Viewer (developed by Ben Schneiderman and Chris Ahlberg and shown in Figure 15.3) is a generic interface which brings together a number of ideas. The viewer displays a collection of data as a scattergram using two of the properties of the data to define the x- and y- positions of the resulting icons. The appearance (size, color and so on) of each icon may depend on further properties.

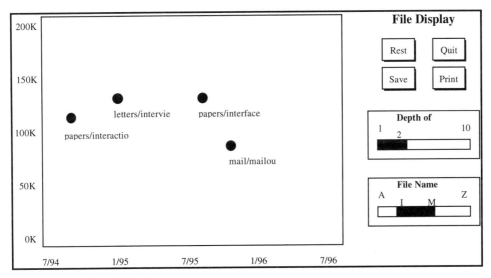

Figure 15.3 Starfield Viewer.

The data that is displayed may either be the whole collection or a selection drawn from the collection by a query, which is specified by using a number of sliders. Each slider controls the selection of one property, restricting the values chosen.

In the figure, data drawn from a user's file directory are shown with the size of the file as the y-axis and the age of the file as the x-axis. There are two sliders specifying the query. The upper one restricts the depth of the file in the directory to the hierarchy so that only files in the top two levels of the hierarchy are shown. The lower slider restricts the name of files to begin with letters between "I" and "M". Four files were found and these are displayed together with their names.

The sliders are operated using the arrow buttons which can be moved to restrict either end of the range of the property. If many files are retrieved, the icons used to display the objects will be kept simple – in this case, a single dot. As fewer objects are displayed more information about them appears, so that, in this case, there is room to show the file names as well. Furthermore, at any time, it is possible to select one of the icons in the display and bring up a form containing all of the property values of that object.

The Starfield Viewer is typical of the kind of complex generic interface tool that can be provided and which would be very suitable for an OODBMS. The framework is the scattergram and the primitives are the sliders which can be associated with properties and the functions which render the data as icons in the scattergram and as displayed forms.

■ 15.4.3 Double Helix

Double Helix is a relational database system which is available on the Macintosh and makes impressive use of direct manipulation techniques to support database work. Figure 15.4 shows the interface at work.

In the screenshot, three windows can be seen – a database window labeled *Collection*, a relation window, labeled *Student* and a query window labeled *Query*. The database is created by a menu option and is then displayed as a two-part window. The left-hand side is a relation factory. New tables are created by dragging the little rounded box into the right-hand side and typing in a name, such as "Student". Tables are deleted by dragging them back over the wastebasket icon.

The *Student* icon can then be opened to reveal the relation window. The structure of this is similar, with a series of icons in the left-hand side which, if dragged into the right-hand side, create components of the relation, such as fields, indexes and queries. Each of these may be opened for editing – a query window is seen as a small example.

Although Double Helix is not an object-oriented system, this kind of interface can equally well be used in the object-oriented context to permit simple data definition and data manipulation tasks to be carried out easily.

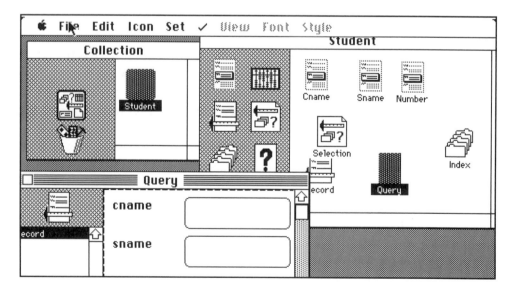

Figure 15.4   Double Helix on the Macintosh.

▨ 15.4.4 The STYLE workbench

STYLE stands for Systematics of TYped Language Environments and the STYLE workbench is a component of the Tycoon system, whose language was described in Section 11.3.3. The intention of the STYLE implementors is to create an interface which integrates the use of data modeling with programming techniques in a manner which maintains the integrity of the two techniques.

STYLE supports the development of an application in the following steps:

1. A graphical schema design tool creates a coarse description of the schema structure, using a data model called OM1.
2. A textual schema description is automatically generated from the graphical representation of the schema.
3. The textual representation is then edited to produce a more detailed schema description. This includes the addition of a variety of additional constraints.
4. A Tycoon Language representation of the schema is automatically generated from the textual schema description. This includes the creation of those parts of the schema code which can be generated systematically, including set and get methods which respect the constraints asserted in the previous phase.
5. The rest of the application is coded by extending the code generated in this way.

This layered system provides several points at which users of different sophistication can contribute to application design, but in a way that ensures that their efforts do not conflict. The provision of multiple views of a database and its schema are an essential component of the DBMS approach and one which is increasingly important as the structure of the data becomes more complex.

One other aspect of the STYLE implementation is important. There are a number of ways in which application code could be generated for a schema and one of the contrasts is in the level of the code generated. One approach is to take a template containing detailed low-level operations and to instantiate this for each class encountered. The STYLE workbench is implemented in the opposite way, by coding data model facilities as functions in the language and thus permitting a direct mapping between schema components and calls to these operations.

■ 15.4.5 Amaze and Drive

There are many experiments currently being undertaken on three-dimensional data visualization and this section describes two projects in this area. The Amaze system is being built in Aberdeen by a group led by Peter Gray and John Boyle to provide 3D schema and data visualization and querying. The work originated in the context of a protein modeling database. This was extended with a 3D end-user interface to data manipulation and in which the protein molecules could be displayed with an interface that permitted the user to rotate and move through the space that the protein occupied.

This background encouraged the group to move the 3D interaction up a level of generality to cover data definition and querying. Part of a 3D schema is shown as Figure 15.5. The user has tools to move through the schema viewing it from a variety of angles and to carry out schema design using it. There is also a

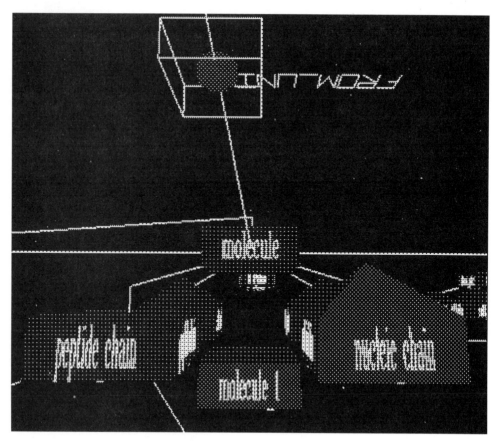

Figure 15.5 A 3D schema in Amaze.

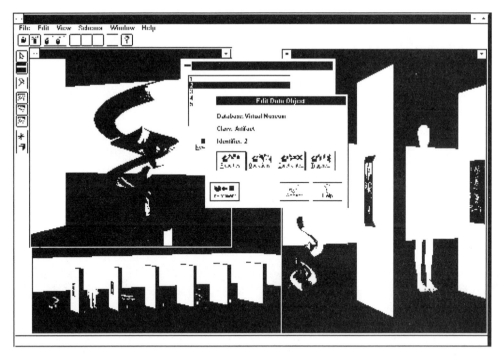

Figure 15.6 An interface to a museum database in Drive.

component which allows queries to be built up using the 3D schema and another which renders the results as blocks in a 3D world.

Drive has been developed at Napier University by the group led by Jessie Kennedy to provide 3D interaction with an object database. The data is described in a data model called NOODL and implemented in POET. The resulting visualization attempts to place spatial data in a simulation of a realistic setting. Figure 15.6, for instance, shows a museum database being displayed in a virtual museum. The user can navigate about the museum and summon data about the artefacts that are encountered.

These two examples demonstrate (imperfectly given the use of two dimensional black-and-white images) that 3D interfaces are viable as long as the data being used has an intrinsic three dimensional quality – molecules or objects in the real world, for instance.

15.4.6 Iconographer

Section 15.3.4 provided a discussion of the elements of visualization. Using this analysis it becomes possible to build a tool in which the components are provided in such a way that they can be used to create the visualization of choice. Iconographer is one experimental system which demonstrates how this might be done. Written in Smalltalk, Iconographer allows the user to connect data with the required methods of visualizing it. The controlling interface to Iconographer is shown in the center of Figure 15.7.

Iconographer uses a switchboard metaphor to allow the user to connect up collections of data with queries and presentation mechanisms. Internally, Iconographer represents all data in a simple Entity Relationship form. It can however, take data from a wide variety of file structures and turn these into this internal form. It can then present this data in a wide variety of ways. The elements of the system are:

- a set of input adapters, which take the data from a file and create a set of entities and attributes;
- a set of filter primitives which allow simple selections to be made on the data;
- a set of picture adapters, which take data of some type and display it in some form;
- a set of compositors, which are the presentation styles of the system;
- the switchboard which permits the internal data to be connected to picture adapters and a compositor to be chosen.

In the figure, the switchboard screen is shown in the center. This shows the effect of three kinds of user action:

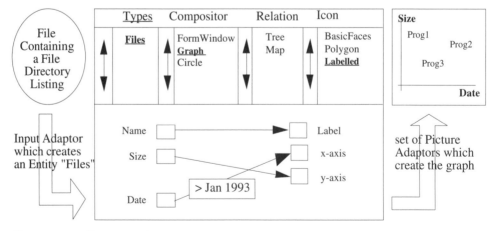

Figure 15.7 Iconographer.

- the selection of the entity type *Files*, the compositor for graphs and picture adapters for labeled icons;
- the introduction of a filter to restrict the display to files after January 1993;
- the connection of the attributes of *Files* to picture adapters for labeled icons.

Thus the user is given a simple direct manipulation interface to connect up the database with appropriate visualization primitives. The context of the use of Iconographer is shown to the left and right of the main window. On the left-hand side is shown a (UNIX) file which holds the result of an *ls* command and for which an input adapter has been written. This creates a single entity type with three attributes – file name, size and date of last modification. On the right-hand side is the result of the connections – a screen showing a graphical display of the file names.

■ 15.5 Summary

This chapter has looked at user interaction for object databases. In doing so it has emphasized the following points:

- The advanced applications involve new kinds of interaction task not seen in previous DBMS, among which are data visualization, imprecise querying and application building.
- There is an increasing body of human–computer interaction research which is usable in the database context, and which has mainly developed using object orientation as an implementation framework.
- This results in the creation of new interface styles including window systems, direct manipulation and three-dimensional interfaces.
- The OODBMS approach promises the availability of a wide range of user-interface tools in the form of class libraries which can be bought in and installed seamlessly alongside the DBMS classes.
- The elements of user interaction are increasingly understood and promise the possibility of decomposable and customizable interfaces for visualization and for database access.

16 A survey of other OODBMS products

This chapter will look at the products which are bringing the ideas contained in this book to the marketplace. There are already several systems which have been made available and many more which have been proposed. Even some of the proposals that were not fully implemented would be interesting to re-examine, but space has limited the discussion here to the products of the companies which are contributing to the Object Database Management Group as voting members. The chapter will not, however, discuss O_2, since this has already been extensively dealt with in Chapter 7.

The chapter starts with a short historical introduction, indicating how and when OODBMS products were developed and became available. This will be followed by a description of the important distinguishing facets of OODBMS, before sections on each of the products are given.

■ 16.1 Historical introduction

The recognition of the usefulness of an object-oriented logical DBMS data model occurred to many researchers in the early 1980s and attempts to create working

OODBMS date from that time. The early attempts to implement a system were carried out by research groups in three kinds of organization:

- universities and research institutes;
- mainstream computer manufacturing companies;
- small start-up companies.

Universities and research institutes are the traditional place for exploratory "blue sky" research into the feasibility of seemingly attractive ideas. Many of the best database techniques can be traced back to university groups, both for ideas and prototypes – not least in the area of relational systems. In addition, object orientation was taken up enthusiastically by many university researchers, notably in the area of human–computer interaction (HCI). Among the many relevant university projects which attempted to bring object orientation and database research together, Encore at Brown University, Cactis at the University of Colorado at Boulder, Mneme at the University of Massachussetts at Amherst, Thor at MIT, Exodus at the University of Wisconsin, the COMANDOS Esprit project and PISA at the universities of St. Andrews and Glasgow were all working on OODBMS or, at least, on the object stores which underpin them.

The Oregon Graduate Institute (OGI), the Microelectronics and Computer Technology Corporation (MCC) in Austin, Texas and INRIA in Paris were among the leading research institutes researching OODBMS issues. It is primarily from these institutions that four OODBMS arose, which are among the main OODBMS products – Gemstone based on OGI research, ITASCA and UniSQL based on MCC research, and O_2, which developed out of INRIA's Altaïr project.

The main computer companies also investigated the area and some of them devoted a considerable research effort to producing prototypical systems. Most notable in this respect were Hewlett-Packard, who produced the IRIS system and DEC with Trellis/Owl. Both of these were the source of many of the techniques now common in OODBMS. Whereas this effort has influenced later company products, the major companies have left the creation of commercial OODBMS to newly created start-up companies.

These start-up companies have, indeed, produced the major delivery of OODBMS in practice. The first companies to put a product into the marketplace were Graphael, with G-Base in 1986; Servio-Logic, with Gemstone in 1987; Symbolics with Statice in 1988; and Ontologic Ltd with Vbase, also in 1988. Some observations can be made of the early OODBMS prototypes. First, they were almost totally unusable – they were slow and, at best, single user, easily becoming zero user by crashing. They did not provide distribution, effective security or resilience. There was very little work on supporting querying, apart from Object SQL, produced by the IRIS project, as described in Section 9.3.1. Surprisingly, the early OODBMS did not even exploit object-oriented HCI research to produce state-of-the-art interfaces.

Another surprising feature was the almost total avoidance of C++. It was recognized early on that C++ poses serious problems in the database context and the first OODBMS avoided it. G-Base and Statice used Lisp, Gemstone used Smalltalk, while Vbase came with both a novel definition language, TDL, and a novel implementation language, COP. Research groups also avoided C++, preferring to generate new languages which more directly expressed the ideas they were researching. Exodus (the language E), MCC (FAD), PISA (PS-algol and then Napier88) and DEC's Trellis/Owl all developed their own persistent object-oriented languages. There were three resulting realizations from this: forcing customers to learn a new language was bad, forcing them to use two new languages was even worse; and failure to support C++ significantly reduced market acceptance.

The early start-up companies soon had some new rivals. Objectivity, Object Design and Versant started trading in the late 1980s, all with the intent of producing a C++-based OODBMS. Ontologic abandoned Vbase and switched instead to a C++ product called ONTOS. In Europe, O_2Technology was formed to exploit the results of the Altaïr research group and BKS Software began the development of POET. In the 1990s, UniSQL and Itasca developed as companies building upon MCC research.

The current situation is that there are about 10 companies who are producing products which are designated OODBMS. Each has its own flavor, stemming partly from the experience of its developers, but largely from the requirements of its intended customers. Each company has its sights set on a different mix of applications drawn both from those arising in the context of traditional commercial data management and those which involve the manipulation of design and multimedia data.

■ 16.2 OODBMS issues

In describing the products, the discussion will center on a few issues which are the most important in analyzing the usefulness of an OODBMS.

The DBMS *architecture* is an important consideration – how the data are physically stored and how they are delivered to users as objects in a database. In all of the cases to be considered here, a client/server architecture is used, but within this general term, there is a fair amount of difference. In particular, systems differ in how they partition the system behavior between clients and servers –

some preferring to keep the servers simple since they must serve many clients, others preferring to move the work to the server since it has all the data to hand. A complementary distinction is the nature of the network traffic generated by the client/server interaction. In some systems, objects are found by the server, batched together and sent to the client. In others, the client requests pages and finds the objects itself. Again there is a payoff between time spent at either end and the quantity of network traffic generated.

Clustering and caching are two other techniques of which heavy use is made. Objects which tend to be used at the same time can be clustered together on the same or adjacent disk partitions, so that they are more efficiently recovered together. Caches holds groups of objects or pages which are frequently accessed close to the process which is using them. A cache might be maintained by the client or the server or both. Thus if a client process is continuously making use of a number of objects, these will be held in a cache on the client machine, rather than be fetched from the server repeatedly.

The *database facilities* provided are those described in Chapter 1. Each section will examine how extensively the systems provide these. In particular, the transaction mechanism, indexing, schema evolution, version control and event notification will be discussed.

The persistence mechanism determines how the programmer indicates which data are to be stored and how they are then stored. The techniques described in Chapter 3 (explicit storage commands, using the *new* operation, persistent classes and reachability) are the options available to system designers.

All of the systems are primarily used via a *programming interface*, but which programming languages are provided and how they are integrated with the DBMS differs from system to system. The emphasis is on C++ and Smalltalk, since these are the languages initially supported by the ODMG. Some questions which arise here are: does the system accept code written in a standard version of the language or are there DBMS extensions to the syntax; which system classes are provided; can other, third-party, classes easily be used; which development environments are supported; and can data developed in programs written in different languages coexist?

The systems are all more than just a DBMS plus programming languages. They each come with a variety of *support tools*. Some of these are intended for database administrators, others for application developers and others for end-users.

Finally there are two related issues – how *querying* is carried out in the system and how *legacy data* can be accessed. In particular, which flavor of SQL is supported and how does the system interact with data being held in record-based DBMS? These are, in a sense, two halves of the same problem. Querying tools allow external software to treat the object database as if it were relational – usually by providing an ODBC driver. Legacy data is best integrated by a component which connects to a relational database and then makes each table seem like a class of objects.

Each section will start with a brief introduction to the company and its products, including a brief history, company philosophy, products and customers.

16.3 GemStone

Background

Gemstone was one of the first OODBMS to be made commercially available. It was built by Servio-Logic of Beaverton, Oregon in collaboration with the Oregon Graduate Institute. The GemStone system was originally designed around the language Smalltalk80. Although the initial systems were delivered with a principal language called Opal, it was immediately apparent that this was really persistent Smalltalk and the name, Opal, has since largely been replaced by "GemStone Smalltalk". Interfaces to C and C++ were soon added, but the product available today has maintained a heavy emphasis on Smalltalk, with other interfaces being added on top of Smalltalk. As the company say:

> While many initially thought C++ would be the next business language for client/server development, most businesses are finding that language too complex and difficult to learn to meet business needs.

GemStone 4.1 is the latest version and is the one that this section describes. GemStone is available on Sun SPARC, HP 9000 Model 700 and 800, IBM RS/6000 and Intel-based systems running the Windows NT operating system. Supported clients include: Windows 3.1, Windows 95, Windows NT, OS/2, Mac OS and numerous UNIX-based systems depending upon the client Smalltalk development environment selected.

System architecture

The GemStone system emphasizes a three-tier client/server distributed architecture, in which application processing constitutes a middle layer between the user interaction process and the process which maintains the object store. The importance of this is that application code can be located either with the data storage, if a lot of data is being used (e.g. for a survey), or with the user's process, if this largely consists of many changes to small amounts of data. This architecture reduces the amount of network traffic without overloading the server, and thus speeds up processing.

Maintenance of this architecture depends on a number of interacting processes of which two are predominant:

- A *Stone* process coordinates access to the object store, which is called a repository and is made up of multiple extents, which are either disk files or raw disk partitions and may be distributed over several machines. *Stone* synchronizes activities and ensures consistency as it processes requests to commit transactions. *Stone* processes allocate the object identifiers, object pages and object locks.

- A *Gem* process manages Smalltalk programs as well as object storage and retrieval for application programs developed using any of the GemStone interfaces. A *Gem* process provides the user with a consistent view of the object repository, retrieving objects from the store as needed. It is the responsibility of *Gem* to locate objects on pages and to transmit these pages to and from *Stone*. *Gem* also manages the user's GemStone session and controls the execution of GemStone Smalltalk methods. A user application is always connected to at least one *Gem* process, but may have connections to many *Gem* processes, depending on the application.

A host machine runs a single *Stone* process, which serves multiple *Gem* processes. The *Gem* process responsible for object access can be configured to be "local" to the repository to eliminate network overhead, or it can be configured to be "remote" to take advantage of network processing power. Similarly, client processes can be configured to be either local or remote to their *Gems*. Figure 16.1 shows the way this is organized. The user interaction process is connected to two *Gem* processes – one on the client machine and one on the server. Both of these interact with the *Stone* process on the server machine.

GemStone makes use of both caching and clustering to speed up processing. The shared object cache keeps frequently accessed objects in memory ensuring that large objects do not flush data from the cache. The shared cache can be accessed by several applications running simultaneously on the same object repository. Clustering places objects in the most suitable repository extents to reduce disk accesses, by placing the objects which are used together in the same extent.

Applications can be distributed transparently across networks of a heterogeneous collection of clients and servers including Windows, Macintosh and UNIX clients and both UNIX and Windows NT servers. Network communication between clients and servers consists of remote procedure calls over networks running the TCP/IP protocol.

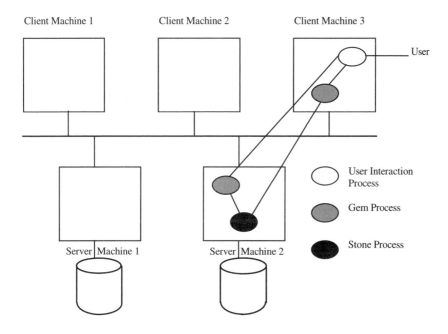

Figure 16.1   The GemStone three-tier architecture.

Database facilities

Concurrency control is maintained, as usual, by a transaction mechanism. This works by viewing each session as managing a local copy of the store and merging any changes at the end of a transaction. This optimistic method of working runs into trouble if others have committed changes to the same data, in which case the task of committing the changes is thrown back to the user. Locking is not carried out automatically, but any user is allowed explicitly to lock an object not previously locked. This will ensure that changes will commit at the end of the transaction.

There are a number of security systems including an interface to Kerberos authentication, password pattern checking, account expiration and password ageing analysis. GemStone provides both user- and group-level security at the object level, so that access can be limited to specific objects or to specific object methods. Each object is assigned to an authorization object that defines which users have access to it and whether those users have read and/or write access.

Recovery from hardware or network failure is achieved through replication, backup and logging mechanisms. Any authorized user may request a full backup or incremental backup, using transaction logs, at any time. After a disk or system failure, restoration begins with a full backup. Log files can then be applied until the object repository is restored to the last committed transaction. Users can also create replicates of extents, which are automatically kept up to date with changes to the original extent.

GemStone guarantees referential integrity among all objects, since it maintains all references through the use of an oid and does not permit objects to which there are references to be deleted. There is also a facility to build indexes to speed searches on frequently accessed collections.

Event notification is a technique in which signals alert either users or processes that pre-defined events, such as object creation, or conditions have occurred. Using this, the application programmer can install code which reacts to events in a systematic way.

Persistence mechanisms

Objects are made persistent by using a kind of persistent root called a connector and then using reachability from connectors. The concepts used are slightly unusual, however. GemStone is said to maintain a GemStone server version of any classes of persistent objects. Thus there will be a class for the programming context and an equivalent class for the database context. The pair are automatically maintained – if a Smalltalk class is created and an object of that class becomes persistent, then a GemStone class for the object is automatically created. Creating a connector makes an instance of the GemStone class equivalent to the Smalltalk class of the object which is to be made persistent. Any object reachable from a connector is automatically made persistent in the same way.

GemStone provides dynamic garbage collection in the form of scavenger processes which automatically reclaim space used by objects, which are no longer referenced.

Language interfaces

GemStone provides the ability to use Smalltalk via VisualWorks, Visual Smalltalk Enterprise or Visual Age, or to use C++, or C. Classes and objects can be created using any of these languages, and objects created in one language can be used in applications written in any other language.

C is provided as a set of functions, together with a set of components which translate between GemStone objects and C structure pointers and literals. C++ is provided as a language pre-processor and a class library.

System classes

GemStone provides an extensive library of predefined classes, many directly inherited from Smalltalk. The class hierarchy includes standard alphanumeric

Object
  Activation
  Association
   StringPair
   SymbolAssociation
  AutoComplete
  Behavior
   Class
   Metaclass
  BlockClosure
   ExecutableBlock
    ComplexBlock
     ComplexVCBlock
    SimpleBlock
   SelectBlock
  Boolean
  ClampSpecification
  ClassOrganizer
  ClusterBucket
  CompiledMethod

Object
  Collection
   AbstractBag
    Bag
    Set
     ClassSet
     Dictionary
      IdentityDictionary
       SymbolDictionary
        LanguageDictionary
      StringPairSet
      SymbolSet
      UserProfileSet
    RcBag
   HashDictionary
    IdentityHashDictionary
    IntegerHashDictionary
    StringHashDictionary
     SymbolHashDictionary
     SymbolListDictionary
   RcHashDictionary
   RcQueue
   SequenceableCollection
    Array
     ClassHistory
     ClusterBucketArray
     CollisionBucket
      IdentityCollisionBucket
     InvariantArray
    OrderedCollection
     SortedCollection
    Repository
    SymbolList
    CharacterCollection
     JapaneseString
      EUCString
       InvariantEUCString
       EUCSymbol
     String
      ISOLatin
      InvariantString
      Symbol

Object ...
  Exception
  Magnitude
   AbstractCharacter
    Character
    JISCharacter
   DateTime
   Number
    DecimalFloat
    BinaryFloat
    Float
    SmallFloat
    Fraction
    Integer
     LargeNegativeInteger
     LargePositiveInteger
     SmallInteger
  Process
  ProfMonitor
  RcCounter
  Segment
  StackBuffer
  StackSegment
  Stream
   BtreeReadStream
    RangeIndexReadStream
   PositionableStream
    ReadStream
    WriteStream
  System
  UndefinedObject
  UserProfile
  VariableContext

Figure 16.2 The GemStone class hierarchy.

types including character strings, numbers and dates; collection classes for arrays and sets; and stream classes for I/O. Available classes also include graphics, sound, and interface components such as forms.

It is useful to compare this set of classes with the ODMG hierarchy shown in Figure 16.2. There are some significant differences – a number of classes which make available many of the components of the DBMS (such as processes, segments and user profiles), a greater variety of collection classes, the dispersal of the scalar classes, and the presence of reduced conflict classes. These have names starting "Rc" and consist of bulk data classes, in which concurrency control will be less rigid, thus permitting faster average access time to the components.

User interfaces and support tools

GemStone includes a set of system administration tools for such functions as establishing user privileges, class management, performance monitoring and backup. GemStone system administration can be performed directly from a client Smalltalk image in conjunction with the GemStone Smalltalk Interface.

Among the many development tools, there is a configuration tool, a facility to inspect the state of objects, an interactive debugger, and browsers for the classes, session and transactions, class versions, symbol lists and system connections.

Querying and access to legacy data

Connections to relational systems, such as Oracle and Sybase, are via gateways. Data are updated automatically in order to keep GemStone and external copies synchronized. These updates may be performed continuously, or on a scheduled batch basis, depending on the environment and degree of synchronization required.

GemStone can also be used to manage information which complies with standards such as CORBA and OLE. Smalltalk can also respond to relational database access methods including SQL and ODBC.

■ 16.4 ITASCA

Background

The ITASCA distributed object database management system is the product resulting from the Orion project at MCC. A series of three prototypes culminated in a multi-client/multi-server architecture which was released by MCC in July 1989. The final prototype was at first developed into the commercial ITASCA system by a Texas start-up company. This company was bought out in 1995 by the IBEX Corporation which runs a group of information technology operations in Europe.

The DBMS architecture

ITASCA provides a distributed architecture with private and shared databases spread across a UNIX-based local area network. Each data value is held at one site, but there is no central control – each server is autonomous. Each server maintains both a page cache and an object cache and services multiple clients managing concurrency control and locking by using the object cache. Clients maintain only an object cache.

Database facilities

ITASCA provides concurrency control using the two-phase commit protocol with serialized transactions and deadlock detection. It also supports long transactions which are started by checking out an object from a shared to a private database. Cooperative working is supported by permitting several users to take part in a long transaction. Intention locks are also provided.

A single schema is maintained for the whole of a distributed database, with sub-schemata being used for private fragments of a database. The data model includes multiple inheritance, classes as objects, class properties and operations, instance operations and properties, integrity constraints and operation overloading. New data, classes, properties and operations can be added at any time. Composite objects can be defined which can be used to control the propagation of operations such as object deletion.

There are two kinds of multimedia data supported: linear long data objects are essentially sequential data such as text and audio; spatial long data objects have two dimensions – images for instance.

Recovery is provided by using an undo log, which permits the effect of half-completed transactions to be reversed after a crash. Committing a transaction results in the server flushing all of the objects changed by the transaction from the object buffer to the page buffer.

There is an indexing mechanism which uses B+ trees. Indexes can be created for a single class on a single property or can use multiple properties from multiple classes.

There are notifiable classes, which allow change notification to occur in one of two forms. Passive notification is achieved by storing when instances of a notifiable class have been updated or deleted. The application can then query the class to see if these events have occurred. Active notification causes an operation to be invoked if update, deletion, version creation, check-in or check-out have occurred. The default behavior is to Email the superuser, although other behavior can be programmed if needed.

Version management is provided using the check-in mechanism, which can create a transient version, a working version or a released version of an object. The version derivation hierarchy can be used to bind versions to each other either statically or dynamically – the latter modifying the bindings automatically as new versions are created.

Security is provided by an authorization mechanism which provides a particular privilege (read access, write access or creation) to a role (which may refer to one user or to a group of users). Privileges can be attached to databases, classes, extents, objects, operations or properties. There is a default authorization which can be inferred for any role and this can be augmented with further authorizations, which can be either positive (i.e. the role is permitted to perform the action) or negative (i.e. the role is debarred from the activity).

The persistence mechanism

In C++, persistence is added by accessing a class library of persistent supporting classes. In CLOS (the Common Lisp Object System), a persistent metaclass is provided. Persistent objects must be members of classes which are instances of this metaclass. Furthermore, it is possible to indicate that some properties of a persistent class are transient.

Programming language support

ITASCA supports C++, Smalltalk, CLOS, Common Lisp and C. The emphasis is on dynamic schema modification without halting the database and without extensive recompiling and re-linking. Each language is accessed through a functional API. In C++, a C++ header file is automatically created and merged with code files to generate the application.

Software engineering support and tools

ITASCA has a sister product – Distributed Archiving and Workflow Network (DAWN) – which is described as a "class library of workflow methods and development tools". Among the components of DAWN are: transparent workflow management, support for multimedia data, a thesaurus tool, the maintenance of document audit trails and an event notification system.

There is also a database administration tool and a schema design tool. The former allows authorized users to create and manage private databases, migrate objects, tune the database parameters, gather statistics and compact the disk. The schema design tool provides a graphical means to add and remove classes, properties and operations.

Querying support and access to legacy data

ITASCA has its own querying capability, which allows a user to query either a private database, a shared database or both. Query optimization and parallel execution techniques are used to improve performance.

16.5 ObjectStore

Background

Object Design Inc. was set up in 1988 with the express purpose of building and marketing the OODBMS that became ObjectStore. Situated in Burlington, Massachussetts, they claim to have 1000 customers world wide, with over 10,000 developers currently using the system. They have become closely involved with IBM as joint marketing partner.

The DBMS architecture

ObjectStore is built on a client/server architecture, in which each server is responsible for controlling access to the object store and for managing the logging of updates, locking, checkpointing, resolving conflicts in the data and for backup and recovery. A server supports multiple clients. A client process takes a higher level view of the data and will typically be responsible for collections, queries and transaction management.

The servers are designed to exploit a virtual memory mapping architecture which uses a virtual memory space that is network-wide and can span multiple servers. Retrieved objects can be batched for data transfer, so that network traffic is cut down. Servers also use a clustering strategy to reduce access time. Each client uses a local cache to maintain the objects which it is using. When an object is brought into the client's workspace, references to it are manipulated so that each access subsequently takes a single instruction.

Database facilities

Concurrency control is provided using a transparent locking mechanism with shared and exclusive locks. Any client requiring data sends requests to the server which keeps track of all locks. Locking is provided at a variety of granularities – on segments of the database, on pages, or on configurations (groups of objects specified by the programmer).

Resilience is achieved by using an after-image log. The transaction manager is responsible for ensuring that all changes are recorded in the log, while a "propagation filter" moves the logged updates into the database where they will be permanently recorded. There is a separate "archive log" use to which the programmer can create backups at fixed intervals of time.

There is a version management facility which supports collaborative working and uses a check-in/check-out mechanism of update, thus allowing for long transactions. For any configuration of objects it is possible to create a version history, which is independent of the type of the objects.

The persistence mechanism

ObjectStore supports persistence through named roots, with object persistence being indicated at creation time. There is a class of databases which is used to support persistence. Databases are created with the *new* operation as usual and are opened and closed with methods of the database class. This class also supports the creation of persistent root objects, which are usually collections into which persistent objects are put.

Here are some examples in simplified C++:

```
OS_BEGIN_TX( Tx1, update )                        // starts a transaction
                                                  //   called Tx1
empDB = os_database :: open("Employment", write)  // opens Employment DB in
                                                  //   write mode
set(Person) People = new set(Person)              // creates a new
                                                  //   collection
PeopleRoot = empDB -> create_Root( "People" )     // creates a new root
PeopleRoot -> set_value( People )                 // makes the root hold the
                                                  //   collection
empDB -> close( )                                 // closes the database
OS_END_TX( Tx1)                                   // ends the transaction
                                                  //   attempting to
                                                  //   commit the changes
```

This first transaction creates a root extent for the class *Person*. It does so by creating a new set to hold the collection and then by making this set the value of a newly created root, one which will be identifiable by the name "People".

The following transaction puts a person in this set:

```
OS_BEGIN_TX( Tx2, update )                         // starts a transaction
                                                   //   called Tx2
empDB = os_database :: open("Employment", write)   // opens the DB again
PeopleRoot = empDB -> find_Root( "People" )        // retrieves the root
set(Person) People =                               // retrieves the
                                                   //   collection from
   PeopleRoot -> get_value( PersonSet )            //   the root
Person john = new( empDB, personType )             // creates a persistent
                                                   //   person object
People -> insert( john )                           // puts this in the
                                                   //   collection
empDB -> close( )                                  // ends the transaction
                                                   //   attempting to commit
                                                   //   the changes
```

After opening the database, the persistent root object is retrieved and then its value is extracted and cast from its dynamically typed form to be a set of *Person* objects. A persistent *Person* object is then created using a different form of the *new* operation, one that requires that the database be specified as a parameter. The same operator can be used to create transient values by setting the value of this parameter to be the memory heap.

Programming language support

ObjectStore supports the use of C++, Smalltalk and C. The languages are made persistent by the inclusion of system classes such as the controlling class, *ObjectStore*, which has a method to initialize the system on start-up, and a class for databases, as described above. ObjectStore also provides collection classes for lists, bags, sets and arrays. These have the usual insertion, deletion and enquiry methods.

The Smalltalk interface has been developed in collaboration with ParcPlace and integrates VisualWorks with ObjectStore. The principal design decision has been to structure the Smalltalk image so that it can contain direct references to persistent objects without the need to transform the persistent objects in any way.

Software engineering support and tools

The ObjectStore Inspector is a class browser, which supports: the display of the class hierarchy in any of four standard object-oriented representations (Booch, OMT, Coad and Yourdon, and Statecharts); instance editing and navigation; the creation of multiple versions; and the ability to create and manage extents of the classes.

The ObjectStore Performance Expert is available to collect data on database use, storing the results in trace files. An analytical tool is then available to produce diagrammatic presentations of the results in a graphical environment. There is also a component which can supply a real-time presentation of metrics of running servers.

Application interfaces can be built using the UTAH C++-based Graphical User Interface available from Viewsoft Inc. of Provo, Utah. This provides object mappers which create editable on-screen representations of the objects in the store. Using UTAH, it is possible to see multiple synchronized views of the data. Utah supports both IBM's SOM and Microsoft's OLE document architectures.

Access to legacy data and query support

ObjectStore provides gateway objects which permit access to relational data and a schema mapping tool which maps a relational schema into an object-oriented version. These are the basis of two system components:

- *Open Access* allows ObjectStore databases to be accessed using SQL, providing an ODBC driver for the purpose;
- *DBconnect* allows relational databases to be used as if they were object databases. Three modes are supported: providing a C++ front-end to a relational database, taking copies of the relational data into ObjectStore, and creating replicates of the relational data which can then be used in parallel with the relational version.

Querying can also be performed using either C++ or Smalltalk. Both of these provide functions which take a string containing a boolean expression, using this to filter the members of a collection.

■ 16.6 Objectivity/DB

Background

Objectivity, which is based in Mountain View, California, was founded in 1988 by engineers from the computer and database industries. Using $25 million raised from venture capital, they set out to build a distributed database system which would exploit object technology, high-speed networking and symmetric multi-processors. Objectivity/DB Version 1.0 was shipped in 1990 and was mainly taken up in the engineering and technical markets. The current release is version 3.0 and it is used for manufacturing control, telecommunications, software management, environmental control and scientific applications.

Objectivity is available on 17 platforms (over which transparent interoperability is claimed), including the NT, VMS, UNIX and Windows operating systems and hardware platforms from Data General, DEC, HP, IBM, Pentium, NEC, Siemens Nixdorf, SGI, Stratus and Sun, with full platform interoperability. Currently listed customers include: Motorola, Fermi Labs, BNR, Boeing, BT, Citibank, ICL, Siemens and Sybase and the company claim approximately 100,000 users.

The DBMS architecture

Objectivity/DB has a client/server architecture in which pages are the unit of transfer. The client is responsible for many of the system functions, including caching, traversal and converting between formats. The server is constructed to exploit multi-threading where this is available. All object references are via a 64-bit object identifier, rather than using virtual memory addressing. The company claims "unlimited scalability" for this architecture.

There is a four-level structure for data. Objects are held in containers. Containers form part of databases and databases may be combined into federated databases. There is also support for partitions, which replicate and distribute the data about the network, in order to provide fault tolerance. Partitions control the locking of the data they contain.

Database facilities

The system supports the ability to change classes and automatically migrate objects to new versions. Objectivity/DB also provides a mechanism for managing "genealogies" of versions of objects.

Objectivity/DB supports both long and short transactions. To do this, the system recognizes both read and write locks, with shared and exclusive versions of each and provides deadlock detection. Collaborative working is emphasized by the provision of the shared locks, object versioning and a check-in/check-out facility for updating objects.

The persistence mechanism and programming language support

Objectivity/DB supports ANSI standard C++ 3.0 and ParcPlace Smalltalk, but the ways in which the two languages are used are rather different. Data modeling, persistence and system classes are all different between the two languages.

In C++, persistence is by inheritance from the class, *ooObj*. Thus, any C++ application must be modified to ensure that the classes of persistent objects inherit from *ooObj*. In Smalltalk, persistence is by reachability from named roots, which are dictionary objects. Object deletion is by garbage collecting unreachable objects in Smalltalk, but by explicit deletion in C++.

Whereas there is a common data model between the two languages, the way it is programmed is slightly different. The common data model includes the support for bi-directional relationships, which may be 1–1, 1–*n* or *m*–*n*. It also supports the management of composite objects by permitting operations, such as deletion, to be propagated.

In C++, data modeling is carried out by using a language extension called DDL. A pre-processor takes a DDL program, using it to create the database and the C++ code to manage it. The main addition in DDL is the way in which relationships are specified. For instance, if an employee object has a relationship to a set of dependents, this would be specified as:

```
class Employee
  ...
  ooRef(Person) Dependents() <-> DependsOn prop(delete);
  ...
end
```

which creates a property of *Employee* called *Dependents*, which is multi-valued (the empty brackets after "Dependents" indicate that); has an inverse property, *DependsOn*, in class *Person*, which is single valued; and will propagate a deletion. That is, if the employee is deleted so will be any dependents that the employee might have. *ooRef* is the class of object references, although objects can also be referred to by normal C++ pointers or by handles, which are optimized references for local use.

In Smalltalk, all development is carried out in the context of a session. Sessions manage transactions and inside transactions updates occur. The schema is created as a set of Smalltalk classes, with a similar mechanism for describing relationships and also a feature for constraining types. It is not clear whether or not operation propagation can be carried out in Smalltalk.

C++ comes with a set of classes derived from the RogueWave library (described in Section 15.3.2), to which has been added array, string and map classes tuned for database work. Smalltalk comes with the normal ParcPlace library, but is also designed for use with the ENVY toolkit.

Software engineering support and tools

There are a set of browsers for data, metadata and queries; performance tuning tools which gather and analyze statistics of the database; and administrative tools to maintain the collection of containers, partitions, databases and federated databases which constitute the data and to permit backup and recovery.

Access to legacy data and querying support

Objectivity/DB supports SQL-89 and entry level SQL-92. This is provided in three forms:

- An interactive querying interface, in which queries and transactions can be specified and where there are facilities for managing a command history, creating batch jobs and escaping to the shell.
- An ODBC driver which allows external relational tools to use the database.
- An application programmer's interface, which contains a set of calling mechanisms to develop and submit queries from within a program.

The approach is to use ODBC to enable the user to use the object database and a relational database in a unified way. It is not clear whether Objectivity/DB permits the users to manage legacy data as though they were object oriented.

16.7 POET

Background

The POET system emerged as the natural progression of products of a German company, initially called BKS Software but now renamed POET Software. Their initial product line consisted of C development tools, from which the company moved to C++ and, in particular, persistent C++. POET Version 1.0 was released in December 1991 and the current release is version 3.0. As well as the distributed multi-user OODBMS, the company sell a stripped down single-user version.

Although it runs on a wide variety of platforms (including SunOS, Solaris, HP-UX, IBM AIX, Windows (95 and NT), NeXTStep and Linux), POET is targeted specifically towards C++ developments for PCs, LANs and workstations. The emphasis seems to be on a product which is itself small and which is intended for clients with applications managing amounts of data which are relatively modest in size, yet possess complex data management problems. The application areas for which it is intended include team based design, group managed document and hypermedia systems, and telecommunications. The company claims the sales of 8000 licenses and lists among its customers, tele-communications companies, such as AT&T, manufacturers such as Ford and SONY, software vendors and consulting companies.

The DBMS architecture and database facilities

The full DBMS version of POET has a distributed client/server architecture, in which the query processing is carried out in the server and network traffic is in terms of objects. Concurrency control is managed using nested transactions and locks which are held on objects. There are locks which prevent others from reading an object, updating an object or deleting an object.

POET provides a distributed event notification system. To achieve this, the programmer can install functions which are activated whenever a particular event involving an object occurs. The events include activities in which the object is stored, deleted or unlocked. The functions are called wherever the event occurs and no matter where the database is located.

POET emphasizes cooperative working, in which the event notification system can be used together with a version mechanism which includes a check-in/check-out facility. There is a mechanism for sharing data between databases by setting up cross-references.

The persistence mechanism

Persistence is specified on classes. Any object whose class is declared using the keyword "persistent" can be stored in a database. The effect of this is that the pre-processor causes the class to inherit from the system class, *PtObject*, which holds all of the storage functions. The *new* operation is then used unchanged, calling *new* on a persistent class creates persistent objects, while calling *new* on a non-persistent class creates transient objects. Storing persistent objects is achieved by placing them explicitly in the database.

Programming language support

POET only supports C++ and provides specific extensions to the syntax to permit database access. The source code is then run through a pre-compiler, which uses the C++ persistent class declarations to achieve four tasks: the creation of the class dictionary for the database, the production of class-specific administration classes to support querying, the creation of an extent for the class, and the creation of a pure C++ form of the class.

Here are some of the extensions:

- the keyword **ondemand** can be used to indicate that the value of a property should only be brought into memory when it is accessed;
- the keyword **lset** is used to indicate that a property is multi-valued;
- the keyword **depend** is used to indicate that deletion of an object should propagate to an object which is one of its properties;
- the keyword **transient** can be used to indicate properties which should not be stored – interactors are given as examples of this;
- the keyword **useindex** is used to indicate that a class has an index, which may be compound and involves object properties and sets.

Here is an example of a POET definition of the class, *Employee*:

```
persistent class Employee
{ private:
  PtDate DateOfEmployment;        // Use of POET system class PtDate
  *char staffNo;
  *Department worksIn;            // Some properties are normal C++
                                  //   pointers
  ondemand<Employee> supervisor;  // Others are not automatically
                                  //   brought in
  depend lset<Person> Dependents; // A multi-valued property which is
                                  //   deleted when the Employee object is
  transient PersonDialog* pDialog; // An interactor set up by the window
                                  //   system
  public:
    Employee();
    ...
  useindex StaffNoIndex
};
```

in which the index is defined as:

```
indexdef StaffNoIndex : Employee
{
   staffNo;
};
```

Software engineering support and tools

The POET Developer's Workbench is an integrated development environment which allows the user to create and edit programs, run POET's pre-compiler, build databases, browse and edit the class declarations and the objects in a database, and run OQL queries.

The POET Administrator's Workbench provides the tools needed for database administration, server administration and user administration. Database administration tasks include on-line backup, database creation, creating database versions, regenerating the indexes, or updating the database format to a new version of POET. Server administration tasks include upgrading the server to permit more users, examining which users are accessing the server, and shutting down the server. User administration controls database protection, for which there are a number of access rights available at different levels of granularity.

Querying support and access to legacy data

It does not seem possible for POET to access relational databases, but the system provides full querying facilities, including an ODBC driver and OLE compliance. The latter means that it is possible for OLE tools to store their documents in POET for improved efficiency of access.

POET also provides two other querying routes – OQL and extended C++. OQL can be submitted using the workbench or can be embedded as strings in C++ programs. Extended C++ includes a class for queries. The query is created by calls to operations of this class which build up predicates, associate result objects and so on.

■ 16.8 Versant ODBMS

Background

VERSANT Object Technology, based in Menlo Park, California, has a primary application focus on the area of network management. Their markets include telecommunications, utilities, transportation, computers, and business process re-engineering. VERSANT have a variety of customers including Alcatel, British

Telecom, Fujitsu Network Systems, GTE, Informix, Panasonic, Scotiabank, Siemens, Texaco, and many other leading organizations worldwide.

The product is supported on a number of platforms including SunSPARC (Solaris and SunOS), Windows NT and 3.1, HP 9000 Series 700/800, * IBM RS/ 6000 and * OS/2.

The DBMS architecture

VERSANT is based on the logical management of data, i.e. of objects, rather than physical representations such as pages. Object location is transparently managed and caching is used to maintain a local store of objects. The VERSANT architecture also supports multi-threading.

The VERSANT Fault Tolerant Server is intended to ensure continuous operation of databases in a distributed environment in the presence of server failures. This is achieved by maintaining two servers (either on the same node or on two different nodes connected by a wide area network) which are kept in automatic synchronization without any change to application code.

Each VERSANT database may contain 281 tera-objects, each object can be of unlimited size and there can be 65,000 databases per network. Tertiary storage of data can be used for archiving data, with operator intervention being automatically requested when an archived object is dereferenced.

Clusters of objects that are used together are continuously maintained, with embedded objects being held within parent objects, thus avoiding fragmentation. Clustering is also used in the front-end cache.

VERSANT attempts to support mobile computing, by allowing the use of personal databases. These may be disconnected, used remotely and then re-attached to commit their updates to the main database.

Database facilities

Locking is provided at the object level, but locks may also be applied to classes, instances or versioned objects. There is a range of different kinds of lock – short and persistent locks to support long transactions, "nolocks" for optimistic working and update locks. VERSANT even supports the ability for users to extend the model to define their own locking rules. VERSANT automatically prevents deadlock by refusing to grant a lock which would close a deadlock loop. Transactions are run using a transparent distributed two-phase commit, with partial cache commits, checkpoints and savepoints. Other transaction types are provided including nested transactions. The check-in/check-out mechanism establishes a persistent lock on given objects, which will deny access to others until a long transaction is completed.

VERSANT provides server-based event management based on research carried out with AT&T and Bellcore. The application registers events with the server together with an operation, which the server invokes when it detects the event. The events which may be registered include updates or deletions of objects or classes, and creations, updates and deletions of class instances.

Resilience is managed by a dual logging facility – both logical and physical logs are maintained. A roll-forward mechanism ensures full recovery of trans-actions, since after the database is restored, committed transactions recorded in the logs are re-applied to the database.

VERSANT provides referential integrity and location transparency in distributed environments, since it makes heavy use of the logical object identifier to manage inter-object references. Objects may migrate about the network to exploit differences in load and yet cause no problems to running applications.

Dynamic schema evolution is provided, so that instances of modified classes are transformed automatically as they are used. The application does not need to be stopped to achieve this, neither does the DBMS have to be halted to add new physical volumes to its store.

VERSANT supports version management in the form of versioning graphs, which provide both transparent and explicit access to versioned objects. From one version it is possible to access its parents, children and siblings. There are also methods of creating configurations which represent transient, working and released status levels.

The persistence mechanism

VERSANT uses a single persistent pointer type to represent relationships between objects in the database. The system supports the invisible transformation between database pointers and standard C++ in-memory pointers. Objects are therefore created and deleted using standard language constructors and destructors.

Querying support

Querying is supported in a number of ways: by providing cursor classes so that data collections can be iterated over, by providing a superset of ANSI-89 SQL, and by providing an ODBC driver so that a range of database software can run on top of VERSANT.

Programming language support

VERSANT supports C++ and Smalltalk, and with both languages the emphasis is on the ability to use standard language systems unchanged. The database capability is added, for instance by automatically generating the database schema directly from C++ header files, thus avoiding the need for pre-processors or special compilers. This conveys two benefits: programmers can continue to work with a familiar environment, and applications will port to the system more easily.

VERSANT supports pointers, user-defined data types, user-defined templates, and also offers a database-aware string class, as well as sets, lists, arrays and dictionaries. The two languages co-exist so that objects created in C++ can be accessible from Smalltalk and vice versa.

Software engineering support and tools

VERSANT supports the use of a number of different additional tools:

- DBA utilities to tune the database, to set up incremental backup, and to monitor performance;
- the ENVY-Developer line of software engineering tools, which brings with it multi-user and multi-version application development support;
- a number of object modeling tools including the Rumbaugh OMT development model and the Jacobson Use-Case methodology;
- graphical user interface builders such as Galaxy, XVT or zAPP, which produce C++ stubs;
- VERSANT Argos – a Smalltalk-based application development environment, which includes an object modeling facility, visual programming tool, team-based design repository, and configuration management tool and which is based on ParcPlace VisualWorks.

Access to legacy data

VERSANT/M is the component of VERSANT which manages the use of relational data. This proceeds in both directions – allowing VERSANT data to look like relations by supporting ODBC, and by providing multi-database support which enables other databases, such as Oracle, DB2 and IMS, to be managed by VERSANT tools. Much of the work carried out in this context has involved collaboration with UniSQL.

■ 16.9 UniSQL

Background

UniSQL have a somewhat different approach to that of the other vendors discussed here. Whereas the others see the object model as central and access to relational data to be a subordinate issue, albeit a vital one, UniSQL describes its approach as object-relational and seeks to unify the relational and object-oriented models. The company mission statement emphasizes the need to "exploit the advantages of object-oriented technology, without giving up relational database features that are relied on". In unifying the data models they seek "to manage all data types with the same level of reliability and consistency that relational-only systems have provided for simple numbers, characters, and strings".

The UniSQL products have developed from the research work of Dr. Won Kim, mainly carried out at MCC. The company, UniSQL Inc., received its initial funds in 1991 from a subsidiary of the Japanese national telephone company and produced its first product in 1992.

The UniSQL approach is based on two core products. UniSQL/X is a database server which is used through an extension of SQL to managed objects and classes as well as records and tables. UniSQL/M is a DBMS which creates a federated database out of a mixture of databases of different kinds – object-oriented, relational and pre-relational. The products run on SunOS, Solaris, HP-UX, OSF/1, Windows (NT and 3.1), among others.

The DBMS architecture and querying support

UniSQL provide a federated database system called the *multi-vendor database system*. This provides a unified view of data which may be held either in a UniSQL database or in one of a number of relational DBMS (currently including ORACLE, SYBASE, Informix and CA-INGRES) and pre-relational systems. Figure 16.3 shows an example of the basic structure. The server is unifying four relational and two object-relational DBMS. Three applications are using this and the second is running in the context of a schema, S, which is made up from fragments (SF1, SF2 and SF3) which describe data held on different DBMS. The UniSQL server integrates the data from these three sources and presents them to the application as though it were using a single database. The user of UniSQL therefore has the illusion of a single database even though this might be constructed by integrating data from a variety of sources.

UniSQL believe that the problems involved in attempting to build a DBMS with full capability on the basis of an entirely novel data model are too severe to succeed (and anyway, the attempt is unnecessary). The UniSQL DBMS is therefore built around an "object-relational" model, which is constructed as a systematic extension to the relational model, rather than as a completely dissimilar alternative. The extension consists of four components:

- properties can be objects not just literal values;
- properties can be multi-valued;

- tables (now called classes) are built into an inheritance hierarchy;
- classes also include operations.

The databases built using this model are accessed using SQL/X, which is a superset of ANSI standard SQL, which includes both object-oriented and relational features. This contrasts with the ODMG proposal for OQL, which avoids the data definition and update parts of SQL. The existence of an object query language which approximates to full SQL permits experienced relational database users to get started with the system immediately and gradually move over to the use of the object-oriented features.

Database facilities

Since the product extends the relational approach, it naturally supports relational facilities such as view definition, query optimization and a transaction manager which serializes the transactions. Concurrency control uses two-phase locking and supports shared and exclusive locks, and also intention locks. Locking can be on pages, objects and classes, and is automatically able to turn a number of locks on individual members of a class into a single lock on the class as a whole.

Recovery is supported by means of a write-ahead log in which both a before image and an after image is maintained. The system can recover from crashes in which the disk is destroyed as well as those in which the disk remains intact.

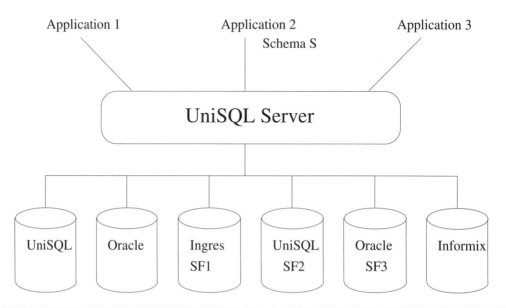

Figure 16.3 The UniSQL architecture.

The persistence mechanism

As befits the company name, SQL is the main interface and persistence is asserted by the usual SQL "create" commands.

Programming language support

UniSQL supports C++ and Smalltalk. In both cases, the languages remain unchanged and DBMS functionality is added through a class library, which includes classes of DBMS objects including: databases, schemata, transactions, iteration cursors, queries, privileges, triggers and exceptions.

There are two complementary approaches to using the languages with the database. The first takes programs written in the language and generates a database schema from the classes. The second takes a schema and generates a language description (C++ header files or Smalltalk class descriptions). Thus it is possible to write code which accesses pre-existing databases and also code which creates new databases. The UniSQL C++ Interface also supports the embedded use of the execution of SQL statements for querying.

As well as the database-oriented classes already discussed, the system provides: scalar classes for characters, money and various kinds of number, string, date and time; collection classes for arrays, bags, sets and lists; and multimedia classes.

The C++ Interface can use any standard C++ compiler. UniSQL Smalltalk Interface integrates ObjectWorks (the ParcPlace version of Smalltalk) with the UniSQL Server.

Software engineering support and tools

The VisualEditor is a WYSIWYG database schema and data definition, management and viewing tool. It provides the means to interact with the data from a variety of perspectives: through the class-instance relationship, through the inheritance hierarchy, or through an object composition hierarchy.

■ 16.10 Summary

This chapter has examined a range of OODBMS products currently on the market. The survey has necessarily been brief and the reader is urged to visit the Websites of the various companies to find more details on each of the products – full addresses are given in the further reading appendix.

In general, there are a number of features which are common to all of the systems and which may therefore be taken to have become a consensus preference between the alternatives:

- a client/server architecture, since this permits the distribution of workload between the nodes of the network;
- commitment to C++ and, with the exception of POET, to Smalltalk, since these are the industry standard languages;
- support for both competitive and collaborative modes of concurrent working (and thus short and long transactions), since there is a need to provide both for traditional applications and design applications;
- some form of versioning for the design market;
- provision of an SQL-like querying facility;
- integration with relational data;
- a commitment to continuous working, even if a schema evolves and if nodes in the network become unavailable.

On the other hand, there are issues on which no consensus is yet forthcoming. These include:

- how to distribute the workload between clients and servers;
- the unit of network traffic (page or object);
- the way in which the language is integrated with the database (by extending the syntax or providing a class library);
- the class libraries supported;
- the way in which event management is provided;
- the intended size of database managed – POET is targeted at small PC-based applications, while Objectivity is among those which intend to support massive applications.

To some extent, these differences are due to the expected clients of the systems, since each vendor has a particular user-base in mind. However, there is an obvious growing together of the products. Each product cannot expect to sell if it omits features that its competitors have provided and so every feature becomes generally supported. In the future, a further coming together can be expected, which will provide either a consensus choice between the differences still evident, or systems providing all alternatives and then allowing a degree of customization.

17 Conclusions

This final chapter pulls together the strands of the previous text, summarizing the most important ideas, discussing the strengths and weaknesses of the approaches examined and looking at the future directions which might be expected.

17.1 Summary

The *DBMS approach* to data management has brought enormous benefits to our society in the form of fast access to securely held and relatively reliable information. Many crucial enterprises depend for their effectiveness on access to a database and the implementors of mainstream DBMS products have provided these enterprises with appropriate and effective support for their information-processing needs. The success has, however, been achieved by simplifying the data and the means of its manipulation. While this has been a supportable cost for managing the greater part of commercial data, it is less so for the management of the more complicated data which occurs in design, hypermedia and geographic applications. Such applications are characterized by their need to use more complex data structures, to integrate the code with the data, to use multimedia data and to support cooperative modes of working.

Consequently, there is an emerging new class of database systems which are built around object models and which are better equipped to handle complex data. *Object-oriented database management systems* replace the record-based models which underlie traditional DBMS with an object-oriented model. Object orientation as a structuring paradigm for data and applications arose variously in the fields of artificial intelligence, programming languages and data modeling. This text has emphasized the last of these since the logical models, which are at the heart of OODBMS, are the natural extension of semantic data models.

An *object-oriented model* contains support for objects – which provide a one-to-one mapping from real world objects to their computer representations – classification, inheritance, encapsulation, information hiding and late binding. An object class takes the place of a relation, enhancing its features with non-atomic properties, encapsulated operations, information hiding and inheritance. Taken together these provide an extensive set of constructs which make the direct modeling of application information considerably easier.

An OODBMS combines an object data model with persistence. *Persistence* is the ability of a system to retain data between the process executions. An OODBMS provides a means by which objects are stored between runs of program which are written in an object-oriented language. There are a number of different methods for storing objects including explicit storage commands in the language, partitioning the class hierarchy between classes for transient objects and classes for persistent objects, maintaining two versions of each class – one persistent and one transient – and using reachability to assert that all objects accessible from named persistence roots are also automatically persistent.

There are many currently available OODBMS which provide persistent object management and some of the more prominent ones were surveyed. They have a commitment to a client/server architecture, access to legacy data and support for C++ in common, but otherwise there are considerable differences in the particular features which are provided, in implementation techniques and in the expected capabilities of the systems. These differences largely stem from the vendors focussing on different client groups and different user needs.

Unfortunately, this lack of uniformity has, until recently, been noticeable most strongly among the object models used. Unlike *the* relational model, it is not possible to point to *the* object model. One response to this has been a concerted effort by the major OODBMS vendors to develop a consensus on the issues involved. The *Object Database Management Group* was set up for this purpose and has brought out proposals for a core data model and access to a DBMS built around this in the form of a data definition language, a query language and bindings to the languages C++, Smalltalk and (soon) Java.

Each of these was discussed in depth (except Java, for which such a discussion would have been premature) and the OODBMS O$_2$ was chosen to provide a practical example of the use of a system which aims to comply with this standard. The *ODMG data model* included support for literals as well as objects, for relationships as well as attributes, and for bulk data types and domain types. It also supports named values in the database from which programming database access can start, although it does not presume that these are persistent roots. The *query language, OQL*, is an extension of the querying part of SQL to cover object querying. It can be used either by a stand-alone interpreter or by embedding calls into the programming languages. The discussion of the *C++ binding* showed how the data model could be implemented, mostly by creating a set of classes which implement the various parts of the data model. The *Smalltalk binding*, although less well-defined, implemented some parts of the data model in different ways from the C++ version – the differences being due to differences in the features of the two languages leading to some contrasts in "natural" ways of using the languages.

In looking at the O$_2$ system, a practical implementation of the data model was seen, but one which is more than that. O$_2$, in common with other compliant systems, starts from a slightly different model. O$_2$ supports applications, sessions and schemata as fundamental objects not in the ODMG model. O$_2$ also supports persistence by reachability, which extends the ODMG proposal. Furthermore, there are O$_2$ components, such as the O$_2$*Look* interface, the graph library and the version management component, which are integrated on top of the ODMG model.

In the discussion of OODBMS, the need for multiple user interfaces was particularly evident. A programming interface can be seen to be more important in a OODBMS than in an RDBMS, but the need for a querying interface does not disappear. The language OQL is provided to allow users who are experienced with SQL access to a method of using the DBMS which is relatively familiar. A variety of techniques for user interaction showed that forms are still useful, graphical interaction is more necessary, and control over the ways data is to be visualised increasingly vital. Furthermore, the application has to move from being an extra built on top of the database to being integrated with the data. Application components are just one more part of the metadata which an OODBMS expects to manage.

The brief description of OODBMS implementation revealed a number of issues in which consensus has been achieved, but more on which the available systems differ. All use a layered implementation and provide a client/server architecture usually with multiple clients and multiple servers coexisting. The precise nature of the layering and the partitioning of functionality between client and server processes varies widely. The ways in which caching and clustering are used varies, as does the way the object identifier is implemented and used. The way in which data transfer is organised also varies in two respects – how traffic een the disk and memory is organized, and what gets passed across the network (objects or pages). For each of these issues, it is not yet clear whether one of the options is demonstrably the best or whether the appropriate mechanism depends on context, in which case, the ability to configure the appropriate mechanism would be valuable.

■ 17.2 Discussion

In this section, some attention is given to some of the more problematic aspects of OODBMS. This starts with a discussion of the transition from relational to object systems and continues with an evaluation of what the major benefits of object orientation are. The section is completed with a discussion of issues related to implementation and to the user interface.

■ 17.2.1 Objects versus relations

The relationship between OODBMS and RDBMS is much debated. An OODBMS can either be seen as a revolutionary alternative or as the result of evolution from a relational system. After all, a class can be thought of (as in the UNISQL model) as a table with non-atomic elements, an associated extensible set of operations and links to other classes by inheritance relationships. Conversely, the switch to object orientation can be seen as a *paradigm shift* in the sense popularized by Thomas Kuhn. Certainly the division of the database world into camps, each of which brings forth its own manifesto to defend their position, resembles Kuhn's description of the behavior of scientists during a paradigm shift. The relational devotees having fought a long and successful battle to replace network systems and they have been placed in a difficult position when confronted with the new kids on the block.

For a potential customer, this tends to have the worrying effect that OODBMS seem so new and difficult that the customer cannot be expected to manage the transition. In the products on sale, a much less daunting prospect is provided. Certainly, the object model is a considerable extension to the relational model and one that is not precise and whose theory is not completely understood. However, the ways in which object management is delivered to users deliberately use familiar patterns. An OODBMS supports a tabular view of the objects, an SQL-like interface, schema design tools and easily achieved access to relational data. Moreover, the operational constructs, such as distribution, resilience and concurrency, are provided in ways with which the users will be familiar. The old methods of working are, in general, supported and new ways of working can be incrementally mastered. Thus, access to multimedia data, the ability to work cooperatively and to exploit advanced interfaces can be achieved after the user is comfortable with using the new DBMS in familiar ways.

Furthermore, the implementation of OODBMS, although requiring additional techniques, builds strongly on those methods which have so successfully been used in record-based database systems. In this sense, the change does not resemble a Kuhnian paradigm shift at all. Very little has been thrown away when moving from relations to objects. Indeed, it would be very worrying if 30 years of hard research, which has amply demonstrated its value, were to be thrown away. All that has been thrown away when moving from relations to objects is the restricted and low level view of data with which users are forced to comply.

■ 17.2.2 A critique of the object-oriented model

The object-oriented paradigm has many aspects. Which are the most important? The fundamental change which delivers the most benefit is the maintenance of a single computer representation for a single real world concept. The notion of *object identity* frees the user from a great deal of unnecessarily low-level work in maintaining the coherence of complex data. Any computer system which provides objects which are referred to by pointers with sharing semantics has a considerable advantage when used to manage data, particularly long-lived data.

Of the other aspects of the model, *classification* is not at all new. Tables in relational systems and types in programming languages are examples of the fact that no computer system which manages lots of data can afford to support a different description for every value.

Inheritance is an important advance, however, since it both saves a great deal of coding and provides a structuring mechanism with which people are familiar from the real world. Unfortunately, the semantics of inheritance and its relationship with subtyping have not been fully worked out. Moreover, inheritance is a heavily-used mechanism. It is used in different systems for specializing, generalizing, subsetting, extending a class without recompiling a great deal of code, and for providing multiple implementations. That there are so many uses for the same mechanism, although valuable in a tool such as the Swiss Army Knife, is problematic in a descriptive device. It is desirable that when a description is made, the meaning of each fragment is clear through the syntactic structures used. Inheritance as currently provided does not do this.

Overriding and *late binding* are vital measures in order to prevent the inheritance hierarchy from becoming too inflexible. If, in inheriting from a class most of whose features were useful, the programmer was forced to inherit those features which were not, then the value of inheritance would be much diminished.

The value of *encapsulating* code with the data has been emphasised at a number of points in the text. Often much of the semantics of the data is much more easily expressed by programming than by structural data modeling and keeping the two separate is less and less acceptable. Coding the application as methods of classes has the significant benefit of utilizing a coherent structure for the complex task of integrating code and data. Moreover, object-oriented design methodologies provide an increasingly usable method of application design which can be mapped into an OODBMS easily. However, some aspects of the code do not fit comfortably into this structure and it seems that more flexible structures will ultimately be found necessary.

Information hiding is both vital in the DBMS context and extremely difficult to provide in an easily used way. The provision of "friends" in C++ is one indication of how difficult it is to incorporate protection in the object-oriented model and stick with it. It seems inevitable that what needs, in general, to be hidden will, in some circumstances, need to be revealed. Improved protection mechanisms would be useful but it is not all clear how they can be developed from the object-oriented model as it currently stands. Given that, the current facilities are just about sufficient.

In summary, object identity is the crucial benefit which object orientation provides and encapsulation is also vital in supporting the need to integrate code with the data. Inheritance is a labour-saving device which also has data modeling benefits and requires overriding facilities to make it fully usable. Information hiding is also a valuable protection mechanism. However, the ultimate forms of inheritance, information hiding and the integration of code with data have not yet been developed.

■ 17.2.3 Implementation issues

The first OODBMS were unusable. They were slow, limited in data size, prone to failure and did not attempt to provide most of the important DBMS facilities such as multi-user access. Currently available OODBMS, by contrast, are close to providing full DBMS functionality efficiently. It has taken a great deal of effort from the companies to bring about this transformation.

Improvements in implementation are achieved by re-using the best of the previous work and by carefully measuring performance to determine where the bottlenecks are. Just as the use of an OODBMS is designed to allow relational users to migrate easily, so the implementation is also evolutionary. Much of the work on access methods, indexes, query optimization and generic user interface creation, which was carried out to make relational DBMS, successful can be taken over by OODBMS manufacturers and developed in the object context. O_2's use of a record manager to underlie object management is one example which indicates that many of the techniques developed for record-based DBMS have practical application in OODBMS.

However, some implementation issues are not fully solved and the potential customer should be careful to verify that any particular product meets all requirements. Although current products are practically usable, further improvements continue to be made.

■ 17.2.4 User interaction

Following surveys by some of the leading database practitioners in 1989 and 1993, it is common to read that improving facilities for user interaction is the most pressing problem for DBMS developers. Now the situation in this area seems to be getting a great deal better. Partly, this is because object orientation has long been held to be a suitable paradigm for developing user interaction techniques for all kinds of software, and so OODBMS are starting to provide high-quality user interfaces, building on the object-oriented techniques which have been developed elsewhere. However, improvements to the user interface are prevalent in all kinds of DBMS. The movement of the DBMS from mainframe systems to workstations and portable computers has put them in the same environment as tools, such as spreadsheets and word processors which have, for some time, been exhibiting user interfaces which are much easier to use than those provided by old-fashioned DBMS.

It seems, however, that a lot of this work is relatively *ad hoc*. Too little work on user interfaces is built on a clear conceptual model of the data or is backed up by appropriate experiments on user acceptance of the interface. A user interface should allow the user to interact with what he or she believes to be in the database, rather than being driven by the data structures actually used (even the logical ones). Often these two views of the data are the same, but sometimes the user interface needs to support a more high-level and abstract view of the data than that used to implement it. For some classes of user, it is no better to visualize the data as a set of inter-connected records than it would be to show them rows of 1's and 0's representing the bits in the file holding the data. This is a problematic area, and one which can only be satisfactorily resolved by collaboration between database experts, HCI researchers and cognitive scientists. Fortunately, the move to object systems reduces the likely gap between concept and implementation.

Once completed, an interface should not be given to users without suitable testing and evaluation. HCI research has developed suitable methodologies for achieving this, but too much research into new interfaces still stops at the design and implementation level. Just as system implementation should be backed up by performance measurement, so interface construction should be backed up by user evaluation.

Research in the area of database interaction is still patchily reported in the main database conferences. Fortunately there are now three continuing series of workshops in which new work can be reported: the IFIP Visual Databases series; Advanced Visual Interfaces and Interfaces to Database Systems. Further developments on user interfaces can be expected.

■ 17.3 The future

Although database systems have evolved considerably, they are still some way from their ultimate form. In this section, three areas for improvement will be examined: the need for better programming languages; the need to bring uniformity to the ways in which code and data are managed; and the need to provide an increasing number of customizable options in the implementation and user interface areas.

■ 17.3.1 Database programming languages

Chapter 1 started with a claim that databases were successful. They have proved to be appropriate tools for managing large amounts of data, which can be used by a wide variety of users for an increasingly wide variety of purposes. The same is far from true about programming languages. The object-oriented paradigm is a highly suitable structuring device for software development. The languages which provide object orientation are not. Whereas programming is intrinsically a difficult task to master, the languages that programmers are forced to use all include compromises in their design decisions which complicate the task. Programming is not going to go away and so the design of good quality languages is a vital concern.

In looking at the programming interfaces, C++ and Smalltalk were chosen because they have one overriding advantage – familiarity. The strength of the object-oriented paradigm is shown by the fact that languages which implement it are comparatively weak and yet are increasingly used. C++ has an unsafe type system and gives the programmer facilities with which the DBMS can be undermined. Smalltalk is entirely dynamically typed. However, because they support the object-oriented paradigm, both provide a suitable basis for database work.

A good quality language should combine simplicity and power. Java seems to be a step forward. Although it has its own compromises, it seems simpler to use than many languages. Design of a programming language is primarily an HCI issue, in which programmers are the users. It is important that there be increased effort to create and evaluate better languages – ones which more directly present the constructs being managed, are simpler and are more powerful. Given that programming is now important in the database arena, this is particular important for the next generation DBMS.

■ 17.3.2 Code and data

OODBMS bring code into the database in highly constrained ways. This is beneficial in that it provides an intelligible structure for the programmer, but restrictive in that there are other ways in which code and data could appropriately be structured. The essential insight which is required for progress is to remove any unnecessary distinction between code and data management.

Currently there are several constrained ways in which code and data can co-exist as methods, free-standing functions, by providing ways of referred-to external functions, as exceptions or in active databases with triggers. All of these point to an increasing need for access to different kinds of code object. If these are added to the computational model of the DBMS in a piecemeal fashion, an unnecessarily complex environment will result. Providing code as data which is subject to the same kinds of structuring and management mechanisms, would allow any of these techniques to be added without complicating the structure. Ultimately, the differences between code and data management will be forced to disappear in order to keep system complexity at manageable levels.

■ 17.3.3 Customizing the DBMS

In Section 17.1, a question was raised concerning the best techniques for implementing some of the object management problems, such as identifying the best way of using caching, the appropriate elements of network traffic, and so on. Is there a "best" version of these components, or does suitability change with context? One answer to this would be the development of a toolkit approach to OODBMS development. This would use the same kinds of ideas as Exodus, the extensible DBMS generator built at the University of Wisconsin at Madison. In Exodus, the DBMS developer is given a toolkit which includes various parameterized flavors of query optimizations, a set of different access methods etc. Using this toolkit, a complete DBMS can be built. It seems likely that this will be the way forward for OODBMS, allowing the combination of a number of different techniques to create a system.

A similar situation exists for the user interface. Components for managing user interaction can be expected to be added to DBMS. The Iconographer system discussed in Section 16.4.7 shows how this can be achieved with data management and user interaction elements being integrated by a tool, which enables them to be combined in appropriate ways, thus achieving suitable forms of visualisation, querying and data manipulation operations.

Another alternative is to build DBMS which are increasingly self-optimizing. Proposals have been around for some time to build systems which analyze patterns of usage and re-organize the data and the data management to achieve the same results more efficiently. Such systems will start to appear in order to maximize efficiency in the widest number of settings.

For all of these reasons, OODBMS development can still be considered work in progress. Current products are usable now, but will improve in a wide variety of ways. Database management of complex information is increasingly becoming a reality. Database systems for design information, office information, spatial information and for the internet are becoming more powerful and more prevalent. Although development will continue, most of the most important structures are already in place. Their enhancement is the work of the next phase of DBMS development.

Appendix A The electronic mail application in C++

A.1 Class headers

```
class User {
   private:
      d_String name;
      d_String login;
      d_String password;
      Mailbox incoming;
      d_Set<Mailbox> stored;
   public:
      User(const char* userName; const char*
            userLogin, const char* userPassword);
      void sendmail();
      void receive( d_Ref<Message> theMessage );
      void summarise();
      void readMail();
      void deleteMsg();
      void createMbox();
      void removeMbox();
      void flushMbox();
      void displayLogin();
      static d_Set< d_Ref<User> > theUsers;
      static void restart(int);
      static void clear();
};
```

```
class Superuser : User {
    public:
        Superuser();
        void makeUser();
        void deleteUser();
        void statistics();
};


class Mailbox {
    private:
        d_String name;
        d_List<d_Ref<Message>> holds;
                inverse Message :: heldIn;
    public:
        Mailbox( const char* theName );
        Unsigned Long  number();
        void insert( d_Ref<Message> newMessage );
        void showHeaders();
        d_Ref<Message>
                getMessage(Unsigned Long number);
        void delete( d_Ref<Message> theMessage );
        void flush();
        void display();
};


class Message {
    private:
        d_String subject;
        d_Timestamp timeSent;
        d_String body;
        d_set< d_Ref<Mailbox> > heldin
                inverse Mailbox :: holds;
        d_Ref<User > sender;
        d_Set< d_Ref<User> > recipients;
    public:
        Message( d_Ref<User > sendingUser );
        void summarise( d_Short number );
        void display();
        void reply( d_Ref<User> sender,  d_Ref<User>
                replier,const char* oldSubject);
};
```

■ A.2 Creating and setting up the database

Database creation cannot be achieved in C++. It is carried out using O_2 system commands as follows:

```
create schema EMAIL
create base Email
```

The next program creates the persistent roots:

```
main() {
        d_Session theSession;
        d_Database theDatabase;
        if (theSession. begin( argc, argv,
                "Mail System", "Mail Server", "/usr/bin/o2", OL_ALPHA ) );
            { showSnl( "Connection error" );   exit(1);    };


        d_Transaction  TXcreateRoots;
        *char databaseName = getString
                ( "Which database do you want to set up?  " );
        theDatabase . open( databaseName );
        TXcreateRoots . begin();
        theDatabase . create_persistence_root
                ( "The Users",  "d_Set< d_Ref<User> >" );
        theDatabase . create_persistence_root
                ( "Super User",  "d_Ref<SuperUser>" );
        d_Ref<SuperUser> superUser( "Super User" );
        superUser = User( "Jane Brown", "jbrown", "????" );
        d_Set< d_Ref<User> >  theUsers( "The Users" );
        theUsers . insert_element( superUser );
        TXcreateRoots . validate();

        theDatabase . close();
        theSession . end();
}
```

■ A.3 The application

```
d_Set< d_Ref<User> >  theUsers;
d_Ref<Superuser>  superUser;


void printMenu( )   {
    showSnl( "Choose one of the following:" );
        showSnl( "  1: Log In" );
    if  (currentUser != NULL)
        { showSnl( "  2: Log Out" );
          showSnl( "  3: Send ShowSnl" );
          showSnl( "  4: Summarise Mailbox" );
          showSnl( "  5: Read ShowSnl" );
          showSnl( "  6: Delete ShowSnl" );
          showSnl( "  7: Create a Mailbox" );
          showSnl( "  8: Remove a Mailbox" );
          showSnl( "  9: Flush a Mailbox" );
        };
    if (currentUser == superUser)
      { cout "  10: Create a User" );
        cout "  11: Delete a User" );
        cout "  12: Statistics of Usage" );
        };
    showSnl( "0 : quit" ) );
}
```

```
void  loginFacility( )  {
    d_Ref<User>  theUser;
    d_String  uLogin = getString( "Give login name: " );
    d_String  uPassword =getString("Give password: ");
    theUser  = findUser( uLogin );
    if ( theUser  != NULL &&
        theUser . password == Upassword )
                currentUser = theUser;
        else showSnl( "Login incorrect" );
    printMenu( );
}

void  logoutFacility( )  {
    currentUser = NULL;  }

void   sendMailFacility()  {
     if (currentUser != NULL)
         currentUser .sendMail();  }

void  summariseFacility()  {
     if (currentUser != NULL)
         currentUser .summarise();   }

void  readMailFacility()  {
     if (currentUser != NULL)
         currentUser .readMail();   }

void  deletMailFacility()  {
     if (currentUser != NULL)
                currentUser .deleteMsg();   }


void  createMailboxFacility()  {
     if (currentUser != NULL)
         currentUser .createMbox();  }

void  removeMailboxFacility()  {
     if (currentUser != NULL)
         currentUser .removeMbox(); }

void  flushMailboxFacility()  {
     if (currentUser != NULL)
         currentUser .flushMbox();  }

void  createUserFacility();  {
    if (currentUser == superUser )
        superUser . createUser();  }

void  removeUserFacility()  {
    if (currentUser == superUser )
        superUser . removeUser();  }

void  statisticsFacility( )  {
    if (currentUser == superUser )
        superUser . statistics();  }

int menu( )  {
    int choice = -1;
    int top = 9;
```

```
    if (currentUser == superUser) top = 12;
    while (choice < 0  or choice > top)
        choice = getInt(
            "Choose an option between 0 and " +
                top + ": ");

  switch    (choice) {
      case 1: loginFacility(); break;
      case 2: logoutFacility(); break;
      case 3: sendMailFacility(); break;
      case 4: summariseFacility(); break;
      case 5: readMailFacility(); break;
     case 6: deleteMailFacility(); break;
      case 7: createMailboxFacility(); break;
      case 8: removeMailboxFacility(); break;
      case 9: flushMailboxFacility(); break;
      case 10: createUserFacility(); break;
      case 11: removeUserFacility(); break;
      case 12: statisticsFacility(); break;
      default {};          // Do nothing if quit is requested
    }
    return choice;
}

main() {
  d_Session theSession;
  d_Database theDatabase;
  if (theSession. begin( argc, argv, "MSystem",
      "MServer", "/usr/bin/o2", OL_ALPHA ) );
    { showSnl( "Connection error" );  exit(1);     }
  *char databaseName =
      getString( "Choose the database to use:  " );
  theDatabase . open( databaseName );
  User :: restart();
  printMenu();
  while ( menu() > 0 )    {};
  theDatabase . close();

  theSession . end();
}
```

■ A.4 Utility functions and queries

OQL queries

```
d_OQL_Query    findMbox( "element(
    select M from M in $1 where M.name = $2 )" );

d_OQL_Query    findUser( "element(
    select U from U in theUsers
          where U.login = $1 )" );
```

Free-standing functions

```
d_Ref<Mailbox> chooseBox( const *char prompt )   {
   d_Ref<Mailbox> theBox;
   d_String boxName = getString( prompt );
   if (boxName == "Incoming" || boxName = "" )
     return  incoming;
   else {
      findMbox << stored << boxName;
      if (d_oql_execute( findMbox, theBox) ) {
         showSnl("No box with that name found");
         return NULL;  };
      else return theBox
   }
}

d_ref<User> getUser( const *char aLogin )  {
   d_ref<User> aUser;
   findUser<<  aLogin;
   if ( d_oql_execute( findUser, aUser ) )
      return NULL;
      else return aUser;
}

d_RString subString( d_String input,
      Unsigned Short first, Unsigned Short last )  {
   ... returns a substring of the input parameter;
}

void showS(  const *char input ) { .. prints the input .. }
void showI( Unsigned Long input) {.. prints the input ..}
void showSnl( const *char input ) {.. adds a newline .. }
void showInl(Unsigned Long input) {.. adds a newline ..}
integer getInteger( const *char prompt )
               {requests a number }
*char getString(const *char prompt) {..requests a string.. }
integer yesNo(const *char prompt) {..returns whether or not user responds
               with a "y"..}
```

■ A.5 Class implementations

Implementation of the class User

```
User :: User(const char* userName; const char*
      userLogin, const char* userPassword) {
   name = userName;
   login = userLogin;
   password = userPassword;
}

void User :: sendmail() {
   d_Ref<Message> theMessage( this );
}
```

```
void User :: receive( d_Ref<Message> theMessage ) {
  incoming . insert( theMessage );
}

void User :: summarise()  {
  d_Ref<Mailbox> summariseBox = chooseBox(
      "Give name of mailbox to summarise: " );
  if (summariseBox  !=  NULL)
      summariseBox . showHeaders();
}

void User :: readMail()  {
  d_Ref<Mailbox> readBox =
    chooseBox("Give name of box to read from: ");
  if  (readBox != NULL)  {
    readBox . showHeaders();
    int messageNum = getInt("Which message?  ");
    while (messageNum < 1 || messageNumber >
           readBox  . number() )
      messageNum = getInt(
        "Bad Message Number, Try Again: " );
    d_Ref<Message> theMessage =
      readBox . getMessage( messageNum );
    theMessage . display();
    if ( yesNo( "Reply to this message?" ) )
        theMessage . reply( this );
    if ( yesNo( "Store this message?  " ) )
       if ( stored.is_empty() )
         showSnl( "No storage boxes - sorry!" )
       else  {
       d_Ref<Mailbox> storeBox = chooseBox(
         "Give name of box to store in: " );
       if (storeBox  !=  NULL)
          storeBox . insert( theMessage );
          };

    if ( yesNo( "Delete this message?  " ) )
       readBox . delete( theMessage );
  };
}

void User :: deleteMsg()  {
  d_Ref<Mailbox> removeBox = chooseBox(
      "Give name of mailbox to remove from: " );
  if (removeBox  !=  NULL) {
    removeBox  . showHeaders();
    int messageNum = getInteger(
      "Which message do you want to see?  " );
    while (messageNum < 1 ||  messageNumber >
           removeBox  . number() )
      messageNum = getInteger(
        "Bad Message Number, Try Again: " );
    d_Ref<Message> theMessage =
      removeBox . getMessage(messageNum);
    removeBox . delete( theMessage );
  }
}
```

```
void User :: createMbox()  {
  d_Ref<Mailbox> oldBox;
  d_String newName  :=
      getString( "Give new mailbox name: " );
  findMbox << newName;
  if (d_oql_execute( findMbox, oldBox) )
     { d_Ref<Mailbox> newBox =
         new( this ) Mailbox( newName );
    TXcreateMbox.  begin();
      stored . insert_element( newBox );
      mark_modified();
    TXcreateMbox.  validate();   }
  else showSnl("Box with this name already exists");
}

void User :: removeMbox()  {
  d_Ref<Mailbox> removeBox = chooseBox(
      "Give name of mailbox to remove: " );
  if (removeBox  !=  NULL) {
    TXremoveMbox.  begin();
      stored . remove_element( removeBox );
      mark_modified();
    TXremoveMbox.  validate();   }
}

void User :: flushMbox()  {
  d_Ref<Mailbox> flushBox = chooseBox(
      "Give name of mailbox to flush: " );
  if (flushBox  !=  NULL)   flushBox  . flush( );
}

void User :: displayLogin(  ) {
  showS( login );
}

static void User :: restart(int)  {
  theUsers = new d_Set< d_Ref<User> >
        ( "The Users", OL_WRITE );
  superUser = new d_Ref<superUser>
        ( "Super User", OL_WRITE );
}

static void User :: clear()  {
  superUser = User("Jane Brown", "jbrown", "????" );
  d_Set< d_Ref<User> >  emptySet;
  theUsers = emptySet;
  theUsers . insert_element( superUser );
}
```

Implementation of the class Superuser

```
void Superuser :: makeUser( ) {
  if (currentUser ==  superUser ) {
  d_String uLogin =
    getString( "Give login name for new user: " );
  Ref<User>  aUser = findUser( uLogin );
```

```
    if ( aUser == NULL )
      showSnl( "User already exists" );
    else {
      d_String uPass =
        getString("Give password for new user: " );
      d_String uName =
        getString("Give real name for new user: " );
      Ref<User>  newUser( uName, uLogin, uPass );
      d_Transaction  TXcreateUser;
      TXcreateUser  .  begin();
        theUsers . insert_element( newUser );
        theUsers . mark_modified( );
      TXcreateUser  .  validate();
    }
  }
}

void Superuser :: deleteUser( ) {
  if (currentUser ==  superUser ) {
    d_String uLogin =
      getString( "Give login for user to delete: " );
    d_Ref<User>  theUser = getUser( uLogin );
    if ( theUser == NULL )
      showSnl( "User does not exist" );
    else {
      d_Transaction  TXdeleteUser;
      TXdeleteUser  .  begin();
        theUsers . remove_element( theUser );
        theUsers . mark_modified( );
      TXdeleteUser  .  validate();
    }
  }
}

void Superuser :: statistics( ) {
  if (currentUser ==  superUser ) {
    d_Iterator<User>  uIter = theUsers . createIterator();
    d_Ref<User> aUser;
    d_ref<Mailbox> aBox;
    while ( uIter.next( aUser) ) {
      aUser . displayName();
      showS( "Number of incoming messages" );
      showI( aUser . incoming . number() );
      showSnl( "Storage mailboxes" );
      d_Iterator<Mailbox>  mbIter =
          aUser . storage . createIterator();
      while ( mbIter.next( aBox ) )  aBox . display;
    };
  }
}
```

Implementation of the class Mailbox

```
void Mailbox :: Mailbox( const char* theName ) {
  name := theName;
}
```

```
Unsigned Long Mailbox :: number() {
  return holds . cardinality();
}

void Mailbox :: insert( d_Ref<Message> newMessage )
  d_Transaction  TXstoreMessage;
  TXstoreMessage.  begin;
    holds. insert_element_last( newMessage );
    mark_modified( );
    newMessage . mark_modified( );
  TXstoreMessage.  validate();
}

void Mailbox :: showHeaders() {
  d_Iterator<Message> mIter = holds . createIterator();
  Unsigned Long  N := 0;
  d_Ref<Message> aMessage;
  while ( mIter.next( aMessage) ) {
    N += 1;
    aMessage . summarise( N )  };
}

d_Ref<Message> Mailbox ::
      getMessage(Unsigned Long number) {
  return holds[number];
}

void Mailbox :: delete( d_Ref<Message> theMessage ) {
  d_Transaction  TXremoveMessage;
  TXremoveMessage.  begin;
    holds . .remove_element( theMessage );
    mark_modified( );
    theMessage . mark_modified( );
  TXremoveMessage.  validate();
}

void Mailbox :: flush() {
  d_Iterator<Message> mIter = holds . createIterator();
  d_Ref<Message> aMessage;
  d_Transaction  TXflushMailbox;
  TXflushMailbox.  begin;
    while ( mIter.next( aMessage) ) {
      holds . .remove_element( aMessage );
      aMessage . mark_modified( );  }
    mark_modified( );
  TXflushMailbox.  validate();
}

void Mailbox :: display() {
  showS( name );
  showInl( number() );
}
```

Implementation of the class Message

```
void Message:: Message( d_Ref<User > theSender) {
  sender = theSender;
  subject = getString( "Subject: " );

  recipients = d_Set< d_Ref<User> >( );
  *char  uLogin = getString( "Give first recipient: " );
  while (uLogin == "")  {
    d_Ref<User >  receiver := getUser( uLogin );
    if ( receiver == NULL )
      showSnl( "Cannot find that user" );
    else recipients . insert_element( receiver );
    uLogin = getString(
  "Give next recipient (or empty string to quit): " );
      }

  heldIn = d_Set< d_Ref<Mailbox> >( );
  body = getString( "Body of message: " );
  timeSent = d_Timestamp :: current();

  for (U in recipients) U . receive( this );
}

void summarise( Unsigned Long number ) {
  showI( number );
  sender . displayLogin();
  showSnl( subject );
}

void display() {
  showSnl( body );
}

void reply( d_Ref<User> sender,  d_Ref<User> replier,
            const char* oldSubject) {
  d_ref< Message > replyMessage();
  sender = replier;
  if ( substring( oldSubject, 1, 4 ) == "Re: " )
    subject = oldSubject;
    else  subject := "Re: " + oldSubject;
  timeSent = d_Timestamp :: current();
  recipients = new List<User>;
  recipients . insert_element( receiver );
  sender . receive( this );
}
```

Further Reading

■ Chapter 1

Database systems are one of the areas of computer science best supported by first-class textbooks. Of the many that are available, the author is personally familiar acquainted with [Elmasri and Navathe, 1994], [Silberschatz *et al*, 1997], [Date, 1995] and [Connolly *et al.*, 1996], all of which are outstanding pieces of work. Readers requiring further discussion of the points discussed in section 1.1 should start with one of these. More detail can be found in primary references for the following topics: the ANSI/SPARC architecture [ANSI, 1975], ACID transactions [Haerder and Rothermel, 1987], distributed databases [Ceri and Pelagatti, 1984; Bell and Grimson, 1992], the network data model [Olle, 1978] and the relational data model [Codd, 1970]. The requirements of advanced applications is discussed in [Catell, 1991]. The modeling shortcomings of the record-based model are described in [Kent, 1979] and [Hull and King, 1987]. The impedance mismatch problem was first discussed in [Atkinson, 1978].

Semantic data modeling is the subject of two excellent surveys [Hull and King, 1987] and [Peckham and Maryanski, 1988]. The following individual models have seminal papers written about them: the ER model [Chen, 1976], the extended ER model [Elmasri and Navathe, 1994], the functional data model [Shipman, 1981], the semantic data model [Hammer and McLeod, 1981], IFO [Abiteboul and Hull, 1987] and TAXIS [Mylopolous *et al.*, 1980]. These and other papers are gathered in [Zdonik and Maier, 1990]. The mapping of an ER schema to relations is described in [Teorey, 1994].

Further reading on the advanced kinds of DBMS discussed in section 1.3 can be found in the following: [Rowe and Stonebraker, 1987] on POSTGRES; [Verso *et al.*, 1986] on complex object DBMS; [Ullman, 1988] on deductive DBMS in general; [Ceri and Gottlob, 1989] on Datalog; [Ramakrishnan *et al.*, 1992] on CORAL; [Barja *et al.*, 1995] on Rock`n'roll, an integrated OO and deductive system; [Atkinson and Morrison, 1995] is the best coherent account of persistent programming languages and the whole of the volume 4, number 3 of *VLDB* contains articles on that approach; [Dayal *et al.*, 1995] discuss active database systems; [Peuquet and Marble, 1990] discuss the different aspects of GIS; while [Tansel *et al.*, 1993] discusses temporal DBMS. [Paton *et al.*, 1994] contains long expositions on the functional, deductive, persistent and object-oriented approaches to database systems.

Object orientation has a long and detailed history. Among the programming languages which have been written about are Simula [Dahl and Nyberg, 1966], Smalltalk [Goldberg, 1989], C++ [Stroustrup 1991] and Eiffel [Meyer, 1992]. Fundamental papers on OODBMS are collected in [Zdonik and Maier, 1990]. The first comprehensive textbook was [Catell, 1991], while among the many other accounts, [Khoshafian, 1993] and [Bertino and Martino, 1993] stand out. [Kim, 1995] discusses many of the important areas of modern database design. Finally the transition from record-based to object systems is clearly described in [Delobel *et al.*, 1995].

The World Wide Web holds many interesting papers on database systems. There is only room here to mention [WebLaz] which gives a clear description of the value that database research has been and [WebUllman] which discusses the necessary future research. The ACM SIGMOD home page [WebSIGMOD] and sites held at the universities of Berkeley [WebBerkeley] and Massachussetts [WebUMass] are good start points for discovering much more about database systems. There is an enormous bibliography of all kinds of computer science subject matter maintained by Alf-Christian Achilles, of which the database specific information is at [WebDBresearch].

■ Chapter 2

For further details on object orientation there are a number of standard design methodologies, each of which describe the basic concepts of object orientation in more detail than space permitted here. [Meyer, 1988] describes object orientation in the context of the Eiffel language. [Booch, 1995], [Rumbaugh *et al.*, 1991] and [Coad and Yourdon, 1991a and 1991b] all describe particular methodologies. [Gamma *et al.*, 1994] discusses patterns.

There is a web site [WebOOFAQ] which maintains frequently asked questions about object orientation and is a good start point for finding out about object-oriented techniques and systems.

■ Chapter 3

The issues surrounding persistence were first discussed in [Atkinson, 1978]. Subsequent work by the same author and his colleagues is summarized in [Atkinson and Morrison, 1995] and [Atkinson, 1997]. Much of the important research issues are discussed in the proceedings of two interleaved series of conferences: Persistent Object Systems [Atkinson *et al.*, 1988; Rosenberg and Koch, 1989; Dearle *et al.*, 1990; Kanellakis and Schmidt, 1992; Atkinson *et al.*, 1994] which describes implementation techniques and Database Programming Languages [Bancilhon and Buneman, 1990; Hull *et al.*, 1990; Beeri *et al.*, *1993*] which discusses description techniques.

■ Chapter 4

The details of the discussion in this paper largely resides in the publications of the various standardizing bodies themselves. These are best accessed through the web sites of the organizations concerned [WebISO, WebANSI, WebOMG, WebODMG, WebOpenDoc].

■ Chapters 5 and 6

The bulk of the material here is taken from the ODMG-93 report [Catell, 1994]. Updates are available through the ODMG web site [WebODMG].

■ Chapters 7 and 8

Most of the detail of this chapter comes from the various manuals which come with the O_2 system. Each component comes with its own manual. Much of the history is to be found in the O_2 book [Bancilhon *et al.*, 1992]. The proceedings of the major database conferences over the past ten years contain a large number of papers referring to specific design decisions. Many of these are available from the O_2 web site [WebO2].

■ Chapter 9

The standard database textbooks each have at least a chapter devoted to query languages. [Date, 1989] and [Melton and Simon, 1993] are entirely devoted to SQL. Object SQL is described in [Beech, 1988], while ReLoop is described in Chapter 12 of [Bancilhon *et al.*, 1992]. Chapter 11 of the same book describes other query language experiments at O_2. The development of SQL is best monitored at the web site [WebSQL].

■ Chapter 10

This chapter describes OQL partly using descriptions in [Catell, 1994] and partly using updates on this standard which will be available as the next release.

■ Chapter 11

The primary source for the material discussed is the Atkinson and Buneman survey [Atkinson and Buneman, 1987]. Cardelli's early work on the development of a suitable type system for object databases is [Cardelli and Wegner, 1985]. Much of Cardelli's later work is available from DEC SRC [WebDECSRC]. There are many textbooks for the various object-oriented languages, including ones on: Eiffel [Meyer, 1992]; CLOS [Bobrow *et al.*, 1988]; Modula-3 [Harbison, 1992]; Beta [Madsen *et al*, 1993; and Java [Arnold and Gosling, 1995].

Of the various system described here, details about DBPL, Galileo, Fibonacci, Tycoon and Napier88 are all available via the FIDE ESPRIT Project web site [WebFIDE]. Amber is described in [Cardelli, 1984].

■ Chapter 12 and 13

There are very many text books on C++ and Smalltalk. The primary reference for C++ is [Stroustrop, 1991]. [Goldberg, 1989] is the source Smalltalk textbook, while [Goldberg, 1984] describes the interactive environment.

■ Chapter 14

The author is not aware of any textbook dealing wholly with the implementation of object databases. The persistent object stores workshops (see Chapter 3) and the web sites of the manufacturers, listed under Chapter 16, provide much detail.

Distributed and concurrent system textbooks abound. Of principal interest to OODBMS are [Coulouris *et al.*, 1994] and [Mullender, 1993] in which fundamentals are discussed; [Ozsu *et al.*, 1994] which includes papers on distributed object management; and [Bacon, 1993] on concurrent systems. Client/server architectures are discussed in [Loomis, 1992]. A more complete introduction to garbage collection techniques can be found in [Wilson, 1994], with more detail in [Jones, 1996].

■ Chapter 15

There is a growing body of work on interfaces to database systems, largely to be found in three series of workshops: the IFIP Visual Database series; the Advanced Visual Interfaces series [Catarci *et al.*, 1993; Catarci *et al.*, 1994]; and the Interfaces to Databases series [Cooper, 1993; Sawyer 1995; Kennedy and Barclay, 1996].

[Paton *et al.*, 1994] and [Kirby *et al*, 1989] discuss the idea of bringing the interface into the database. [King and Novak, 1993] describes one approach to customizing the interface. Of the systems described in Section 15.4, Visual Works is described at the web site of ParcPlace Digitalk [WebPP]; the Starfield Viewer is discussed in [Ahlberg and Schneiderman, 1994]; STYLE in [Wetzel *et al.*, 1997]; Amaze in [Boyle *et al.*, 1993]; Drive in [Mitchell *et al.*, 1996]; and Iconographer in [Draper and Waite, 1991].

The web site of the FADIVA [WebFADIVA] working group is an entry point for three-dimensional interfaces.

■ Chapter 16

The ODMG web site [WebODMG] is a good start point, while each of the manufacturers has its own web site [WebGemStone; WebIBEX; WebO2; WebObjectivity; WebODI; WebONTOS; WebPOET; WebUniSQL; WebVersant].

■ Chapter 17

The theory of paradigm shifts is expounded in [Kuhn, 1970]. Exodus is described in [Carey and DeWitt, 1987].

References

Abiteboul, S. and Hull, R. (1987). IFO: A formal semantic data model. *ACM TODS*, 12:4, 525–565.

Ahlberg, C. and Shneiderman, B. (1994). Visual information seeking: tight coupling of dynamic query filters with starfield displays. In *Proceedings CHI'94: Human Factors in Computer. Systems*. Also in Baecker, R., Grudin J., Buxton, W., and Greenberg, S. *Readings in Human-Computer Interaction: Toward the Year 2000*, 2nd edition. Morgan Kaufmann Publishers.

Andrews, T. and Harris, C. (1990). Combining language and database advances in an object-oriented development environment. *Proc OOPSLA*, (Orlando, Florida, September 1987). Also in Zdonik and Maier, 1990.

ANSI(1975) American National Standards Institute Study Group on Data Base Management Systems *Interim Report, FDT, 7:2*, ACM.

Arnold, K. and Gosling, J. (1995). *The Java Programming Language*. Addison-Wesley.

Atkinson, M.P. (1978). Programming languages and databases. In Yao, S.P., (ed.) *Proc 4th International Conference on Very Large Data Bases*, (Berlin, September 1978) pp 408–419, IEEE.

Atkinson, M.P. and Buneman, O.P. (1987). Types and persistence in database programming languages. *ACM Computing Surveys*, 19:2, 105–190

Atkinson, M.P., Buneman, O.P. and Morrison, R. (1988). Data types and persistence. In *Topics in Information Systems*. Springer-Verlag, 1988. ISBN 3 540 18785 5.

Atkinson, M.P., Bancilhon, F. , DeWitt, D., Dittrich, K., Maier, D. and Zdonik, S. (1990). The object-oriented system manifesto. Reprinted in Bancilhon *et al.*, 1992.

Atkinson, M.P., Maier, D. and Benzaken, V. (eds.) (1994). *Proc. Persistent Objects Systems 7*, Tarascon. Workshops in Computer Science, Springer-Verlag. ISBN 3 540 19912 8.

Atkinson, M.P. and Morrison, R. (1995). Orthogonal persistent object systems. *VLDB Journal*, 4:3.

Atkinson, M.P. (1997). *The FIDE Project*, (in press). Springer-Verlag.

Bacon, J. (1993). *Concurrent Systems: An Integrated Approach to Operating Systems*. Addison-Wesley. ISBN 0 201 41677 8.

Bancilhon, F. and Buneman, O.P. (1990) *Advances in Database Programming Languages*, edited proceedings of the Workshop on Database Programming Languages (Roscoff, France, September 1987), Frontier Series, ACM Press

Bancilhon, F., Delobel, C. and Kanellakis P. (eds) (1992). *The Story of O₂: Building an Object-Oriented Database System*. Morgan Kaufmann. ISBN 1 55860 169 4.

Bannerjee, J., Chou, H.T., Garza, J.F., Kim, W., Woelk, D., Ballou, N. and Kim, H-J. (1987). Data model issues for object-oriented databases. *ACM TOOIS*, 5:1. Also in Zdonik and Maier, 1990.

Barja, M.L., Fernandes, A.A.A., Paton, N.W., Williams, M.H., Dinn, A. and Abdelmoty, A.I. (1995). Design and implementation of ROCK & ROLL: a deductive object-oriented database system. *Information Systems*, 20:3, 185–211.

Beech, D. (1988). A foundation for evolution from relational to object databases. In Schmidt *et al* (eds.) *Proc. Extending Database Technology Conf.*, pp. 251–270.

Beech, D., Bernstein, P., Brodie, M., Carey, M., Lindsay, B., Rowe, L., and Stonebraker, M. (1991). Third-generation data base system manifesto. In Meersman, R.A. *et al* (eds.) *Object-Oriented Databases: Analysis, Design and Construction* (DS-4) North-Holland.

Beeri, C., Ohori, A. and Shasha, D. (eds) (1993). *Database Programming Languages*. Springer-Verlag.

Bell, D. and Grimson, J. (1992). *Distributed Database Systems*. Addison-Wesley. ISBN 0 201 54400 8.

Bernstein, P.A., Hadzilacos, V. and Goodman, N. (1987). *Concurrency Control and Recovery in Database Systems*. Addison-Wesley.

The Laguna Beach Participants (1989). Future directions in DBMS research. *ACM SIGMOD Record*, 18:1, 17–26.

Bertino, E. and Martino, L. (1993). *Object-Oriented Database Systems: Concepts and Architectures*. Addison-Wesley. ISBN 0 201 62439 7.

Bobrow, D.G., DeMichiel, L.G., Gabriel, R.P., Keene, S.E., Kiczales, G. and Moon, D.A. (1988). Common LISP Object System specification X3J13. *ACM SIGPLAN Notices*, 23.

Booch, G. (1995). *Object-Oriented Analysis and Design with Applications,* 2nd edition. Benjamin Cummings. ISBN 0-8053-5340-2.

Boyle, J., Fothergill, J. and Gray, P. (1993). Design of a 3D user interface to a database. *Database Issues for Data Visualization.* Workshop at IEEE Visualization. Springer-Verlag.

Brodie, M., Mylopolous, J. and Schmidt, J.W. (eds), (1984). *Conceptual Modelling,* Springer-Verlag.

Buneman, O.P. and Nikhil, R. (1984). The functional data model and its uses for interaction with databases. In Brodie, M., Mylopolous, J. and Schmidt, J.W. (eds), *Conceptual Modelling,* Springer-Verlag.

Cahill, V., Balter, R., Harris, N.R. and Rousset de Pina, X. (eds) (1993*). The COMANDOS Distributed Application Platform.* ESPRIT Research Reports, Project 2071, COMANDOS, Vol 1. Springer-Verlag. ISBN 3 540 56660 0.

Cardelli, L. (1984). *Amber,* AT&T Bell Labs Technical Report, AT&T, Murray Hill, NJ.

Cardelli, L. and Wegner, P. (1985). On understanding types, data abstraction and polymorphism. *ACM Computing Surveys,* 17:4, 471–523.

Carey, M. and DeWitt, D. (1987). An overview of the EXODUS project. *IEEE Database Engineering,* 10:2. See also Zdonik and Maier, 1990.

Catarci, T., Costabile, M.F and Levialdi, S. (eds) (1993). *Advanced Visual Interfaces.* World Scientific Series in Computer Science, vol.36, World Scientific.

Catarci, T., Costabile, M., Levialdi, S. and Santucci, G. (eds) (1994). *Proc. Second Int. Workshop on Advanced Visual Interfaces, AVI'94,* ACM Press.

Cattell, R.G.G. (1991). *Object Data Management: Object-Oriented and Extended Relational Database Systems.* Addison-Wesley. ISBN 0 201 53092.

Cattell, R.G.G. (ed) (1994). *The Object Database Standard: ODMG-93.* Morgan Kaufmann. ISBN 1 55860 302 6.

Ceri, S., Gottlob, G. and Tanca, L. (1990). *Logic Programming and Databases.* Springer-Verlag.

Ceri, S. and Gottlob, G. (1989). What you always wanted to know about Datalog (and never dared to ask). *IEEE Transactions on Knowledge and Data Engineering,* 1, 146–66.

Ceri, S. and Pellagatti, P. (1984). *Distibuted Databases: Principles and Systems.* McGraw Hill. ISBN 0-07-Y66215-0.

Chen, P.P. (1976) The entity-relationship model – toward a unified view of data. *ACM TODS,* 1:1, 9–36.

Coad, P. and Yourdon, E. (1991a). *Object-Oriented Analysis,* 2nd edition. Prentice Hall. ISBN 0 13 629981 4.

Coad, P. and Yourdon, E. (1991b). *Object-Oriented Design.* Prentice Hall. ISBN 0 13 630070 7.

Codd, E.F. (1970) A relational model of data for large shared data banks. *CACM* 13:6, 377–387.

Codd, E.F. (1979). Extending the relational model to capture more meaning. *ACM TODS.* 4:4, 397–434.

Connolly, T., Begg, C. and Strachan, A. (1996). *Database Systems: A Practical Approach to Design, Implementation and Management.* Addison-Wesley. ISBN 0 201 42277 8.

Cooper, R.L. (ed) (1993). *Interfaces to Databases.* Workshops in Computer Science, Springer-Verlag. ISBN 3 540 19802 4.

Coulouris, G., Dollimore, J. and Kindberg, T. (1994). *Distributed Systems: Concepts and Design,* 2nd edition. Addison-Wesley. ISBN 0 201 62433 8.

Cox, B.J. (1991). *Object-Oriented Programming, An Evolutionary Approach.* Addison-Wesley.

Dahl, O. and Nygaard, K. (1966). Simula, an algol-based simulation language. *CACM,* 9:9, 671–678.

Date, C.J. (1989). *A Guide to the SQL Standard,* 2nd edition. Addison-Wesley.

Date, C.J. (1995). *An Introduction to Database Systems,* 6th edition. Addison-Wesley. ISBN 0-201-82458-2.

Dayal, U., Hanson, E.N. and Widom, J (1995) Active database systems. In Kim, W. (ed.), *Modern Database Systems – The Object Model, Interoperability and Beyond.* Addison-Wesley. ISBN 0 201 59098 0.

Dearle, A., Shaw, G., and Zdonik, S. (1990). Implementing persistent object bases: principles and practice. In *Proc 4th International Workshop on Persistent Object Systems,* (Martha's Vineyard, MA, September 1990). Morgan Kaufmann. ISBN 1 55860 168 6.

Delobel, C., Lécluse, C. and Richard, P. (1995). *Databases: From Relational to Object-Oriented System.* International Thomson. ISBN 1-850-32124-8.

Draper, S.W. and Waite, K. W. (1991). Iconographer as a visual programming system. In Diaper, D. and Hammond, N. (eds) *HCI'91 People and Computers VI: Usability Now!.* Cambridge University Press.

Elmasri, R. and Navathe, S.B. (1994). *Fundamentals of Database Systems,* 2nd edition. Addison-Wesley. ISBN 0 8053 1753 8.

Fishman, D.H., Beech, D., Cate, H.P., Chow, E.C., Connors, T., Davis, J.W., Derrett, N., Hoch, C.G., Kent, W., Lyngbaek, P., Mahbod, B., Neimat, M.A., Ryan, T.A. and Shan, M.C. (1987). Iris: An object-oriented database management system. *ACM TOOIS,* 5:1, 48–69.

Gamma, E., Helm, R., Johnson, R., and Vlissides, J. (1994) *Design Patterns: Elements of Reusable Object-Oriented Software.* Professional Computing Series, Addison-Wesley. ISBN 0 201 63361 2.

Goldberg, A. (1984). *Smalltalk-80: The Interactive Programming Environment.* Addison-Wesley.

Goldberg, A. (1989) *Smalltalk-80: The Language.* Addison-Wesley. ISBN 0 201 13688 0

Haerder, T. and Rothermel, K. (1987). Concepts for transaction recovery in nested transactions. *Proc ACM SIGMOD.*

Hammer, M. and McLeod, D. (1981) Database description with SDM: a semantic database model. *ACM TODS*, 6:3, 351–386. Also in Zdonik and Maier, 1990.

Harbison, S. (1992). *Modula-3.* Prentice Hall. ISBN 0 13 596396.

Hornick, M. and Zdonik, S.B. (1987). A shared, segmented memory system for an object-oriented database. *ACM TOOIS*, 5:1, 70–95.

Hull R. and King R., (1987). Semantic data modeling: survey, applications and research issues. *ACM Computing Surveys*, 19:3, 201–260

Hull, R., Morrison, R. and Stemple, D. (1990). Database programming languages. In *Proc 2nd International Workshop on Database Programming Languages,* (Salishan Lodge, Gleneden Beach, Oregon, June 1989). Morgan Kaufmann.

Jones, R. (1996). *Garbage Collection: Algorithms for Automatic Dynamic Memory Management.* John Wiley. ISBN 0 471 94148 4.

Kanellakis, P. and Schmidt, J. (1992). Database programming languages: bulk types and persistent data. In *Proc 3rd International Workshop on Database Programming Languages,* (Nafplion, Greece, August 1991). Morgan Kaufmann.

Katz, R.H. and Chang, E. (1987). Managing change in a computer-aided design database. In *Proc 13th International Conference on Very Large Databases,* (Brighton, September 1987), pp 339–346.

Kennedy, J. and Barclay, P. (eds) (1996). *Interfaces to database systems. (IDS96),* (Napier University, July 1994). Workshops in Computing, Springer-Verlag. ISBN 3-540-76066-0.

Kent, W (1979). Limitation of record-based information models. *ACM TODS*, 4:1, 107–131.

Khoshafian, S. (1993). *Object-Oriented Databases.* John Wiley.

Khoshafian, S.N. and Copeland, G.P. (1990). Object Identity. In *Proc OOPSLA.* Also in Zdonik and Maier, 1990.

Kim, W (ed.) (1995). *Modern Database Systems – The Object Model, Interoperability and Beyond.* Addison-Wesley. ISBN 0 201 59098 0.

Kim, W. and Lochovsky, F. (eds) (1989). *Object-Oriented Concepts, Applications, and Databases.* Addison-Wesley. ISBN 0 201 14410 7.

King, R. and Novak, M. (1993). Designing database interfaces with Facekit. *ACM TOOIS*, 11:2, 105–132.

Kirby, G., Cutts, Q. Dearle, A. and Marlin, C. (1989). *WIN – A Persistent Window Management System.* Tech Report PPRR-73-89, Universities of Glasgow and St. Andrews.

Knudsen, J.L., Lofgren, M., Madsen, O.L., Magnusson, B. (eds.) (1996). *Object-Oriented Environments: The Mjolner Approach.* The Object-Oriented Series, Prentice Hall. ISBN: 0-13-009291-6

Kuhn, T.S. (1970). *The Structure of Scientific Revolutions*, 2nd editon. Chicago University Press. ISBN 0-226-45804-0

Leler, W. (1988). *Constraint Programming Languages: Their Specification and Generation.* Addison-Wesley.

Loomis, S. (1992). Client-server architecture. *J. Object Oriented Programming.* 4:9

Madsen, O.L., Møller-Pedersen, B., and Nygaard, K. (1993) *Object-oriented Programming in the BETA Programming Language.* Addison-Wesley. ISBN 0 201 62430 3

Maier, D. and Stein, J. (1990). Development and implementation of an object-oriented DBMS. In Zdonik, S.B. and Maier, D. (eds) *Readings on Object Oriented Database Systems.* Morgan Kaufmann. ISBN 1 55860 000 0.

Melton, J. and Simon, A.R. (1993). *Understanding the new SQL: A Complete Guide.* Morgan Kaufmann. ISBN 1 55860 245 3.

Meyer, B. (1988). *Object-oriented Software Construction.* International Series in Computer Science, Prentice-Hall. ISBN 0 13 629031 0.

Meyer, B. (1992). *Eiffel: The Language.* Prentice Hall. ISBN 0 13 247925 7.

Mitchell, K.J., Kennedy, J.B., and Barclay, J. (1996). DRIVE: an environment for the organised construction of user interfaces to databases. In Kennedy, J. and Barclay, P. (eds) *Interfaces to database systems.(IDS96),* (Napier University, July 1994). Workshops in Computing, Springer-Verlag. ISBN 3-540-76066-0.

Moon, D.A. (1989). The Common Lisp Object-Oriented Programming Language Standard. In Kim, W. and Lochovsky, F. (eds). *Object-Oriented Concepts, Applications, and Databases.* Addison-Wesley. ISBN 0 201 14410 7.

Morrison, R., Brown, A., Carrick, R., Connor , R. and Dearle, A. (1989). *The Napier Reference Manual.* Computational Science, University of St. Andrews.

Mullender, S. (ed.) (1993). *Distributed Systems,* 2nd edition. Addison-Wesley. ISBN 0 201 62427 3.

Mylopolous, J. Bernstein, P.A. and Wong, H.K.T (1980). A language facility for designing database-intensive applications. *ACM TODS*, 5:2, 185–207. Also in Zdonik and Maier, 1990.

O'Brien, P.D., Halbert, D.C. and Kilian, M.F. (1987). The Trellis programming environment. In *Proc OOPSLA*, Orlando, Forida, October 1987.

Olle, T.W. (1978). *The CODASYL Approach to Data Base Management.* John Wiley.

Ozsu, M.T., Dayal, U. and Valduriez, P. (1984). *Distributed Object Management.* Morgan Kaufmann. ISBN 1 55860 256 9.

Paton, N., Cooper, R.L., England, D, al-Qaimari, G. and Kilgour, A.C. (1994) Integrated architectures for database interface development. *IEE Proc. Comput. Digit. Tech.*, 141:2.

Paton, N., Cooper, R., Williams, H. and Trinder, P. (1994). *Database Programming Languages.* Prentice Hall. ISBN 0-13-508434-2.

Peckham, J. and Maryanski, F. (1988). Semantic data models. *ACM Computing Surveys*, 20:3, 153–189.

Peuquet, J. and Marble, D.F. (1990). *Introductory Readings in Geographic Infomation Systems.* Taylor and Francis. ISBN 0-85066-856-5.

The PS-algol Reference Manual, 4th edition. Persistent Programming Research Report 12, Universities of Glasgow and St. Andrews, 1987.

Ramakrishnan, R., Srivastava, D., and Sudarshan, S. (1992). CORAL – control, relations and logic. In *Proc 18th VLDB*, pp 238-250.

Richardson, J. and Carey, M.J. (1987). Programming constructs for database system implementation in EXODUS. In *Proc ACM SIGMOD International Conference on Data Management Systems*, (San Francisco, May 1987), pp 208–219.

Rosenberg, J. and Koch, D. (eds) (1989). *Persistent Object Systems.* Springer-Verlag. ISBN 3 540 19626 9.

Rowe, L. and Stonebraker, M. (1987). The POSTGRES data model. In *Proc 13th VLDB*, 1987, pp 83–97.Also in Zdonik and Maier, 1990.

Rumbaugh, J., Blaha, M.,Premeriani, W., Eddy, F. and Lorensen, W. (1991) *Object-Oriented Modeling and Design.* Prentice Hall. ISBN 0 13 630054 5.

Sawyer, P. (ed.) (1995). *Interfaces to Database Systems, Proc 2nd International Workshop on Interfaces to Database Systems (IDS94)*, (Lancaster University, July 1994). Workshops in Computing, Springer-Verlag. ISBN 3-540-19910-1.

Schmidt, J.W. (1977) Some high-level language constructs for data of type relation. *ACM TODS*, 2:3, 247–261.

Schmidt, J.W. and Matthes, F. (1992). *The Database Programming Language {DBPL} Rationale and Report.* FIDE Report 92/46.

Shipman, D.W. The functional data model and the data language DAPLEX.*ACM TODS*, 6:1, 140–173. Also in Zdonik and Maier, 1990.

Silberschatz, A., Korth, H.F. and Sudarshan, S. (1997). *Database System Concepts*, 3rd edition. Addison-Wesley. ISBN 007044756X.

Stonebraker, M., Beech, D., Bernstein, P, Brodie, M., Carey, M., Gray, J., Lindsay, B. and Rowe, L.A. (1990). Third-generation database system manifesto. *ACM SIGMOD Record*, 19:3.

Strachey, C. (1967). Fundamental concepts in programming languages. Lecture notes for International Summer School in Computer Programming, Copenhagen, August 1967.

Stroustrup, B. (1991). *The C++ Programming Language*. Addison-Wesley.

Tansel, A., Clifford, J., Gadia, S., Jajodia, S., Segev, A. and Snodgrass, R. (eds.) (1993). *Temporal Databases: Theory, Design, and Implementation*. Benjamin Cummings.

Teorey, T.J., (1994). *Database Modelling and Design: The Fundamental Principles*, 2nd edition. Morgan Kaufmann.

Teorey, T.J., Yang, D. and Fry J.P. (1986). A logical design methodology for relational databases using the extended entity-relationship model. *ACM Computing Surveys*, 18:2, 197–222.

Ullman, J. (1988/89). *Database and Knowledgebase Systems* (2 vols). Computer Science Press, Rockville, MA.

Verso, J., Abiteboul, S., Bancilhon, F., Bidoit, N., Delebarre, V., Gamerman, S., Laubin, J.-M., Mainguenaud, M., Mostardi, T., Pauthe, P., Plateau, D., Richard, P., Scholl, M., and Verroust, A. (1986) *VERSO: A Database Machine Based on Non 1NF Relations*. Springer-Verlag.

Wetzel, I., Matthes, F., and Schmidt, J.W. (1997) The {STYLE} Workbench: Systematics of typed language environments. In Atkinson, M.P. (ed.) *The FIDE Project*, (in press). Springer-Verlag.

Wilson, P.R. (1994). *Uniprocessor Garbage Collection Techniques*. University of Texas Technical Report, January 1994.

Wirfs-Brock, R., Wilkerson, B. and Wiener L. (1990). *Designing Object Oriented Software*. Prentice Hall.

Zdonik, S.B. and Maier, D. (1990). *Readings on Object Oriented Database Systems*. Morgan Kaufmann. ISBN 1 55860 000 0.

Zloof, M.M. (1977).Query-by-example, a new database language. *IBM Systems Journal*, 16:4, 324–344.

Web Sites

Since web sites tend to move from time to time, the list of web sites given here is merely a guide to the current positions.

WebANSI	http://info.gte.com/ftp/doc/activities/x3h7.html
WebBerkeley	http://s2k-ftp.cs.berkeley.edu:8000/postgres/ otherdbms.html
WebC++	http://www.cs.monash.edu.au/~damian/ c++FAQ.html
WebCORAL	http://www.cs.wisc.edut/coral
WebDBresearch	http://liinwww.ira.uka.de/bibliography/database/ index.html
WebDECSRC	http://ftp.digital.com/pub/DEC/SRC/research-reports
WebEiffel	http://www.eiffel.com
WebFADIVA	http://www-cui.darmstadt.gmd.de/visit/Activities/ Fadiva/
WebFIDE	http://www.dcs.gla.ac.uk/fide/default.html
WebGemStone	http://www.gemstone.com
WebIBEX	http://www.iprolink.ch/ibexcom
WebISO	http://www.iso.ch/
WebJava	http://java.sun.com/faq2.html
WebLaz	http://www.cs.washington.edu/homes/lazowska/ cra/database.html

WebModula3	http://www.research.digital.com/SRC/modula-3/html/home.html
WebNapier88	http://www-fide.dcs.st-andrews.ac.uk/
WebO2	http://www.o2tech.com
WebObjectivity	http://www.objectivity.com
WebODI	http://www.odi.com
WebODMG	http://www.odmg.org/
WebOMG	http://www.omg.org
WebONTOS	http://www.ontos.com
WebOOFAQ	http://iamwww.unibe.ch/~scg/OOinfo/FAQ/oo-faq-toc.html#TOC
WebOpenDoc	http://www.opendoc.apple.com/
WebPOET	http://www.poet.com
WebPP	http://www.parcplace.com/index.htm
WebRocknRoll	http://www.cee.hw.ac.uk/Databases/rnr.html
WebSIGMOD	http://bunny.cs.uiuc.edu/README.html
WebSmalltalk	http://st-www.cs.uiuc.edu/
WebSQL	http://www.jcc.com/sql_stnd.html
WebTEMPORAL	ftp://ftp.cs.arizona.edu/bib/time.bib
WebUllman	http://db.stamford.edu/pub/ullman/lagii.ps
WebUMass	http://www-ccs.cs.umass.edu/db.html
WebUniSQL	http://www.unisql.com
WebVersant	http://www.versant.com

Index